Child and Family Practice

Also available from Lyceum Books, Inc.

Advisory Editor: Thomas M. Meenaghan, *New York University*

CHILDREN AND LOSS: A PRACTICAL HANDBOOK FOR PROFESSIONALS
edited by Elizabeth C. Pomeroy and Renée Bradford Garcia

DIVERSITY IN FAMILY CONSTELLATIONS: IMPLICATIONS FOR PRACTICE
edited by Krishna L. Guadalupe and Debra L. Welkley

BEST PRACTICES IN COMMUNITY MENTAL HEALTH: A POCKET GUIDE
edited by Vikki L. Vandiver

UNDERSTANDING AND MANAGING THE THERAPEUTIC RELATIONSHIP
by Fred R. McKenzie

THE COSTS OF COURAGE: COMBAT STRESS, WARRIORS, AND
FAMILY SURVIVAL
by Josephine G. Price, Col. David H. Price, and Kimberly K. Shackleford

CHARACTER FORMATION AND IDENTITY IN ADOLESCENCE
by Randolph L. Lucente

THE RECOVERY PHILOSOPHY AND DIRECT SOCIAL WORK PRACTICE
by Joseph Walsh

CIVIC YOUTH WORK: CO-CREATING DEMOCRATIC YOUTH SPACES
edited by Ross VeLure Roholt, Michael Baizerman, and R. W. Hildreth

THE USE OF SELF: THE ESSENCE OF PROFESSIONAL EDUCATION
by Raymond Fox

HOW TO TEACH EFFECTIVELY: A BRIEF GUIDE
by Bruce Friedman

Child and Family Practice

A Relational Perspective

Shelley Cohen Konrad
University of New England

LYCEUM

BOOKS, INC.

Chicago, Illinois

© 2013 by Lyceum Books, Inc.

Published by
  LYCEUM BOOKS, INC.
  5758 S. Blackstone Ave.
  Chicago, Illinois 60637
  773 + 643-1903 fax
  773 + 643-1902 phone
  lyceum@lyceumbooks.com
  www.lyceumbooks.com

6 5 4 3 2 1   13 14 15 16 17 18

ISBN 978-1-933478-44-9

Cover: Artwork by students in the School of Social Work, University of New

Printed in the United States of America.

Library of Congress Cataloging-in-Publication Data

Cohen Konrad, Shelley.
    Child and family practice : a relational perspective / Shelley Cohen Konra
New England.
      pages   cm
    Includes bibliographical references.
    ISBN 978-1-933478-44-9 (pbk. : alk. paper)
    1. Social work with children.   2. Family social work.   I. Title.
HV713.C6394   2013
362.7—dc23
                                                          2012036452

Contents

Boxes

Preface

Dear Shelley,

I hope this note finds you and not the junk file. My name is Sarah Lawler, and several years ago (circa 1998) I was a client in your care. I wanted to say thank you for all that you did for me.

I know my departure from therapy was abrupt, and I'm sorry it took so long to get back in touch. To catch you up, shortly after high school I left the state for good and never looked back. I got a degree in microbiology and then entered "the working world," not using my degree one bit. In 2004, on the very same date only 6 years earlier that my dad kicked me out, I bought my own home. This was a major triumph given, as you know, I never felt like I belonged anywhere or to anybody. I lived there for 6 years and then sold it to use the money to get an advanced degree in occupational therapy.

I'm proud to say that this fall I am taking anatomy, physiology, and sociology, and also three different psychology courses. All the psychology classes have reminded me of you and the help that you gave me through my high school years. You believed in me and that made a difference. So I did a little Internet digging and found your e-mail. Hope you are well and thank you again.

Many Smiles,
Sarah

When I first read Sarah's note, I thought, What is she thanking me for? What did I *do* to help her become the capable adult portrayed in the e-mail? I recalled our final conversation nearly nine years earlier. Sarah called me from a phone booth to say good-bye. She was leaving home, and there was no turning back. In truth I felt I had failed her. Yet at the same time, I was confident that Sarah's resilience ran deep. Remarkably and despite all the adversities she had faced, Sarah had never lost faith in herself.

In hindsight there is no doubt that Sarah's situation was fraught with multiple losses and missed opportunities. She spent her early years negotiating divided loyalties, and endured bumpy, cross-continental transitions. The only child of never-married parents, she was caught in the endless battle

between two very different family systems. At thirteen, her residency unexpectedly shifted from her mother's home to her father's, leaving Sarah
grappling with a whole new set of rules and expectations. She became a
client of mine because the strains of her new life began to erupt.

As Sarah's letter implies, the change in households was not successful
and ended in yet another relational loss. This was not for lack of trying on
anyone's part. Relocation proved to be a bad fit for all concerned. Despite
the placement failure, however, Sarah emerged a success. In the end, she
cultivated her strengths, coped with adversity, and discovered a promising
future. When she phoned to tell me she was leaving, I was frustrated that I
could *do* nothing more to mend broken fences. Now, so many years later, I
recognize it wasn't what I did *for* Sarah but rather what we did together that
made the difference.

In many respects, Sarah's brief, heartfelt update exemplifies the essence
of this book. The relational perspective described throughout this text
emphasizes the power and enduring nature of human relationships. In
regard to child and family practice, relational practitioners highly value the
quality and meaning of relationships established between children and their
primary caregivers and also those fostered among children, families, and
helping professionals. These caring connections bear the potential for
growth and employ many kinds of intervention. In the end, relationships
empower transformational change and lead to hopeful futures.

Although *relational connection* is at the core of this practice perspective, it is only one of several critical components that make up effective child-
and family-centered practice. The use of relationship in therapeutic work is
never random but is thoughtfully guided by scientific evidence and theoretical frameworks, and informed by reflexive contemplation. In Sarah's situation, for example, I mined the *scholarly literature* available on high-conflict
divorce and relocation to understand her predicament and its potential
impact on adolescents in her situation. I scoured the research for *evidence-
guided* practice suggestions, including those that might help families adapt
to unexpected residency changes. I also had to take stock of my own values
and opinions. Readers will come to recognize this process as a reflexive
practice strategy. In Sarah's case, the *reflexive practitioner* in me continually
and critically evaluated attitudes and biases that might unduly and adversely
affect our work. Would the ghosts from other contentious divorces get in the
way of building open and effective relationships with Sarah and her kin?

To avoid unhelpful presumptions, I used journaling and consultation to
understand Sarah's circumstances. Doing so allowed me to assess her situation from multiple perspectives. As a result, I could maintain clarity and
avoid becoming caught in the clashes between Sarah and her families. The
combination of scholarship, research, and reflexive practices prevented
compassion fatigue, a common pitfall for child-centered practitioners who
work in unremittingly high-conflict situations. In the end I like to think that

I was able to sidestep the inevitable emotional repercussions of contention and keep Sarah's needs at the forefront of our work together.

Stories like Sarah's provided the inspiration for this book. Techniques for practice may come and go: some endure, others evolve or go by the wayside. What remains true is that relationships matter: even when little can be done to effect tangible change, people are empowered by the connections made with those who care.

The changing health and mental health landscape in America provides additional impetus for writing this book. In the twenty-first century, the importance of caring is promoted in health-care marketing, but the enactment of caring relationships has been all but lost to efficiency, technology, and bottom-line economics. Although caring and relational rhetoric pervades health education and practice, very little time is allotted to teaching relational paradigms or to fostering caring attitudes that can be applied with intention to our work with clients and patients. Years of working in mental health, health-care, and educational systems have taught me that learning about relational and caring practices does not necessarily happen on its own. My intention in this book is to raise awareness of relational principles for practice not simply as a nice gesture, but as a conscious strategy that promotes positive change for individual children, parents, families, and communities.

The book begins by outlining knowledge, skills, and attitudes essential to the relational perspective as applied to practice with children and families. Its basic tenets—relational connection, evidence-guided knowledge, and reflexivity—are explained, examined, and exemplified in chapter 1, providing a conceptual guide for the content that follows. Chapters 2 and 3 focus on early-childhood research and attachment theory, both of which inform relational child- and family-centered practice.

Chapters 4 through 7 describe skills for building respectful and productive therapeutic relationships with children and their caregivers. Case examples based on my thirty years of experience as a clinical social worker and community-resource builder illustrate the application of these skills with child clients of different ages and from diverse family structures and backgrounds. It is my hope that these examples will put a human face on the challenges children and families encounter and breathe life into the concepts and skills presented in the book.

The remaining chapters highlight populations and common issues presented by children who are seen in a range of mental health centers, community clinics, educational institutions, and social service settings. Chapter 8, for example, concentrates on adolescents as a distinctive group and sheds light on specific issues they grapple with during this transitional phase of life; chapter 11 addresses children's understanding and responses to death. Each chapter integrates relational principles, highlighting their contributions to understanding and working with children and families affected by a range of life events. As is the case with any book, not every pertinent issue affecting children and families could be addressed. Indeed, colleagues and other authors may prioritize different populations, areas of practice, skill sets, and dilemmas. This does not imply that the missing content is less important or that alternative perspectives on child and family social work practice are not equally valid. It is my hope, however, that readers will be inspired to write about how they've applied relational principles to children and other groups that they work with.

As I reflect upon the content of this book, I am reminded of the musings of Ted Andrews: "No music is totally 'pure,' and the vitality of a tradition can be measured by its ability to integrate new contributions." Concepts and perspectives put forth in this text are in no small way influenced by many interwoven voices, old and new. I therefore want to thank my teachers and mentors: those I have known in real time as well as those whose writings and legacy have inspired my philosophy and practice. Many of their words and ideas infuse these chapters, and I hope I have done them justice. I especially appreciate Kim Strom-Gottfried's diligence in connecting me with David Follmer at Lyceum Books. There is no doubt that this book would never have appeared without her belief in me and her unrelenting advocacy. Martha Wilson and Stephen Rose also provided me with "on the ground" support through kind words, author guidance, and excellent lunches. Many thanks also extend to Clay Graybeal, who taught me how to write for publication.

I've been fortunate to work with amazing children and families throughout my career, many of whom provided inspiration for the stories in the book. Collectively they've taught me to never, never, never give up. I've learned that hope dwells in unexpected places and growth emerges in surprising and beautiful ways. Harder lessons have also been demonstrated by these children, especially those who fought hard battles and lost and those who from the get-go knew that their time on earth was limited. To them I offer gratitude for disclosing how to tolerate uncertainty, to bear witness to suffering, and to appreciate the small things in life. I'm also blessed to have had rich and diverse experiences teaching and learning from my graduate students at the University of New England's School of Social Work. They graciously gave me opportunities to practice what I'm preaching to a wider audience through this book.

My husband, Richard Konrad, deserves daily thanks for having sustained me through the writing process by serving me nutritious dinners and providing gentle reminders to come to bed when I lost time in front of the computer screen. Many thanks also to my dearest friend, Sara Gilfenbaum, whose belief in me transcends reality, and to my brother Harry Cohen, who still can't get over that his "little sister" is a published author and academic.

My children, Justin and Hilary, have provided inspiration beyond simply having grown into wonderfully distinctive adults. They have shown me that adversity can transform people in positive and life-affirming ways and that love is essential to life.

Finally, this book is dedicated to the memories of my mother and brother Albie, who loved and cared for children, and given to Zoe, whose light is a beacon toward a hopeful future.

1

Practice with Children and Their Families

A Relational Perspective

Reaching for the heart is equally important as healing with the hands.

Suzanne M. Peloquin, "Embracing Our
Ethos, Reclaiming Our Heart"

THE LEGACY OF THE RELATIONAL PERSPECTIVE

The social work profession has from its inception identified relationship as the heart of social work practice (Perlman, 1979). Other health professions likewise promote relationship as critical to healing practices. Relational-cultural theory developed by psychiatrist Jean Baker Miller (1976) suggests that authentic and mutual connection is at the core of therapeutic healing. Similarly, the professions of physical and occupational therapy promote caring and helpful human encounters as essential not only to health but also to human dignity, the latter being a foundational ethic in social work practice as well. Nursing also has a legacy of relationship-centered caring, highlighted in the works of Jean Watson (2009), whose "caring science" upholds the essential nature of interpersonal connections with patients and clients, regardless of health field.

So why write another text about relational perspectives, in this case focused on practice with children and families? Given their seeming embeddedness in the theories and ethics of social work and other health and human service practices, why is it timely now to reassert the essential value of relational skills and attitudes?

Three decades ago in his review of Helen Harris Perlman's (1979) seminal social work text, *Relationship: The Heart of Helping People*, Herbert Strean (1980, p. 71) wrote: "At a time when clients are frequently perceived as units in micro- and macro-systems, when they are manipulated by rewards and punishments, when their 'tasks' are considered to be more important than their wishes, anxieties and defenses and when they are given limited professional attention under the guise of short term treatment, it is refreshing to be presented with a book by an eminent scholar, lucid writer, and compassionate person who views the client-worker relationship as the heart of practice."

Thirty years later, Strean's comments on Perlman's work profoundly resonate with what many clients and workers face in today's health and mental health systems. Targeted approaches to evidence-guided practice, fiscal conservatism, restrictions in mental health reimbursement, and increasing use of corporatized health management models have become serious obstacles to the application of relational and caring practices. Although the words *caring* and *relationship* are consistently used in health-care marketing, their importance within active practice models is often elusive. All too many contemporary educators believe that the relational aspects of the work we do is supplemental or implicit and thus less important to study than the techniques and strategies we use to produce tangible and thus reimbursable outcomes.

Given the current health-care landscape, it is evident that educators, scholars, and mentors must reaffirm the value of empowering and therapeutic relationships with children and families. Following the lead of Perlman and other relational theorist-practitioners, we need to train future social workers and other mental health and social service practitioners in relational skills that transcend settings and that contribute to useful intervention strategies. Relational perspectives are relevant to community and organizational practice as well. Principles for relational practice build interpersonal skills and encourage reflective insight grounded in thoughtfulness, respect, and collaboration.

Relational practice emanates from critical thinking and self-reflection that invites workers to be aware of the ways in which their professional and personal knowledge shapes how they interpret the world. In the end, social workers and other relationally prepared professionals reengage with what we've always held to be true—that the quality of our relationships matters. Or as Perlman (1979) argued so many years ago, relationships, no matter how brief, can be catalysts that enable people to engage in their own healing and enact positive and enduring change in their lives and in their communities.

THE BOY IN THE WAITING ROOM: PART 1

The following case narrative illustrates how knowledge, relational experience, practice wisdom, and personal assumptions guide how we interpret human experience. Two workers take different approaches to the case. Both workers are competent, observant, and well-intended. Neither is considered to be right or wrong. But each one relates differently to "the boy in the waiting room," and uses her knowledge to construct a case theory based on observation.

Two intake workers walk into the waiting room of a busy urban clinic to greet a four-year-old boy who is there for assessment. The first worker notices that the boy's clothes fit badly. She sees that his face is clean but his ears are dirty, and she worries about his frail appearance. Is he malnourished? Perhaps he is neglected or suffers from ill effects of early adversities or material deprivation. Is there trauma or abuse in his past? Will he need special education services and costly resources?

The young African American boy is cuddled next to an older Caucasian man, who is reading him a book. Where is the boy's mother, she wonders, and what kept her from bringing him to this appointment? Who is this man, and what is his relationship to the boy? They are of different races and thus are not likely to be biologically related. Perhaps he is a caseworker or the mother's boyfriend? Will the worker need to make a referral to child protective services?

A troublesome case for sure, she reflects to herself. However, knowing that her agency is a research site for trauma-focused cognitive-behavioral therapy alleviates some of her fears. If indeed the child has met with hard times, she will be prepared with an appropriate intervention strategy to guide his successful treatment. Knowing that she has a plan in sight assures the worker that she will have something positive to offer this youngster.

The second worker's first impression is quite different from her colleague's. She observes that the boy is absorbed in looking at a picture book, aided by the older man. She stops for a moment and enjoys their shared interaction. The child's body language is relaxed yet curious. What factors in this child's life have afforded him the assuredness he seems to possess?

Like the other worker, she wonders about the older man's connection to this child. Given that the boy seems African American and the older man Caucasian, she speculates that he might be a relative, friend, partner to the child's mother, or adoptive or foster parent. Or perhaps he's the bus driver who brought him from preschool? She holds back from assuming too much; she doesn't want to leap to conclusions.

Like her colleague, this worker notices the boy's frailty and wonders whether he has an undetected medical condition or perhaps suffers from hunger. It's also possible that the family body type is slender. She reminds herself to check into his family and medical history to add detail to these observations.

As she ponders making her approach, this worker notices that she is not the only one assessing the situation. The boy has been watching her too and now cautiously meets her gaze. What is he thinking? she wonders. What have his experiences been with his mother and other female caregivers in his young life, and how will these influence their alliance? An interesting child, she thinks to herself as she waits just one more minute before interrupting them.

Early Assessments

These brief yet distinctive impressions have begun the child assessment process. From the very first encounter, both workers began gathering data to construct a case theory or hypothesis about the child who will become a client in their practice setting. Each took notice of "evidence" that will guide their diagnostic formulations and case planning. As they get to know this child better, these initial observations will be confirmed or disconfirmed, and transformed into narratives that will assist him with the challenges that he brought to the waiting room today. In the end, this child's story will be archived in a case record that will follow him throughout his childhood.

As is evident from the brief scenarios, these two workers are likely to choose different aspects of this child's story to prepare their assessments, develop case formulations, and recommend interventions. What do you notice about their observations and musings? What different assumptions might guide their thinking? How will their perspectives influence assessment, and how will their relationships be affected by their unique standpoints? Finally, what theories about problem causation do they convey, and why is identifying these important to the work they will do?

The first worker's tentative case theory is primarily influenced by concerns about the boy's frailty and possible adversity and traumas. She is therefore relieved to know that her agency is piloting a particular treatment approach—trauma-focused cognitive-behavioral therapy—that has been effective with children like the boy in the waiting room. Over time, as she comes to know the boy and his significant family and community systems, she will discover whether her early speculations are accurate and her chosen intervention protocol beneficial.

One question to consider is how her relationship with the boy, his family, and his community will influence or transform her initial assumptions. Let's consider, for example, that she learns that the man is the boy's grandfather and primary caregiver and that they share a close and caring relationship. Although their economic circumstances are insecure, their love is not.

The boy's struggles, however, are significant; he's lost both his mother and father. As it stands, he can't quite control his behavior, though he has many resources to draw upon, not the least of which are his intelligence and resilience. Would this first worker be willing to adapt her approach and shift gears to accommodate the boy's assets into a revised treatment plan? What additional evidence would she seek to update and revise her original line of thinking?

The second worker views her case theory as a work in progress. This does not imply that she doesn't have thoughts and feelings about the boy and his circumstances; she does. However, she is aware that her knowledge is at best partial and that her case theory will evolve over time. She knows that if invited into the family's confidence, she will achieve greater understanding of the factors and circumstances influencing the young boy's current challenges. Moreover, if allowed into the child's relational world, she will become even more effective. Gaining relational access will require specialized child-centered skills, including openness, respect, and playfulness.

Yet even though the second worker knows that she has much to learn from her child client and his family, she is confident that she has beneficial knowledge and skills to share. Perhaps her greatest asset is being aware that she doesn't have to know everything and that, as the relationship unfolds, she will make new discoveries. These will lead her to investigate evidence and empirical research that will ultimately inform her case theory and practice. They may also bring her into relationship with providers outside her own discipline who will collaborate on behalf of the boy and his family. She is excited and looks forward to getting to know this child within the context of his life.

While formulating her initial impressions, the second worker is simultaneously reflecting upon her observations and taking stock of her behavior and responses. She knows that *how* she responds to this child and his family will be as important as *what* methods and resources she uses. Their relationship will in many ways predict whether any chosen intervention strategy will succeed. Thus this worker will be responsive to the boy and his caregivers, hoping that they will see that she is sincere and includes them as vital members of their health and wellness team.

Comparative Analysis

There is no doubt that both workers are well intended and responsibly doing their job as best they can. Let's take a moment, however, to reflect upon critical differences in the process, attitudes, and perspectives they bring to their work with children and families. The first worker's assessment is primarily problem focused. She's primed to see deficits in the young boy's presentation. Her problem-based perspective is evident in what she observes (ill-fitting clothes, dirty ears), the language she uses (troublesome case for sure), and the assessment questions she posits (Is he neglected, malnourished, or intellectually disabled?). Few if any of her deliberations identify or seek out the child's strengths and capabilities.

Because of her problem-based perspective, this worker is likely to see what is wrong, not what is right. This naturally leads her to a preliminary assumption that the child will need a therapeutic approach designed to address trauma. This worker may be right in her deductions; addressing traumatic circumstances and early adversity in this child's life may provide relief from the challenges he faces. What is absent in her initial impressions, however, is recognition of the strengths and assets he and his family/caregivers will bring to the therapeutic process. Missing as well is any hint of uncertainty in the trend of her thinking. There are many risks in thinking from a single paradigm, and in the case of this young boy, the social worker's presumptions could lead to unintended assessment errors and therapeutic missteps that will impede rather than promote his growth and healing.

The second worker's approach is measured and deliberate. She observes that this four-year-old brings strengths as well as probable challenges to the therapeutic encounter. Her internal dialogue takes note of the positive behavior she witnesses (absorbed, relaxed, curious) and her descriptive language acknowledges his diverse qualities (frailty, assuredness). The questions she raises show that she is well aware that she doesn't know much. Her queries also seek to find out what is helping this boy adapt (What factors in this child's life have afforded him the assuredness he seems to possess?) as well as what may be contributing to his struggles (undetected medical condition, economic insecurity).

Unlike her colleague, this worker is circumspect about making quick assumptions. Eventually a treatment protocol will be determined, but she wants to get to know this child and the context of his life before taking actions that will impact his world. He might remind her of other four-year-olds she's met, but she wants to respect his uniqueness. She notes her earliest impressions (she reminds herself to check into his medical and body-type background) and contemplates her own thinking (she doesn't want to leap to conclusions). Through self-reflection, she recognizes the impact that her knowledge, values, and beliefs and the relationship she will ultimately form with this child and family will have on her practice choices. One should not mistake this worker's thoughtful restraint for lack of confidence. She is simply employing a distinctive way of understanding this child's circumstances, one that is based on a relational perspective for practice with children and families.

THE RELATIONAL PERSPECTIVE: AN OVERVIEW

This book explores tenets of relational practice and how they pertain to work with children, families, and their interacting community systems. Relational practice is based in social work, developmental psychology, and psychoanalytic theories for practice; however, it can readily be implemented in work with children and families across caring disciplines, including mental health, social service, psychology, pediatrics, counseling, nursing, and occupational therapy. It can also be applied to the ways in which we work with colleagues as members of interprofessional teams. In the end, building thoughtful and mutually respectful relationships with other health and mental health professionals, as well as teachers and other professionals, benefits the children and families who become our clients.

The relational perspective values human relationships, particularly those that children establish with primary caregivers and helping professionals across settings. Within the relational paradigm, children are viewed as distinctive, unique human beings. At the same time, they depend on adults who directly care for them or perform vital roles, such as teachers and caseworkers. Children are responsive not only to their primary attachments but also to the relationships that link family members to others. Such relationships include those between parenting partners, those joining parents with extended-family members, and those that establish a family's connection with people and institutions in their community.

Children and families are also affected by their relationships with a larger sociocultural landscape. They are influenced by institutional and sociopolitical forces, such as policies that decide who is privileged and who is not (e.g., immigration laws) and regulations that determine who and what is safe (e.g., child protection and safety regulations), and by social standards that dictate what is normal and what is deviant (e.g., mental health diagnoses). Altogether, children's relationships to their families, significant adults, peers, educational and social institutions, and the broader culture have complicated and intersecting effects on their lives.

Significant relationships in children's lives are diverse. Positive relationships are perceived as protective and serve to buffer or counteract childhood adversity. Conversely, ill-formed or destructive relationships can contribute to children's already difficult circumstances. It is typically at times of adversity or difficulty that mental health or human services practitioners come into children's worlds.

Child-centered practitioners understand the complexities of working with children and families. They know that communicating with children requires special approaches that differ from communicating with adults. For example, child-centered workers must be well versed in using expressive and play-based modalities. Along with building relationships with child clients, workers must also develop strong, open ties with the significant adults in their worlds. Skills for constructing relationships with a host of divergent people and personalities are therefore critical for effective child and family practice.

The relational perspective informs both attitudes and skills for establishing these meaningful and productive relationships. Within this framework the therapeutic relationship, rather than a specific intervention strategy, is seen as the primary tool for understanding child clients' circumstances (assessment) and for effecting desired change in broader client systems (intervention). In effect, relational practice principles can be applied in conjunction with almost any evidence-guided therapeutic method as long as the selected method fits the needs of the child client and his or her family system. Developing strong relationships with children also relies on respectful and culturally responsive communication and on faith in children's capacity for resilience and self-correction. Thus, relational practice is distinguished not only by *what* the worker says or does, but also by what clients and workers do together.

Building strong and affirming relationships with children and families is not simply a nice idea. The therapeutic advantages of client-worker alliances have been recognized for decades. Robust empirical evidence suggests that 30 percent of therapeutic success is attributable to the qualities inherent in therapeutic relationships (Lambert & Barley, 2001). Such qualities include the worker's capacity to be responsive and empathetic and to convey belief in the client's capacity to heal. In child-centered practice, alliances between workers and parents are also instrumental to genuine therapeutic change.

Moreover, qualities and assets that child clients bring to treatment play significant roles in therapeutic outcomes. In Lambert and Barley's (2001) study, 40 percent of positive therapeutic results were attributable to the strengths and capabilities clients brought to the therapeutic encounter. Successful therapeutic outcomes in child-centered work manifest in the client's enhanced self-perception, behaviors, and overall performance. For parents, positive outcomes include better communication with their children, increased confidence in child rearing, and improved interactions in the community (Duncan, Miller, & Sparks, 2007).

Relational and communication competencies are also relevant to those working in social service and health-care settings who interact daily with children and their families. For instance, parents of critically ill and dying children consistently report that how well they cope depends in large part on the quality of their relationships with health professionals (Contro, Larson, Scofield, Sourkes, & Cohen, 2002). As we will see in chapter 8, adolescents in the child welfare system say that their resilience is enhanced by the availability of caseworkers who listen to them and prove their relational mettle (Laursen & Birmingham, 2003).

In the text that follows, readers will come to appreciate that relational practice is a perspective, not a distinctive theory or modality. Relational practice is grounded in the belief that children are doing the best they can with the skills they have and that most parents are doing the same. It offers a way of understanding children and their families within the contexts of their lives while reflecting upon ourselves within the context of the work we do.

Relational principles set the tone for the attitudes we hope to attain in practice: openness, humility, and willingness not to presume, prejudge, or pathologize that which we do not yet understand. At the same time, relational principles promote lifelong learning through ongoing investigation of contemporary research findings and theories of practice. In combination such attitudes and knowledge inform skills used in the context of the relationships we develop with child clients.

Like resiliency theory (Masten, 2001) and the strengths perspective (Saleebey, 2009), which focus attention on the capacities and resources that clients possess, relational practice seeks to identify clients' capabilities, understand their challenges, and collaboratively develop tools they will need to cope in often tumultuous times. It is consistent with values and ethics of a number of caring professions, especially those that emphasize human dignity, cultural humility, and meeting clients wherever they happen to be. In this way it informs but does not prescribe the techniques and models selected for intervention. Relational perspectives thus lead practitioners to respectfully perceive the client's needs as *the* central focus of care.

GUIDING PRINCIPLES OF THE RELATIONAL PERSPECTIVE

The relational perspective is distinguished by three unifying principles that will be applied throughout this book. First, it affirms that children are resilient and can grow and change if given opportunities and resources. Second, it underscores the interdependency and interrelatedness of children and their caregivers and of human beings and their social environments. Third, it emphasizes the prominence of the client-worker relationship in the change process (Borden, 2000).

Principles of the relational perspective conform to those historically found in social work and other helping professions. This symmetry is not coincidental. The relational perspective derives from philosophies and strategies that have worked well for clients and workers in the past. Relational principles, perspectives, and strategies presented in this book are in essence being reasserted, reaffirmed, and reincorporated into current, mainstream micro- and macropractices.

Workers who subscribe to the relational perspective will cultivate these skills (Borden, 2000; Pozzuto, Arnd-Caddigan, & Averett, 2009; Tosone, 2004):

- Understand that human experience is complex, affected by multiple and interacting variables that include biological, psychological, relational, social, political, phenomenological, and spiritual factors.

- Recognize that the therapeutic relationship is interactive and dynamic and that workers and clients of all ages affect and transform one other.

- Work with clients to establish safe relational environments that promote openness and healing.

- Appreciate the uniqueness of each child and family system, the context of their lives, and the circumstances that they face.

- Seek to establish a bidirectional working relationship in which the expertise of the other is respected and used to its best advantage.

- Be curious and pursue new knowledge to stay current and informed.

- Use a reflexive approach that incorporates self-reflection and examination of knowledge claims.

RELATIONAL PRACTICE AND ORGANIZATIONAL/ COMMUNITY PRACTICE

Relational practice principles are relevant to organizational and community practice. Simply put, human beings make up organizational and institutional structures. Communication and relational proficiencies are therefore essential to advocating on behalf of children, youth, and families in a myriad of agencies and social institutions as well as in legislative and policy-making forums (Pozzuto et al., 2009). Effective advocacy depends to a large extent on the worker's capacity to organize and sustain productive interactions with decision makers, especially those who determine child- and family-related outcomes. Such decision makers may include representatives from child protection agencies, medical and health-related systems, the courts, and educational institutions, among others. Critical thinking and the capacity to consider multiple perspectives help workers step outside their paradigms in the service of understanding institutional priorities. By seeking to understand rather than dismiss others' claims, workers become more persuasive in negotiating critical decisions on behalf of child clients and their families.

Although this book focuses on direct service with children and families, it embeds a strong invitation to workers to see themselves as assertive and active agents of broader change. Frontline workers see firsthand the impact of programming and policies developed without knowledge or input from the constituencies they serve. Children and families, particularly those who live under the radar of public opinion, are too frequently invisible to or dismissed by decision makers. Workers are positioned to join with these silenced populations: to bear witness to their experiences and to represent their causes. Assertive practitioners act as links between micro- and macro-practices and must promote programs and policy changes that better meet the true needs of children, families, and the communities in which they live and should thrive.

EVIDENCE, SCIENCE, AND THE RELATIONAL PERSPECTIVE

Relational child and family practice is grounded in rich and diverse theories and traditions. It is informed by varied disciplines such as psychodynamic theories, social work, neuroscience, cognitive psychology, feminism, behaviorism, cultural anthropology, family systems theories, philosophy, and educational theory. It is consistently reshaped and refined by new knowledge and evidence-guided research designed to improve how we interact with our child clients, their families, and communities and how we build therapeutic alliances that contribute to productive and enduring change. Child and family practice is also significantly influenced by ongoing political and cultural trends that contribute to public perceptions and definitions of childhood, family, and good-enough parenting. Evidence suggests that how practitioners relate to one another also significantly affects health and mental health outcomes across populations. In other words, client and family healing appears to be enhanced by the collective relational capacities of interprofessional care teams (Konrad & Browning, 2012).

Relational practice principles in child-centered work inform how scientific knowledge, new discovery, and evidence are translated into practice. For example, it has been suggested that best practice relies on best evidence. In contemporary mental health and social service practice, much emphasis is placed on the use of evidence-guided knowledge and approaches. Evidence-guided practice is grounded in the thoughtful and discriminating use of scientific and evaluative research to make practice decisions.

From a relational perspective, evidence-guided knowledge is one of many reliable sources used to develop a theory for understanding child clients and addressing their circumstances. Evidence may derive from empirically based research or from qualitative or first-person studies. It may also be found in studies that use mixed-methods designs. Data derived from empirical or quantitative research offers an overview of how large participant groups respond to certain situations, events, or interventions. Qualitative or first-person research seeks to learn in more detail how smaller cohorts of people make sense of a shared phenomenon.

Neuroscience discoveries contribute evidence for developing theories of practice relevant to child- and family-centered work. Advancements in neuroscience research over the last two decades, for example, have changed the way we think about early attachments and the possibilities for change (see chapter 3). Although Freud, Winnicott, and others surmised the importance of a child's earliest bonds, substantive scientific evidence now backs their claims (Schore & Schore, 2008; Zeanah & Smyke, 2008). Furthermore, neuroscience research now suggests that the brain is continuously responsive to positive relationships and thus repairable throughout life. These findings contradict previous work that predicted dire, lifelong consequences for children whose early attachments were insufficient or missing altogether.

Evidence also comes directly from clients' lived experiences. Recognizing, acknowledging, and integrating client and client-family expertise into all aspects of practice adds to our understanding of people's strengths and challenges. Relational practice assumes that workers, child clients, and their families share complementary knowledge that informs therapeutic choices as well as other critical child-focused decisions. It could be said that sharing complementary knowledge contributes to best practice by ensuring an ongoing dialogue between evidence-guided practice and client-based evidence. Client knowledge used as worker feedback provides immediate evaluative input about the efficacy of practice protocols, and improves the likelihood of successful treatment outcomes (Duncan et al., 2007).

Workers' collective practice wisdom and intuitive sensibilities further contribute to evidence. Like our clients, we have acquired a storehouse of knowledge from the many people we meet and from our educations and ongoing studies. In some instances when child clients and their families come from unfamiliar nations and cultures, workers seek out evidence from cultural brokers or other community informants. Critical evidence is also gleaned by workers within the context of their relationships with children and families, whereby verbal and nonverbal information is exchanged.

As can be surmised, practitioners who have a relational perspective see evidence as a thoughtful and well-balanced compilation of science, intuition, conversation, and artfulness. In Graybeal's (2007, p. 514) words, evidence used for practice provides us with "a balance between the structured, general knowledge that prepares the practitioner for categories of concern, and the intuitive, improvisatory understanding that is expressed in the immeasurable details of being fully present to another human being."

In many respects every new child client presents us with a research dilemma to investigate. Some aspects of the child's situation may resonate with general knowledge; he or she may display behaviors seen in youngsters diagnosed with a certain health condition, for example, autism. But how one child's autism diagnosis interplays with a variety of factors, including temperament, family systems, material circumstances, lived experiences, and/or educational environments, will make his or her situation unique.

Thus, knowing about autism, or for that matter any health condition or life circumstance, from the research literature alone is not sufficient to ensure best practice or predict whether outcomes will be positive. Indeed, much of what we know about positive outcomes is hard to predict without longitudinal (ongoing) data collection. Take Sarah, for example, whom you met in the preface. It isn't lost on me that had therapeutic outcomes been evaluated just before Sarah left her family, the treatment would have been considered severely lacking. Over the life course, however, Sarah incorporated aspects of the work we did together in ways that positively shaped her life. Sarah's story is testimony that measuring treatment efficacy can be more elusive and nonlinear than evidence-guided researchers might hope.

There are also times when a child's thoughts and actions defy known diagnostics or psychosocial explanations. When faced with puzzling situations in relational practice, workers must ask themselves what they are missing, what they have not considered or noticed in this child's unique set of circumstances. What might hold the key to productive intervention and change? Embracing inquiry helps workers avoid viewing problems as residing in their clients. Seeing people as problems all too often leads to blaming them or their caregivers for their predicament. When workers, children, and families view *problems* as problems, they are much more likely to pursue further knowledge than to defer to simplistic solutions.

REFLEXIVITY WITHIN A RELATIONAL PERSPECTIVE

It is natural for people to have beliefs and assumptions, especially when trying to make sense of human suffering. It is also natural to have opinions about almost everything: right and wrong, normal and deviant, good parenting and bad parenting, and so on. Relational perspectives promote reflexive strategies to circumvent the natural inclination to impose our beliefs upon others. Reflexivity engages practitioners in an ongoing process of identifying and analyzing the influence of personal beliefs, professional knowledge, and social and cultural values on how we practice. Maintaining awareness of our opinions and biases helps reduce their unintended impact on the work we do. Being conscious of what we do *not* know is equally important to reflexive practice. Hence reflexivity is a multifaceted and active process that requires workers "to sift through and sort out different impressions, layers of meaning and awareness as we concurrently learn about others and ourselves" (Dean, 2001, p. 625).

Attuned attitudes and guiding values are particularly important for child-centered practice. This is because working with children inevitably evokes conscious and unconscious responses to our childhoods. When these default reactions go unrecognized and unaddressed, they can unduly influence our work. Lack of reflexivity can result in assessment errors and ineffective treatment or service planning.

Over time, it is natural for practitioners to accrue portfolios of experience with child clients and their families. These impressions are beneficial, in that they contribute to practice wisdom. It is also true, however, that experience can make workers presumptuous about clients' problems or incurious when they believe that they've seen it all. When this happens, workers run the risk of seeing what they expect rather than what is before them.

Continuous reflexivity encourages workers to maintain critical attitudes toward their practice knowledge and values. In assessment, it helps workers resist the temptation to quickly classify clients or to rely exclusively on unchecked intuition or anecdotal experiences. When engaged in case planning, reflexive workers refrain from deferring to familiar techniques or approaches. Instead they actively seek intervention methods that best fit the children and families engaged in treatment processes.

When working with people from unfamiliar cultures or situations, reflexivity invites workers to be open to learning about clients' individualized influences and cultural practices. Openness actively directs workers' attention to their lived culture and how it inevitably informs internalized assumptions. Awareness of these assumptions helps counter unrecognized bias and promotes authentic and effective relationships with diverse children and families.

THE BOY IN THE WAITING ROOM: PART 2

Let's revisit the young boy in the waiting room for a snapshot of how to apply the relational perspective. We now know his name is Roger. Imagine that according to four-year-old Roger's case file, at age two he lost his mother to a drug overdose. His father, a disabled Iraq war veteran, was unable to adequately care for him because of war-related disabilities. With no extended family to speak of and few if any economic resources, Roger's father made the difficult choice to relinquish his parental rights when his son turned three. That was when Roger became a ward of the state. His caseworkers had every hope that he would quickly be adopted. As a side note, the gentleman seen reading to Roger in the waiting area is the bus driver who regularly takes him from Head Start to his therapy appointment. They have known each other for about a year and reportedly share a warm and friendly relationship.

As it happens, Roger is now in his third foster home. His first placement fell apart because the foster family was not prepared to manage his irregular and sometimes explosive behaviors. According to case records, Roger has been diagnosed with attention-deficit/hyperactivity disorder (ADHD) and separation anxiety. He has trouble with transitions of any sort. He sleeps fitfully and wets his bed.

Roger's second placement ended because a fifteen-year-old boy living in the foster home lost his temper, called Roger a racist term, and blackened his eyes. After this incident, Roger was placed with a single, African American woman, Dora Miller, who has two married daughters. Thus far he seems content in this home, and Mrs. Miller reports that she and Roger are slowly learning about each other.

According to Head Start staff, Roger is a quick learner who is capable of self-directed play. His reported behavioral difficulties occur primarily during transitions, for example, at the beginning of the day when he first separates from his foster mother, at recess, and at the end of the day when it's time to clean up. His teachers say that, once out of control, Roger has a hard time settling down; it can take up to half an hour for him "to get back to himself."

Roger reportedly expresses remorse about these incidents. One teacher states that Roger is extremely hard on himself and is constantly aware of how he is perceived by others. He asks everyone he meets, Do you like me?

Notes in the case file indicate that Roger's teachers and previous case-workers have had concerns about his slow growth and frail appearance. Roger's record holds no evaluations or summaries from his medical providers. The worker will follow up with Mrs. Miller to glean her thoughts about Roger's stature and health condition. If appropriate, she will work with her to obtain an up-to-date medical assessment.

Let's pause for a moment to reflect upon your initial impressions of young Roger. From the information provided, do you have tentative theories that might shed light on his behaviors? Where does evidence for these working hypotheses come from? What aspects of Roger's story do you consider relevant to relationship building? What information is missing? What steps might you take to engage Roger in his healing?

It's the worker's job in the beginning to learn about Roger within the context of the unique relationship they will form with one another. This is not to say that the worker enters this relationship as a blank slate. This would be both impossible and inappropriate. Everyone enters relationships with assumptions and expectations. In this worker's case, for instance, knowledge of attachment and relational theories guides her to pay particular attention to whether Roger has difficulty forming and/or trusting a relationship. If so, loss may be a significant factor in his troubles. The worker will also take note that as a white woman working with an African American child and foster parent, race may be a factor in establishing their relationship.

The worker will stay acutely aware that at the outset of this unique therapeutic encounter her hypotheses are working assumptions, not facts or truths. She speculates that Roger may need to reject her many times before he accepts her. Having made these reflective notes, the worker will also be open to the possibility that Roger will be nothing like the child described in the case file.

Another part of her preparation for working with Roger is to examine current evidence on the etiology and treatments for childhood ADHD. In this case, the worker ponders whether Roger's behaviors conform to an ADHD diagnosis. She leaves open the possibility that his dysregulation may have more to do with relational insecurities and despair than with neurological inattentiveness.

The worker will compare the evidence she gathers with what she learns about Roger in their direct encounters, in his play, and from his caregivers. She will notice whether his actions conform to those seen in other children who present with ADHD symptoms. If they do, she will apply techniques (e.g., cognitive-behavioral therapy) that have proven successful with this set of behaviors. She might also investigate the utility of medication to help Roger access his strengths, if ADHD is diagnosed. If a diagnosis of ADHD doesn't appear appropriate, she will seek methods that fit best with Roger's unique constellation of temperament, behaviors, and needs.

From what she has read as well as from her work experience, the worker has come to believe in the importance of developing a positive working relationship with Roger's foster mother. Thus she will do her best to establish a collaborative relationship with Mrs. Miller, grounded in mutuality and respect. The worker will listen with keen interest to Mrs. Miller's assessment of Roger's talents and challenges, while validating any frustrations that his behavior may prompt. She will impart her ideas, including those concerning Roger's multiple losses, attachment, and ADHD.

The worker will also seek out the foster mother's thoughts and theories. She will do her best to determine how variables embedded in the circumstances of Roger's young life are affecting his present functioning. She will elicit Mrs. Miller's thoughts about Roger's health, growth, and wellness and determine if further medical work-ups might shed light on his current situation. Based on their shared expertise, they will determine a treatment plan aimed at helping Roger achieve optimal functioning.

As previously mentioned, the worker is aware that race and class differences may play a role in relational trust building with Mrs. Miller. Furthermore she speculates that cultural differences may surface in regards to child-rearing and disciplinary practices. The worker will gently raise issues of power and difference as they go about cementing their relationship. Honest exchange, she believes, will ensure an effective working alliance.

Finally, the worker knows that Roger will profit if she is able to communicate effectively with his teachers, service providers, and other significant people in his life. Therefore she will establish lines of communication with Head Start staff, his caseworker, community members, and if appropriate, other professional caregivers invested in Roger's health and success. In the end, she will embrace the old Japanese proverb, None of us is as smart as all of us.

SUMMARY

In the late 1970s, Helen Harris Perlman reignited interest in relational principles for social work practice. At the time, Perlman was concerned that the essential relational connection was being replaced by contemporary approaches that promised briefer treatments and better outcome without the benefits of human exchange. She did not discount the utility of these approaches but sought to remind practitioners that relationship is critical to any successful therapeutic intervention.

Relationship plays a central role in social work practice with children and families. Relational principles underscore the critical healing potential of human connection. They are grounded in the belief that children, and most parents, do the best they can. Children's attachments to parents and other primary caregivers form the basis of health and well-being. When troubles befall children and families, relational practitioners offer guidance and support to reduce and overcome the effects. Relationships sustain hope in children and families that supports them through often difficult times.

Relational practitioners appreciate that every child who comes to their attention is uniquely responsive to the many relationships present in his or her life. They recognize that children and parents live in families and communities and are influenced by their connections or disconnections to broader social and economic forces. They know too that *how* they form relationships with child clients and their families is at the heart of positive change.

A relational perspective informs the knowledge, skills, and attitudes brought to the practice environment. It promotes thoughtful use of evidence-guided research while acknowledging the complementary knowledge that clients bring to therapeutic encounters. Relational practice requires that workers be reflexive about personal beliefs and biases to avoid imposing them on clients. In Roger's case, the second worker took time to reflect upon her initial impression; she considered self-reflection a mandatory component of child-centered assessment. She also knew that as she reflected upon Roger, he was speculating about her. It would take both of them to foster a safe-enough relationship in which healing and growth could occur.

In today's world, access to appropriate and effective mental health and social services for children and families is undermined by downturns in the economy. At the same time, more children and families are being identified as needing complex therapeutic interventions. Agencies in the second decade of the twenty-first century are responding like those in Perlman's generation, investing in brief treatment protocols and increasingly promoting pharmaceutical solutions.

It is times like these that inspire reconnection to the roots of social work and relational practices. Meaningful relationships enhance the benefits and sustainability of all forms of therapeutic intervention. The extra time it takes to build a meaningful relationship may in the end reduce costs by preventing or reducing the likelihood of future problems for young clients. The cost of not caring is much higher.

References

Borden, W. (2000). The relational paradigm in contemporary psychoanalysis: Toward a psychodynamically informed social work perspective. *Social Service Review,* 74(3), 353–379.

Contro, N., Larson, J., Scofield, S., Sourkes, B., & Cohen, H. (2002). Family perspectives on the quality of pediatric palliative care. *Archives of Pediatric and Adolescent Medicine,* 156(1), 14–20.

Dean, R. G. (2001). The myth of cross-cultural competence. *Families in Society,* 82(6), 623–630.

Duncan, B. L., Miller, S. D., & Sparks, J. (2007). Common factors and the uncommon heroism of youth. *Psychotherapy in Australia,* 13(2), 34–43.

Graybeal, C. T. (2007). Evidence for the art of social work. *Families in Society,* 88(4), 513–522.

Konrad, S. C., & Browning, D. M. (2012). Relational learning and interprofessional practice: Transforming health education for the 21st century. *Work,* 41(3), 247–251.

Laird, J. (1998). Theorizing culture: Narrative ideas and practice principles. In M. McGoldrick (Ed.), *Revisioning family therapy: Race, culture and gender in clinical practice* (pp. 93–110). New York: Guilford Press.

Lambert, M. J., & Barley, D. E. (2001). Research summary on the therapeutic relationship and psychotherapy outcome. *Psychotherapy,* 38(4), 357–361.

Laursen, E. K., & Birmingham, S. M. (2003). Caring relationships as protective factors for at-risk youth: An ethnographic study. *Families in Society,* 84(2), 240.

Masten, A. S. (2001). Ordinary magic: Resilience processes in development. *American Psychologist,* 56(3), 227–238.

Miller, J. B. (1976). *Toward a new psychology of women.* Boston: Beacon Press.

Peloquin, S. M. (2005). Embracing our ethos, reclaiming our heart. *American Journal of Occupational Therapy,* 59(6), 611–625.

Perlman, H. H. (1979). *Relationship: The heart of helping people.* Chicago: University of Chicago Press.

Pozzuto, R., Arnd-Caddigan, A., & Averett, P. (2009). Notes in support of a relational social work perspective: A critical review of the relational literature with implication for macro practice. *Smith College Studies in Social Work,* 79, 5–16.

Saleebey, D. (2009). *The strengths perspective* (5th ed.). Boston: Allyn and Bacon.

Schore, J. R., & Schore, A. N. (2008). Modern attachment theory: The central role of affect regulation in development and treatment. *Clinical Social Work Journal,* 36, 9–20.

Strean, H. S. (1980). [Review of the book *Relationship: The heart of helping people* by H. H. Perlman]. *Social Work,* 25(1), 71–72.

Tosone, C. (2004). Relational social work: Honoring the tradition. *Smith College Studies in Social Work,* 74, 475–487.

Watson, J. (2009). Caring science and human caring theory: Transforming professional practices of nursing and health care. *Journal of Health and Human Service Administration,* 31(4), 466–482.

Zeanah, C. H., & Smyke, A. T. (2008). Attachment disorders in family and social context. *Infant Mental Health Journal,* 29(3), 219–233.

2

Early Experiences Matter

If we love science we can love it for its commonness, its everyday presence in the form of observing, questioning, examining—its everyday practice in our clinical work.

Selma Fraiberg, "The Muse in the Kitchen"

SCIENCE IN ACTION

This chapter focuses on evolving scientific or evidence-guided knowledge that underpins our understanding of children, family systems, and their sociocultural realities. Scientific study is a systematic process that organizes and evaluates what we know about a phenomenon at any given time. Such inquiry tests and retests theoretical knowledge and encourages breakthroughs and innovations in our scholarship and professional practices. Sir Karl Popper, a twentieth-century science philosopher, was famous for asserting that scientific knowledge consisted primarily of learning from our mistakes. That is, new knowledge disproves and replaces existing knowledge, thereby changing our theories and beliefs about human behavior and the social environment.

Childhood researchers include neuroscientists, public health researchers, epidemiologists, behavioral scholars, and community action researchers who pursue discovery in tandem with relevant community partners. Whether investigating brain development, the effects of maternal alcohol use, or the impact of economic insecurities, these laboratory-based, population health and social scientists are united in their search for salient factors that contribute to health and childhood well-being. Moreover, their research is typically used and appraised by critical stakeholders. For instance, social strategists and legislators use up-to-date social science metrics to improve policies for social and child welfare programs; mental health providers use evidence-guided protocols to upgrade preventive services and other interventions; and educators determine curriculum based on current knowledge of learning outcomes.

Families, too, rely on contemporary research findings. One has only to surf the Internet to gauge the vast impact that the science of childhood has on everyday life. For example, expectant parents do a Google search for information about the best birthing techniques; parents seek out Internet resources to help their depressed teen; and families respond to news media reports on recent child-focused research.

How is scientific knowledge useful and applicable to real-world child- and family-centered practice? Consider the following conversation that I had several years ago with a second-grade teacher in the school cafeteria. (I had many such conversations during my work in three schools.) As you will see, the teacher was investigating her own theory about Amanda and her behaviors. What evidence made her deduce that Amanda's mother was lax in her discipline? Why was she skeptical about the student's ADHD diagnosis? Before responding to this or any other teacher's queries, I begin by asking myself, what does he or she really want to know? My first step therefore was to gain a better understanding of the teacher's perspective before inserting my own.

> TEACHER. Do you really think that Amanda has an attention-deficit disorder? I think her mother is simply too permissive.
>
> ME. Can you describe Amanda's behaviors? I ask because there are many explanations for why children are inattentive.
>
> TEACHER. I thought ADHD was a straightforward diagnosis. All I know is that Amanda can't seem to focus on her work. She looks dreamy and distracted. I read somewhere that when kids don't get good structure at home, they do poorly in school and can become ADHD. I think that may be Amanda's problem.
>
> ME. That could explain Amanda's inattention, but over the years I've learned there are so many opinions out there about what causes ADHD.
>
> TEACHER. Really? I thought it's pretty obvious that it's either the child's brain or his parents.
>
> ME. Yeah, I wish it was so clear cut.
>
> TEACHER. Well, what do you think?
>
> ME. It's been my experience that in most situations parenting isn't usually the only cause. There are so many parents who provide little structure for their kids, yet not all of those children end up with attention problems or ADHD.
>
> TEACHER. Oh. I never thought about it that way.
>
> ME. Because of the work I do, I've done a lot of reading about child behavior, and what I've learned is that kids with ADHD have different

levels of brain activity than those who don't. I also found out that typically children with true ADHD tend to have focus problems early on. I wonder . . . has Amanda always seemed dreamy and distracted?

TEACHER. Hmmm . . . now that you mention it, she seemed to be more put together at the beginning of the school year. Her mother got a new boyfriend around Christmas time, so I assumed Amanda isn't getting all the attention she needs. Boy, her mother can pick them.

ME. That may be important information . . . sometimes kids can become distracted by tensions in the family. They're so preoccupied with things at home that they're unable to concentrate on their schoolwork.

TEACHER. You know, Amanda mentioned that she didn't like her mother's new boyfriend, but I just chalked that up to being jealous of her mother's time. By Amanda's accounts this new guy sounds like a bully. I wonder . . . she did seem so much better last fall.

ME. You know Amanda better than I do. But I think your questions are really thoughtful and important. Amanda's attention problems could be attributable to many things, but one thing I do know is that ADHD doesn't suddenly happen. So it's insightful that you noticed the changes that have taken place in her over the course of the school year.

TEACHER. Perhaps I should talk with her mother and see if she'd be willing for Amanda to meet with you.

ME. An assessment might be helpful to you, Amanda, and her mother. That way we'd all be more certain about what we're dealing with.

The conversation above represents how complementary knowledge, including relevant research findings associated with inattention, ADHD, and family systems, can be shared in practice settings. On one hand, teachers, school administrators, and staff have considerable information and insight into their students' lives. They know about the triumphs and hardships children and families face. They're keyed into the neighborhood and understand the culture of the community in which their students live. On the other hand, practitioners, in this case the school social worker, also have expertise. The teacher knew Amanda. I knew about various psychosocial and neurological conditions associated with children's inattention. Together we explored the evidence and proposed a plan based on observation and science. Our evidentiary collaboration and shared investment in Amanda would, in the end, serve her best.

I hope this example conveys how empirical knowledge is thoughtfully integrated into the daily discourse of practice. What follows is a sampling of scientific discoveries relevant to work with children and families. The chapter begins by focusing on infant brain and neuroscience research. Such research describes how an infant's brain development is influenced by human relationship. This research is important to understanding human relationships, separation issues, attachment, and the regulatory system. We will also examine efforts to integrate early-childhood research findings into early-childhood programs and policy.

The chapter continues by looking at the effects of stress and adversity in childhood, including hardships incurred by economic and social insecurities. Many of the children who become our clients enter mental health and social service settings because of complex and problematic interactions they and their families are having with their environments. Knowledge of how economic disadvantage and stress influence emotional, social, and behavioral development is thus critical to effective child-centered practice.

The chapter concludes with a discussion of research that examines human resilience, defined for our purposes as a person's or system's capacity to adapt and thrive amid life's challenges. In particular we will look at qualities and conditions associated with resilience in children and their families. Knowledge of resiliency factors is foundational for conducting useful assessments and developing beneficial intervention plans with the children and families we serve.

RELATIONSHIP AND THE BRAIN

Over the past forty years, investigators across disciplines, including developmental biology, education, neuroscience, genomics, epidemiology, and mental health, have pooled their expertise to significantly advance our knowledge of early childhood. These advances offer a scientific foundation to what many already surmised—that early-childhood relational experiences matter, in many different ways.

Scientific trends associate the development of children's regulatory capacity and relational competency with the quality of their earliest caregiving relationships. Neuroimaging discoveries illustrate that the growing child's brain and neurological development are highly responsive to caregiver feedback (Schore & Schore, 2008). Thus infants whose cries are met with reassurance and responsiveness become confident that they will survive. As a result their brains learn how to wait, delay gratification, and trust in relational security. Children whose needs are inconsistently or rarely met are apt to flounder; their brains have not received consistent enough feedback to assure them that relationships are trustworthy. Without reliable input, these infants do not learn how to effectively communicate their needs, self-soothe, or develop skills that help them maintain internal harmony. As will be further explained in chapter 3, the qualities of infants' and caregivers' earliest attachments have wide-reaching effects on short- and long-term development.

If infants' development relies on caregivers, then it is logical that mothers, fathers, and other primary caregivers also need to receive positive feedback from their children to feel validated and nurtured. Without relational reinforcement, parents may become uncertain of their skills or feel rejected by their children. In the case of infants born with disabilities or temperamental irregularities, their needs may be difficult to read even for the most seasoned parents. Moreover, parents who themselves have not received adequate nurturing in childhood may not have the skills and know-how to be sufficiently responsive to their babies.

Even secure adults struggle with new parenthood, so it is not surprising that vulnerable parents may find caring for their young children highly stressful. Such stress is exacerbated by economic adversity as well as by co-occurring conditions such as insufficient shelter, unemployment, and medical or mental health problems. Preventive assistance and early intervention can significantly benefit these children and families.

INFANT MENTAL HEALTH RESEARCH

Selma Fraiberg (1987) and her colleagues were some of the first clinician-researchers to methodically observe and record interactions between vulnerable infants (from birth to age three) and parents in their home environments. They witnessed the interconnectivity between infants' demands and parents' needs. They speculated that parents of infants, especially those born with congenital differences, required nurturing themselves in order to adequately care for their high-need children.

Weatherston (2000, p. 3) describes the work of these clinician-researcher pioneers: "Each practitioner returned to 'the source,' the home where the infant and parent lived, to observe first-hand, the infant or toddler within the context of the emerging parent-child relationship. Sitting beside the parent and infant at the kitchen table or on the floor or sofa, the Infant Mental Health practitioner watched and listened carefully in an effort to understand the capacities of the child and family, the risks they faced, and the ways in which the practitioner might be helpful to the infant or toddler and the family."

Fraiberg's (1987) research is recognized as foundational to the development of the infant mental health (IMH) field. IMH practitioners focus on relationships between infants and parents, between families and practitioners, and between family systems and communities. Through methodical, direct observations, these interdisciplinary practitioners learned about the importance of nurturing for both infants and parents. They concluded that parents who feel secure and cared for are better equipped to nurture their infants. According to these parents, feeling *secure* meant access to obtainable economic and material resources. Feeling *cared for* included the availability of people who listened to their concerns, responded with compassion, and came to their emotional aid when needed.

EARLY-CHILDHOOD DEVELOPMENT

Some thirty years after Fraiberg and her colleagues conducted their studies, the National Research Council and the Institute of Medicine initiated a broad-based review of existing scientific knowledge on early-childhood development, which came to be titled *From Neurons to Neighborhoods* (*FNTN*; Shonkoff & Phillips, 2000). These eminent organizations brought together investigators spanning a range of disciplines, including medicine, mental health, education, human services, engineering, and public health. The committee's charge was to update and integrate what was then known about the nature of early childhood and, in particular, the role and impact of early experiences on the growing child. Their tasks were to clarify and separate evidence-guided knowledge from popular and often politicized beliefs about young children (from birth to age five); to learn more about trends in childhood and child rearing; and to consider and apply this knowledge to the development of policy, practices, training, and research that affected children and their families.

Overarching themes that emerged from the extensive and multilevel *FNTN* study substantiated and expanded upon past observational findings and contemporary neuroscience and attachment research. In sum, findings validated the influential and enduring nature of children's earliest relationships and experiences. *FNTN* editors Shonkoff and Phillips (2000) offered the following consolidation of the review's most prominent findings:

- All children are born wired for feelings and ready to learn. Early life experiences matter.
- Nurturing relationships are essential to children's health and development.
- Needs of children and families change over time, and society must be responsive to these changes.

Core concepts from *FNTN* are presented in a modified form in box 2.1.

FNTN investigations emphasized that childhood development is a dynamic process influenced by complex and interacting factors. These include the differential effect of an array of early and ongoing relationships as well as the pervasive influence of physiological, psychosocial, socioeconomic, relational, and environmental factors, and cultural diversity. Early adversity and material insecurities are seen as significant contributors to childhood vulnerability. Environmental conditions, including toxicity and other health hazards, also play key roles in children's health disparities and vulnerabilities. Factors of safety and the predominance of community and

BOX 2.1
Core Findings about Early Childhood

- Human development is shaped by a dynamic and continuous interaction between biology and experience.

- Culture influences every aspect of human development.

- The growth of self-regulation is a cornerstone of early-childhood development and cuts across all domains of behavior.

- Children are active participants in their own development.

- Human relationships and their interactional effects are the building blocks of healthy development.

- The broad range of individual differences among young children makes it difficult to distinguish normal variations from transient or persistent impairments.

- The development of children unfolds along individual pathways characterized by continuities and discontinuities, as well as by a series of significant transitions.

- Human development is shaped by the ongoing interplay among sources of vulnerability and sources of resilience.

- The timing of early experiences can matter, but more often than not, the developing child remains vulnerable to risks and open to protective influences throughout the early years of life and into adulthood.

- The course of development can be altered in early childhood by effective interventions that change the balance between risk and protections, thereby shifting the odds in favor of more adaptive outcomes.

Shonkoff & Phillips, 2000.

family violence are also viewed as influential in even the youngest children's wellness.

Because of the confluence of so many variables, *FNTN* researchers advised that children's development must be considered with attention to individualization rather than normalization. *FNTN* concluded by stating that the care and protection of young children should be shared by adults at all relational levels, including parents, families, institutions, and the greater society. Accordingly, *FNTN* emphasized that children need something from all of us: "At their most intimate level, they require the investment and attention of a limited number of adults. In their broadest context, they depend on an environment that supports the child-rearing function of families. In the final analysis, healthy child development is dependent on a combination of individual responsibility, informal social supports, and formalized structures that evolve within a society" (Shonkoff & Phillips, 2000, p. 337).

Although *FNTN* recognized the many stresses and challenges young children and their families face, it is infused with hope for their futures. It is a perfect blend of science and advocacy, and in the end, it recommends that program developers, policy makers, and child-centered practitioners commit to early and effective interventions that can benefit all children and families, and most particularly those identified as vulnerable.

EARLY INVESTMENT IN CHILD DEVELOPMENT

The Center on the Developing Child (CDC) at Harvard University in Cambridge, Massachusetts, extends the work of *FNTN* by applying the science of early childhood to the design of intervention programs, programmatic evaluation, and child-focused policy development. Their mission is to use findings from early-childhood science to enhance the welfare of children and families on a broad-based societal scale. Underlying their research is the operating assumption that early investment in children has both short- and long-term benefits for human health and well-being.

One example of CDC's research was an investigation into conditions and resources that contribute to the quality of early-intervention programs, particularly those accessed by families and children considered to be at risk. Research goals were to better identify specific environmental and human factors that underlie a child's burgeoning capacities for learning, socialization, and positive physical and mental health. Effectiveness factors associated with successful child- and family-centered programs were identified, and are outlined in box 2.2.

Although it could be said that these factors would benefit any child, the study underscored that economically disadvantaged and otherwise vulnerable children need optimal educational, relational, and environmental structures to circumvent resource disparities. The researchers emphasized that poorly designed programs have little or no benefit and may in fact incur greater costs to families and society in the long run. Alternatively, well-constructed early-intervention services offer benefits to children and families that can last a lifetime.

So what does the CDC's research tell us, and what social and political decisions does it inform? One example of its utility in decision making is represented by discussions that address the economic crisis in the United States. In 2011, proposed cuts in funding for early-intervention programs such as Head Start were being considered to reduce federal spending. Since 1964, Head Start, a federally funded program for children age three to five, has reliably provided a range of educational, health-based, and family

BOX 2.2
What Children Need: A Science-Based Framework for Early-Childhood Policy

FINDINGS

- Positive and enduring early relationships influence children's brain architecture.
- Positive relationships, rich learning opportunities, and safe environments support optimal learning.
- Early and positive experiences prior to school entry produce better health, learning, and behavioral outcomes than later remediation services.
- Programs and policies that support early relationships create sturdy foundations for later academic, social, and economic achievement.
- Programs composed of underskilled staff for cost-saving purposes will not be effective.
- Up-front costs for early intervention generate a strong return on investment.

FACTORS THAT PROMOTE CHILD DEVELOPMENT

- Access to basic health care for parents and children.
- Reduction in levels of neurotoxins in the environment.
- Early-childhood programs staffed by highly skilled and relationally responsive staff that offer language-rich and stimulating environments with age-appropriate ratios.

EFFECTIVE INTERVENTION STRATEGIES FOR AT-RISK AND LOW-INCOME CHILDREN AND FAMILIES

- Intensive in-home support for first-time parents.
- High-quality, center-based, early education programs to enhance cognitive and social development.
- Cross-generational programs that provide support and guidance for parents and early education for children.
- Specialized service-specific programs for young children who experience adverse childhood experiences,* to promote better brain development.
- Work-based income supplements for economically disadvantaged families.

Modified from Center on the Developing Child, 2007. Retrieved from www.developingchild.harvard.edu

*Includes abuse and neglect, severe maternal depression, parental substance abuse, and family violence.

resource services to children and families across the nation. The US Department of Health and Human Services has oversight of Head Start programs, but some states also contribute dollars or enhance programming through additional state-level early-intervention initiatives.

Head Start meets criteria cited by CDC to provide early, high-quality services to economically disadvantaged and vulnerable children and families who would otherwise not have access to preschool, child care, and health-related services. There is no doubt that funding cuts targeting early-intervention programming will have significant and potentially devastating effects on the health and welfare of children and families who now participate in Head Start. What CDC research also tells us, however, is that such cuts will increase costs to society in the long run. This is because children exposed to positive early experiences are more likely to be healthier, to learn more effectively, and to have stable regulatory capacities that contribute to better adult health outcomes. Better health means lower health-care costs over time. Thus when advocating on behalf of early-intervention services, strong empirical evidence like that being discovered at CDC is available to support the argument that early investments in children profit everyone; preventing problems is always less expensive in human and financial costs than solving problems later in life.

EARLY-CHILDHOOD ADVERSITY AND HEALTH

The Adverse Childhood Experiences (ACE) study is a large-scale, ongoing project that asks the following question: do early-childhood experiences affect health in later life and, if so, in what ways? (Dube, Felitti, Dong, Giles, & Anda, 2003). In a collaboration between the US Centers for Disease Control and Prevention and Kaiser Permanente's Health Appraisal Center in San Diego, California, ACE researchers look at the impact of child abuse, family violence, and other detrimental life experiences on lifelong health outcomes. Thus far, study findings suggest that there are predictable links between deprivation and trauma in early childhood and the advent of chronic illnesses and other life-affecting conditions in adulthood (Dong, Anda, Dube, Giles, & Felitti, 2003; Shonkoff, Boyce, & McEwen, 2009). Moreover, adverse experiences are more often than not interrelated. This means that a child who is sexually abused may simultaneously experience exposure to physical or emotional neglect and other household strains and stressors.

ACE research proposes that children living in poor, disadvantaged environments are more likely to experience cumulative effects of adversity. This is due in part to their limited access to healthy resources, for example, nutritious food and stable shelter. It also results from less exposure to resource-rich learning and social institutions. Furthermore, in the United States, no- or low-income families are often without adequate health insurance, and as a consequence, they also experience disparities in health-care access and provision.

Concurrent with material insecurities and resource disparities, parents living in insecure environments are more likely to be distracted and distressed and therefore less able to meet the multifaceted demands of their growing children. These wide-ranging early adversities negatively affect health early in children's development as well as across the life course. ACE factors identified in the study are highlighted in box 2.3.

Findings from the ongoing ACE study support and reinforce the importance of early intervention with children and families. Congruent with findings from *FNTN* and CDC, they serve as strong scientific impetus for advocacy and activism on behalf of children in these harsh economic times. Indeed they explicitly bring present and future voices of children and families to the forefront of public attention, highlighting that shortsighted cost savings now may produce long-term costs for years.

STRESS AND ITS IMPACTS

The studies highlighted thus far in this chapter have emphasized the potentially damaging effect that cumulative, persistent, and uncontrollable adversity has on human health. When such adversity is neither addressed nor buffered, it can lead to both immediate and lifelong physical and psychobiological problems for children, as well as for adults (Shonkoff et al., 2009). It

---

BOX 2.3
Adverse Childhood Factors

- Recurrent physical abuse
- Recurrent physical neglect
- Recurrent emotional abuse
- Recurrent emotional neglect
- Contact sexual abuse
- Household substance abuse
- An incarcerated household member
- A person with mental illness in the household
- Domestic or family violence
- Parental disruption and loss

From Adverse Childhood Experiences study. Modified from Dube, Felitti, Dong, Giles, & Anda, 2003.

is also true, however, that children need to master certain levels of controlled adversity in order to learn new tasks and develop resilience to life's challenges.

To better understand the intersection of stress and resilience, the National Scientific Council on the Developing Child (2005) developed a taxonomy that describes three categories of stressful life experiences. These include positive, tolerable, and toxic stress and their relative impact on developing children.

Positive stress occurs when children are faced with acute events that are frustrating or anxiety-producing. For example, on the first day of kindergarten a five-year-old may experience short-term, acute stress or some level of separation anxiety. The ability to endure this stressful experience depends in part on the context of supportive relationships that help children master anxiety. When children master stress, it leads to increased self-worth ("I did it. And I got a sticker, too") and, on a physiologic level, restores the body's stress-response system to baseline. Each time children negotiate stressful transitions, they gain mastery that generalizes to other experiences of change.

Tolerable stress occurs when a child's physiological state is disrupted by a major, life-altering event. For example, the loss of a loved one or a sustained period of environmental instability (e.g., divorce, homelessness) constitutes a stressor that could potentially disrupt a child's neurological development. If stress is not mediated by support, it is more likely that the child will experience short- and/or long-term adverse effects.

Even a one-time traumatic event that is not dealt with effectively can leave lasting physiological and emotional scars. For example, children who experience violence or abuse that is neither named nor believed may struggle with lifelong anxieties, fears, and mistrust. Conversely, positive resources and relational buffers help mediate the damaging effects of such stressors on the developing child.

Temperamental factors also influence how the child negotiates and integrates stress-producing situations. Thus an easygoing youngster may be able to take an unexpected relocation in his stride, whereas a child who has ongoing difficulties with transitions might find it highly disruptive to his emotional and physical well-being.

Excessive, persistent, or uncontrollable adversity is at the root of *toxic stress*. Extreme poverty, chronic neglect, ongoing parental physical or mental illness, and recurring family and community violence are examples of chronic situations known to provoke toxic stress. Often these stressors take place simultaneously, leaving little room for physiological or emotional reprieve. In other words, there is insufficient stress-free time for the brain to restore or repair the effects of unremitting stressful assault.

Children experiencing toxic stress may appear distracted and detached, and are often misdiagnosed as having psychiatric conditions, neurologic disabilities, or attentional disorders. Over time, toxic stress interferes with healthy brain development and relational trust. As a result, damage to other organ systems may occur, causing chronic physical and mental health problems that persist throughout life. Toxic stress and its effects are consistent with the kinds of situations identified by the ACE research described above.

ECONOMIC DISADVANTAGE AND CHILDHOOD

The robust association between economic disadvantage and higher rates of early adverse experiences is noted by researchers across disciplines (Dube, Felitti, et al., 2003; Galster & Santiago, 2006; Schilling, Aseltine, & Gore, 2008; Shonkoff et al., 2009). Collectively speaking, economic hardship imposes tremendous burdens on children and parents. This is true for those living in urban settings or in rural communities. Thus studies find that children living in low-income urban neighborhoods have poorer health, lower levels of academic achievement, and fewer employment opportunities than same-age youngsters living in economically stable and advantaged areas. These youngsters are also likely to have greater exposure to community and family violence.

Children and families living in rural settings are also found to suffer greatly because of economic insecurities. Rural poverty is deeply embedded in the fabric of especially remote communities. It is often intergenerational and endures in families for longer periods than in comparable urban populations. Like their urban counterparts, children from disadvantaged rural areas lack access to health care and have limited recreational and social opportunities. Lack of money and transportation keeps them from obtaining needed services, most of which are located in distant towns and cities.

Financial disadvantage for all children and families is associated with tangible burdens in obtaining basic necessities of life, such as housing, food, medications, and clothing. It is also linked to emotional and relational consequences brought about by cultural marginalization and social stigma.

In his seminal work, Erving Goffman (1963) proposed that individuals and groups are stigmatized when they present characteristics or behaviors considered outside socially preferred norms. People living in poverty are often assumed to bring on their own problems and thus may receive little empathy or support from the general public. One has only to stand in line at the supermarket behind a young family paying for their groceries with food stamps to witness the marginalizing effects of material disadvantage. As the cashier publicly sifts through the family's purchases eliminating items not covered by their food stamps, you can sometimes hear the judgmental comments of others standing in line. These already vulnerable and struggling families are further targeted by uninformed attitudes and hostile reactions.

Economic disadvantage and children with health conditions

Economic disadvantage is especially felt by families of children with chronic health conditions. According to some estimates, families raising children with medical and developmental disabilities incur nearly three times the costs of those raising nondisabled children. Family budgets are overwhelmed by the limits of the reimbursement rates of the US health insurance system as well as by rising health-care costs (Parish, Rose, & Andrews, 2010; Sloper & Beresford, 2006). This is true for those with private insurance as well as for those with public insurance or without any insurance at all. According to Sloper and Beresford's (2006) study, up to 90 percent of US families caring for children with disabilities identify state benefits as their sole support. Financial burdens are exacerbated when the primary caregiver must reduce hours or leave employment altogether to stay home and care for his or her children (Parish, Rose, & Andrews, 2010).

In Canada approximately 500,000 children under the age of twenty are affected by disabilities (Kohen, Uppal, Khan, & Visentin, 2010). As in the United States, the medical costs for these children can range from two and a half to twenty times more than average childhood health-care costs. Moreover, costs to health and welfare for Canadian families caring for a child with a disability are significant, due to lack of resources such as respite, appropriate educational programming, and health-related support (Kohen et al., 2010).

According to American researchers, these families report a higher level of stress and a lower level of well-being than those raising healthy children. It is interesting to note, however, that families do not consider their caregiving duties or children's medical needs to be primary stressors. Instead, stress is associated with economic and resource inequities, insurance failure, and society's lack of understanding for the experiences of families whose children live with chronic medical conditions (Sloper & Beresford, 2006).

Therese's story helps illustrate these points. Magdalena, her daughter, was born with Leigh syndrome, a congenital cell disease that damages human cells that are essential for converting nutrition to energy. Leigh syndrome is usually diagnosed before age two, and physical deterioration is often rapid and leads to death. By the age of four, Magdalena's symptoms included seizures, feeding and speech difficulties, heart problems, and muscle weakness. By age five, she required medical technology assistance and twenty-four-hour care for basic activities of daily living. For the most part, Therese lovingly cared for her daughter as well as for her two younger children. In addition to home and child-rearing responsibilities, she worked at a Laundromat three mornings a week to supplement her husband's salary.

When asked about Magdalena, Therese would say that she was courageous, loved to read, and taught everyone in the family about gratitude. She would also tell you that being a parent to a child with a chronic health condition was hard work that few people outside of the disability world understood. At one particularly frustrating juncture, Therese made a list she called "Things People Don't Understand about Parents with Children with Life-Threatening Illnesses." Box 2.4 is a modified version of this list.

Therese's story exemplifies many of the common dilemmas shared by families of children with disabilities and chronic illnesses. Unlike poor or low-income families of healthy children, however, paid work is not the sole solution to the fiscal concerns faced by parents of children with chronic health conditions. Therese needed to be home to care for Magdalena. Although insurance paid for some home health service, it did not nearly cover all her health-care needs. Nor did Therese want others to care for her beautiful yet vulnerable daughter. Rather, she wanted to have as much time as possible with Magdalena, as she knew her life would be all too brief.

Therese aptly observed that few people recognize or seek to understand the experiences of parents whose children live with chronic medical conditions. Researchers report that family members, friends, and health professionals frequently misunderstand parents or avoid them altogether (Konrad, 2008). Like financially disadvantaged families, those caring for ill and disabled children are often judged as being somehow responsible for their plight. Parents are well aware that no one can truly know them unless they "walk in their shoes."

POVERTY AND STIGMA: THE CHILD'S VIEW

Socioeconomic differences are keenly felt not only by adults but also by children. In a culture that privileges wealth and celebrity, being poor represents the quintessential form of stigmatization, especially for children and youth embroiled in forming their identity. Many of these youngsters are well aware of the barriers to success they face.

As noted above, ample evidence associates poverty with adversity, social stigma, and negative health outcomes for children. However, very little of this research comes directly from the children themselves. Research conducted with children in America and the United Kingdom enlightens us to the day-to-day lived effects of growing up poor (Sutton, Smith, Dearden, & Middleton, 2007). For example, children tell us that being seen as economically disadvantaged makes them targets for bullies. According to children, when they are perceived as poor, they become susceptible to harassment and insult from their financially better-off peers.

Children's perceptions of stigmatization are confirmed by research findings. For example, in a study conducted by Sutton and colleagues (2007), middle-class children used disparaging terms to describe lower-income

BOX 2.4
Things People Don't Know about Parents of Children with Life-Threatening Illnesses

- We don't get uninterrupted sleep—ever.
- We can't keep jobs very well, because of the chance that our child will get sick.
- We don't have a social life.
- We have a *ton* of garbage.
- Our other children often have to wait.
- We don't like pity in people's voices.
- The day-to-day strain of the illness affects family life tremendously.
- Other people spend more time with our children than we do.
- Our phone bills are huge.
- We look at our calendars at least twenty-five times a day—no kidding.
- We feel like we're running a three-ring circus sometimes.
- We get a crash course in nursing, whether we want to or not.
- We can have ten to twenty people in our home per day working with our children.
- We have to deal with nursing agencies that JUST DON'T GET the fact that having seven different home health aides is not beneficial to our family's sanity.
- Giving up on dreams is frequent.
- Leaving our other children to go for daylong or monthly treatments for our sick child is very painful.
- The amount of coordination it takes for one of us to work full-time and the other part-time is exhausting. And finding child care at odd hours or coverage for sick children is nearly impossible.
- Our other children have needs that require meetings, too.
- Professionals don't understand that we need them to communicate with us in order to set up things like child-care and work schedules. It is important to ask parents and to keep them in the loop regarding any and all aspects of their child's care.
- It is difficult for us to ask for help.
- Because we need the help, we often put up with people whose personalities aren't necessarily compatible with our own. A little common courtesy would help.
- It is difficult to have much private time or space.
- Physicians expect us to get to their offices, while we have to find child care and sometimes transportation.

- Physicians think that parents can easily do medical procedures at home without taking into account siblings, mess, time, and so on.
- The amount of necessary medical supplies and equipment takes over the home.
- We constantly have to beg and plead for insurance to reimburse our health-care costs.
- We are dependent on a health-care system that is getting weaker by the day.

Therese Gaetjens, personal communication, March 28, 2012.

classmates. Furthermore, these youngsters assumed that economically vulnerable families had lower moral standards because they received state welfare subsidies. Children targeted by these disparaging views describe internalizing negative opinions. They report feeling defeated and hopeless about future prospects, which in the end, made them feel isolated or turn to negative means to gain status in their community.

Equally difficult for low-income children are the barriers to engagement in the world of their middle-class peers. Social-class chasms are created when activities of childhood are simply out of the reach of poor children. Lack of money and transportation impedes their ability to participate in athletic activities or academic extracurricular opportunities that could potentially level the social playing field. Moreover, many disadvantaged youngsters care for younger siblings or assume household responsibilities while their parents work multiple jobs.

In an attempt to belong, some youth find social/relational connection by joining gangs or otherwise marginalized groups. Messerschmidt (2000) found that incarcerated youth reported engaging in crime to be part of a social enterprise. They noted that socially sanctioned group memberships were more often than not unattainable for them, due to economic and cultural barriers and racism. Along with lives of economic deprivation, many of these youth experienced other early adversity, including multiple losses, early abuse, and chronic intrafamily conflict representative of the toxic stress described above.

FAMILY RESILIENCE

It is important for child- and family-centered workers to recognize that although adversity and poverty impose enormous burdens on children, parents, and families, one should never assume that there is a direct trajectory to negative outcomes for these youth. Why do some families do well while others succumb to the hardships imposed by harsh living circumstances? Social scientists agree that resilience explains this difference.

Resilient families support one another and find benefit in the shared experience of enduring and mastering life's difficulties. Researchers suggest that resilience is a dynamic process that is fostered by positive interaction and interrelationship with others, both within and outside the family system (Infante, 2001; Masten, 2001). Resilient families are characterized by a combination of individual qualities that include positive outlook, religious faith, communication and problem-solving capacities, planned time together, and other functional capabilities that enable families to manage and deal with hard times (Black & Lobo, 2008). Anticipating needs and avoiding risky behaviors also help families avoid crises and cope with challenges. Community-level factors that promote family resilience include involvement with and support from neighborhood and community networks, including faith-based institutions. Other protective community assets include living in safe environments and having access to high-quality education, child care, and health care (Bana & Bachoo, 2011).

How families perceive their circumstances also influences adaptation. Optimism, humor, and confidence are at the heart of dealing with adversity. Capacities to positively appraise difficult circumstances, find value in small successes, and cope with uncertainty helped families combat despair and hopelessness. Researchers Black and Lobo (2008) found that relational warmth between family members created security, which fostered courage and endurance to move past helplessness toward better lives and better futures.

There is no doubt that all children fare better when caregivers provide reliable emotional support and clear behavioral structure, and model socially acceptable behaviors. These qualities are especially important when raising youth at risk for social marginalization due to poverty. Family ties to neighborhood, school, and community are also protective factors for poor children.

Take Diego, age eight. His mother, Soledad, was determined that he receive all the educational resources necessary to address his learning and behavioral differences, despite their limited economic resources. Soledad knew that her son was bright, charming, and learning disabled. She witnessed his computer savvy and intense interest in a broad range of sophisticated subjects. Diego also loved sports and was physically adept at anything involving running and a ball. However, Soledad did not ignore the fact that Diego was a handful and challenged most of his classroom teachers. She observed daily how easily he was distracted at home even with just two parents and his dog, Pescado.

Soledad had to use personal days from her job to meet with Diego's teachers at the beginning, middle, and end of each school year. She checked his assignments and communicated with his teachers on a regular basis. She followed up with the assistant principal when Diego reported a reprimand. She made sure that Diego's father, who could not leave work to attend these meetings, knew of all school events and meetings.

Soledad wanted Diego to know that she and his father were aware of his activities and that they mattered. She found ways to refurbish old athletic equipment so that he could play on the district's youth soccer and hockey teams, especially important activities for youth living in Toronto.

Soledad convinced school decision makers that their educational assessment tools were biased against poor Hispanic kids who couldn't take advantage of software, expensive learning opportunities, and English-only instruments geared for those more economically privileged. And when the time came, she adamantly and successfully advocated that Diego be placed in the school's gifted and talented program even though he didn't meet the traditionally required criteria.

Soledad and Frank, his father, wanted to give Diego every chance possible to escape material hardship. Their efforts illustrate the diligence and perseverance it often takes to optimize learning and social opportunities for children without economic resources or social standing. Their efforts paid off. Diego did well in elementary and secondary school and went on to be successful in technical college.

Diego's story is one of family resilience and determination against adversity. However, family researchers caution that while a resiliency perspective emphasizes assets, one should never lose sight of poverty's negative effects or dismiss the tenaciousness of its intergenerational stronghold (Vandsburger, Harrigan, & Biggerstaff, 2008). Resilient parents like Soledad and Frank are not superhuman, nor are they immune to the harsh impact of stress and adversity. Child and family workers should thus never romanticize stories of success or minimize the ravages of economic hardship. Instead they must join in the struggle against economic injustice and disparities in systems that should treat all children as equally deserving of access to resources provided by schools, the community, and the wider society.

SUMMARY

Scientific study continually informs the work we do with children and families. Relational practitioners stay abreast of new knowledge to ensure that best practices are being used in the best interests of the people who become our clients. Workers are also encouraged to remain curious and to pursue studies of their own. Over the years, practitioner-researchers like Selma Fraiberg, Jean Baker Miller, and Judith and Allan Schore have translated client-centered wisdom into critical scientific discoveries.

The science of early childhood consistently reminds us that what happens in children's earliest years is highly influential throughout the life course. Furthermore, as Fraiberg and colleagues first learned in the kitchens of family homes, the quality of parents' lives also has ramifications on developing children. In all respects early-childhood science reinforces what most already know: that we are relationally interconnected, that children rely on their parents, that parents are responsive to their children, and that the quality of these interactions matter.

This chapter highlighted only a handful of important research endeavors. These included the groundbreaking *From Neurons to Neighborhoods* study supported by the Institute of Medicine and the National Research Council. *FNTN* synthesized existing knowledge about the effects of early experience on childhood, its underlying neurobiology, and the critical importance of investing in children and families as early in life as possible (Shonkoff et al., 2009). Since then, other important studies, including the ongoing ACE study, research at Harvard's CDC, and neuroscience inquiries conducted by a number of eminent researchers, have reinforced evidence supporting the importance of early attachments and the efficacy and agency of early interventions. For relational workers, this compelling and continually advancing evidence is part and parcel of the knowledge brought to micro- and macropractice and to program and policy-development initiatives. By the time this book reaches you, new discoveries will inform the work you do.

Therese's and Soledad's stories remind us of the critical importance of client-centered evidence. Indeed, these women bring life into what studies are meant to inform us about. They also illustrate how knowledge is translated into real-world experience and emphasize the radical imperative of advocacy and activism on behalf of all children. Their strength and tenacious spirit compel us to never be complacent about the needs of children and families, especially those whose resources are limited and whose circumstances are vulnerable.

References

Bana, A., & Bachoo, S. (2011). The determinants of family resilience among families in low- and middle-income contexts: A systematic literature review. *South African Journal of Psychology, 41*(2), 131–139.

Black, K., & Lobo, M. (2008). A conceptual view of family resilience. *Journal of Family Nursing, 14*(1), 33–55.

Center on the Developing Child. (2007). A science-based framework for early-childhood policy. Retrieved from www.developingchild.harvard.edu

Dong, M., Anda, R. F., Dube, S. R., Giles, W. H., & Felitti, V. J. (2003). The relationship of exposure to childhood sexual abuse to other forms of abuse, neglect, and household dysfunction during childhood. *Child Abuse and Neglect, 27*, 625.

Dube, S. R., Felitti, V. J., Dong, M., Giles, W. H., & Anda, R. F. (2003). The impact of adverse childhood experiences on health problems: Evidence from four birth cohorts dating back to 1900. *Preventive Medicine, 37*(3), 268–277.

Fraiberg, S. (1987). The muse in the kitchen: A case study in clinical research. In L. Fraiberg (Ed.), *Selected writings of Selma Fraiberg* (pp. 65–99). Columbus: Ohio State University Press.

Galster, G. C., & Santiago, A. M. (2006). What's the hood got to do with it? Parental perceptions of how neighborhood mechanisms affect their children. *Journal of Urban Affairs, 28*(3), 201–226.

Goffman, E. (1963). *Stigma: Notes on the management of spoiled identity.* New York: Simon and Schuster.

Infante, F. (2001). *Five open questions to resilience: A review of recent literature.* The Hague, Netherlands: Bernard van Leer Foundation.

Kohen, D., Uppal, S., Khan, S., & Visentin, L. (2010). Access and barriers to educational services for Canadian children with disabilities. Health Analysis and Measurement Group, Statistics Canada. Canadian Council on Learning. Retrieved from http://www.ccl-cca.ca/pdfs/OtherReports/201009KohenUppalKhanVisentinFullReport.pdf

Konrad, S. C. (2008). Mothers' perspectives on qualities of care in their relationships with health care professionals: The influence of relational and communicative competencies. *Journal of Social Work in End-of-Life and Palliative Care, 4*(1), 19–53.

Masten, A. S. (2001). Ordinary magic: Resilience processes in development. *American Psychologist, 56*(3), 227–238.

Messerschmidt, J. (2000). *Nine lives: Adolescent masculinities, the body and violence.* Boulder, CO: Westview Press.

National Scientific Council on the Developing Child. (2005). Center on the Developing Child, Harvard University. Retrieved from http://developingchild.harvard.edu/index.php/activities/council/

Parish, S., Rose, R. A., & Andrews, M. E. (2010). TANF's impact of low-income mothers raising children with disabilities. *Exceptional Children, 76*(2), 234–253.

Schilling, E. A., Aseltine, R. H., & Gore, S. (2008). The impact of cumulative childhood adversity on young adult mental health: Measures, models and interpretations. *Social Science and Medicine, 66*(5), 1140.

Schore, J. R., & Schore, A. N. (2008). Modern attachment theory: The central role of affect regulation in development and treatment. *Clinical Social Work Journal, 36,* 9–20.

Shonkoff, J. P., Boyce, W. T., & McEwen, B. S. (2009). Neuroscience, molecular biology, and childhood roots of health disparities: Building a new framework for health promotion and disease prevention. *Journal of the American Medical Association, 301*(21), 2252.

Shonkoff, J., & Phillips, D. (Eds.). (2000). *From neurons to neighborhoods: The science of early-childhood development.* Committee on Integrating the Science of Early Childhood Development, Board on Children, Youth, and Families. Retrieved from http://www.nap.edu/catalog/9824.html

Sloper, T., & Beresford, B. (2006). Families with disabled children. *British Medical Journal (International edition), 333*(7575), 928.

Sutton, L., Smith, N., Dearden, C., & Middleton, S. (2007). *A child's-eye view of social difference.* York, UK: Joseph Rowntree Foundation.

Vandsburger, E., Harrigan, M., & Biggerstaff, M. (2008). In spite of it all, we make it: Themes of stress and resilience as told by women in families living in poverty. *Journal of Family Social Work, 11*(1), 17–35.

Weatherston, D. J. (2000). The infant mental health specialist. *Zero to Three, 20*(4), 3–10.

3

Learning How to Love

Once there was a little bunny who wanted to run away. So he said
to his mother, "I am running away."

"If you run away," said his mother, "I will run after you. For
you are my little bunny."

Margaret Wise Brown, *The Runaway Bunny*

WHAT IS ATTACHMENT?

In Margaret Wise Brown's (1942) classic children's story *The Runaway
Bunny*, the little bunny embarks on many adventures, trusting that his
mother will always be there whether he succeeds or fails, whether he's
naughty or nice. His adventures take him into uncharted territory—climbing
a mountain, sailing the seas, walking a tightrope. Each time he takes on a
new adventure, his mother watches and waits, hoping for his success and
being there in case he fails. She is steadfast, attentive, and ever present.
Knowing that he is safe and loved provides the little bunny with the security
he needs to take calculated risks, learn from experience, and venture out
into the world.

The relationship between mother and bunny in Brown's tale exemplifies in a playful way the very serious role of attachment in early childhood.
Attachment refers to the enduring and reciprocal relational bonds between
children and primary caregivers. When children derive a sense of security
from their earliest attachments, they feel safe to explore the world. When
successful, infants and caregivers develop a kind of synchronicity: reliable
relational communication ensures that when hungry, babies are fed; when
soiled, diapers are changed; and when tired, infants are soothed to sleep.
Over time, relational reliability guides infants to learn how to trust themselves, and they become skillful at delaying the immediacy of their urges
and soothing themselves. Their hungry cries are now calmed simply when
mother or father enters the room; they can play contentedly in their cribs,
knowing that someone will eventually be there to welcome them into the
day.

Similarly, when healthy attachments form, caregivers fall in love with their babies. Strong connections make it possible for parents to endure the rigors of child rearing with all its challenges. Thus relational security gets mothers and fathers through the long colicky nights when nothing seems to console their squalling infant. Relational attunement also ensures that as children grow, their caregivers grow with them. Thus as toddlers begin to explore their world, parents allow them to do so within a safety net of care. Such caring watchfulness continues into adolescence and eventually transforms into warm and mutually satisfying relationships between parents and their adult children, capable of weathering the normal ebb and flow of life's changes and transformations.

Alternatively, when early infant/parent bonds are continually distressed, disconnected, or disorganized for whatever reasons, children do not learn to rely on being cared for. These babies tend to have difficulty with self-regulation and mastery of normative developmental tasks. Irritability and inconsolability are two hallmarks of infants who have experienced relational insecurity. Those who experience chronic neglect or persistent environmental adversity may express more severe and life-affecting behavioral challenges. As these youngsters grow, emotional and physical dysregulation may interfere with their capacity to learn and impede their social and emotional well-being. Such children especially need caring adults and responsive caregiving systems to teach them regulatory and socialization skills they didn't learn earlier.

This chapter begins with a history of attachment theory. The importance of human bonds has been observed by practitioners and tested by researchers over time, yet theories of attachment are not without their critics. I integrate concepts from chapter 2, examining how ongoing neuroscience studies have produced greater insight into the role of the brain in building human connection, and discuss how these studies are reshaping approaches to health and healing across the life course.

Scientific investigation and practice wisdom have also informed how we understand patterns of attachment. Although there is never a simple link between early attachment and later relational outcomes, understanding variability in early attachment experiences helps us appreciate how people relate to one another. Moreover, understanding such patterns contributes to developing empathy for challenging youngsters whose early lives are characterized by confused or neglected attachments.

The chapter then looks at the enduring nature of human bonds, including the effect that our own attachments may have on practice with the children and families who are our clients. Comments on the relevance of attachment theories and relationship to human rights and child advocacy wrap up the chapter.

HISTORY OF ATTACHMENT THEORY

Attachment theory has its origins in interdisciplinary scholarship, systematic research, and anecdotal observations. Its roots can be traced back to a range of evidence-guided and social science fields, including biology, psychology, social work, behaviorism, anthropology, and ethnology. Pioneering psychoanalytic theorists first recognized the importance and tenacity of bonds between infants and mothers. Sigmund Freud was one of the earliest theorists to note the importance of early relational connections and the meaning they have throughout the life course. Attachment theory further evolved through the combined works of British practitioner-researchers such as D. W. Winnicott and W. R. D. Fairbairn. Winnicott, a pediatrician by training, initially observed the power of interactional behaviors between mothers and infants in the waiting room of his busy pediatric practice. Over time he concluded that the quality of the mother/child relationship was central to the growing child's healthy development. Winnicott posited that positive relationships contain traits of parallel engagement and responsivity, and he coined the phrase "good enough mothering" (Winnicott, 1986) to describe the quality of relationship that resulted when a caregiver was attuned and responsive to her infant's physical and emotional needs.

Although there was an early flurry of interest in maternal-child bonds, John Bowlby (1983) is credited by most as the originator of modern attachment theory. Bowlby dedicated his life's work to the scientific investigation of early attachment, viewing it not only as beneficial to the quality of later human connections but also as an essential evolutionary survival skill. He argued that without human connectedness, people can neither thrive nor endure.

Bowlby (1969) identified four determinants of attachment relationships, all of which are exemplified in Brown's story of the little bunny and his mother. They are (1) *proximity maintenance*, or the desire to be close to those we feel attached to; (2) *safe haven*, the inner knowledge that one can return to secure relationships when faced with uncertainty, threat, or fear; (3) *secure base*, the reliable presence of another who acts as a source of stability and comfort when the child explores his or her world; and (4) *separation distress*, exemplified in anxiety or stress in the absence of the primary attachment figure(s).

Bowlby's work coincided with that of another esteemed researcher, Mary Salter Ainsworth, whose inquiry focused on variations in infant-caregiver attachment patterns. Ainsworth and her collaborators wondered whether parents' attachment styles were intergenerational in nature. That is, like Fraiberg (1987b; see chapter 2) she suspected that the ways in which mothers and fathers were parented would influence and affect their own caregiving.

It is worth noting that social workers, among other professionals, were initially wary of attachment theory. They did not want it to obfuscate the very real effects that resource inequities and economic disadvantage play in people's lives. They argued that although early relations are important, they nevertheless occur within a social context that influences how well or how poorly people can experience them. Feminist practitioners in the early 1970s and 1980s were especially concerned that attachment theory lays too much of the blame for children's developmental and relational failures on women. Furthermore, attachment theory was critiqued for not recognizing fathers' role as a primary attachment figure.

Beginning in the 1970s, feminist scholars like Jean Baker Miller and Carol Gilligan revisited the merits of attachment theory and its relevance to human development. Until this point psychological health was primarily defined by the capacity to separate and be independent from the critical relationships in one's early life. Miller and Stiver (1997, pp. 2–3) observed: "The notion of separation as a goal has become the standard by which, we are told, we should define ourselves as healthy human beings. Independence and self-sufficiency are considered the hallmarks of maturity . . . Thus, for instance, we learn that children must begin from a very early age to separate from their parents, especially their mothers, in order to move successfully into adolescence and adulthood." Feminist scholars argued that this description of health not only missed the critical nature of human relationships but in fact denigrated the importance of human connection in people's lives. It furthermore privileged the roles that men traditionally held as "breadwinners" and dismissed the importance of caregiving and child rearing, roles primarily assumed by women during those decades.

In response to what they perceived as a static and relatively insufficient understanding of emotional and relational health, Miller and other practitioner-researchers revised attachment theory, integrating it into what they termed relational-cultural theory (RCT). RCT asserts that independence and relational connection are complementary aspects of human health and thus constitute hallmarks of functional adult development.

Tenets described by Bowlby and others reemerged in RCT, but this time, they were considered within a broader context of human experience that embraced individual, systemic, and cultural factors. Terminology such as "psychological mutuality" and "human connection" conveyed participatory rather than passive engagement by all people in promoting growth-fostering relationships, and these qualities of relationship were considered relevant to people regardless of age or gender, and within all settings and contexts (Miller & Stiver, 1997). From a resilience standpoint, RCT presupposed that all people can strive for and obtain connection. Thus those who lacked early connection as well as those who had suffered traumatic disconnections were believed to have the ability to regain the capacity for relational success with self and others (Hartling, 2008).

ATTACHMENT AND THE BRAIN: SCIENCE AND PRACTICE

Early theorists and researchers such as Freud, Bowlby, Ainsworth, and Fraiberg assumed that the brain held yet-to-be discovered secrets about qualities of attachment, relationship, and regulatory functioning that were formed in early childhood. As already discussed in chapter 2, contemporary scientific evidence has supported the view that children's brains are indeed born wired and ready for relationship and connection to those who care for them. Moreover, robust evidence indicates that the brain and regulatory systems of infants are highly responsive both to their relationships with primary caregivers and to environmental conditions that support their learning and social ties.

Scientists have recently begun investigating ties between the formation of these same early brain structures and later capacities for social intelligence and empathy (Banks, 2011). According to Banks, mirror neurons located throughout the brain are thought to help people observe and interpret the feelings and behaviors of others. Thus, in combination, human capacities for communication, intimacy, social acuity, self-preservation, and emotional/behavioral regulation are thought to be tied in with early attachments and caregiver responsivity.

Parents and infants naturally get to know each other in the earliest days and months after birth. It is during this period that primary caregiver(s) become familiar with the infant's cues and emotionally attuned to her or his signals and needs. Factors found to nurture positive infant-caregiver attachments include reciprocity, attunement to the unique child's needs, empathy, temperamental fit, and consistency in both affect and response.

In neuroscience terms the primary caregiver acts as a regulator for the infant's developing brain and central nervous system. This requires that she or he be attentive to the infant's verbal and nonverbal solicitations and responses. Schore and Schore (2008, p. 11) describe this process from a psychobiological perspective: "In this dialogical process the more the mother contingently tunes her activity level to the infant during periods of social engagement, the more she allows him to recover quietly in periods of disengagement, and the more she attends to his reinitiating cues for reengagement, the more synchronized his interactions."

In the end, such synchronistic responsiveness promotes healthy development of the right brain (Schore & Schore, 2008). According to neuroscience researchers, the right brain plays a significant role in controlling regulatory functions, advancing higher cognitive processes, and promoting social/relational connection.

At the same time that the primary caregiver is effectively tutoring the infant's developing brain, the infant is regulating and guiding the caregiver. Each infant has a different pattern of communication, and parents cannot simply impose their knowledge or style on the developing child. Ask any parent of two or more children, and they will tell you how different their children are from one another.

Like many other aspects of relationship, what fits one individual does not always fit the next. When a caregiver is attuned to her unique infant, she can more often than not distinguish his needs by the nuance of his cry. For instance, one cry may signal hunger while another one signals fatigue, and so on. Thus caregivers establish individualized synchronicity that provides stabilizing feedback to their growing children's brains.

Some caregivers cannot read their infants' cries or determine what it is they need. When disharmony occurs in the feedback loop, caregiver and infant become frustrated and unable to regulate. Both experience a constant state of uncertainty. The result is that the infant's brain receives inconsistent messages; the infant does not achieve regulation or internal homeostasis. This interference with attachment, if left uninterrupted, may have cognitive, behavioral, and emotional ramifications for the growing child.

Selma Fraiberg (1987a) noted this type of early relational discord in her depiction of Karen and Nina, an adolescent mother and her infant daughter. She writes: "The depression of the mother is mirrored in the baby's face. The baby is silent, stares off into space, uninvested in her surroundings. She rarely turns to her mother for a social exchange or for comfort . . . we see a limited number of attachment indicators . . . Nina has a limited repertoire of attachment behaviors but they are muted and joyless. Similarly Karen show some signs of affection for her baby, but she sinks back into depression and solitude after each exertion" (pp. 175–176).

In this case, Fraiberg recognizes that Karen is still a child herself, and having an infant of her own presents her with overwhelming responsibilities. In addition clinical depression impairs Karen's ability to be responsive and affectionate with her daughter. We also learn from Karen's story that her own early attachment patterns were disconnected and that her parents were still unsupportive during her pregnancy and new motherhood. There was no doubt, however, that Nina was ready and seeking connection with Karen; she simply didn't yet know how to engage her. Nina needed her mother to guide her, and Karen needed to feel loved by her infant. Fraiberg understood that both mother and child had to learn how to love and be loved. They were clearly interdependent and responsive to one another. Nina's growth and well-being was highly dependent on Karen's capacity to be in relationship to both herself and her child.

Understanding the connectivity between attachment theory and infant brain research is critical to child- and family-centered relational practice.

Both areas of study provide insight into why some children manage the rigors of early childhood with aplomb and resilience while others cannot. They also help explain why some children who become our clients have more difficulty than others building and maintaining relational trust. Workers familiar with attachment theories are also more apt to be conscientious about engaging parents in the therapeutic process. This is true whether or not the parents are currently actively involved in the child's life.

Psychobiological implications of attachment theory also inform how we work therapeutically with children. Like infants and caregivers, child clients do best when workers key into their nonverbal cues. Sensitivity permits the worker to detect when regulation is unraveling and to know when to intervene in timely and child-centered ways. It is at these difficult junctures that workers and children engage together in transformational, brain-changing interventions.

Given the challenges faced by many children and families, perhaps what is most important about attachment and infant brain research is that it inspires hope. Viewing the brain as a repairable organ is a relatively new concept. It challenges the long-held belief that emotional and relational health are determined in the first five years of life and relatively unresponsive to permanent change. Evidence now suggests that the brain is more receptive to change than previously thought. Relational therapies targeting right-brain processes appear to improve clients' regulatory and relational capacities across the life course (Schore & Schore, 2008). Qualities inherent in such therapies emulate those seen in healthy early attachments, including affective responsiveness, unconditional acceptance, and consistent relational engagement provided by workers who are fully present. Whitehead (2006, p. 624) refers to this level of therapeutic contact as "deep contact."

One final unexpected and equally hopeful consequence of infant brain research is that it explains children's "bad behavior" to those who might otherwise be unsympathetic. For example, teachers, principals, caregivers, and others in day-to-day relationships with often difficult children can now associate the problematic behaviors with something tangible. Seeing problems as "real" and situated in the brain, rather than simply "emotional," increases the likelihood that compassion rather than blame will be extended to these youngsters. In the best of all circumstances, child-centered workers from all persuasions benefit from understanding the interrelatedness of positive relationships and child health and wellness.

PATTERNS OF ATTACHMENT

Speaking to the World Health Organization (WHO) in 1952, John Bowlby asserted, "The quality of the parental care which a child receives in his earliest years is of vital importance for his future mental health" (Zeanah &

Smyke, 2008, p. 220). More than six decades later, scientific discoveries have affirmed his assertions. When he gave this speech, attachment theories were predominantly based on anecdotal and clinical observations and thus had yet to gain credibility in the scientific world. As noted earlier, the first systematic studies of attachment behaviors were conducted by Mary Salter Ainsworth in the 1960s and 1970s. The most famous of these, "the strange situation" procedure (SSP), examined whether there were patterns of attachment linked to specific styles of maternal/infant interaction (Ainsworth, Blehar, Waters, & Wall, 1978). Ainsworth and her colleagues speculated that there were.

The first stage of the SSP study observed infants responding to their mothers in an unfamiliar situation. The second stage had the same infants responding to a stranger in an identical environment. On the basis of these systematic observations, three patterns of attachment were distinguished: secure, insecure/avoidant, and insecure/resistant. A fourth pattern, disorganized attachment, was later identified by Mary Main (1991) and her collaborators.

Secure Attachment

A *secure attachment style* typically results when the primary caregiver is attuned, relationally connected, and responsive to the child's initiatives. Relational attunement provides consistent feedback to the infant, which in turn helps her or him regulate physical and affective responses. As a result the infant can negotiate development milestones, adjust to transitions, and tolerate the normative frustrations that growth and development bring.

Underlying the infant's confidence is the security of knowing that his or her needs will met and that when distressed, he or she will be soothed. This early knowledge also contributes to the infant's capacity to tolerate frustration and delay gratification, thus freeing up energy to pursue developmental tasks involving motor, language, intellectual, emotional, and social growth. As the child matures, a stable regulatory system helps him or her accept behavioral limits and social rules.

All in all, secure attachments promote the child's psychobiological regulation, allowing him or her to navigate separations and explore the world. When infants and young children trust in their attachments to caregivers, they develop relational confidence, which translates to the capacity to form positive and productive relationships with others. Securely attached youngsters are able to practice autonomy, knowing that their mother is available if she is needed.

Mahler, Pine, and Bergman (1975) called this expansion of developmental skill *rapprochement.* Rapprochement typically begins between fifteen and eighteen months of age during the separation-individuation phase of development. As observed in the securely attached youngsters in Ainsworth's study, after achieving motor prowess, the toddler wants to explore realities beyond her or his mother's reach, but needs her to be within sight in order to have the confidence to explore (fathers may also be primary caregivers). An example of rapprochement is the eighteen-month-old child who gleefully runs away from his caregiver, checking back to make sure she or he is close at hand.

Securely attached children are thought to be better able to traverse "stranger danger" than their less secure peers. Stranger danger, sometimes referred to as stranger anxiety, occurs at approximately seven to eight months of age when the infant becomes aware of his or her separateness from the primary caregiver. In effect the ability to differentiate primary caregivers from other people is evidence that the child is developing appropriately; it signals the infant's first steps toward healthy differentiation and represents the child's emotional connectedness or attachment to his or her caregivers.

Separation anxiety is typically observed in securely attached infants until they reach what is called object constancy. Object constancy is the capacity to maintain the caregiver's image even when she or he isn't present. Securely attached children on average learn to thrive in a variety of environments and caregiving situations because they trust implicitly that their caregivers will return.

Insecure Attachment: Avoidant and Resistant Styles

Children develop insecure/avoidant attachments when their caregivers are inconsistent or extreme in their responses. Children in the SSP study who had insecure/avoidant attachment styles seemed indifferent to the comings and goings of their mothers. They were interested in play with a stranger or focused their attention on inanimate objects, such as toys in the playroom. At times these children appeared to be detached and disinterested toward their caregivers. The SSP researchers speculated that these youngsters developed this attachment style as a protective mechanism in response to repeated and chronic exposure to angry, unreliable, or overly controlling caregiver feedback.

Alternatively, insecure/resistant attachment styles are characterized by clinginess and highly distressed responses to separation from caregivers. Once distressed, such infants are often inconsolable and difficult to soothe. They appear to simultaneously have a strong desire for attention from their caregiver and resist it when it becomes available.

Ainsworth and colleagues (1978) speculated that resistant attachment styles emanate from experiences with caring that are inconsistent and sometimes remote. These children's caregivers were thought to be distracted from child rearing by physical or emotional distress, substance misuse, domestic violence, or other significant stressors. Inconsistency implied that sometimes these caregivers were attuned and appropriately responsive to their infants, while at other times they were not. Such unreliable responsivity made infants confused and unsure whether their needs would be met.

Let's use the example of a hungry infant to explain the differences between secure and insecure attachments. If an infant has experienced consistent caregiving and as a result feels genuinely secure, she trusts that she will be fed even if feeding is somewhat delayed. She may briefly whine because of hunger pangs, but she is ultimately able to regulate and delay her need—she can handle the wait.

A hungry infant who has experienced inconsistent care has less faith that her basic needs will be satisfied. She has learned that often she must loudly protest before she is heard. Insecurely attached children do not intrinsically possess flexibility or confidence in their worlds. Experience has taught them that they may be chastised rather than soothed when they are distressed. Depending on their temperament, insecurely attached children will use a range of strategies to deal with their hunger. They may be inconsolable even after they are fed. They may cry out for more even when physically satiated. In extreme cases, infants may become apathetic or withdrawn and uninterested in being fed at all. Highly withdrawn infants may become malnourished, cease to grow, and suffer from a medical condition called *failure to thrive*, the outcome of which can be death.

As they mature, insecurely attached children develop survival skills aimed at ensuring that their needs are met. They may appear inattentive, distracted by inner needs or outer opportunities. Like the infants in the SSP studies, they desire attention from adults but don't particularly understand relationship. These youngsters are often seen as difficult and even unlikeable. Understanding the origins of their relational and regulatory difficulties helps adults, especially those in caregiving or instructional positions, develop compassion for these children who do not have the regulatory or relational skills necessary to keep their emotions or behaviors under control.

Disorganized Attachment Style and Reactive Attachment Disorder

Ainsworth's student Mary Main (1991) unearthed the fourth attachment style. Disorganized attachment is distinguished by the child's inconsistent and contradictory responses in interaction with his or her caregiver. Unlike infants and children whose attachment behaviors are strategic, those with disorganized attachments show behaviors that are unpredictable, often aggressive, and primarily disconnected. Main hypothesized that these children developed fear in response to their caregiving, which left them in a state of disorientation. Accordingly their attachment behaviors showed little rhyme or reason; actions and reactions were unpredictable and insufficient in response to normal, everyday stresses.

Children with disorganized attachment patterns are often those whose early lives are characterized by crisis, chaos, and disruption, and sometimes abuse and neglect. Even when proper caregiving is eventually available, children with disorganized attachment styles demonstrate extreme reactivity, relational confusion, and intense distrust. Seemingly opposing behaviors are often observed; for example, foster parents may be initially taken with these charming children, who without warning violently erupt over the slightest infraction. They are loving one minute and hostile the next.

Children with attachment styles characterized by extreme and inappropriate social interactions may receive a diagnosis of reactive attachment disorder. This disorder can take the form of chronic failure to engage in or initiate social relationships. It can also result in indiscriminate and undifferentiated attempts to get close to even relative strangers. These behavioral patterns may fluctuate within the same child or they may be stable. Either way, the child lacks effective relational strategies.

This was the case with seven-year-old Marianna and her foster parents. Marianna and her siblings suffered extreme, chronic neglect and abuse in early childhood. Marianna first came into care at seven months of age. In her first two years she transitioned multiple times between her parents' home and foster care. When she was two and a half, Marianna's parents lost their parental rights. This led to four foster placements in four years, culminating in what was expected to be her permanent placement with Lucy and Annie Carlisle-Tedford. Although the couple knew Marianna's previous placements ended because of extreme behavioral outbursts, they believed that their love, dedication, and patience would lead to successful adoption.

Initially Marianna was loving and compliant. But it was not long before Lucy saw her being violent with the family dog. Soon after, the parents noticed that even gentle limit setting provoked extreme tantrums and self-directed aggression. They consulted a social worker, who offered cognitive-behavioral suggestions. The behavioral plan backfired, however, sending Marianna into even more violent and lengthy outbursts.

Within six months Lucy and Annie wondered whether they were suited to be Marianna's caregivers. Her behavior put great strain on their relationship. Their social life was at a standstill, and both of them lost days at work.

Within the year Lucy and Annie, reluctantly and with great feelings of guilt, decided to end their dreams of adopting Marianna. Instead they advocated that she be placed in a long-term therapeutic foster home. The couple continued to visit Marianna weekly throughout her childhood and adolescence. Lucy described their relationship as turbulent, one-sided, yet committed.

Working with children and families who manifest insecure, disorganized, or otherwise problematic attachment styles is understandably demanding. Because interventions with these families are arduous and often viewed as futile, some workers may blame parents for children's distress. Others may urge parents to take control, even when control may be impossible or perhaps even damaging to the children. Either way, one should never minimize the difficulties of day-to-day life when raising a child who is unresponsive or highly reactive to transitions, limit setting, and social interactions. This is true for biological parents as well as foster parents and kin, whose caring and compassion may be pushed to their limits.

In the best of situations, children struggling with extreme attachment difficulties get therapeutic interventions geared toward relearning regulatory and relational skills. Parents, too, need specialized support to help them become attuned and effectively responsive to their children's complex needs. Parents also benefit from ongoing support from workers familiar with their unique struggles. Like their children, these parents need workers to believe in their capacity to heal and find hope in their futures.

Variations in Attachment Styles and Confounding Factors

Classifying patterns of attachment is meant to help practitioners make sense of social and relational behavioral styles. But there are many variations in attachment, and not every parent-child bonding experience can be explained by attachment styles. Workers must be especially careful not to seek information simply to confirm the presence of a particular attachment style or its expected antecedents. Like any form of categorization, attachment classifications should not be used to blame or judge parents or override positive and hopeful qualities of infant-caregiver relationships and lifestyles.

Human responsivity and relational attachments are highly varied, affected by factors such as the child's temperamental proclivities, the family's cultural practices, goodness of fit between parent and child, and the child's developmental capacity and health. Family stressors can also affect the quality of early and ongoing attachments. In order to appreciate the interaction of such factors, let's examine possible attachment patterns that might occur between a child with autism and his parents.

From the outset, youngsters with autism spectrum disorders (ASD) may be atypical in their sensory, communicative, and relational responses. Parents with even the best of intentions may find it difficult to interpret or connect with their infants, because of their unusual reactions to stimulation and input. Nurturance may thus be thwarted, and subsequently parents may feel rejected by their children's denial of affection. Parents may respond to disconnection in a number of different ways; for example, they may distance themselves to avoid upsetting their youngsters, or they may feel shame for somehow having caused relational failures.

From a practice standpoint, it is essential to know about attachment theory and the autism spectrum while working with these families. Understanding the social-communication deficits implicit in autism helps parents revise their relational expectations. Children with ASD *are* capable of forming attachments, but these relationships will look different from those of neurotypical children and will differ according to the level of the child's social-communication functional impairment (chapter 9 expands on this point). Workers can provide parents much-needed education and support as they reconstruct relational hopes and develop skills for newly formed connections.

Mateo and his parents offer an example of reformulated attachment patterns. Helen and Luis came to see me at the request of a Child Development Services' caseworker who observed their discouragement at Mateo's lack of emotional responsiveness.[1] He was their only child, born late in their lives, at a particularly difficult time in their family. He was diagnosed at age four with Asperger's syndrome, which is on the higher-functioning end of the autism spectrum.[2]

Mateo, age five, was referred to Child Development Services because of reported preschool adjustment problems. He was observed to be a bright, attractive, and energetic youngster who talked nonstop without seeming interest in feedback or interaction. He was fluent in English, French, and Spanish, his father's first language. Like many youngsters with ASD, Mateo had little awareness of the people around him and could neither initiate nor read social interactions. At the time of his referral, he was having significant social problems with aggressive outbursts, and there was concern that he might be dismissed from preschool.

Helen was an engaging and intelligent woman who had never expected to have children. She worked from home as a seamstress, but given the economy, work was scarce. Upon learning of her pregnancy, Helen, then forty-one, was surprisingly ecstatic. Luis was also pleased with the unexpected news, but like Helen, he too was struggling with keeping his computer repair business afloat.

The couple's excitement tempered after Mateo's birth. Their beautiful infant seemed uninterested in their affections. Friends assured them that what they were experiencing was normal, given their surprise parenthood. Rather than improving, however, Mateo's responses seemed increasingly detached. Helen worried that he instinctively knew that she hadn't wanted children. Luis blamed Helen for not being maternal. New parenthood and Mateo's unexpected behavior put additional strains on the already stressed pair.

My brief work with Helen and Luis focused on teaching them about autism and its multilevel effects. They quickly understood that what they had assumed to be attachment failures were instead the consequence of Mateo's neurodevelopmental social-communication challenges. Knowledge of autism and its manifestations helped ease the couple's feelings of inadequacy while it directed them to think creatively about how to develop relational bonds with their much loved child.

Full of ideas, Helen revised her relational expectations and engaged with her son in new and rewarding ways. Instead of getting angry and frustrated with Mateo's disorganization, she created a highly structured, reliable schedule that helped him navigate the daily routine. Mateo consequently felt increasingly secure in his environment and became less reactive. Mateo and his parents learned to relax more and enjoy each other's company.

Mateo's care and intervention, however, took much of Helen's time and energy. After difficult deliberation, the couple decided that she would quit working to concentrate on caring for their son. The change in family income put strains on their budget, especially because Mateo's therapies were for the most part not covered by Medicaid. Thus Luis concentrated on the difficult task of trying to meet their financial obligations, which kept him working away from home for long hours.

On the positive side, Mateo began initiating relational opportunities with his mother, father, and some of his teachers at preschool. Helen reported great joy over progress made in these relationships. She dedicated her time to work with Mateo's teachers to develop effective social/behavioral strategies.

These considerable social improvements, however, did not completely dispel Helen's feelings of grief over the loss of the responsive child she imagined during her pregnancy. Luis, although he loved Mateo deeply, never fully accepted the ASD diagnosis and relied on Helen to do most of the parenting. Like other parents of children with chronic health conditions, the family struggled to maintain a good quality of life.

ENDURING BONDS

The long-term effects of early bonds are durable, whether secure or insecure. For example, children separated from their primary caregivers for whatever reasons may long for and seek connection to these earliest relationships. While some adopted children do not seek out their birth parents, others are impelled to find them even when attachments to their adoptive parents are affectionate and stable. Children living in foster families may not be able to quell their desires to return to original families, despite the adversity they may have faced with them. The strength and tenacity of children's attachments to neglectful, abusive, or otherwise unavailable parents is often baffling to workers and other child-centered health professionals. Yet these bonds, whether realized or potential, have important meaning to youngsters.

Complicated and ambiguous feelings of loss can also arise when relational disconnection is less observable but deeply felt. This may occur when a parent is psychologically absent yet physically present, as in cases of parental substance abuse, physical or mental illness, developmental disability, or post-traumatic stress disorder (PTSD). Boss (2004) defines this type of ambiguous loss as when a loved one is physically present but not functioning in their expected or familiar role. Ambiguous loss may also be felt when children are separated from parents due to incarceration, deployment, hospitalization, or other ongoing disruption in the continuity of relational ties. Because ambiguous loss is typically unidentified, it is often unaddressed by significant others in the child's life. For children who experience multiple separations, disruptions, and transitions, the pileup of ambiguous losses may be substantial. If left unattended, such losses may result in psychosocial or other health problems.

The ways in which children are cared for and loved affect how they eventually understand themselves. These early attachment messages are absorbed and integrated into the child's evolving formation of identity. Thus a child's internalized self-worth is influenced by whether he or she has felt seen, listened to, and heard. Children's self-efficacy and hope originate from being affirmed in their strengths and having their missteps forgiven. Simply stated, it is difficult for children to believe in themselves if their primary caregivers have not had the opportunity to express a belief in them.

This does not imply that these youngsters will not succeed. Rather it suggests that the road to success will likely be more difficult. These are often the children in need of relational repair and reaffirmation who come to the attention of mental health and social service workers. Qualities of secure attachment—for example reliability, patience, responsiveness, and positive regard—are critical to these healing alliances.

A final common theme represented in the lives of children who have experienced disrupted or lost attachments is the meaning of family ties (Siu & Hogan, 1989). Workers are often taken aback by the tenacity of children's attachments to parents who they have never met or who have intentionally or unintentionally harmed or abandoned them. Workers must appreciate the strength and endurance of these children's early attachments, even those that could not possibly have been consciously experienced by the child. Whether these ties are real or idealized, it is nonetheless essential that workers acknowledge and recognize them.

Sarina's story is a case in point. Sarina was fifteen when I first met her. She had been in foster care since age four. Her initial foster placement occurred after her sleeping mother's cigarette burned down the family trailer. The family was lucky to have survived, as the trailer was in an isolated, rural location. Smoke from the blaze was noticed by a police officer who just happened to be in the trailer park looking for kids who had robbed a local convenience store.

After the fire, Sarina, four, and her sister, Katie, six, were placed in separate foster homes. Their mother, Marlene, thirty-three, was sent to the local hospital's psychiatric unit to detox from alcohol and prescription medications.

During the following two years, child protective services attempted many times to reunify the sisters with their mother. Marlene was able neither to maintain sobriety nor to adequately demonstrate ability to provide appropriate care for her young daughters. Just prior to the termination of parental rights (TPR) hearing, Marlene was given a dual diagnosis of polydrug addiction and schizoaffective disorder. This diagnosis enabled Marlene to receive much needed health insurance and disability benefits, including Section 8 housing. In combination, however, the diagnosis and TPR led to multiple losses and transitions for Sarina and Katie.

When I met Sarina eleven years later, she was still longing for reunion with her mother. She had lived in five different foster homes. Each placement had been disrupted because of Sarina's impulse to locate her mother and "take care of her." Similarly, Sarina and Katie found and lost each other multiple times, in part due to episodic changes in their residencies.

When asked about these disruptions, Sarina told me that she loved her mother and knew in her heart that her mother loved her, too. She truly believed that they were meant to be together. Sarina insisted that she was grateful to all the foster parents who tried to "give me a family." Yet she knew that she was unable to genuinely accept their caring. When I last heard about Sarina, she was nineteen and had a baby of her own, a little girl named Marlena. She was studying for a GED and hoped to get work in the future as a counselor helping kids in foster care.

Unlike Sarina, who could readily articulate her longing to reconnect with her family of origin, many children and youth simply act on their impulses. They may react defensively and inexplicably to the efforts of even the most caring people. In many respects they are vigilantly self-protective, prepared for hurt and rejection. In contrast to securely attached children, who tend to be adaptively flexible in their relationships, children who have met with multiple losses often have difficulty modifying or changing their response to new relational situations. In addition they do not have the skills to read or evaluate relational efforts made by others on their behalf.

Workers' attitudes toward such children's parents may also lead them to dismiss the meaning and endurance of family ties for these youngsters. Workers are understandably wary of parents who abandon or harm their children. One does not have to accept the behaviors of parents, however, in order to appreciate and respect that their children desire to be loved by them. Ironically, workers must honor these critical relationships while helping children relinquish them.

In the spirit of full disclosure, I acknowledge that I spent considerable time with a seasoned supervisor to process my feelings and reactions to

Sarina's unrelenting desire to be with Marlene. In the end the only remedy was for me to do my best to see the world through her eyes. She simply yearned to love and be loved by her mother. That was a sentiment I could genuinely understand. I was also well aware of the devastating toll substance abuse and mental illness had taken on Marlene's health and well-being. Over time I managed to develop true empathy for her, and in doing so, I was able to work more effectively with Sarina.

However, knowledge, understanding, and compassion have their limits. In Sarina's case I consistently bumped up against one of the cruel and unsolvable dilemmas of child and family work—you can't meet everyone's needs or resolve the unresolvable, especially in matters of the heart. Although appreciative of Sarina's longings, I had to take sides and advocate for her safety, which meant setting firm and clearly undesired boundaries around her contact with Marlene. Unfortunately Marlene simply did not have the capacity or skills to be a "good enough" mother to Sarina.

Sarina eventually took leave of our relationship to continue the search for her mother's love. On the positive side she took with her strengthened self-worth, enhanced anticipatory skills, and future plans. While I couldn't circumvent her choice to be a teen mother, I knew that she had the capacity to love and care for her daughter. I don't know where Sarina is now but hope that it is a place that she can call home.

ATTACHMENT THEORY AND ADOLESCENTS

Applying principles of attachment theory to practice with adolescents is especially challenging. Creating positive therapeutic connections is understandably difficult for any teenager because they are ensconced in separating and differentiating themselves from the significant adults in their lives. In many respects, relationship building with adults presents adolescents with an existential dilemma. On the one hand, they long for connection with caring adults, and on the other, they strive for autonomy. Establishing working alliances is further complicated for youth who have never experienced stable and secure attachments.

Research on adolescent resiliency offers important findings about youth and their desire for connection with adults. Evidence strongly suggests that adolescents not only want relational attention but thrive when it is supplied in ways that mimic qualities of secure attachment. Laursen and Birmingham's (2003) study found that youth favored authentic and reliable relationships with adults. Adolescent participants in their research reported that genuine connections with caring workers promoted and enhanced their resilience and restored their faith in themselves and others.

Other studies affirm that many youth seek out confiding and caring relationships with adults (Spencer, Jordan, & Sazama, 2004). Qualities viewed as essential to such relationships included trust, attention, empathy, affirmation, respect, virtue, and availability. It is interesting that these same attributes mirror those identified as contributing to infants' secure attachments. Interactional qualities such as conveying genuine interest, active listening, and expressed empathy were seen by adolescents as relational links to bridging mistrust and promoting productive and trusting alliances (Spencer et al., 2004).

Adolescents in these studies reported feeling reassured when workers were willing to disclose personal aspects of their own youthful mistakes. As one girl in Spencer and colleagues' (2004, p. 358) study noted: "Yeah, like, if you tell an adult something, like a problem that you have, and they are a nice adult and helpful adult, they will relate to it and they will say, 'Oh yeah, in my life that happened to me and I can relate to it and this is what I did to deal with that.'" Workers' honest and reciprocal communication helped these adolescents to develop a sense of belonging and to feel less alone in their trials. When adolescents knew that workers had been through similarly confusing and hard times, they permitted them to have access to their worlds.

ATTACHMENT THEORY AND REFLEXIVE PRACTICE

Knowledge of attachment theory prepares practitioners to be compassionate toward those we might otherwise disdain, for example the nine-year-old foster child who, despite the worker's best efforts, continues to steal from classmates. It underpins training for tutors, respite workers, and adoptive or foster parents who need to develop tolerance to remain calm and collected during the inevitable emotional storms that their children display. Furthermore, appreciation for the impact of early attachments, for better or for worse, lends workers the strength to bypass harsh and often divisive judgments toward those that society has forgotten.

Best practice requires us to know ourselves in the context of our own attachments and relational worlds. In everyday practice, such knowledge helps explain practice choices and actions. Without this self-awareness, workers run the risk of overstepping relational boundaries or of erecting barriers that keep us emotionally distanced from our clients' troubles.

The story of one caseworker illustrates how boundary violations can occur when attachment issues remain unexamined. This worker had been in the field for many years and clearly loved her work. She would often say that every one of her clients was like *her own child*. She thus rationalized the little gifts and treats she gave to some of her clients as a "workplace benefit." It became her custom during the holiday season to buy lavish gifts for a selected child from disadvantaged circumstances. These were always much more than the child's family could possibly afford.

This workers' actions, though well intended, were clearly inappropriate. Her supervisor eventually placed her on a year's probation for prioritizing her own needs over those of the children and families she served. The worker's desire for connection, to be loved and feel loved, had replaced her ethical and professional responsibilities. Thus she put children in harm's way and unintentionally denigrated the role of their parents.

Practice with children and families by its very nature renders us vulnerable to being overwhelmed by the many stories of suffering, despair, and loss that we bear witness to on a daily basis. These stories furthermore tap into our own experiences of being cared for and, in some cases, of being parents to our own children. Reflective practice ensures that workers take time to pause and consider how clients' stories resonate with personal attachment histories and thus affect our perspectives and practice choices.

ATTACHMENT AS A HUMAN RIGHT

The Convention on the Rights of the Child (UN General Assembly, 1989) recognizes that children have rights to protection of their relationships with family members and community (Melton, 2010). The right to be nurtured, to belong and be loved, is written into this basic human rights doctrine. According to Melton (2010), governments have a responsibility to ensure that all children have the opportunity to be nurtured by their families, and when relational failures occur, they are equally responsible for taking appropriate measures to promote and sustain children's health and personal security.

Human rights advocates understand the intrinsic meaning and importance of children's relational connections. Recent discoveries from cognitive, neuroscience, and early attachment research therefore can, and must, be used to inform and strengthen child- and family-centered advocacy efforts and policy initiatives. Such evidence-guided knowledge underscores the importance of building, supporting, and maintaining high-quality early-childhood and family-centered programs. As noted in chapter 1, evidence from scientific inquiry asserts that building poorly resourced early-childhood programming is insufficient and perhaps even detrimental to children's welfare. Doing nothing at all in the way of prevention or early intervention, especially for at-risk children and families, inevitably creates greater financial and human costs to society.

Community programs that incorporate attachment theories into models for practice have been found effective for disenfranchised or marginalized populations who commonly experience chronic societal disconnection. One such program, the Relational Psychotherapy Mothers' Group (RPMG), serves mothers recovering from addiction. RPMG focuses on building interpersonal, parenting, and problem-solving skills. In addition, the women work on developing stronger self-regulation with directed attention to managing stress. This relationally based model for change has been found to be more successful than standard abstinence-focused drug counseling, insofar as it improves maternal-child bonds and decreases the likelihood of future child maltreatment (Suchman, McMahon, & Luthar, 2004). Like Fraiberg's (1987b) kitchen therapy, it respects the needs of the mothers, who also need nurturing as well as relational skill building in order to love themselves and, by extension, to love their babies.

Unfortunately, early-childhood and family-centered services for children are often the first programs that face local, state, and federal budget cuts. In part this is because children cannot advocate for themselves, and when they do, they are not taken seriously. Moreover, vulnerable families are rarely empowered to advocate on their own behalf; their energies are caught up in day-to-day survival. Not having the power or language to describe their experience contributes to the marginalization process. Thus child-centered practitioners are in the best position to act with and on behalf of children and families to make their voices heard.

Regrettably, there are more subtle and insidious barriers to using attachment models to design therapeutic services for marginalized groups. Society harshly judges people, especially caregiving parents, who fall into difficult times or struggle with intergenerational insecurity or dysfunction. These people are generally served by time-limited programs aimed at symptom reduction or crisis diversion rather than at in-depth recovery or healing. In general, reluctance to use longer-term attachment-based approaches with disenfranchised child clients and families seems grounded less on theoretical rationale and more on lack of social investment.

Advocacy thus begins by raising decision makers' awareness of the relevancy of human attachment to children's growth and development and to families' overall well-being. Also critical is lending insight into what happens when early bonds are disrupted because of adversity and relational disconnection. Child-centered workers are poised to raise such awareness because, as a profession, we value relational connections and understand the power and endurance of interactions that occur between infants and caregivers and between families and their communities (Azzi-Lessing, 2010).When policy makers and legislatures recognize the costs of insufficient early relationships, they may recognize the value of efforts that improve and expand early-intervention services to young children, especially those affected by risk factors such as poverty and other emotional, relational, and social insecurity (Azzi-Lessing, 2010).

SUMMARY

Principles of attachment theory are consistent with relational practice. Relational workers fully recognize the interdependency and complexity of human relationships, especially those between infants and caregivers, workers and clients, and people and their communities. Although attachment theory helps us understand human experience across the life course, it by no means implies that change is easy. Early relational experiences and memories of being cared for, for better or for worse, are durably held. Despite best practice efforts, some children and adults are never entirely released from the influence of early relational images and experiences. Sarina's and Marianna's cases illustrate how the influence and meaning of early relational ties are unconsciously transported into new relationships. That is to say, the work we do with children and parents is often very complicated and messy.

Attachment theory and knowledge offers ways to conceptualize human relationships. Its principles suggest strategies that enable workers and the children and parents they work with to revisit, revise, and hopefully make meaningful sense of the past. Selma Fraiberg exemplified how to do this in her relationship with Karen and Nina. Within the therapeutic relationship, Fraiberg focused on helping Karen deconstruct her own experiences of parental rejection and replace them with feelings of worthiness as both a child and a mother. Once nurtured herself, Karen was able to nurture her daughter. As a result, Nina was able to "become a loving, intelligent person who gave her mother huge rewards for motherhood" (Fraiberg, 1987a, p. 181).

Finally, it is incumbent on legislators and policy makers to recognize that children have the right to secure and reliable relationships. The drafters of the Convention on the Rights of the Child foresaw the elementary value of protecting children's ties to their families. Accordingly they underscored that relational attachments "are critical to purpose in life, sense of personal fulfillment, and identity as both an individual and a member of a family or a clan, a religious community, and a nation or an ethnic group—in effect, the ingredient in personhood" (Melton, 2010, p. 165). Child- and family-centered practitioners are therefore charged to protect children's rights to relational health by advocating early-intervention programs that foster support for young families, provide opportunities for and empower vulnerable families, and promote the rights and resources for all children and families, so that they can thrive.

Notes

1. Child Development Services provides early intervention (birth to two years) and free appropriate public education for children age three to five years under the supervision of the Maine Department of Education.

2. The revised *Diagnostic and Statistical Manual* (scheduled for release in May 2013) is proposing to eliminate Asperger's syndrome as a standalone diagnosis. Instead it will be integrated as a high-functioning form of ASD.

References

Ainsworth, M. S., Blehar, M. C., Waters, E., & Wall, S. (1978). *Patterns of attachment: A psychological study of the strange situation.* Hillsdale, NJ: Erlbaum.

Azzi-Lessing, L. (2010). Growing together: Expanding roles for social work practice in early-childhood settings. *Social Work, 55*(3), 255–263.

Banks, A. E. (2011). Developing the capacity to connect. *Zygon, 46*(1), 168–182.

Boss, P. (2004). Ambiguous loss. In F. Wash & M. McGoldrick (Eds.), *Living beyond loss: Death in the family* (2nd ed., pp. 237–246). New York: Norton.

Bowlby, J. (1969). *Attachment and loss: Vol. 1. Attachment.* New York: Basic Books.

Bowlby, J. (1983). Attachment and loss: Retrospect and prospect. *Annual Progress in Child Psychiatry and Child Development, 69*, 29–47.

Brown, M. W. (1942). *The runaway bunny.* New York: Harper and Row.

Fraiberg, S. (1987a). The adolescent mother and her infant. In L. Fraiberg (Ed.), *Selected writings of Selma Fraiberg* (pp. 165–182). Columbus: Ohio State University Press.

Fraiberg, S. (1987b). The muse in the kitchen: A case study in clinical research. In L. Fraiberg (Ed.), *Selected writings of Selma Fraiberg* (pp. 65–99). Columbus: Ohio State University Press.

Hartling, L. M. (2008). Strengthening resilience in a risky world: It's all about relationships. *Women and Therapy, 31*(2–4), 51.

Laursen, E. K., & Birmingham, S. M. (2003). Caring relationships as protective factors for at-risk youth: An ethnographic study. *Families in Society, 84*(2), 240.

Mahler, M., Pine, F., & Bergman, A. (1975). *The psychological birth of the infant.* New York: Basic Books.

Main, M. (1991). Metacognitive knowledge, metacognitive monitoring, and singular (coherent) vs. multiple (incoherent) model of attachment: Finding and directions for future research. In C. M. Parkes, J. Stevenson-Hinde, & P. Marris (Eds.), *Attachment across the life cycle* (pp. 127–159). New York: Tavistock/Routledge.

Melton, G. B. (2010). It's all about relationships! The psychology of human rights. *American Journal of Orthopsychiatry, 80*(2), 161–169.

Miller, J. B., & Stiver, I. P. (1997). *The healing connection.* Boston: Beacon Press.

Schore, J. R., & Schore, A. N. (2008). Modern attachment theory: The central role of affect regulation in development and treatment. *Clinical Social Work Journal, 36*, 9–20.

Siu, S., & Hogan, P. T. (1989). Public child welfare: The need for clinical social work. *Social Work, 34*(6), 423–428.

Spencer, R., Jordan, J. V., & Sazama, J. (2004) Growth-promoting relationships between youth and adults: A focus group study. *Families in Society, 85*(3), 354–362.

Suchman, N. E., McMahon, T. J., & Luthar, S. S. (2004). Interpersonal maladjustment as a predictor of mothers' response to a relational parenting intervention. *Journal of Substance Abuse Treatment, 27*, 135–143.

UN General Assembly. (1989, November 20). *Convention on the Rights of the Child* (United Nations, Treaty Series, 1577:3). Retrieved from http://www.unhcr.org/refworld/docid/3ae6b38f0.html

Whitehead, C. C. (2006). Neo-psychoanalysis: A paradigm for the 21st century. *Journal of the Academy of Psychoanalysis and Dynamic Psychiatry, 34*, 603–627.

Winnicott, D. W. (1986). The theory of parent-infant relationship. In P. Buckley (Ed.), *Essential papers on object relations* (pp. 233–253). New York: New York University Press.

Zeanah, C. H., & Smyke, A. T. (2008). Attachment disorders in family and social context. *Infant Mental Health Journal, 29*(3), 219–233.

4

Child-Centered Assessment

Lives in Translation

And I learned there are troubles
Of more than one kind.
Some come from ahead
And some come from behind.
. . .
But I've bought a big bat.
I'm all ready, you see.
Now my troubles are going
To have trouble with *me!*

Dr. Seuss, *I Had Trouble in Getting to Solla Sollew*

CHILD-CENTERED ASSESSMENT AND FORMULATION

The overarching objective of a relationally based child-centered assessment is to truly get to know one child, to see the uniqueness in his or her situation, and to work with assets to relieve discord and suffering. To do this well, practitioners must understand child-centered assessment as a process, not a fact-finding mission. This process involves getting information, formulating case theory, and planning intervention.

Helpful assessments gather information from a range of sources and provide a diversity of perspectives. Sources naturally include parents and caregivers, child clients, and observations and insights from people who care for and work with children in their natural environments. Altogether, data gathered for assessments help evaluators, families, and others make sense of wide-ranging, often conflicting, and always complicated evidence.

Formulation is the process of integrating and synthesizing a body of wide-ranging information and devising a hypothesis or case theory about what is causing or sustaining a child's problems. During the formulation phase, an evaluator brings together evidence-guided knowledge, practitioner wisdom, and contextual knowledge about this particular child's life circumstances. Themes developed from this body of evidence are integrated into an individualized case theory that should fit this child only (Bisman, 1999).

The case theory guides recommendations and planning that determines the child's course of therapy and other interventions. For example, a case theory may propose that a child is suffering from anxiety and recommends approaches that are best suited to anxiety reduction. If the child's anxiety is caused or exacerbated by social or environmental factors, recommendations to address these are also included in the intervention plan. In some cases, getting information, formulating a case theory, and determining an effective intervention plan is seamless. In more cases, however, case theories are continuously revised and interventions reformulated as new information emerges and as the child's and family's circumstances change.

In the sections that follow, you will be exposed to domains of information used for child-centered assessments and to strategies used to gather this information. The assessment process typically begins with a series of conversations between the evaluator and the child client and family. Information is also acquired through standardized assessment questionnaires required by agencies and other practice settings.

When assessment is a first-time experience, evaluators start with a clean slate. Many workers encounter children who have already had multiple evaluations, however, and they may find themselves combing through rich and extensive case files.

Child-centered assessments differ from those conducted with adults in a number of ways. First, data that informs the assessment is acquired in several co-occurring ways, including verbal exchange, general impressions, observations, and dynamic interactions. Second, expressive modalities such as artwork and play are used to elicit insight into inner experience that children may not be able to put into words. Evaluators should always have art supplies and toys on hand, so that children can tell their stories in ways that conform to their ability, proclivity, and developmental stage. Third, child-centered evaluators often communicate directly or indirectly with relevant collateral contacts, such as teachers, caseworkers, pediatricians, and others who have had encounters with the child and family. Finally, relational connections take place not only with the child client, but also with his or her biological, foster, or kin-related caregivers. All in all, those working with children must be prepared to engage in assessments that are more versatile than the one-to-one exchanges they have with adult clients.

When the evaluator is also the intended worker, assessment and intervention go hand in hand. In some settings the evaluator may begin the assessment process and then refer the child to a long-term provider. When this occurs, evaluators should not minimize the importance of relational connection with the child and family. Positive and respectful engagement even in a one-time exchange ensures a more useful and productive assessment outcome.

This chapter opens with an exploration of the domains of experience relevant to child-centered assessment. Such domains include the psychological, social, biological, relational, and cultural/spiritual aspects of children's lives. As will be discussed, domains are not standalone: they interact and influence one another in both positive and challenging ways. The chapter goes on to discuss multiple perspectives brought into child-centered assessments, and then identifies common errors that occur in assessment.

The remainder of the chapter applies and critiques child assessment models. The stories of Laura and Oscar illustrate how theories, language, and attitudes influence the assessment process. Because knowledge guides our interpretations of human experience, assessments are influenced, for better or for worse, by our chosen theories for practice.

CHILD-CENTERED ASSESSMENT

Data gathered for assessment illuminate biological, psychological, social, relational, and cultural/spiritual domains of a child's life (see figure 4.1). Assessment examines factors within each domain to understand how they might contribute to and maintain problematic situations. It also explores attributes and resources that promote the child's resilience and enable family members to manage adversity and adapt.

During the assessment process, parents and caregivers are continually encouraged to be active participants. These are the people who know the child best, and their expertise should be explicitly acknowledged. Their active participation is essential because successful health outcomes are more likely to occur when families perceive recommendations and goals to be in line with their stated needs and desires.

Biological Domain

Biological data include relevant information about health and developmental growth of the individual child and relevant family health and mental health history. Evaluators explore the development of gross and fine motor skills, speech and language capabilities, and other physical and cognitive milestones (see box 4.1). They look for mastery of early routines that indicate the development of healthy regulatory functioning. For example, evaluators may ask parents about the child's sleeping patterns, feeding schedules, eating preferences, and toileting habits, all basic functions of life that work together to help the child master developmental milestones.

FIGURE 4.1 Child-centered assessment factors

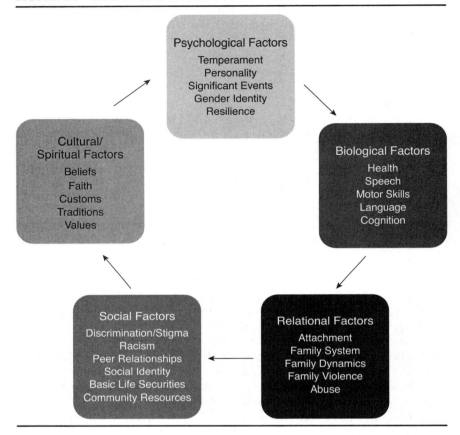

Knowledge of child development is invaluable to the evaluator during this assessment phase. Awareness of developmental stages and patterns helps evaluators determine whether the child is within the normal range of growth for his or her age group. Healthy children develop at different paces, however, and evaluators should not be hasty to make assumptions based solely on developmental time lines. As an example, one child may walk at nine months while another may not take his first step until fourteen months. Both youngsters, however, will enter kindergarten perfectly capable of walking, running, and playing. Another child late to develop language may suddenly erupt in full sentences at age three. Conversely, the three-year-old who inexplicably loses language skills may be facing significant problems. Developmental growth must thus be considered carefully within the context of the child's life and in view of what might be simple delays or growing concerns.

BOX 4.1
Generalized Child Development

BIRTH TO SIX MONTHS (INFANCY)

- Building attachments to caregivers
- Early development of regulatory skills
- Early social-interaction skills
- Early development of motor coordination
- Early language (social babbling)

SIX TO TWENTY-FOUR MONTHS (TODDLERHOOD)

- Beginning to organize world
- Recognition of self as separate from other
- Exploration and mastery of environment
- Separation and stranger anxiety
- Increased language and motor development
- Early social-skill development and curiosity

TWO TO FIVE YEARS (PRESCHOOL)

- Continued growth of individuality and emergence of personality
- Increased capacity for social interaction and play
- Increased self-regulation and memory
- Increased capacity to use language to express thoughts and feelings
- Regulation of bodily functions

SIX TO EIGHT YEARS (EARLY CHILDHOOD)

- Rapid physical and cognitive growth
- Developing peer and social relationships
- Early moral development and empathy
- Increased impulse control
- Beginning sense of identity, competence, and mastery

NINE TO TWELVE YEARS (MIDDLE CHILDHOOD)

- Rapid and uneven physical growth

- Increase in physical strength and motor coordination
- Growing cognitive and social proficiency
- Developing sense of identity and self-evaluative skills
- Broadening sense of the world
- Stronger identification with peer/social group
- Sexual awareness

THIRTEEN TO EIGHTEEN YEARS (ADOLESCENCE)

- Strengthening cognition and abstract reasoning
- Growing autonomy with ambivalent adult attachments
- Identity formation through connection with peers, groups, and community
- Sexuality
- Experimentation with relational intimacy, drugs, and alcohol
- Ability to move about independently (driver's license)
- Growing recognition of mortality
- Risk-taking behaviors

Knowing the family's customs, practices, and needs is essential to child- and family-centered assessment. This is because developmental milestones are influenced by cultural and material necessity. Let's take the example of sleeping arrangements. Eurowestern child-development experts typically view the family bed as inappropriate if not harmful for infants and children. Most experts recommend that infants sleep independently by age six months or younger.

In other cultures, children traditionally sleep in the family bed until late childhood. Placing infants in a separate bed might be viewed as premature if not neglectful. In other circumstances worldwide, children sleep with parents and siblings because they live in homes where there is only one bedroom for multiple family members. Thus it is not appropriate for evaluators to have one standard for sleeping arrangements for all children.

An individualized baseline is also needed to establish when the child's problems began or when changes in development occurred. If a six-year-old is referred due to tantrums, the evaluator should determine whether the child has always had a feisty temperament. Perhaps the youngster's reactivity is indicative of sensory or temperamental sensitivities.

If the child was initially easygoing and changed gradually or suddenly, however, the evaluator would then explore events on the time line of these changes. A sudden change might indicate that something triggered the child's irritability, whereas a child who has always been somewhat volatile may be dealing with inherent, biological regulatory difficulties.

Gathering information about pregnancy and the family's birthing experiences is also germane to child-centered assessment. Parents' stories of conception, gestation, and birth provide a backdrop to understanding factors that may potentially influence both the child's health and the parents' relationship to the child. Questions about the pregnancy might include whether it was planned or unplanned. Were there previous miscarriages or prenatal losses? Were there any concerns about the mother's health during gestation? How did the father or parenting partner participate in the pregnancy? What was the birthing process like? Were there anticipated or unanticipated complications during birth?

Finally, it is also useful to ask an open-ended question about parents' first responses to their newborn. Answers may reveal important information that routine check-off questions may miss. This was true in the case of Barbara, the mother of Anthony, a three-year-old who was being assessed for behavioral difficulties. Barbara was seeking recommendations to help parent her highly active preschooler. Anthony's father was recently incarcerated, and Barbara also had a newborn daughter to tend to.

Anthony was born with a severe cleft palate, a birth defect affecting the formation of the upper lip and roof of the mouth. The faces of children with cleft palates can initially appear quite deformed, which was the case with Anthony. Over the short course of his life, Anthony had had seven surgeries to repair his lip, and he continued to receive speech and occupational therapy to assist with his feeding and language delays.

When asked about her postpartum responses, Barbara commented that the nurses seemed "horrified" by Anthony's appearance. Her own reaction was quite the contrary. She told the evaluator that when Anthony was placed in her arms, all she saw was "the most beautiful ugly baby in the world." This information spoke volumes about Barbara's attachment to Anthony and made sense of her vigilance and advocacy on his behalf.

Biological data also include intergenerational trends; for instance, does diabetes or bed-wetting run in the family? Do other family members exhibit behavioral or cognitive patterns or problems similar to the child being assessed? Genograms can be used to illustrate inter- and intrafamily patterns of health and systems functioning. When evaluators and clients create genograms, the product can be both helpful in identifying common themes and therapeutic in forging a connection between worker and client(s).

The genogram in figure 4.2 illustrates Anthony and Barbara's family. As one can see, Barbara has a significant history of family disruption on her side of the family. John and Barbara, however, have stayed together despite adversity and geographic separations. One might ask, how has the couple maintained this connection, and what do their relational ties mean for Anthony's and his sister's experiences of being a family?

FIGURE 4.2 Anthony's genogram

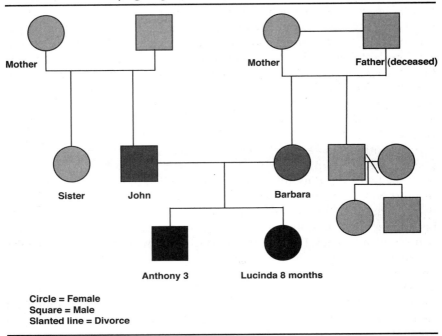

Circle = Female
Square = Male
Slanted line = Divorce

Psychological Domain

Psychological data gathered for child assessment explore factors of temperament, personality, sexuality, gender identity, and the impact of significant individual and family events on the child's emotional and identity development. Resilience and the child's strengths, talents, and capacities to cope with adversity and stress are also explored as part of this domain.

Like biological predispositions and characteristics, psychological makeup interacts with the relational and social domains in a person's life. Attachment, for example, is influenced by the fit between a child's temperament and that of the parent. A highly energetic girl may be difficult for a low-key mother to parent, whereas an athletically oriented family may find themselves worried about a son who always has his nose in a book.

A child's sexual orientation and gender identity have implications for overall identity formation. Evaluators sometimes make the error of inferring heterosexuality and gender conformity without asking questions about these factors. Indeed, many workers are uncomfortable addressing these issues at all unless the child or family raises them.

For this reason Edward, age twelve, was reluctant to discuss his attraction to boys with the evaluator. A veteran of psychotherapy since the age of six, he was astute at detecting adults' discomfort and judgments. None of his previous evaluators mentioned sexual orientation or gender identity, so Edward simply kept quiet about these matters. His four previous evaluations (all of which he'd read) contained an array of diagnostic speculations about why this bright, handsome, athletic youngster did not live up to his potential or thrive. None mentioned sexual orientation, gender identity, or sexuality as related to Edward's development.

When asked by this new evaluator about sexual orientation and gender identity, Edward refused to answer. When his parents were asked, they seemed insulted; their son was "all man," his father reported. Once a safe-enough relationship was established, however, Edward came back to the issue of sexual orientation with his worker and asked if it was "normal" for him to like boys "in that way." The initial assessment questions about sexual development had left the door open for him to be candid.

Background history about the child's mental health is another routine aspect of assessment. Questions might include, Does this youngster adapt well in the face of strains and challenges? Does he or she have difficulties with mood or behavior even in the best of circumstances? Has the child received psychological counseling or been prescribed psychotropic medications? The evaluator should ask about family history of mental health or behavioral problems to assess for the child's possible genetic predisposition.

Evaluators should be familiar with the most current version of the *Diagnostic and Statistical Manual of Mental Disorders* (DSM). They need to understand diagnoses that may have been applied to the child or the child's family members. A diagnosis, however, should never be used as a substitute for fully knowing an individual. Diagnosis, like case theory, represents a hypothesis about why a person is experiencing a range of symptoms or acting in a particular manner. In some cases a diagnosis can be helpful to parents and children trying to make sense of diverse and complicated behaviors.

The child's adaptational style is another component of the psychological profile. Children are resourceful. They survive seemingly insurmountable odds. Knowing how they have coped and survived challenges in the past offers insight into their capacity for change and future growth. As part of any assessment process, the child client should be asked to identify his or her strengths and capabilities.

Often the child's reported problematic behaviors or symptoms indicate coping strategies that have outlived their usefulness. For example, a child who has experienced neglect may seem demanding to his foster parents or seeking negative attention from his teachers. In the past this youngster may have had to strongly draw attention to himself in order to survive. He will likely continue to use these familiar survival skills until he learns new, more functional behaviors. In the meantime it is helpful for evaluators to note the functional nature of these seemingly dysfunctional behaviors.

As a rule, assessments typically focus on what is wrong rather than what is right or good about the child. As part of any assessment process, parents and caregivers should explicitly be asked to name children's strengths. How they respond to this query is always illuminating. Parents who can easily identify a child's strengths ("she's a wonderful artist") and virtues ("he's so kind") know their children well. Those who cannot come up with positive attributes to describe their children tell a different story. They may be overwhelmed by the child's presenting problems or perhaps with life in general. In either case, how parents and caregivers respond to this line of inquiry says a lot about the psychological environment of the parent-child relationship and the family.

Social Domain

The social component of assessment investigates individual, family, and community-based aspects of the child's social world. Infants and toddlers may enjoy the company of other children, but typically they play in a parallel way. Questions in the social domain for this age group might focus on whether the child is exposed to other children and, if so, what his or her responses are. Can the child spend time with adults other than parents without too much separation anxiety? Is there a special adult (or adults) in the child's life to whom he or she is attached?

If the child is old enough to have an active life outside the home, is he or she able to identify a cohort of friends? Does he or she have a "best friend," interpreted as someone to rely on or share interests with? Conversely, does the youngster describe experiences of social isolation or marginalization? Has he or she been bullied? How have adults responded to such harassment?

Evaluators should also ask about the child's capacity for give-and-take. For example, does the child need to be in control of the play, or can he or she be flexible? When playing games, is the child able to lose gracefully, or does loss prompt a tantrum or other behavioral fallout? Do the parents remedy all social disappointment, or is the child encouraged to develop coping skills that help manage conflicts in peer relations?

Childhood is often thought of as a playful time, and healthy children are typically viewed as those who socialize with others and make friends. Thus children content with their own company are often suspected of being deficient. Yet some youngsters enjoy focused tasks and have interests that are self-contained. If this is the case, the evaluator might want to inquire whether the child occasionally enjoys the company of peers without experiencing distress. If the child cannot engage with peers in any way, then further evaluation of social communication capacities is warranted.

As noted in chapter 2, children are well aware of where they sit on the sociocultural spectrum. Once engaged in the world outside of the family, they compare their lives and resources to others'. Like adults, children's social troubles may in part reflect life in an unjust society. Social ostracism may at times be a consequence of class discrimination, racism, heterosexism, and other forms of societal oppression. Racism and ethnocentrism also affect children's social well-being.

Evaluators must be sensitive to the powerful role that discrimination plays in children's lives. Regardless of age, people's social experiences shape how they see themselves as well as how they are seen. Parents, too, are affected by discrimination, including discrimination by mental health, social service, and educational systems. Families experiencing material insecurities or health-access disparities are often blamed for not adequately taking care of their children. Indeed, some become so disenfranchised that they are unlikely to feel safe enough to be honest with evaluators about the child's and family's experiences. Engaging authentically with these families during the assessment phase is especially important for developing useful intervention strategies.

Lastly, the evaluator inquires about social resources available to the child and family. These include internal family social supports, extended family ties, connections to community resources, and faith-based connections. Families may have close or complicated ties with any or all of these resources. Some families may have no family ties, social resources, or community connections at all, perhaps because of relocation, intergenerational conflicts, or isolation caused by fear of domestic violence. Given the interlocking relationships between children, their caregivers, and social resources, it is important for evaluators to ask about supports and resources, and why they are or aren't available.

Relational Domain

Relational connection is a hallmark of health. For young children, relational connection can make the difference between survival and failure to thrive, between healthy regulation and interruptive dysregulation. As noted in chapter 3, strong ties between infants and caregivers more often than not lead to secure attachments, which guide children toward positive identity and social acuity. Insufficient or absent ties result in insecure attachments that can impede a child's growth across developmental domains. In essence, relational factors interact with all aspects of a child's life and predict where strengths or problems may reside.

The importance of relational factors compels evaluators to do a thorough inquiry into the child's early and ongoing ties to caregivers, other adults, and peers. Open-ended questions about early relational attachment are best, for example, "Tell me about Billy as a baby." Follow-up prompts ask about the quality of the parent-child bond: Was Billy cuddly and fun to play with? What is the parent's relationship with Billy now, and has it always been thus? If not, what happened to change the course of their relationship? Were there specific incidents that caused the relationship to break down?

Evaluators should ask about events known to distress or complicate attachment relationships. Child maltreatment and sexual abuse erode relationships between parents and children. They also disturb the child's capacity to trust in relationships with others within and outside of the family. Domestic violence also affects relational trust, as does chronic conflict within families, divorced or otherwise.

Relational qualities should also be gleaned from the child. Young children play out aspects of relational connection or disconnection or make them explicit in drawings or sand trays. Relational connections may also be observed between the child and parent during times of separation, reconnection, or participation in the assessment process itself.

Age and developmental factors must be considered when assessing the relational domain. For example, it's not unusual for a young child to need a parent to be in the room during an assessment conversation, whereas it's less common for an adolescent to be unable to separate from a parent or caregiver unless developmental or intellectual disabilities are factors.

Evaluators should determine whether significant people outside of immediate caregivers have or have had meaning to the child. Foster parents, siblings, kin, coaches, counselors, and teachers, among others, can provide foundational support to children who may be relationally afloat. Such was the case for Phillip, sixteen, who spoke warmly about his foster mother during our assessment conversation. Although caring for as many as ten foster children at any given time, she always made sure she checked in with Phillip daily. The fact that his foster mother consistently sought relational connection with him made all the difference in the world to Phillip. "She reminded me that I mattered—that I wasn't invisible," he said.

Cultural/Spiritual Domain

Cultural and spiritual factors influence the fabric of daily life for children and families. Such factors include the family's customs, personal beliefs, and faith traditions; their rituals; ties to family and community; and shared histories. Although common threads run across different cultures, races, ethnicities, and religions, each child and family is distinctive in the way they weave these together. In some instances, children's customs may diverge from their family of origins. This is seen most clearly in immigrant and refugee children, who may acculturate to their new environs much quicker than their parents do, because of immersion in schooling and other child-centered cultural activities. Foster children may struggle in the cultural/spiritual domain because they possess beliefs and practices that differ from those of their fostering families.

Sometimes children deeply adhere to cultural traditions or religious convictions that are misunderstood by evaluators. David Hodge (2002) points out that Muslim youth are often misunderstood by educators and service providers who expect them to readily conform to Western customs. He comments that Muslim adolescents tend to socialize with family rather than peers because they highly value family interconnectedness. Prayer rituals and clothing traditions are sometimes misread by non-Muslim evaluators as signs of oppression rather than as highly regarded cultural traditions. Hodge (2002) makes it clear that not all Muslim youth embrace their traditions, but many do. His work reminds us to explore the meaning of culture and spirituality from multiple standpoints and to integrate these into formulations and intervention planning.

Ethical dilemmas for evaluators can arise because of the child's or family's cultural and religious practices. This occurs most often in child protective cases, when clashes arise over disciplinary practices, child rearing, or health care (see chapter 13). It can also occur in mental health settings when families from diverse cultures hold very different perspectives, on the causes and treatments for mental illness, for example, or on ways to deal with violence within families.

Family customs may also collide with the personal values of the evaluator or with agency practices and policy mandates. Cultural differences are keenly felt and must be respectfully addressed in the course of an assessment. Thus evaluators must become proficient in conducting culturally sensitive assessments and be open to learning from children and families about their traditions, beliefs, and values (Webb, 2001).

MULTIPLE PERSPECTIVES AND ASSESSMENT ERRORS

As described above, child-centered assessment requires solicitation of multiple viewpoints and diverse opinions. These are gathered from the child as well as a range of people with whom the child has had significant contact. It should be expected that the information assembled may be contradictory, sometimes polarizing, and often confusing. For example, parents and school personnel frequently have very different ideas about a child's problems and strengths. Similarly, parents who do not raise their children together may disagree about the source of a child's difficulties. To add to the confusion, prior evaluations, school reports, and other written documents may clarify or altogether complicate the assessment process.

How do evaluators remain open to divergent opinions and viewpoints? To begin with, it is important to remember that data generate only a partial portrait of any child. Evaluations, interviews, and conversations offer snap-shots that contribute to a much larger story. It is therefore critical that evalua-tors remember that children grow and change, circumstances evolve, and there is always more to be known. As I emphasize throughout this chapter, workers must take care not to rush to conclusions or favor one person's accounts over that of another. Logging their thoughts during the assessment process can help evaluators keep track of ideas that can later be confirmed or disconfirmed as they gather more information.

Waiting for comprehensive data before constructing a formulation and developing recommendations is not only good practice but also prevents assessment errors that may impede good outcomes. Jerome Groopman (2007), an author and professor of medicine at Harvard Medical School, reports that it takes most physicians on average eighteen seconds with a patient to determine a diagnosis. One might ask how much one can know about another person in eighteen seconds? How accurate can one be with-out assessing the complicated and interactional biological, psychological, social, relational, and cultural influences that affect people's lives?

Costly errors naturally result when evaluators issue diagnoses without in-depth, individual inquiry. Not the least of these costs is the loss of pre-cious time and money spent on ineffective protocols and medications. More disturbing, however, is when incorrect assumptions lead to mistakes that have long-term consequences for the client's health and well-being.

Assessment errors commonly occur when practitioners leap to diagnos-tic conclusions before all the data are in. Erroneous judgments also result when single causes are used to explain complex problems. These are rein-forced when evaluators, having drawn a conclusion from partial information, ignore or exclude the potential impact of disconfirming evidence.

The consequences of erroneous judgments may be slight or significant, depending on how they affect the children's relationships and well-being. Quick and mistaken judgments are frequently seen in child welfare cases where the impact of material insecurities, discrimination, and violence may be ignored or minimized in favor of a simple diagnostic solution. Sometimes children are assumed to have ADHD when they are in fact inattentive because of chronic family violence. Oppositional defiant disorder (ODD) is a common diagnostic label readily assigned to disadvantaged young males of color. These youngsters, like those diagnosed with ADHD, may be vigilant and angry due to real-life circumstances, including discrimination that affects their capacity to self-regulate. In the end, youngsters may end up on compli-cated medication regimens that do little to address the essential problems and inequities in their young lives.

Assessment errors also transpire when workers base conclusions on information from only one source. This often happens when children are brought for evaluation by one parent and information is not obtained from the other parent or significant family caregivers. An evaluator may erroneously assume that the nonreporting parent is uninterested or uninvolved when in fact he or she either does not know about the assessment or has limited access to the child. Evaluators should always err on the side of getting information from all parents and caregivers. Obtaining multiple views will result in a more useful and ethical assessment.

At times, even accurate and valid data may seem discrepant. Children can behave differently in response to their caregivers or act in distinctive ways in different environments. Children's lives, like adults', are messy. Thus evaluators must avoid the mistake of oversimplifying their assessment and making recommendations based on only one aspect of the child's varied life. A more comprehensive and helpful assessment is drawn when all perspectives are considered.

Lulu, age six, will help illustrate the value of integrating multiple perspectives into a comprehensive child-centered assessment. Lulu's kindergarten teacher was highly concerned because she rarely spoke up in class. The school's speech therapist was equally worried because, despite her best efforts, she could not get a word out of Lulu during their sessions together. Only the music teacher heard Lulu's voice. "She sings like an angel," he reported. School personnel believed that Lulu suffered with anxiety and a language-processing problem. The school social worker was assigned to meet the family.

Lulu's mother and father were baffled by the school's reports. According to them, they couldn't get Lulu to stop talking at home. "She's a little chatterbox," said her mother. "She doesn't shut up," reported her nine-year-old brother. Her father and live-in grandmother both described Lulu as a lively little girl who engaged even the shyest children in dramatic backyard productions.

The school social worker concluded that all reports of Lulu's behaviors and attitudes were valid. Having heard from everyone, she was able to formulate a case theory that yielded recommendations that would help Lulu access her strengths and talents in the school environment. Once aware of her capabilities, teachers and other school personnel were more confident in building bridges between school and home. By the end of kindergarten, Lulu's teachers were more concerned with how to quiet her than how to help her open up.

THE CHILD'S PERSPECTIVE

Evidence for child-centered assessment is gathered not only from pertinent adults, but also from children. This begs the question—how does one gather helpful information from children and interpret it meaningfully? Indeed, children's perspectives have been criticized by some as being immature, inconsistent, and too changeable to have relevance. One might argue, however, that adults also change their stories frequently and are at times inaccurate reporters.

Respecting the voices of children is a deeply rooted principle of relational practice and applies to all aspects of child-centered assessment. Children are no doubt experts in their own lives, and like people of all ages, they deserve to be listened to, respected, and heard. Although there's a paucity of research with children engaged in the assessment process, studies find that children enlighten and deepen the assessment process (Smart, 2006). Children's accounts tend to be multilayered, capturing the intricate details of day-to-day life. Although information gleaned from children alone is not sufficient, it adds much to data provided by parents and other adults involved in the assessment process.

Engaging children in the assessment process begins with knowing that conversations will be considerably different in content, style, and focus than those taking place between adults. Therefore, evaluators need specific knowledge and skills for child-centered communication (see chapter 5). They must feel genuine respect for the child and his or her viewpoint. Empathy helps evaluators imagine what an assessment session might look like through the eyes of, say, a five-year-old girl. What is she thinking as she sits on a big chair, in a strange room with an unfamiliar adult? Or for that matter, what might a surly twelve-year-old be feeling about an unfamiliar adult asking about his poor grades? Perhaps even more daunting is the waiting-room anxiety of a frightened but well-defended ten-year-old whose abuse disclosure has divided her family and sent her mother's boyfriend to jail?

Given the anxieties and skepticism children might bring to assessment, the evaluator should do her or his best to create a conversational and developmentally sensitive environment in which the child can feel safe enough to share his or her story. From a logistical standpoint, the child and evaluator should be on the same level, without desks separating them. Language needs to be child-centered without being infantile, and jargon must be avoided. Overall, evaluators must convince children that their opinions matter.

Hearing children requires many skills, including the capacities to listen and observe (Webb, 2003). Listening necessitates a host of attitudinal skills, including patience, flexibility, humor, playfulness, and tolerance for ambiguity. For some children assessment begins with verbal interaction, while for others it may start with art activities or games. The use of familiar expressive methods helps children feel comfortable enough to express their thoughts and feelings (see chapter 7).

Evaluators' interest in what children have to say is critically important. Without such assurance, children may say what they've been told to say, they may withhold facts, or they may simply tell you what they think you want to hear. Such information does not advance the assessment process. When children feel respected and safe enough, however, they provide invaluable insight into their inner and outer lives, which in the end promotes more accurate formulations and fosters recommendations that are more likely to be in children's best interests.

THE FINAL PRODUCT

The culmination of the child-centered assessment is a written report to be shared with adults concerned with the child's welfare. In some situations, children old enough to grasp the intent and language of an assessment report will also be privy to its content. Language used in these documents is highly influential. It records perceptions of the child, including diagnostic impressions that have both short- and long-term effects. It describes the role of the family in the child's problems and the recovery process. Language has multiple intrapersonal implications as well. It shapes the child's sense of self-worth. It affects how parents experience and interpret their caring, competence, and culpability. It also influences workers' initial perceptions of the child client and family.

To illustrate the impact of language, let's look at three statements potentially used to describe Laura, age six, who is having relational difficulties with her mother and younger brother, Miles, age four. Consider these descriptions of Laura used in a hypothetical case record: (1) "She's a bad girl." (2) "She has oppositional defiant disorder" (ODD). (3) "Laura loses control at times, and her behavior becomes irritating to her mother and brother."

The first example, "She's a bad girl," implies an identity that assumes that being bad is who Laura is. The second example, which claims that Laura has ODD, applies an attribute to Laura that becomes part of who she is and frames how she's viewed by others. This diagnostic label may become part of her individual and collective identity, whether or not it ultimately proves to be a valid assumption. Furthermore, electronic record keeping could ensure that the attribute ODD will remain in Laura's profile for a lifetime. In any case, being labeled ODD will affect both how Laura sees herself and how others judge her.

The last statement, "Laura loses control at times, and her behavior becomes irritating to her mother and brother," is descriptive. It names a specific behavior that occurs and how it affects those around her. It does not deny that she possesses other, more positive characteristics. The descriptor does not state who Laura is or what disorder she has but tells us what she does that seems to get her into trouble. The actual ways in which Laura enacts "being irritating" are not yet known and need to be explored.

The more behavioral statement also implies a reciprocal/relational process that, when scrutinized, may contain valuable information that can be used to prompt further inquiry. For example, what actions are characteristic of Laura's irritating behaviors? How do Laura's mother and brother respond to her loss of control? What happens following their responses, how is it handled, and by whom?

Each of the above statements represents assumptions that influence how this six-year-old's behaviors will be perceived and responded to. There are relational risks in assessing Laura as a "bad girl"; it's a potential setup for disconnection from her mother and brother. It also immediately influences the tenor of developing relationships with helping professionals. Knowing she's been referred to as "bad" also may contribute to Laura's negative self-appraisal and feelings of hopelessness. And while the diagnostic label ODD may be helpful to her parents or therapeutic workers to explain behavioral patterns, it simultaneously creates an obstacle to seeing more positive aspects of Laura, including her hilarious sense of humor, her love of reading, and her capacity for gentleness and compassion when she is not overly stimulated.

The variable effects of these statements emphasize that assessment reports are most constructive when they are descriptive, not categorizing or reductive. The natural response to a descriptive statement is to ask for clarification: "So what happens when Laura loses control and becomes irritating?" Her four-year-old brother replies, "Mom lets her watch TV because she becomes such a pain." Miles offers useful information, as does his mother's response, "Well I have to keep her quiet because Dad gets very mad when you two fight."

Now Laura's irritating behavior takes on another meaning. It is one step removed from her identity as "bad" and becomes part of an evolving story within the context of this family's life. Such details contribute to beneficial formulation and open up additional entry points for intervention. These can now be incorporated into useful recommendations that include engagement of the couple, parents, and sibling. Indeed, the variations of language used for Laura's assessment emphasize that *how* information is reported may be as or even more important than *what* is reported.

CONTEMPORARY CHILD-CENTERED ASSESSMENTS: LIMITATIONS AND ACCOMMODATIONS

Applying the relational assessment process described in this chapter to "real-life" practice is a growing challenge for mental health practitioners across settings. Assessment models are increasingly adapted to predetermined intervention protocols used by agencies. Some are geared to electronic health check-off formats with minimal space for qualitative narratives. Moreover, clients who seek services from publicly supported health and mental health systems do not get to choose preferred models for assessment: reimbursement systems prescribe evaluative protocols and time lines whether or not they are useful to clients or practitioners (Ballou, Hill, & West, 2008).

In addition, many social service and mental health agencies are limited by standardized or culturally restricted definitions of such terms as *family, health,* or *wellness* (Ballou et al., 2008). Assessments may be influenced by the constraints of these definitions, resulting in pathologizing identities or delegitimizing family structures. For example, an agency's understanding of the term *family* may be bound to norms that do not recognize the broad range of people who raise children, including kin in Native and African American families, single parents, same-sex parents, and grandparents. The growing racial, ethnic, linguistic, and cultural diversity of children in the United States and Canada demands that all child-centered programs and services recognize the wide variety of families they now serve. Such applied diversity is not always the case nor are cultural factors consistently integrated into standardized assessments.

While it is true that institutional resources are constrained by economic realities, these should not diminish efforts made to apply relational principles to our practices. Changing institutional culture involves shifting attitudes within systems while actively campaigning for critical policy changes in administration and legislation. We must continually remind ourselves that institutions are made up of people striving for similar goals but constrained by different directives.

Relational child-centered assessment is continuous and multifaceted. It seeks to expand and improve upon an understanding of the child, the family, and the context in which they live, so that effective interventions can be put into place. Like science, which is a process of ongoing discovery, assessment is meant to instigate fresh ways of thinking about a child that will improve the quality of her or his life.

APPLICATIONS OF CHILD-CENTERED ASSESSMENTS: OSCAR

Let's look at how child-centered assessment translates the vast and varied information received at referral and beyond. In two examples, you will meet Oscar and his family. The first example represents a traditional assessment model; the second integrates the relational perspective into an assessment framework developed by Ruth Dean and Nancy Poorvu (2008).

When you review the case of Oscar, compare the two examples. Note the language used in each assessment. What information is needed to formulate a useful case theory? What feelings do you notice as you learn more about Oscar, his family, and his life circumstances? What personal reflections would you add to the discussion as you contemplate Oscar's future and hopes for success?

Traditional Assessment

Oscar Winters is a seven-year-old boy with a Native American mother and Caucasian father. Oscar just returned to his mother's home after living for two months with his aunt and cousins on a reservation just south of the Canadian border. His mother, Nancy Dana, thirty-two, sends her children to be with relatives when she feels too stressed to parent. Oscar currently lives with his mother and sister, Mary, thirteen. The whereabouts of Oscar's father, Edmund Winters, sixty-two, is unknown. His last known residence was in a cabin not far from Oscar's current rental home. Edmund travels to find work and is often out of touch with his children.

Most of the time Oscar's family lives in a one-bedroom rental cottage in a coastal tourist town. Their cottage is heated by an old propane stove, and Nancy is responsible for supplying the heating fuel, which she says is very expensive. In the summer, the family usually moves north and lives in a tent. They return to the coastal community just before Labor Day, so the children can stay in the same school administrative district even though they have to move quite frequently. According to the referral materials, Oscar has moved sixteen times in his young life. The case report submitted by the school social worker states that Oscar's favorite activity is "making houses out of any and all art and play materials provided" (figure 4.3).

Oscar's referral was prompted by the school nurse, who is concerned about Oscar's inconsistent toileting. She suggests that he suffers from encopresis, a condition that causes involuntary defecation. The school nurse reports that they keep a supply of clothes in her office for children who wet or otherwise soil their clothes during the school day. However, school policy requires that children who defecate in their pants be automatically sent home to be showered and changed. According to the nurse's notes, Oscar's mother does not have a reliable phone number and therefore cannot be reached during school hours. The school nurse states, "I'm at a loss as to how to deal with Oscar's soiling problem."

Nancy Dana works at The Pines, a local nursing home. She tells school personnel that she is concerned about Oscar but that she will lose her job if she leaves work too often. Her solution is to send Oscar to school in training pants so that his clothes won't be soiled and he can remain in class. She prefers that Oscar be embarrassed by his behavior, because she believes being ashamed will help him "quit crapping his pants." "He's a big boy," she says. "It's time he acts like one."

Oscar's case file is thick, filled with evaluations for mental health and learning challenges. The speech therapist's report indicates significant delays in receptive and expressive language skills. The physical therapy report says that his gross motor skills are lagging. Both reports speculate that Oscar's development is affected by insufficient nutrition, resulting in failure to thrive, a medical condition that results in a child's not growing or gaining weight at expected rates. The psychological examiner questions possible sexual abuse and neglect.

His file also includes case notes from Child Protective Services (CPS). CPS has received numerous calls from school personnel and from anonymous callers with reports of alleged abuse and neglect of both Oscar and

FIGURE 4.3 Oscar's home

Mary. CPS has not yet opened a case because there has been insufficient evidence of neglect or physical or sexual abuse. Although Nancy Dana reaches out to her extended family when circumstances get too difficult for her or for the children, CPS has not contacted the extended family.

The school psychological examiner (PE) interviewed Nancy Dana in the fall of Oscar's kindergarten year. The case summary states that "Nancy Dana arrived on time for her appointment to discuss her son, Oscar Winters, 7. She appeared neatly dressed and open to discussing the school's concerns about her son." The PE concluded: "Oscar's family history is significant for early neglect, single-parenthood, multiple losses and transitions, and domestic violence. Oscar suffers from encopresis and occasional enuresis; cause unknown at this time." The PE comments: "The mother is passive and noncompliant. She admits Oscar is slow and has problems, but she does not seem motivated to follow through on recommendations for medical evaluations, occupational therapy services, or family counseling."

The notes also report that "Nancy Dana states that she enjoys partying with friends" and does not deny occasional alcohol consumption. In his concluding comments, the PE questions if Miss Dana is "in denial about her substance misuse." He also suggests looking into the mother's cognitive capacity, as "she appears to have cognitive and communicational limitations." He writes, "Nancy Dana had difficulty in school and thinks she may have undiagnosed learning disabilities." His final conclusion focuses on Miss Dana's attachment to Oscar: "problematic attachment is assumed due to frequent maternal-child separations."

The PE's diagnostic suggestions include reactive attachment disorder; encopresis of unknown etiology; developmental delays in cognitive, behavioral, and emotional functioning rule out mental retardation; and possible attention-deficit/hyperactivity disorder. He recommends evaluation for sexual abuse.

Prognosis

Oscar's mental health diagnoses, poor physical health, and cognitive disabilities define him as academically and socially at risk. Antisocial behaviors, potential substance misuse, and academic failure are predicted unless intervention occurs as soon as possible in multiple psychosocial domains.

Recommendations

1. Oscar is eligible for Title 1 services because the family's income qualifies him for free snacks and reduced lunch.

2. Oscar will receive two hours of group math skills per week with an educational technician.

3. The school social worker will provide a half hour of individual counseling for Oscar per week and consult with the classroom teacher as needed.

4. Oscar's situation will be evaluated by the student assessment team next month to determine his eligibility for referral to special education services.

5. Miss Dana will be referred to the Community Counseling Center for family counseling and parenting classes.

6. Miss Dana is strongly encouraged to seek a medical evaluation for Oscar's encopresis.

7. If family recommendations are not acted upon within six weeks, the family will be referred to Child Protective Services.

Applying Relational Child-Centered Assessment

Oscar is a seven-year-old boy of mixed ethnic and racial parentage. His mother, Nancy Dana, thirty-two, is Native American; her tribe is Micmac (Mi'kmaq), and she has family living in Nova Scotia and on lands in northeastern Maine. Oscar's father, Edmund Winters, sixty-two years old, is Caucasian and of German descent. Mr. Winters's whereabouts is currently unknown. His last known residence was in a cabin not far from Oscar's current home. Mr. Winters travels to find work and is often out of touch with his children. This means that Miss Dana has primarily raised and provided for Mary, thirteen, and Oscar as a single parent.

Oscar recently spent two months living with his mother's sister and cousins on the reservation in northern Maine. Miss Dana is grateful to have relatives willing to help her out when life gets too hard for her to feel like a good-enough mother. Oscar is now back with his mother and sister in a winter rental in the southern part of the state. The children's education is very important to Miss Dana. She is adamant that their schooling be consistent, and she believes that the children receive an excellent education in the town where they live during the school year. Because of limited income, however, the family can live in this school administrative district only when rents are low. In the summer they move north and live in a tent or stay with relatives.

There are downsides to the family's transient living situation. First, because of traveling back and forth during the summer and needing to locate new housing for each school year, Oscar has had to move approximately sixteen times in his young life. Second, staying in the same school district requires the family to live a great distance from Miss Dana's nearest family and cultural supports. Third, because the family has limited income, adequate housing has been hard to find. Living conditions in the Dana/Winters household are currently affected by small living space and by the high cost of propane for their only source of heat, a space heater. Miss Dana is used to being independent and is reluctant to seek financial aid to help cover her heating costs.

The present referral was prompted by the school nurse. She was concerned about Oscar's inconsistent toileting and has tentatively diagnosed encopresis, a condition of involuntary defecation of unknown origin. According to the school nurse's report, the school keeps a supply of clothes for children who wet or otherwise soil their clothes during the school day. However, school policy requires that children who defecate in their pants be automatically sent home to be showered and changed. The report also indicates that Oscar's mother does not have a phone and therefore cannot be reached during school hours. The school nurse is at a loss as to how to deal with Oscar's soiling problem.

Miss Dana has struggled with how to handle Oscar's problems. Her older daughter was easily toilet trained, and she has had no experience with encopresis. She is also worried that she could lose her job if she has to leave it to pick up Oscar too often. Given the family's already meager income and Mr. Winters's lack of child support, losing her job will have very serious repercussions for the Dana/Winters family.

At the time of referral, Miss Dana voiced frustration and anger about Oscar's soiling problem. She thought that sending Oscar to school in training pants would keep his clothes from being soiled. She also thought that having to go back to diapers would be embarrassing, thus providing Oscar with greater incentive to keep from defecating in his pants.

There are many reports and case notes in Oscar's school file. Each chronicles the difficulties Oscar has had as a result of many adverse early experiences in his life, including chronic poverty, food and shelter insecurities, inadequate nutrition, and multiple losses, including a highly inconsistent relationship with his father.

Developmental assessments reveal that Oscar has language and gross motor delays. His current overall IQ score is 75. His growth chart indicates inhibited growth for both height and weight. The literature on adverse childhood experiences indicates that multiple stresses can delay biopsychosocial growth factors in young children. However, early-infant brain research finds that the brain has the capacity for continuous development over the life course. Although Oscar's skills are currently below average, it is premature to predict what his future will look like after appropriate and consistent interventions are put into place.

Case notes from CPS are also included in Oscar's case file. They indicate that CPS has received reports of concern about Oscar and Mary. They have interviewed Miss Dana and the children on multiple occasions and have thus far concluded that although the family experiences many material strains and stresses of living, there is no abuse or neglect occurring in the Dana/Winters home.

Miss Dana feels sure that she can count on her family. The Micmac tribe values collectivity, and extended-family care and housing is given to any child of any family member from the tribe. Miss Dana has considered relocating back to the reservation, but jobs there are scarce. Furthermore, she wants Oscar and Mary to have opportunities that are not available living in such a remote area of rural Maine.

A psychological case note is included in the school file. This documents that Miss Dana reliably showed up for scheduled appointments. It also states that she believes that she probably has undiagnosed learning problems. She's never been evaluated for learning disabilities, but she has trouble reading and paying attention. She also thinks that Oscar may have inherited some of her learning difficulties. Miss Dana hopes that Oscar will do better in school than she did.

Miss Dana was candid in her discussion and acknowledged that she has been unable to follow through on many of the recommendations offered by professionals. In part this is because she believes that she and her family should handle their own problems. She has never accepted welfare and has managed to keep the children out of CPS despite the strains and burdens of single parenting on a very limited budget. The other reasons Miss Dana cites for not following the school's recommendations relate primarily to fear of losing her job. Miss Dana has no health insurance, no car, no sick days or personal leave. Losing her job would be devastating for the Dana/Winters family.

On a personal note, Miss Dana acknowledges that she occasionally drinks alcohol with friends. When prompted about this, she stated that she needs to have a break from the kids and doesn't see anything wrong with having a few drinks at the local pub. She is aware of the dangers of substance abuse, as it is a factor in her family history.

The most recent psychological assessment states that Oscar has a diagnosis of attachment disorder with development delays in cognitive, behavioral, and emotional functioning. He also has encopresis, which is thus far of unknown etiology. One should be careful not to assume its causes before a full physical and psychological workup are conducted.

Factors outlined in this psychological assessment offer a snapshot of Oscar that describe immediate and long-term problems and situations that affect his overall functioning. However, these should not be used to preclude possibilities for growth and change. Life has been difficult for Oscar and his family. He has experienced multiple health-related problems and the ramifications of chronic poverty. In addition he has suffered many losses and transitions in his young life. However, at seven years old, Oscar possesses the ability to be responsive to appropriate interventions aimed at improving his physical health, cognitive growth, and emotional/social functioning. For example, Oscar enjoys play therapy with the school social worker. He loves to use toys and art supplies to make houses. This may be Oscar's way of trying to master the multiple moves and losses he's had in his life.

Miss Dana's strengths are noteworthy. They include a strong desire for her children to get a good and consistent education, ability to reach out to family for respite, candidness, a positive employment record, and resourcefulness.

Miss Dana's inability to follow through on proposed recommendations seems to stem in part from very real barriers. Her desire to see her children succeed provides a strong base from which she can connect with professionals.

Relevant Writing and Research

The literature concerning adverse early experiences and their implications for poor families is well documented (see chapter 2). In addition, early-attachment and infant brain research suggests the importance of working with both mother and child within the context of empathetic therapeutic and service relationships.[1]

Although problems must be addressed as early as possible, parents need validation for what has gone right as well as nonjudgmental support to address the problems they face. Finally, the research on encopresis and its causes is mixed. Therefore ongoing assessment should address medical, psychological, and environmental factors that may be contributing to Oscar's current health difficulties.

Goals and Interventions

1. Improve knowledge of encopresis. Miss Dana would benefit from assistance in understanding and managing Oscar's encopresis. It is important that professionals who work with her on this matter appreciate the constant stress she is under in being the sole provider and caregiver for her two children. Recognition of her learning and cultural differences should be integrated into effective health education.

2. Support Miss Dana's strengths. She has made it possible for her children to remain in the same school district. There is therefore ample opportunity for the school social worker, school nurse, and other support personnel to develop an enduring working alliance with the Dana/Winters family.

3. Expand and strengthen local supports. Miss Dana receives support from her extended family. Because they are at a great distance, however, Oscar and his immediate family will benefit from resources that are closer to home, perhaps through family counseling. The social worker will help Miss Dana explore appropriate local resources and investigate case management options. Transportation and reimbursement concerns will also be looked into.

4. Address cultural components of working with the family. *Culture* in this case refers to the family's Micmac heritage and customs as well as the distinctive family style that Miss Dana has established. Understanding barriers to accepting help from others will be useful in formulating intervention strategies.

5. Medical causes for Oscar's encopresis need to be explored. This requires that the social worker, school nurse, and Miss Dana collaboratively identify obstacles to obtaining a medical assessment. The possibility of providing transportation to and from medical appointments will be explored. Scheduling medical evaluations and appointments during Miss Dana's nonwork hours will also be investigated.

6. Explore available educational and social support opportunities. Oscar is eligible for Title 1 services. In his school district, this means that he can have free breakfast and lunch during the school week. The school social worker will discuss this option with Miss Dana. Arrangements for morning transportation will be explored. In addition a student assessment team meeting will be convened to determine appropriate educational and in-school support services for Oscar. These will include but not be limited to individual play therapy and counseling with the school social worker, assessment for occupational and physical therapies, and educational assessments to determine discipline-specific interventions. The school social worker and teacher will maintain ongoing communication about Oscar's problems and his progress. The school social worker will communicate weekly with Miss Dana at a time when she is not at work. Assessment of Oscar's progress and needs will be ongoing.

Treatment Relationship

It will be important for the social worker to embrace the importance of working with both Oscar and his mother. Ongoing supervision will be instrumental to reduce the potential to dichotomize care. It will also be useful to address aspects of treatment that may affect the social worker's attitude toward and relationship with this child and family.

Once a good-enough therapeutic relationship is developed with the worker, it will be constructive for her to respectfully ask about Miss Dana's experiences of growing up. Learning from Miss Dana about her culture will also be helpful.

Miss Dana's goals and wishes for Oscar should be determined, so that the social worker does not make personal, professional, or culturally insensitive assumptions. It will be especially important for the social worker to understand that maintaining trust and openness with Miss Dana and Oscar will be an ongoing process.

Reflection on the Scenarios

Mental health practitioners often meet parents for the first time during assessment. Acknowledging that your child has a problem worthy of professional scrutiny is difficult. For all parents, anticipating a child's assessment understandably conjures stress and fear. Assessment can reopen old wounds, especially for those who have been previously marginalized by social institutions. The challenge for workers during assessment is to transcend negative expectations, providing instead a respectful opportunity for conversation, mutual dialogue, collaborative meaning making, and useful intervention planning. Equally important is for workers to remember that these earliest connections establish a relational orientation that has far-reaching implications for future alliances with helping professionals.

The traditional assessment of Oscar provides psychobiomedical shorthand to describe the deficits embedded in Oscar's short life, and speculates on the trajectory of these problems if interventions do not occur. The language used might be interpreted as too personal (first names of mother and father), and descriptors may seem judgmental ("The mother is passive and noncompliant").

This model of assessment is well-intended and is full of important and useful information. However, its focus on deficits offers a partial representation of Oscar's complicated life. It misses important information about child and family assets and culture, both of which could increase the likelihood of positive outcomes. Further, its problem-only focus has the potential to demoralize both Miss Dana and the professionals working with Oscar by rushing to judgment and predicting dire consequences for this little boy.

The second assessment provides a broader view of Oscar's life and struggles. It is narrated in language that is respectful without minimizing the reality of Oscar's problems. Miss Dana is portrayed descriptively, and her responses are recorded to illuminate her perspective alongside those of professional evaluators. As Webb (2003) and Graybeal and Konrad (2008) note, useful assessments with children and families considered to be marginalized or pathologized should begin with an emphasis on the child's and parents' strengths. The second assessment brings Miss Dana vividly into focus; she is more fully dimensional as a mother who has tried to do the best she can in very trying circumstances. Her decisions have not always been effective, but they have been thoughtfully constructed using her own personal/sociocultural lens.

The recommendations in the second assessment use Dean and Poorvu's (2008) framework for social work assessment and formulation. They parallel those of the first but are more specific in not only the *what*, but also the *how* and *why* of follow through. For example, the traditional assessment recommendation for family counseling is fine, but it ignores the barriers that Miss Dana will likely encounter. It is wide open for harsh judgment of the mother if she is unable to comply. The relational assessment recommends family counseling and identifies possible barriers to counseling because of resource insecurities and social inequities. It proposes that the school social worker and Miss Dana work together to determine the necessary supports for family counseling.

A relational orientation to assessment can be applied across settings with children of any age and with a diversity of family constellations and cultures. In the short term it provides a child- and family-sensitive framework aimed at respectfully ushering children and parents into the world of mental health service, special education, or other psychosocial or health-related interventions. In the longer term it offers mutuality, collaboration, guidance, and support to children and families that increase the likelihood of successful interventions and of good health and healing.

SUMMARY

Useful assessments consider the wide variability of human experience. Different families and different children make meaning of the same experience in different ways. Even within families, perceptions of the same event may widely diverge. Children can carry identical diagnostic descriptors though their behaviors present in many forms and variations. Families' socioeconomic circumstances may be the same, but how they perceive their life situation can make all the difference in how they tackle adversity.

Such phenomenological, factual, and behavioral diversity makes mental health, social work, and social service professionals humble about what we think we know. It prompts us to check our assumptions, to practice reflexively, and to investigate evidence-guided research to learn what others have discovered. Such factors can then be filtered into an assessment process that is responsive to each child and useful to his or her family.

As we enter into the second decade of the twenty-first century, there are economic and political pressures to streamline and codify most aspects of health-care practice. Child-centered mental health workers have struggled to keep pace with health-care advancements while maintaining core ethical principles and values. As such, relational practices require a broad-based and inclusive approach to assessment and formulation that conceives of human behavior as influenced by many factors, not the least of which reside in biopsychosocial, cultural, and political domains (Dean & Poorvu, 2008). Respecting the diversity of human experience is as foundational to child-centered assessment as is staying current with approaches to intervention that are in the best interests of children, their families, and their cultures.

At the heart of relational practice is a shift away from an exclusively deficit-based approach toward a perspective that views behavior as a constellation of capacities and vulnerabilities, triumphs and sorrows, hopes and disappointments. Though we recognize clients' assets and resiliency, we must also acknowledge and validate clients' very real struggles and pain. To ignore their distress is to disrespect their experience.

Note

1. Thanks to Ruth Dean for allowing me to reference this assessment and formulation framework.

References

Ballou, M., Hill, M., & West, C. (2008). *Feminist therapy, theory and practice: A contemporary perspective*. New York: Spring.

Bisman, C. D. (1999). Social work assessment: Case theory construction. *Families in Society, 80*(3), 240–246.

Dean, R. G., & Poorvu, N. L. (2008). Assessment and formulation: A contemporary social work perspective. *Families in Society, 89*(4), 596–604.

Graybeal, C. T., & Konrad, S. C. (2008). Strengths-based child assessment: Locating possibility and transforming the paradigm. In M. Calder (Ed.), *Contemporary risk assessment in safeguarding children* (pp. 185–197). London: Russell House.

Groopman, J. (2007). *How doctors think*. New York: Houghton Mifflin.

Hodge, D. R. (2002). Working with Muslim youths: Understanding the values and beliefs of Islamic discourse. *Children and Schools, 24*(1), 6–20.

Smart, C. (2006). Children's narratives of post-divorce family life: From individual experience to an ethical disposition. *Sociological Review, 54*(1), 155–170.

Webb, N. B. (Ed.). (2001). *Culturally diverse parent-child and family relationships: A guide for social workers and other practitioners*. New York: Columbia University Press.

Webb, N. B. (2003). *Social work practice with children* (2nd ed.). New York: Guilford Press.

5

Therapeutic Conversations with Children

Piglet sidled up to Pooh from behind.
"Pooh!" he whispered.
"Yes, Piglet?"
"Nothing," said Piglet, taking Pooh's paw. "I just wanted to be sure
   of you."

                                    A. A. Milne, *The House at Pooh Corner*

BEING SURE OF YOU

Many of the children we meet in practice have experienced significant adversity in their young lives. Single or cumulative negative events may initiate their referrals. Some have been targets or witnesses to violence, violation, and intense conflict. Others may never have felt wanted or loved. Children also see practitioners because of stress caused by behavioral or other disabilities. Whatever the precipitant, it is critical that workers can hear and understand children's stories. It is also critical that they have faith in children's capacity to adapt and heal. When children can "be sure of you," they are more likely to share their private worlds.

Like Piglet, children aren't necessarily forthcoming in communicating their feelings and needs. Often they can't find the words to explain themselves, or they assume that adults can read their thoughts and thus naturally know what it is they desire. A. A. Milne, the author of the Winnie-the-Pooh series, clearly understood the subtleties of child-centered communication. Piglet's modest whisper and tender gesture are acts one might observe in any small child.

As with Pooh, how child-centered practitioners listen and respond to such simple communications sets the stage for further interaction. Conveying genuine curiosity about what children have to say and assuring them that they have been heard lays the groundwork for frank conversations. Responses can be as simple as a nod or as complicated as tolerating a child's distress without losing your footing. In either case, the ways in which adults create opportunities for children to tell their stories make a difference, especially for those who have difficult stories to tell.

This chapter begins by describing qualities and skills necessary to create an environment of trust, or what some refer to as a safe place for child-worker conversations. Attitudes and the capacity for genuine connection are the bricks and mortar of this environment. The sections that follow discuss how to prepare children for participating effectively in therapeutic conversations and how to use child-centered knowledge to design such conversations. Case examples illustrate and critique the qualities of listening, clarifying, and responding in child-worker conversations.

We go on to examine the interpretation of children's words and behaviors. Child-centered communication is quite different from that with adults. In many respects, working with children is a bicultural process: practitioners must enter into this work equipped with culturally sensitive attitudes and skills. Requisite as well is willingness to venture into the world of childhood and become familiar with its customs, language, and perspectives. Toward this end, we explore how children use metaphor, art, and other expressive modalities to convey their feelings and thoughts. The work of Michael White and David Epston using narrative therapy techniques with children exemplifies how a particular theory of practice can be applied in child-centered communication.

The final section of the chapter focuses on the critical role of reflexivity in child-centered communication. Listening to children's stories affects even the most seasoned workers, sometimes in unexpected ways. The story of Avner illuminates why a reflexive stance is especially important in child-centered work.

ENVIRONMENTS OF TRUST

Relational workers create environments of trust where children can openly share their thoughts, feelings, and ideas, knowing that they will be tolerated and contained. This requires setting limits and maintaining a structured and accepting demeanor that assures children that workers can manage even their most difficult emotions and deepest fears. Acceptance does not, however, imply unconditional approval. Practitioners must be honest and help children modify or change actions that have caused problems. Over time children come to rely on the guidance of workers and to believe that their concerns and troubles will be met with compassion and care.

Environments of trust live within relationship and thus are transportable to any physical site. Veteran practitioners know that child-centered venues are rarely ideal; even when offices are designed to be child-friendly, the best conversations may take place outside of their doors. One of the offices I occupied as a school social worker was a former shower stall, complete with a large drain in the middle of a slightly sloping, tiled floor. I managed to convert the room into a private and playful space with toys, books, and colorful posters. Many powerful conversations took place in that room; however, it was a rare first visit when a child or parent did not comment on the drain with a bit of trepidation. Yet children, parents, and teachers managed to find their way to the "shower office," and by all accounts, they were comforted there in times of stress and distress. I now imagine that they knew that within those walls, they would be listened to and comforted. There I learned that *how* we listen and respond is much more important than *where*.

Environments of trust are also established in homes, treatment facilities, clinics, and hospital rooms, wherever children and families seek guidance and consolation. They can go for walks or climb trees, as when a spunky nine-year-old preferred to talk with me while she sat on the lowest limb of a tree.

So how do workers create relational environments that bridge the inevitable generational divide? What specific knowledge, skills, attitudes, and attributes make it possible for children to trust that they will be understood, particularly when they have formerly been disrespected, betrayed, or harmed by adults? How can we reassure children that their perspectives will be considered valid and true? And finally, what methods do we use to transform children's narratives into helpful therapeutic conversations?

QUALITIES OF CHILD-CENTERED CONVERSATIONS

In child-centered practice, successful therapeutic conversations are measured by whether clients show up for their next appointment. Research shows a high dropout rate for children and youth from psychotherapy and counseling services. According to Kazdin's (2004) research, 40 to 60 percent of youth referred for psychotherapy drop out early in the process. Duncan, Miller, and Sparks (2007) found that if child clients and parents do not experience a positive connection with workers within the first few sessions, it is likely that they will discontinue treatment.

While these findings are discouraging, they also implicitly highlight the difference that positive relational connections can make. Actions that promote *effective* child-centered communication include being attentive to subjects that interest the child; conveying genuine curiosity about children's expressed thoughts and feelings; never being dismissive of their opinions, fears, or worries; and inviting them to exchange ideas. Attitudes that set a positive relational tone include patience, flexibility, humor, tolerance for ambiguity, and playfulness.

Another important aspect of child-centered communication is validation. Validation is an active process of letting children know that what they feel is real and deserves respectful consideration. Validation recognizes children's struggles and accepts their views as credible. Toward this goal, workers must reflect upon what it means to be a child in an adult-oriented world. When they understand, they are better able to join with children and youth in their fantasies, hopes, and dreams.

Adolescents, too, need validation. Thus workers should stay abreast of contemporary media trends and not be too quick to dismiss youthful broken hearts. Adolescents need therapeutic and supportive relationships that are steady and reliable, honest and real (see chapter 8). Qualities of interaction should convey to every youngster, no matter their actions or trials, that he or she is worthy.

Child-centered communication requires knowledge and skills for entering children's real and imagined worlds. This is especially the case with young children. For example, workers instinctively want to allay children's fears and ameliorate their distress. However, one shouldn't be *too* quick to dismiss the reality of "robbers hiding in the closet" to calm a worried child. Although such dismissal may seem the right thing to do, it doesn't validate or recognize the child's experience ("But there are robbers in the closet— you just can't see them"). Prematurely quelling children's fears rather than first taking them seriously may worsen the problem and weaken the relational alliance. This is not to say that workers should encourage children's fearful yet fanciful beliefs. Rather, such fears need to be validated, explored, and understood as preparation for solution building.

Often children entering into relationships with unfamiliar adults expect to be in vulnerable if not powerless positions. In their daily lives, children most often encounter adults in positions of authority. Many adults have used this clout in ways that have been at the very least discomforting. Thus from a child-centered perspective, respect and validation are not presumed relational qualities. Children expect to be talked at, not spoken with.

Having meaningful and reciprocal conversations with adults is therefore quite unfamiliar to most children, and they are understandably wary when a stranger (the worker) expresses genuine interest in what they think and feel. It will take time and persistence to convince even the most trusting children that their opinions matter. It's the worker's role to carefully and repeatedly explain in developmentally appropriate terms what the relationship is all about and how it works.

PREPARATION FOR THERAPEUTIC CONVERSATIONS

Ideally, parents collaborate with workers to prepare their children for therapeutic conversations. Such preparation is best codeveloped during an initial session or intake without children present. This allows parents to ask questions and share information that familiarizes them with the process and individualizes it for their child and family. Information and connection are reassuring to parents and caregivers, so they are better equipped to help children get ready for their first conversation.

If workers cannot engage with parents prior to the first meeting, it's critical to check in with children about whether and how they've been prepared. Some children might have been told what to say and what not to say ("Dad said I was coming to you because I'm in trouble, but he doesn't want you to know that he spanks me when I'm bad"). Other parents may soft-pedal the objectives of counseling or therapy ("You're just going to play with a nice lady"). Some youngsters indicate that they didn't know they were seeing a worker until minutes before the meeting, while others have been carefully prepared with explanations such as "My foster mom said I was seeing a *feeling doctor* to talk about my anxieties."

Having heard what has or has not been shared, it is then important to validate the child's understanding. The worker might gently prompt for more detail to get a clearer sense of what the child assumes or believes. As Webb (2003, p. 54) asserts, "Children, like adults, deserve to be treated with honesty and respect as the basis for an effective helping relationship." These early conversations set the stage for such valuable alliances.

THE FIRST MEETING

The first conversation with any child is influenced by many factors, including age; previous experiences with helpers, counselors, or human service workers; and the circumstances that initiated the referral. Language should be developmentally and culturally appropriate as well as respectful; workers must never talk down to even the youngest clients. Workers should be friendly yet maintain clear boundaries, so that children do not feel overwhelmed. Prior knowledge of what previously worked well in similar experiences is useful but doesn't necessarily guarantee that conversational pitfalls will be totally avoided.

After greeting the child and allowing time for thoughtful transition to the meeting room, workers should clarify who they are and what they do. If the child has already used descriptive language as in the case of "the feeling doctor" or of adolescents who prefer the term "shrink," that language will be used in introductions.

After these simple introductions, workers expand upon who they are and the role they will play. For younger children, the description might include content like this: "I'm the kind of feeling doctor called a social worker. I spend time listening and talking to children about things that interest them. We can also talk about things that might be causing problems or troubles. What are your thoughts about being here today?" Clearly, language used to break the ice with older children and adolescents is more sophisticated. The content would be similar—introduction, explanation of the worker's role, and an open-ended question to glean what expectations the youth has brought to the meeting.

If the child responds to the open-ended inquiry with questions, concerns, or interests, then these will initiate and guide the therapeutic conversation. The worker will listen, ask questions, and make sure that he or she understands what the child has just conveyed. During early meetings, workers should frequently check in and make sure that the child is comfortable with the course the conversation is taking. Gentle prompts and inquiries for more detail advance the conversation while permitting the child and worker to get to know one another.

It is often the case, however, especially for first-time or skeptical clients, that these initial prompts are met with a shake of the head, a quick "I don't know," or silence. The worker has options at this juncture. With younger children, the worker can invite them to select a toy, art materials, or a game as a way of getting to know each other through an expressive modality (see chapter 7). If the child is older or reluctant to engage in an activity, the worker might ask about the child's interests or activities.

It is not necessary for this first meeting to be long. Silence is also all right, as long as it does not feel onerous or pressure the child to react. It's always best for children to leave first encounters with positive and hopeful feelings. The goal is for them to want to come back.

CONFIDENTIALITY, COMMUNICATION, AND CHILDREN

Most professional organizations have codes of ethics that offer confidentiality guidelines. These include the nature of confidentiality, why it's important, and the parameters of clients' rights to private communication with practitioners. When the client is a child, the boundaries of confidentiality are influenced by the age of the child, the family constellation, mandates of referring agencies or law enforcement, and the power inequities that naturally exist in child-adult relationships.

Workers are obligated to explain and clarify the boundaries of confidentiality when working with children. It is always best to do this early in relationship building, with all parties present to agree what communication will and will not be confidential. With young children it is helpful for parents, guardians, and caregivers to know that pertinent information will always be shared with them and that they are welcome to ask questions or seek advice whenever necessary. If CPS or the legal system is involved, parents and primary caregivers need to know what the worker must report to these bodies. Disclosures of abuse, self-harm, or harm directed toward others are always reported to related authorities and to parents unless there is cause to believe that disclosure might put the child in jeopardy.

Caregivers should also be informed that children will want to keep aspects of their therapeutic conversations private. As might be expected, they are sometimes disturbed or even angered by the idea that their children are not comfortable telling them everything. It is the worker's responsibility to thoughtfully put into words why assurance of age-appropriate privacy aids the goals of therapeutic conversations ("If Johnny thinks I'm telling you everything, he's less likely to be open").

Child clients should be apprised of how confidentiality works. Confidentiality is explained to young children using plain, developmentally informed language. Workers should let them know that they regularly speak with parents and caregivers. Most children are unconcerned, but some might want to know what the worker will share and ask for input into the process. This desire needs to be honored and worked through when children are worried about parental reactions to thoughts, feelings, or experiences. Two examples illustrate how issues of confidentiality might be addressed in child-centered practice with younger children.

Mark, age seven, was fretful that his mother would be angry because he didn't like her new partner. "Mom's so much happier with Margaret than she was with Rose, but I really don't like Margaret. She takes up all of Mom's time."

Mark discussed these concerns with his worker, Hank. Hank validated Mark's feelings while encouraging him to speak with his mother. Hank already knew that Mark's mother suspected he was jealous of her new relationship. Thus he was authentically able to assure Mark that talking with his mother would be helpful. Mark consented to have a conversation with his mother, and with Hank's help they came up with a plan to share more time together.

The situation for Alexa, age eight, was more complicated. She disclosed to the worker that her brother Finn, fourteen, was drinking alcohol most nights. She was reluctant to say anything because she feared Finn would physically hurt her or her mother. In this instance, the worker reminded Alexa of their confidentiality agreement and her obligation to alert her mother to Finn's potentially dangerous behaviors. At the same time she validated the seriousness of Alexa's concerns and assured her of ongoing support.

Alexa was at first angry, but because their relationship was solid, she was willing to give the worker permission to speak first with her mother alone. The worker then carefully navigated conversations between Alexa and her mother. In the end, Finn received needed intervention services, and Alexa was pleased that she was instrumental in her brother's recovery.

Confidentiality with adolescents is more complex than with younger children. Some states have health-care laws that permit minors (ages fourteen to eighteen) to give consent for their own health and mental health care (Society for Adolescent Medicine, 2004), meaning that they're entitled to the same confidentiality rights as adults. Variation in these laws, however, demand individualized confidentiality agreements that are explicitly agreed upon with each adolescent client. Thus workers should discuss the parameters of confidentiality with adolescent clients and their parents or guardians, making sure that all parties understand and agree to the terms.

Sometimes matters such as substance abuse, Internet exploitation, and sexual behavior place adolescents in situations of risk. Workers' discretion in disclosing these potential dangers must consider professional ethical guidelines. These should help determine whether confidentiality must be breached in favor of client safety. The Society for Adolescent Medicine (2004, p. 163) provides justification for such deviations in confidentiality with adolescent clients: "Individual adolescents vary in their levels of psychosocial maturity and economic independence, as well as in their behaviors and family situations. Therefore, it is inappropriate to apply a single moral prescription in all cases. The protection of confidentiality in adolescent health care should be grounded in the moral principle of respect for autonomy, but must recognize that in specific circumstances it may be permissible or even necessary to breach confidentiality to further other important moral principles, such as beneficence or nonmalificence."

The decision was to breach confidentiality in the following situation: Sadie's adoptive parents referred the shy fifteen-year-old for counseling because she seemed depressed and lonely. Their two biological children were honor students and athletes. Sadie was bothered by the fact that she simply could not keep pace with their accomplishments.

One day Sadie reported to the worker that she had a new group of friends, mostly boys, who she met on the Internet. Shortly thereafter her style of dress and makeup changed drastically, and her parents voiced concerns that Sadie's behavior had shifted from compliant to belligerent and challenging. One evening the worker received an emergency call from the parents, frantic that Sadie had run away. She returned home safely but refused to talk to any of her family members about where she'd been or what had happened.

Sadie eventually opened up to the worker. She disclosed that she was meeting these older teens in remote locations without informing anyone of her whereabouts. The worker frankly discussed the danger Sadie was putting herself in. Initially Sadie minimized her concerns, stating that the boys "were really nice people—they would never hurt me." She added, "I'm more like them than my bio-brothers." She was defensive and challenged the worker to trust in her judgment.

However, the worker could not take this chance. Sadie's social judgment was simply too immature. Although she wished to honor her privacy and respect her perceptions, the worker's *first* obligation was to protect Sadie from harm. The worker reminded Sadie of their initial confidentiality agreement and the parameters of mandated reporting. She then invited her to join in speaking with her adoptive parents.

At first Sadie refused, saying they wouldn't understand. But when the time came, she sat in on the meeting and shared information. The process of disclosure proved revelatory for all involved. Sadie was able to see that these youth were not her friends and that indeed she had put herself in physical and emotional jeopardy. Sadie's adoptive parents didn't dismiss her perspective and were receptive to her feelings. Family counseling was suggested to promote further conversation and solidify family connections.

CONVERSATIONS IN PRACTICE: KAHLILA

The following case portrays a home visit as the venue for a first conversation between a worker and child client. As noted above, conversations are affected by many variables. As you read through the following account, reflect upon whether and how the worker establishes an environment of trust with her clients. What client and worker-related factors influence this outcome? Identify the moments of optimal exchange and gaps when opportunities for connections were missed. How would you evaluate the worker's case note? Does it reflect what happened during the visit? Finally, what areas of inquiry need further exploration? As you ponder these questions, direct your attention toward client-worker communication and not to assessment and intervention planning.

Linda Frost was feeling understandably nervous. This was her first home visit and her first child interview as a newly hired child protective worker. Linda, a twenty-five-year-old Caucasian woman, was the only child of older parents. As she sat looking at Kahlila Johnson's file, she reflected on how she had hoped to work with older adults after graduating with her bachelor's degree in social work. She had very little experience with children except for occasional babysitting in high school. But the job market was tight, and she was lucky to get hired as a caseworker for her local CPS office.

Linda read every detail of the case file in preparation for meeting Kahlila Johnson, age four; her mother, Mrs. Johnson; and her thirteen-year-old brother, Gustav Stone. According to the notes, the Johnson family recently moved from another state. The family lived in an apartment complex in one of the city's lower-income neighborhoods. Mrs. Johnson worked as an administrative assistant at a community college.

Linda was sent to meet the family in response to anonymous complaints to CPS over the last few months. The reports focused primarily on alleged supervision gaps for Kahlila. Individually the complaints seemed to have little merit. However, because there had been four calls in the last two weeks, CPS required that a caseworker visit with the family to assess the situation. In Linda's mind, the number of complaints received by CPS increased the likelihood of their legitimacy.

Linda easily found her way to the Johnson's apartment. The doorbell was answered by Mrs. Johnson, a tall, heavy-set, thirty-five-year-old African American woman. Linda indicated that she was from CPS and showed Mrs. Johnson her identification. Mrs. Johnson welcomed Linda into her apartment without exhibiting much reaction. Linda noted that the house had a lived-in quality, with lots of family photos displayed on the walls and tabletops.

Linda informed Mrs. Johnson about the reports to CPS. Because this was a mandated visit, Linda let Mrs. Johnson know that details of their conversation, including conversations with Kahlila and Gustav, would be shared with CPS supervisors. This was routine for CPS visits.

In response, Mrs. Johnson sat back in her chair, smiled, and sighed. She read the informed consent agreement, signed it, and then spoke directly to Linda. She stated in a firm but not unfriendly way that very few young families were living in the housing complex. There were even fewer families of color. As she put it, the neighborhood was one that time forgot. Most of her neighbors were white, elderly women who had raised their families and had watched their homes "go to seed." She commented that the women seemed "bored, cranky and easily irritated by children." According to Mrs. Johnson, "They have shown no interest in getting to know me or my family."

At that moment Linda noticed Kahlila standing in the doorway of a small bedroom. She was taller and slighter than Linda had expected. Her light hair formed a wild, curly mane around her face. "Well hello there," Linda said. Kahlila slowly retreated back into her room. "Get out here, Kahlila. This lady wants to talk to you," her mother teased.

Linda asked permission to meet with Kahlila in her room. Mrs. Johnson showed no signs of hesitation. Linda knocked on the door and asked Kahlila if she could come in. Kahlila looked up from the doll she had been playing with and smiled. Linda looked around the bedroom, noting lots of toys, stuffed animals, and a white-veneered bed and dresser. "Is that your favorite doll?" she asked. Kahlila nodded. "What's her name?" Kahlila shrugged.

Just as Linda began to panic, not knowing what to say next, Kahlila asked, "What's your name?" "I'm Linda—Linda Frost and I came to visit with you and your mom." "She's not my mom," Kahlila quickly retorted. Linda was taken aback. She didn't recall having read anything about Mrs. Johnson being a foster or adoptive parent. She appeared too young to be a grandmother, although Linda had read an article for one of her classes that said more and more African American grandparents were raising their children's children.

"Well then, who is she?" Linda asked. Kahlila looked bored and frustrated. "She's my mama," she replied. Linda was slightly annoyed by Kahlila's correction, but she was determined to fulfill the objective of the meeting, which was to discern whether Mrs. Johnson's children were undersupervised.

"Is it OK for me to ask you some questions?" she inquired. Kahlila shrugged. Linda proceeded, "So, does your mama work a lot?" she asked. Kahlila answered, "She's always at work. I hate when she works. And Gustav is really mean to me. He makes me shut off the lights and I'm scared of the dark."

This was the longest statement Kahlila had made so far. Linda found it difficult to understand Kahlila's speech and wondered if she might have an accent or perhaps speech impairment.

Linda went on to explore Kahlila's comments in more detail. "Is your mama away from the house a long time? And when she's not home, who takes care of you?" Kahlila shrugged again but suddenly turned to Linda and asked, "Do you want to hold Tatiana?" She held her doll out to Linda. Linda politely declined her offer. Kahlila turned away, looking mildly offended.

Linda moderated her tone, using her best child-friendly voice. "It's really important for me to know who takes care of you when Mama's not home, Kahlila. Little children need to be cared for. So I wonder, does Gustav take care of you."

Kahlila retorted, "No. He's always watching TV." Linda quickly responded, "Then who takes care of you when Mama's at work?" "Gustav!" Kahlila shouted impatiently, and as she did so, she turned away from Linda and began brushing the doll's hair. Linda tried one more question, knowing she was on shaky ground with this preschooler.

"Kahlila, I'm curious about what time your mama comes home at night from work?" "How should I know?" Kahlila responded. "Maybe midnight, but I'm only little so I can't tell time." Kahlila then scooped Tatiana up with a flourish, announcing with her body that their time was over.

Linda left the room and proceeded to the kitchen where she found Mrs. Johnson making a fragrant stew. Mrs. Johnson asked if Kahlila had behaved, and Linda said she had. She then asked Mrs. Johnson what time she typically came home from work. "Around 5," she answered. "Why?" "I just need a time line," Linda replied. They set an appointment for Linda to meet with Gustav the following week, and Linda politely said her good-byes.

The following day Linda put a case note in Kahlila Johnson's file.

January 14, 2012
 I met with Kahlila Johnson, age 4, and her mother, Mrs. Monica Johnson, in their home on 32 Stuyvesant Way. Gustav Stone, 13, Mrs. Johnson's son from

a previous relationship, was not available to be interviewed. The Johnson apartment was small, clean but cluttered. Mrs. Johnson was friendly and did not interfere with the visitation and child interview. The interview took place in the child's bedroom. Kahlila had little to say. She avoided most questions and used her doll to deflect communication. Kahlila's speech and language skills were somewhat impaired, thus making it difficult at times to determine her communications.

While Kahlila did not respond directly to questioning about her mother's supervision, she did state: "She's always at work. I hate when she works. And Gustav is really mean to me. He makes me shut off the lights and I'm scared of the dark" The child refused to elaborate further, leaving this caseworker with concerns about the kind of supervision Kahlila does receive when her mother works. Further, there is a discrepancy between Mrs. Johnson's and Kahlila's reports about when the mother comes home from work. Kahlila believes that her mother comes home at "midnight," while Mrs. Johnson insists she's home by 5 p.m. A meeting with Gustav is scheduled for January 19, 2012.

REFLECTIONS ON A FIRST CONVERSATION

Linda Frost is fictitious, but not altogether unrecognizable as a novice worker. She prepared herself for the first conversation with Kahlila Johnson and her mother by reading the case file. She formulated a tentative case theory that equated frequency of complaints with the likelihood of legitimate problems with child supervision in the Johnson household. Wanting to fulfill her role, she stayed focused on the objective of her visit, which was to discern whether reports made to CPS were justified. Her interviews with Mrs. Johnson and Kahlila were directed toward this end, and she conducted them politely. Her case notes report information she gleaned from her time with Kahlila and Mrs. Johnson.

Let's analyze Linda's first conversations with Mrs. Johnson and Kahlila in greater detail.

First, in preparation for the conversations ahead, Linda could have reflected upon potential barriers to getting to know this child and family. For example, she readily acknowledged her inexperience with young children. Therefore, acquainting herself with the child-development literature or asking her supervisor what to expect from an interview with such a young child might have enhanced her readiness. In doing so, she would have better understood how four-year-olds typically see the world. She might have appreciated and even smiled at Kahlila's insistence that Mrs. Johnson was not her mom but her mama. Such specificity is common for four-year-olds.

Linda also might have responded differently and perhaps more effectively to Kahlila's offer of the doll. This was a gesture of generosity and connection, not deflection. If she had accepted the doll, she could have used it to playfully communicate with Kahlila. She could speak soothingly to the baby doll and see if "she" could tell her about who takes care of Kahlila when Mama's at work and what it might be like when Gustav is in charge ("So tell me Tatiana—how do you think Kahlila feels when Gustav takes care of her?").

When offered information, Linda would have learned more if she had paraphrased her responses to make sure she understood and got more detail about what Kahlila was trying to convey. Knowing more about four-year-old language and cognitive development may have averted the conversational misstep that ended the first exchange. When young Kahlila insisted, "I can't tell time," she instructed Linda about the limitations of a four-year-old's capacities. If Linda had known this in advance, she probably would not have asked this question, or she might have approached Mrs. Johnson's time of arrival from a different vantage point.

Opportunities to understand the family situation were missed in Linda's conversation with Mrs. Johnson. In her eagerness to talk with Kahlila, Linda ignored Mrs. Johnson's observations and feelings. Linda's presumptive case hypothesis was therefore one-sided because it considered the claimants' viewpoints only. This could be interpreted by Mrs. Johnson as culturally insensitive, motivated in part by race and class differences between herself and the worker. The fact that Linda's report omitted Mrs. Johnson's perspective altogether is unfair and discriminatory and would likely affect the mother's capacity to trust Linda. It could also influence her future interactions with other social service workers.

Linda's recorded note was well intended but flawed. Her inexperience and insufficiently informed interaction with Kahlila and Mrs. Johnson contributed to a deficit-focused evaluation that used problem-based language only ("deflection," "impaired" language, and "concerns" about supervision). Positive and nurturing attributes such as Mrs. Johnson's pleasant demeanor, the lived-in feeling of the home, the numerous family photos, and Kahlila's toy-filled room are absent from the report. Comments about Kahlila's personality and spirit were also absent.

It is not unusual for social service reports to focus on what is wrong in a family system. Caseworkers are responsible for identifying abuse, neglect, and other potentially harmful situations that affect children. The zeal to uncover problems, however, should not exclude reporting evidence that highlights what is going right. Such omissions as well as misinterpretations of what the child and family have reported, innocent or not, could lead to dire and irreparable consequences for this family.

This case snapshot offers a cautionary tale of what transpires when workers are inadequately prepared for critical conversations with children and families. Attunement to factors of age and culture is essential when communicating about potentially life-changing matters and interpreting their meaning. Essential as well is the attention paid to the strengths and assets children and families possess in the context of the challenges they face. Finally, of equal importance is how information is permanently archived in case documents. Workers wield enormous power in the words they choose and the attitudes and judgments they convey in their reports. How these are read and interpreted by decision makers and other professionals affects the lives of children well into the future.

CONVERSATIONS AS COPRODUCTIONS

Understanding and making meaning of what children tell us is a mutual and interactional process. When talking with children, workers must listen attentively to determine which leads to pursue and when to prompt for further elaboration and feedback. Though trends to increase billable hours and conduct briefer treatments create very real workplace demands, child-centered workers must balance these with patience and perception, careful not to shortchange fruitful communication and interactions that may take a bit more time. Such exchanges may in the end yield profitable results in terms of positive therapeutic outcomes. Workers must also develop comfort with silence and evaluate when it may encourage deeper communication.

As with adults, children make meaning of their world in distinctive ways. Common themes inhabit the world of childhood, but even they will be communicated and acted upon in different fashions by different children. Let's replay the conversation with Kahlila to illustrate this concept. Many children Kahlila's age harbor fear of the dark. In conversations, however, Linda might try to understand what Kahlila's fear of the dark means to *her*. This begins with asking what frightens her about the dark. Her responses would be followed by questions that help elaborate how this fear plays out for her. Artwork, puppetry, or other expressive modalities could be used to aid both the worker and Kahlila comprehend her fears (see chapter 7).

As details emerge, the worker will use them to inform intervention strategies. So if Kahlila's fears of the dark revolve around monsters, ghosts, or zombies, methods to help her master these would be used. Some children benefit from making tangible items like "zombie catchers" to ward off fears. Others may keep a journal by the bedside and record their worries before going to sleep. Once put on paper, the worries are considered put away for the night.

If fear of the dark involves real events that occurred at night, very different protocols would take shape. These would warrant deeper interviewing and potential CPS referrals. However, it may be that Kahlila's fears have to do with missing her mama and longing for her to return home. In that case the worker would assist Kahlila and her mother to develop methods that would be soothing and reassuring while Mrs. Johnson was at work.

Regardless of the source of Kahlila's fears, the worker must take them seriously and engage child, mother, and family in the intervention process. In some instances parents may already know what's bothering their children, but they may feel inadequate to address it properly. Some may feel pressured by friends and family members to respond in certain ways. Others may have already tried methods that have failed. Each of these parent-child situations must be thoughtfully considered. Best outcomes typically involve open communication between children and their parents, and if necessary, these can be facilitated by workers whom the family trusts.

DIFFICULT CONVERSATIONS

Conversations with children take place for reasons other than for formulating and determining treatment plans. Hard conversations arise when difficult or life-changing events occur in families and communities. The desire to shield children from unfairness, suffering, and sorrow is understandable and not uncommon. In the long run, however, avoiding difficult conversations can backfire or cause more harm than good. Although children respond differently than adults, they nonetheless feel the impact of trauma and tragedy in their lives. Thus it is important for workers to become skilled in navigating hard conversations with children and in guiding families in doing the same.

Children of all ages experience a range of responses to hard stories (see chapters 10 and 11). Some feel deep sadness or high anxiety after a tragedy, while others take it in their stride. Most will feel distress intermittently but will carry on with the normal routines of life. Whatever their reaction, children have many ways to let adults know that they have indeed been affected by circumstances that are painful, unfair, or out of their control.

Such unfortunate circumstances occurred for a family who were faced with telling a three-year-old that her father had been murdered. The family did not know how or whether to talk about the circumstances of her father's death, so they consulted their local community services center. The center's outreach worker located a volunteer bereavement counselor.

According to the counselor, when first learning of her father's demise, the child immediately responded by casually saying that she wanted to "kill herself" so she could "visit with Daddy in heaven." This remark was highly concerning because it spoke to the child's powerful feelings of loss and sadness. Yet it also reflected that as a three-year-old, she had yet to understand death's permanence. She assumed that she could visit her father in heaven and then return.

The counselor did not minimize the child's comments. She encouraged the family to gently explain in language that respected their faith and was developmentally appropriate that one cannot simply visit heaven; once there, you can't come back. She also advised them to stay close to the child to circumvent impulsive actions. This was not because she judged the child to be suicidal—that was far from the case. It was because the child could not yet conceptualize death's reality even in relationship to herself.

In speaking with the child directly, the worker explored what she already knew about her father's death. Indeed, the girl made it clear that she knew "somebody killed Daddy" and that they were "bad." Together they colored pictures, and as they did so, the little girl spoke openly about her feelings and concerns. Would Daddy be OK in the ground, she wondered. Would a new daddy come to take his place? Would Mommy have to go to work? Would Mommy and Memé (Grandmother) cry if she mentioned Daddy's name? All these questions were taken seriously and shared with the surviving family members.

In the end the family decided to have the bereavement counselor facilitate a meeting in their home, so that they could respond directly to the child's concerns. They wanted to give her permission to talk about her father and let her know that they would keep her safe.

As noted throughout the book, relational practice encourages workers to stay current with evidence-guided research to determine services that meet children's and families' best interests. In the case above, it made good sense for the bereavement counselor to familiarize herself with the literature on the impact of sudden and violent loss on children. Scholarly inquiry provided important insight; for example, child survivors of homicide are faced concurrently with their own traumatic grief and that of their family members (Salloum, 2008). In addition families are unexpectedly thrust into the public spotlight. Such unwanted attention often impedes resumption of the family's functioning. Although this had not yet happened, the bereavement counselor was now prepared to assist the three-year-old and her family through the rigors of public scrutiny.

The worker further learned that children of homicide victims may be marginalized or viewed as oddities by peers and adults alike (Salloum, 2008). The three-year-old in this case was temporarily protected because of her age and the fact that she was not in a school or day-care setting. However, her mother was sensitive to the community chatter being generated and was thus highly concerned about how rumors and public opinion might affect her daughter for years to come.

Acquiring up-to-date knowledge helped the bereavement counselor understand the impact of a family member's murder on children and families. She was thus able to anticipate factors that could affect well-being and future adaptation. In the end she was an invaluable support to the three-year-old, her surviving parent, the family, and the community.

ACTIONS SPEAK LOUDER THAN WORDS

Children's behaviors, actions, and expressive gestures frequently speak louder than words. Practitioners must thus hone their observational and sensory skills so as not to miss or misinterpret meaningful communication. For example, a child may demonstrate frustration by throwing a ball against a wall. The worker might put words to these actions ("Those are powerful throws; you seem frustrated"). Conversely, workers may simply bear witness and support these expressed feelings. Children may also communicate their emotions through sensory or ritualized modes. For instance, some children pass wind when anxious. Others may clear their throats or pull at their hair when stressed.

Indeed, when tuned into children's nonverbal communication, workers are better equipped to translate their purpose and meaning. Let's take a moment to reflect upon how Charlie used nonverbal means to both communicate and cope with difficulties managing impulsivity and social insecurities. From Charlie's perspective, these behaviors aided his greater good, while from his teachers' vantage points, they were viewed as negative attention-seeking measures.

From a very young age, Charlie, age ten, had trouble maintaining focus and sitting still. Over time he discovered that tapping his pencil or another object helped him control the impulse to move about. Though the constant pencil tapping helped Charlie sit still, his teacher viewed this behavior as an attention-seeking annoyance and violation of classroom rules. She insisted that he stop tapping or go to the assistant principal's office.

Charlie had a dilemma: he knew that he needed to tap to keep himself still, but if he continued tapping, he'd get in trouble. Furthermore, the behaviors that were negatively received by the teacher were reinforced by his classmates. The other kids loved it when Charlie annoyed the teacher. Charlie benefited from their regard because, for the most part, he was ignored or teased by his classmates. Thus from a social standpoint, Charlie thrived as a result of this positive peer attention.

Charlie's tapping dilemma illustrates the behavioral bind that children experience when nonverbal means are used to communicate and master behavior. Charlie could not put into words why he taps his pencil. He could not articulate to his teacher that his attentional difficulties are curbed by tapping his pencil, nor could he express the short-lived joy of getting positive attention from friends.

Adults can help Charlie by first understanding what he's attempting to do and say. They can then discuss or show him how his behavior works in both positive and negative ways. The positive aspects of his communication can be validated as useful adaptational tools for mastering his attention and high levels of energy. The desire for friendship can be redirected away from annoying behaviors and toward alternative possibilities. Together, Charlie and his worker can discuss solution building with his teacher and devise a plan that helps him with regulation while avoiding trouble. Ideas and strategies for improving Charlie's social standing can also be addressed.

Workers can mine the evidence to help better understand and intervene with Charlie's problematic behaviors. Sharing knowledge with teachers and family helps advance and sustain positive change. It might also reduce adults' annoyance with Charlie and perhaps enhance their patience and understanding. Charlie's assets and strengths can then be directed toward learning, playing, and friendship.

NARRATIVE THERAPY: STORIES AS COMMUNICATION

Children are natural storytellers. Thus it comes as no surprise that narrative therapy has been shown to be effective with children and families who are in changing individual and family systems. Developed by Michael White and David Epston in the 1980s (White & Epston, 1990), narrative therapy involves telling and retelling stories and receiving validation and feedback that builds upon and elucidates their meaning and function.

Narrative methods integrate playfulness and creativity into therapeutically driven conversations through the use of images and metaphors. The goal is to help children separate their struggles and problems from their personhood. In narrative terms, the problem is the problem: the person is not the problem. Once the problem takes on its own identity, it materializes as something that children and others can collaborate on solving.

One of Michael White's most famous child-based cases was a young boy, Tom (White, 1984). Tom, like Oscar in chapter 4, was struggling with the problem of encopresis. While White wanted to discuss encopresis with both Tom and his parents, he did not want "soiling his pants" to be seen as defining Tom's identity. Thus in treatment and with Tom's consent, White separated the boy from the soiling problem by naming the encopresis "Sneaky Poo," as in "Sneaky Poo is messing up Tom's life."

White utilized Sneaky Poo to focus on the problem of encopresis. He asked Tom and his family if there had been times when they had fought and won against Sneaky Poo. This question was aimed at helping the family identify factors that, if used with intention, could help reduce Tom's soiling accidents. He asked Tom directly if he could outsmart Sneaky Poo, thus engaging his natural competitive spirit and desire to beat his foe. The act of collectively waging a full-scale effort to control or exterminate Sneaky Poo brought an otherwise divided family together. Tom's encopresis was no longer his problem to fight alone; he had others on his side to advocate for a successful and sustainable outcome.

Benefits derived from the use of narrative methods include teaching parents and children a shared communication model for future problem solving. Having these skills increases the likelihood that gains made in the context of therapy can be generalized and continued in children's natural environments. Such skills enhance family ties and increase a sense of belonging, which is especially important for children whose problem has led to isolation or disenfranchisement.

Narrative methods for communication have been integrated effectively in a variety of child-centered therapeutic protocols. Connie Ostis (2002), for example, used externalizing approaches in therapy with children who experienced sexual abuse. Children who have been sexually abused often feel at fault and internalize their shame in ways that affect their overall functioning and well-being. Ostis found that incorporating children's own words to externalize abuse made it more possible for them to address and recover from their traumas. Children named their abuse in distinctive ways; one child called the abuse the "yuckies," while another simply labeled it "the hurt." Giving sexual abuse a name allowed youngsters to move their trauma from inside to outside and to address it in empowering ways.

The merger of narrative and relational theories has created other innovative practice approaches. Family attachment narrative therapy (FANT; Lacher, Nichols, & May, 2005) is one example. FANT uses storytelling to help adoptive and foster parents communicate and build relational connections with their children. As noted in chapter 3, children who experience insecure attachments are likely to have difficulties forming healthy and enduring relationships. Workers using FANT encourage parents to revise stories of children's early lives, placing emphasis on why, despite harsh circumstances, they are special and loved. By their very nature, these stories communicate to children that they are not in any way responsible for their abandonment or abuse.

FANT practitioners find that storytelling helps adoptive and foster parents communicate and connect with their children in a manner that models new relational behaviors while healing wounds from the past (Lacher et al., 2005). The act of communicating these stories is especially important for those struggling to raise children with reactive attachment disorders or other difficult relational challenges.

METAPHOR, NARRATIVE, AND COMMUNICATION

As exemplified by narrative therapy techniques, symbols and metaphors are natural means of communication and engagement with children. This is because childhood is inhabited by imaginary friends, fantastic creatures, and fairy-tale and cartoon characters, many of whom are as real to children as the actual people in their lives. A metaphor is a word or figure of speech that over time implies or stands for something else. For example, one child I knew referred to his asthma as "the beast." And as noted above, "the hurt" was used to metaphorically describe sexual abuse. Together workers and children create metaphors to tackle difficult or embarrassing issues in therapeutic conversations. Metaphors or metaphoric themes may spontaneously appear in the course of child-worker communication or they may be intentionally created as White did in the case of Sneaky Poo.

In eight-year-old Abigail's case, I noticed a recurring theme in her use of puppets that became a metaphor in our work together. Abigail became a client because she had difficulty getting along with peers and was having a particularly hard time adjusting to her mother's remarriage. She communicated discontent through aggression and noncompliance. Her mother's new partner was unhappy with Abigail's contentiousness, and it was he who insisted on child-centered therapy.

Fortunately my office was equipped with a basket filled with puppets of all kinds, including woodland animals, bugs, butterflies, sea creatures, tropical birds, and characters such as a devil, an angel, and a ballerina.

From day one, Abigail centered her play on the toucan puppet. Toucan was bright, playful, and boisterous, and seemed to always get into trouble with the other puppets. In Abigail's play, Toucan was yelled at and criticized. In response, Toucan would raise her large, colorful, and awkward beak and fight off her foes. When this didn't make things better, Toucan would sulk. Toucan clearly did not know how to make friends or gain approval from her family.

With Abigail's permission, we began using Toucan as a metaphor for identifying behaviors and attitudes that caused problems. We discovered that Abigail had "Toucan behaviors" or that Toucan appeared most often when Abigail felt threatened, hurt, or unsure. Toucan sometimes appeared in the room when Abigail had a hard day or difficult transition. Over time both Abigail and I would identify when Toucan was in the room. She would say things like "I tried to have a good day today, but I couldn't get Toucan off my shoulder." We eventually came up with an acronym to remove Toucan from the premises: slow down (S), think carefully (T), observe (O), and make a plan (P)—STOP (see figure 5.1).

Abigail and I shared the Toucan metaphor with her mother and step-father and with her father and his family, who then used it at home to support her regulatory gains. Now instead of yelling at her or acting disappointed by her behavior, Abigail's families would calmly note that Toucan was in the

FIGURE 5.1 STOP sign for Abigail's door

room and ask her to S-T-O-P. This alerted Abigail to the fact that she was losing control and needed to redirect herself. If she didn't have the resources, family members were permitted to champion Toucan's removal from the room. The use of metaphor helped strengthen Abigail's relationship with her families. The Toucan metaphor was also used at school; over time her regulatory and social skills improved, and she made academic gains and enduring friends.

COMMUNICATING THROUGH ART

Engaging children in art and other expressive modalities is an invaluable communicative tool (see chapter 7 for more detailed discussion of art in play therapy). Inspired by the creative process, children reveal inner thoughts, unspoken feelings, and relational dynamics that may be inaccessible or hard to articulate. As with all forms of communication, children's artwork should be viewed from an individualized and developmental perspective. Big heads and stick legs are common for four-year-olds, but they may indicate delays or disabilities in the artwork of young teens. Care should also be taken not to stereotype children's images or quickly interpret their meaning. The worker should ask children to describe what they have produced, to avoid erroneous assumptions. For example, some children draw clowns and think they're funny; others may create similar images to impart sadness or fear.

Recurring symbols in children's artwork become points of discussion. For example, Oscar repeatedly drew or built houses (see chapter 4). Sometimes his houses were tall and thin, and sometimes they were so big they filled several pages of construction paper. Sometimes they took up only a tiny corner of a 14 × 14-inch sheet. Although they diverged in form and size, Oscar's houses clearly had significant and enduring meaning.

The artwork created by DeShaun Parker, age nine, caused quite a stir with his teachers. They were disturbed by the images of toxic and nuclear waste in his drawings (figure 5.2). School staff viewed DeShaun's parents as good people, but they believed that they were downplaying their son's apparent problems. Because DeShaun was the youngest of six children in a busy African American family, teachers felt that the Parkers simply didn't have time to focus on him or his preoccupations. The school's psychological examiner (PE) recommended an evaluation of DeShaun.

When the PE asked DeShaun about his artwork, his eyes lit up, and he became animated. He reported that he loved toxic and nuclear waste symbols and was trying to learn everything he could about them. The PE was impressed with DeShaun's vast knowledge of the subject. It was clear that the symbols, not the destructive nature of what they represented, were his passion. After speaking further with his parents, the PE encouraged them to stay abreast of DeShaun's special interests to make sure that his intense focus

FIGURE 5.2   DeShaun's radioactivity on a good day

did not deter growth in other areas of his life. To help stay on top of this, he suggested DeShaun meet with the social worker at the school. The parents agreed.

Interest and passion for toxic and nuclear waste symbols helped De-Shaun express his thoughts and feelings. He used them to evaluate his moods and developed skills to deescalate potentially "toxic" situations. As with Abigail, the worker and DeShaun shared this communicative method with his teachers and family, which resulted in their helping him develop more effective strategies for reducing his frustration and distress.

One particular strategy that proved effective was using a tool to measure DeShaun's "toxic stress." Child-centered cognitive-behavioral interventions encourage the use of images to map feeling levels. At times DeShaun found it difficult to manage frustration, which caused occasional behavioral outbursts in class and on the playground. In DeShaun's case we used a thermometer to gauge feelings as a preventative measure and decide whether these might cause him trouble (see figure 5.3). The thermometer was a convenient scaling tool, readily understandable to the adults in DeShaun's life. Teachers or parents would ask DeShaun where he would place himself on the stress thermometer, and when the reading was high, they identified

FIGURE 5.3 DeShaun's scaling thermometer

methods (e.g., time out, breathing techniques, and running in the gym) that would help him detoxify his frustration and stress.

REFLEXIVITY AND CHILD-CENTERED COMMUNICATION

It makes sense that exposure to child clients' struggles and stories evokes varied responses. Children's pain breaks our hearts, and the urgency of relieving suffering may come at the expense of the child's natural course of healing. As noted above, although we may wish children didn't suffer, we must not avoid talking with them about hard subjects, including losses or tragedies they've endured. Nor should workers offer false reassurances that "everything will be all right." Being calm in the face of crisis is helpful, but dismissing disruptive or painful outcomes minimizes and invalidates children's experience.

When we work with children, it is likely that we will experience emotional and experiential fallout. For example, communicating with children about abuse or abandonment may conjure up workers' memories of their own abuse or other traumas or losses. Practitioners whose workplaces are filled with such stories may eventually avoid asking children questions that elicit answers they don't wish to hear.

It is also true that working with children has other types of emotional and behavioral pitfalls. Bluntly stated, sometimes we simply don't like the children we are expected to help. Many people seek work with children because they think of them as cute and sweet. At the very least they assume that working with children yields more hopeful outcomes than working with adults. Yet some youngsters defy the limits of our tolerance and waylay our best intentions.

Reflexive practice asks us to stay in touch with our thoughts, feelings, and reactions. Knowing that conversations with children often reveal uncomfortable information, it behooves workers to schedule daily time for self-reflection and self-care. Such reparative contemplation prevents compassion burnout and secondary trauma, both of which are common by-products of relational child-centered practice.

REFLECTIONS ON AVNER

Let's consider the role of reflexivity in Peggy Fortuin's work with Avner and his family. Reflect upon your responses to Avner or other child clients who may have challenged your tolerance, commitment, and empathy. What would you need to do to take care of yourself in these circumstances?

Avner, age six, wore thick glasses that always seemed to be falling off of his runny nose. Compared to other children his age, Avner was small and slightly overweight. If it weren't for his advanced verbal skills, one could easily have assumed he was a chubby three-year-old.

Avner had exceptionally light skin and an uncontrollable mane of black curls that made him almost attractive. He walked on his toes and had a way of bumping into everything in his path. Although he was highly active, his awkward gait and small stature didn't allow him to keep pace with his classmates.

Avner's intellect, however, was very engaging. He could expound on almost any subject but especially liked the Civil War, time travel, and food channels. One always learned something new when speaking with Avner. It was therefore unfortunate that he also had the habit of being a close talker. During the course of any given conversation, he'd abruptly pull your face as close to his as possible and cover it with spit as he engaged in a nonstop monologue.

Teachers for the most part found Avner's communication style to be off-putting. His desk was often found situated at the back of the classroom. Avner also rubbed his genitals when excited. This could occur at any time, because he was passionate about almost everything. Children teased Avner and called him a pervert, but he didn't seem to notice.

There was no doubt that Avner was an exceptionally gifted child. He skipped kindergarten and was placed in a first-grade classroom. He went to third-grade classes for math. He had vast knowledge of American history and loved science. He could tell you anything you wanted to know about the Human Genome Project. His parents, Martha and Paul Rosen, saw him as a prodigy. He was their much loved youngest child. His older siblings, nineteen and twenty-four, were in college and graduate school.

No one disputed Avner's impressive cognitive skills and ebullient disposition. However, teachers were concerned that his intellect was quickly outpacing his social, emotional, and motor skills. Although pleasant and sometimes charming, Avner also struggled with self-regulation. He had little tolerance for tasks that he couldn't quickly master, and most days he would have meltdowns over minor tussles with peers. His self-care skills were particularly weak, leading to problems with hygiene.

A pupil evaluation team (PET) meeting was convened just prior to spring vacation to assess how to work with Avner's uneven development as he approached second grade. The Rosens were unreceptive to the PET process and declined the invitation to attend. They were willing, however, to review the final report.

PET members recommended that Avner advance to second grade with gifted accommodations in math, reading, and science. They also suggested that he would benefit from an array of occupational and physical therapies to enhance his fine and gross motor skills. To improve social skills, the team suggested that Avner meet twice a week with the school counselor. Participation in a social skill–building group was suggested as a next step. The counselor would also act as a liaison between the school and the family. The Rosens consented to all of the PET recommendations.

Avner immediately fell in love with Peggy Fortuin, the counselor. Peggy was a ten-year veteran of the school system. She had recently moved from the middle school to the elementary school after a redistricting change. She wasn't entirely pleased to be relocated but chose not to complain; it wasn't in her nature to buck the system. Peggy didn't have as much experience working with young children as she did with middle and high school kids, but she looked at the change as an opportunity to expand her horizons. She eagerly pursued learning more about young kids.

Avner would all but fly down the hall on his tiptoes to get to Peggy's office every Wednesday and Friday morning. Once there, he talked nonstop while generously picking his nose. The office was quite small and cluttered. Avner almost always knocked things off the shelves when he moved about the room. Sometimes he would stand so close while talking to Peggy that she felt uncomfortable. She started leaving the door open lest he report to someone that she had inappropriately touched him during his visits.

Peggy was further frustrated by Avner's refusal to do anything but talk during their times together. He refused invitations to play, draw, or engage in board games. He just kept talking. Peggy's one attempt to engage Avner in a social skills group with two similarly gifted peers was, in her words, "a total disaster."

Peggy admitted to herself that she didn't enjoy or even like Avner. She was too embarrassed to acknowledge these feelings to anyone. Instead she simply tolerated the time she and Avner spent together, allowing him to talk without interruption and thinking all the while about other things she needed to do. Some days their brief thirty-minute sessions seemed interminable.

Peggy met monthly with the Rosens. They acknowledged that Avner was frequently noncompliant, and they were amenable to suggestions for managing his behaviors at home. Excited to finally be of help, Peggy recommended a cognitive-behavioral plan and gave the parents a host of behavioral worksheets.

The parents quickly reported back to Peggy that Avner was uninterested in the behavior plan. "He's intellectually beyond that disciplinary method," they said. Later Peggy learned that the Rosens had asked the principal whether there was a more educated counselor in the school district available to work with Avner. Peggy found herself extending the time between visits with the Rosens.

Peggy prided herself on being nonjudgmental. Thus she was disturbed that she found herself disliking this little boy and blaming the Rosens for his problems. Over her career she had worked successfully with youngsters from diverse cultures and circumstances. But Avner, whose family was of Russian Jewish descent, was somehow different. He made her feel like a failure. When she was honest with herself, she had to admit she just couldn't connect with him or his parents—nor did she really want to. Reluctantly she opened up to her supervisor.

Peggy's supervisor asked her what it was about Avner that shut down her curiosity. The question caught her by surprise. She was usually an avid researcher and advocate when it came to the children she worked with. She suddenly realized that she actually knew very little about Avner, his family, and gifted children in general. Furthermore she felt little incentive to learn more. Instead she was taken aback by her uncharacteristic judgmental and unempathetic attitudes.

Peggy used supervision to investigate and reflect upon her work. In the end she acknowledged that unaddressed issues related to her relocation in the school coupled with personal strains were affecting her overall performance. Avner happened to be a complicated youngster, and Peggy was at a point in her life where she needed all the validation she could get. Such validation was not in Avner's repertoire. Thus she would have to find fulfillment elsewhere and more competently and enthusiastically embrace this little boy starting where *he* was in his change process.

SUMMARY

According to researchers, it takes very little time for children to decide whether practitioners are authentic or trustworthy. Thus seeds for relational success must be sown from the very first moments of connection. To blossom, relationship building requires attentiveness, patience, and reliability. In child-centered practice, success is best guaranteed when workers can carefully balance themselves between the world of childhood and the professional skills and wisdom of adulthood.

Child-centered communication begins with reassuring children through both actions and words. Children's author A. A. Milne is credited with saying that one is best advised to watch what people do as well as what they say. Such advice proves quite sage when workers are engaged in creating environments of trust with the children who become their clients. Successful conversations are prompted by keen and committed interest that follows many channels—through spoken and unspoken exchanges, shared expression, and a process of creative and playful endeavors. Therefore, child-centered practitioners must be comfortable engaging with children on their own turf. Knowledge of childhood theories helps workers contextualize what they see and hear, but they must also be prepared to investigate the uniqueness of every child. Even those of the same age, gender, and culture will be distinctive in style and experience.

It seems logical then, in these times of economic hardship and workplace cutbacks, that instead of concentrating on trendy treatment protocols that may not fit their needs, workers should spend time learning how to converse effectively with their child clients. When children feel safe, heard, and validated, they are more likely to trust the change process, regardless of techniques. When parents believe that their opinions matter, they are more apt to support and sustain strategies that benefit children's growth.

Quality connections don't necessarily take more time, yet they yield lasting impressions that extend well beyond brief therapeutic contacts. To paraphrase the author Maya Angelou, children may forget what you say and do, but they will never forget how you made them feel.

References

Duncan, B. L., Miller, S. D., & Sparks, J. (2007). Common factors and the uncommon heroism of youth. *Psychotherapy in Australia, 13*(2), 34–43.

Kazdin, A. E. (2004). Evidence-based treatments: Challenges and priorities for practice and research. In B. Burns & K. Hoagwood (Eds.), *Child and adolescent psychiatric clinics of North America* (pp. 923–940). New York: Elsevier.

Lacher, D., Nichols, T., & May, J. (2005). *Connecting with kids through stories.* London: Jessica Kingsley.

Ostis, C. (2002). *What's happening in our family: Understanding sexual abuse through metaphors.* Brandon, VT: Safer Society Press.

Salloum, A. (2008). Group therapy for children after homicide and violence: A pilot study. *Research on Social Work Practice, 18*(3), 198–211.

Society for Adolescent Medicine. (2004). Access to health care for adolescents and young adults: Position paper. *Journal of Adolescent Health, 35,* 160–167.

Webb, N. B. (2003). *Social work practice with children* (2nd ed.). New York: Guilford Press.

White, M. (1984). Pseudo-encopresis: From avalanche to victory, from vicious cycles to virtuous cycles. *Family Systems Medicine, 2*(2), 150–160.

White, M., & Epston, D. (1990). *Narrative means to a therapeutic end.* New York: W. W. Norton.

6

Working with Parents

First, do not harm; second, make no mistakes.

Harriette Pipes McAdoo, "Parent and Child Relationships
in African-American Families"

PARENTS IN CHILD-CENTERED PRACTICE

Working with parents is an integral component of relational child-centered
practice. The term *parent* is broadly defined and inclusive of a range of
adults and adolescents in parenting roles. It takes into account biological,
adoptive, and foster parents; stepparents, extended family members, and
grandparents; same-sex and gender-nonconforming partners; nonrelated
and fictive kin—all of whom function in primary caregiving roles. Parents
may be legally married or never married, living together or separately.

Parenting styles run the gamut. Some parents effectively coparent and
divide up caregiving functions. Others adhere to culturally gendered roles,
while some apportion caregiving with extended family, hired caregivers, or
tribal and community members. Depending on levels of cooperation and
conflict, divorced or separated parents may coparent, parent in parallel, or
allocate parenting responsibilities. In increasingly rare instances a parent
may be legally awarded sole custodial rights to a child.

Building relationships can be challenging for both parents and workers.
As with child clients, it's the practitioner's responsibility to create and nurture
the working alliance. Establishing a safe atmosphere where parents can
speak openly about their concerns is one of many steps in trust building.
Conveying safety in these relationships is complicated, however, because all
too many parents have had negative experiences with social service, medical, mental health, and educational professionals. For these parents, trust is
elusive and frequently must be reestablished one conversation at a time.

From the worker's view, relational tensions occur when they feel caught
between the priorities of children and of their parents. Ethical, moral, and
personal strains surface most commonly when working with child protection
cases, domestic violence, and contentious family situations. They are also

121

well documented when workers are faced with meeting the needs of dependent children living with parents facing addiction or mental illness. Conversely, practitioners may find themselves allying with parents to the detriment of their child clients. This is seen most often when working with children and youth struggling with relational, temperamental, and behavioral problems.

The requirement to meet people where they are in their parenting process is never simple. It is further compromised by the fact that knowledge of children, parents, and families is always partial. We typically meet with parents episodically, often at times of stress and urgency. We read case records and evaluations that focus on what is wrong rather than what is right or what is working well. As a result, our understanding of parents is susceptible to misinterpretation and unreasonable judgments. To illustrate this point, think for a moment what it would be like if critical life decisions were made for you based solely on your worst days.

Building authentic worker-parent relationships is a dynamic and individualized process. It takes into account the quality of interaction between workers and parents and the strengths and vulnerabilities each brings to developing relationships. Qualities such as respect, commitment, reliability, positive and bidirectional communication, transparency, and equality are foundational to gaining parents' trust.

Effective workers anticipate that parents will *learn* from them, *lean* on them, and at times, take the *lead* in their children's treatment. They understand that parents must frequently be vigilant and advocate on behalf of their children's best interests. There is no doubt that working with some parents is easier than working with others. Some satisfy our desire to feel competent, while some parents test our mettle.

So how do we enter into trusting and trustworthy relationships with a range of parents and parenting situations? How does one "start where the parent is" when he or she may be at the heart of a child's struggles? How does one establish a balance between building trust with children while not trespassing on parents' love and authority? Finally, what knowledge is necessary to work effectively and caringly with parents whose child-rearing practices are especially burdened, unfamiliar, or conflict with our experiences and values?

This chapter begins with a brief exploration of the social construction of parenthood, to illustrate how evolving theory, policy trends, and human rights affect child-centered practice with parents. Included in this overview is a short history of the child guidance movement, which essentially shaped how services to children and parents have been conceptualized and delivered in America over the past century. It then looks at qualities essential for establishing effective partnerships with parents as well as how to maintain and strengthen these alliances.

The chapter concludes by addressing parents in various situations, such as raising children with chronic health conditions. It addresses issues affecting same-sex parents. In a preview to chapter 13, we briefly touch upon the awareness needed for working effectively with parenting populations whose race, ethnicity, and culture are different from our own. The final section describes a case that applies relational perspectives to work with parents.

THE SOCIAL CONSTRUCTION OF PARENTHOOD

Since the 1950s, social science and early-childhood research has emphasized the critical role that parents play in the lives of children. Parental love and the security it provides are seen as essential to healthy child development. The quality of parent-child bonds is viewed as intrinsic to well-being and is understood to be the backbone of emotional security, human mastery, and relational success.

The safety and protection of children is also seen as parents' responsibility. In the United States, the 1974 passage of the Child Abuse Prevention and Treatment Act (CAPTA) cemented children's rights to physical and emotional protection. It authorized state agencies to remove children from homes where parental maltreatment was substantiated. Such universal legislation in the United States was culturally transformative, as it shifted responsibility for children's health and welfare from solely the family's domain to one subjected to government oversight. Passage made a bold statement about children's rights to the effect that no adult, regardless of relationship, had the unexamined authority to misuse or harm a child.

Fifteen years after passage of CAPTA, the Convention on the Rights of the Child (CRC; UN General Assembly, 1989) identified the family as the natural and fundamental group responsible for children's well-being, protection, and safety. Canada ratified the CRC in 1991, and to this day it supports the duty to report (mandated reporting) in matters of child protection. The interdependent nature of children's and parents' bonds was also recognized. Like CAPTA, the CRC mandated that authorities intervene when adults place children in jeopardy.

In today's world, the role parents and caregivers play in keeping children safe and feeling loved seems unequivocal. Yet this conceptualization of parents' roles and children's needs has not always been the case. In the eighteenth century, for example, good parenting was meant to be stern rather than nurturing. At the time, child-rearing philosophies were primarily dominated by Calvinist principles, which said that, unless strictly guided, children would naturally succumb to sinful behavior.[1] In the best interests of their children, well-intentioned parents restrained themselves from expressing affection and instead set strict behavioral limits, minimized nurturance, and when necessary, doled out harsh punishments to protect their children's souls (Jones, 1999).

Views of parenthood evolved during the nineteenth century as a consequence of several cultural trends and influences. Industrialization and perceived economic opportunity enticed families to migrate from rural to urban areas. These families were often the first of their generation to move away from extended family support. Some families benefited from economic prosperity while others did not, and too many ended up suffering unanticipated adverse effects from industrialization and urbanization. Children and youth in the United States shouldered responsibilities for supporting parents and family elders, and it was frequently taken for granted that even the youngest members worked to keep the family afloat. During this same period in Canada, it was assumed that children over the age of seven would contribute to family income.

While these socioeconomic shifts were occurring, Calvinist influence gave way to emerging Enlightenment philosophies. Radically new social constructions of childhood and parenting emerged. Middle- and upper-class families viewed their children as dependent innocents who relied on the goodness of parents and other adults to guide them to secure and happy lives (Jones, 1999). Unlike earlier times when children were considered to be small versions of adults, childhood was now reconstructed as a stage of life distinct from adulthood. Poor families did not have the luxury of such phenomenological revisions. As in earlier times, children in disadvantaged households worked and took on adult roles.

Although this view of childhood promoted kinder and gentler child rearing, it also placed significant responsibility on parents to produce well-behaved, morally upright children. Parents, primarily mothers, were increasingly the focus of scrutiny, judged by whether their children fulfilled cultural expectations.

The child study movement founded by G. Stanley Hall in the late 1890s sought to establish a scientific base for understanding children's cognitive, emotional, and moral development. Its objectives mostly concentrated on advancing early-education models and improving child-rearing methods (Brehony, 2009). Hall's studies corresponded with society's growing interest in the psychoanalytic movement, which was similarly focused on early-childhood development. Influenced by both these social movements, parents with economic means commenced to seek professional advice to help with child-rearing problems. Once the exclusive domain of parents, extended family members, and faith-based advisers, many families now looked to child-centered experts for guidance.

While scholars searched for greater understanding of childhood, concerns about the impact of poverty and urban living on children and families increased. Child advocates and lay reformers witnessed the negative impact of a rapidly changing society. According to Jones (1999, p. 17), the "trouble-some child of the nineteenth century" reflected the ailments of a nation that had lost its course. These youngsters were usually poor, were underedu-cated, frequently broke the law to sustain themselves and their families, and sometimes appeared to be suffering from mental illness or intellectual delay.

Early in the twentieth century, two institutions took the lead in address-ing children's needs: the juvenile justice system sought to aid children con-victed of breaking the law, and child guidance centers were developed in response to the growing number of children identified as mentally and emo-tionally troubled. Dually influenced by the mental hygiene movement of the late nineteenth and early twentieth centuries and psychoanalytic trends brought over from Europe, the child guidance movement supported the practice of child psychiatry. Its mission was to prevent or intervene in child-centered social, emotional, and behavioral problems.

Child guidance was a uniquely American contribution to psychiatry (Richardson 1989). Trained in psychiatric principles, child guidance workers reached out to economically disadvantaged children who, more often than not, were from immigrant families or living with foster families and in orphanages. Workers advocated better living and working conditions for these children and child labor laws to protect youngsters from exploitation.[2] Yet although workers made the connection between health, well-being, and the social environment, they were nevertheless moralistic and judgmental, especially toward these children's parents and families. Children from poor urban families were sometimes removed from homes simply because of the family's economic disadvantage. These youngsters sometimes ended up in rural foster homes and were exploited as child laborers.

By the 1930s the growing popularity and influence of psychoanalytic theory put a virtual halt to community-focused efforts. The problems of childhood were no longer solely linked to social determinants. Child psychi-atry assessed for psychological abnormalities and problems in normal devel-opment. Children's emotional and behavioral struggles were medicalized, now linked to intrapsychic sources caused in part by parenting deficiencies. Blame was particularly cast on mothers.

Outreach models were summarily replaced by child guidance clinics that provided individual, psychodynamically based treatment to children and guidance to their parents. Child psychiatry also gave rise to school-based psychology, family counseling services, and community psychiatry models, and the fields of social work, human services, education, and counseling, among others, integrated its theories into their practices (Richardson, 1989).

Child guidance models were team-based but hierarchical by design. The child psychiatrist (physician), typically male, provided directed treatment to the child, most often in the form of nondirective play therapy (see chapter 7). He was responsible for the case formulation that guided the treatment process, while clinical assessments were conducted mostly by child psychologists. Parents were seen by psychiatrically trained social workers, most often a woman, whose role was to assess child-rearing capacities and breaches. Social workers then guided parents and caregivers in methods to repair parenting failures and protect the needs of their children.

In the early days of child guidance, there were few if any standardized or validated measures to evaluate parental capacity. Accordingly workers' assessments depended heavily on observation, personal experience, and untested theories as guideposts for determining life-affecting decisions. In combination with workers' subjectivity, child guidance often yielded dire outcomes for parents, children, and families, especially those who were economically disadvantaged or otherwise vulnerable. Parents had little say in determining recommendations; most would not question the authority of experts charged with their children's well-being and care. In the end, those deemed to be unfit temporarily or permanently lost guardianship of their children, who were then transferred to substitute or foster caregivers.

In the twenty-first century, child guidance centers have for the most part transitioned to or merged with community mental health and clinic-based centers. Public schools and public housing in some communities offer child-centered counseling services that include parent education in their programming. Medicalized models based in child psychiatry are still in use; however, contemporary practice standards now emphasize the use of evidence-guided models. Ideally, practitioners use both scientific evidence and parent-based expertise to inform their child-centered practice.

Like parent guidance experts of the past, however, today's workers are not immune from the influence of their own assumptions, perceptions, and biases. These affect how they view and interact with parents of children who become their clients. Like their predecessors, such parents often come from intergenerationally poor and disenfranchised groups. Some have been demeaned or maltreated by systems and institutions that are ostensibly there to help them. How do workers navigate these relationships in ways that benefit children?

Partnering with Parents

People enter into parenthood with hopes for their children. They do not anticipate that their children may need therapeutic intervention. By the time most parents reach social work, counseling, or mental health practitioners, they believe that they have in some way failed. They may be well defended, prepared for criticism or blame. Others feel shame. In some cases parents hope for the best and look forward to the prescribed treatment for their children.

The range of parents who seek out services is wide, deep, and varied. Some are veterans of social care institutions; many of these are understandably guarded, having had unhelpful relationships in the past. Parents of highly challenging youngsters may feel exhausted and ashamed for not being able to control their children. Others have little or no experience with these systems, having avoided extrafamilial intervention. Parents whose children become clients may also be from cultural groups that do not ordinarily interact with professional helpers.

How parents access services is also variable. Some are self-referred, eager to get help for their children. Some get referred because they have temporarily or permanently lost custody of their children due to neglect, abuse, or other harsh circumstances. Those who are mandated by the courts or other authoritative bodies may be reluctant, frightened, or angered by having no choice in the process.

Foster parents may also seek out or be required to participate in supportive counseling, especially for therapeutic foster-care placements. Counseling may also be sought by adoptive parents, particularly those with older children or youngsters who struggle with emotional, relational, behavioral, and/or developmental challenges.

Engaging effectively with parents takes time, humility, and patience. This is true whatever the parents' circumstances. Understanding and compassion are especially important when the parents' lives contained few if any models of connection or trustworthiness. Adversity informs their experiences, and despite their best efforts, they are likely to reenact familiar yet insufficient relational patterns.

Ongoing life factors may create obstacles to building worker-parent partnerships. People subjected to repeated relational violence or other forms of abuse may be unable to engage because of realistic fears of harm to themselves or their children (see chapter 12). In other instances, parents are distracted from the tasks of raising children because they are simultaneously caring for aging parents. Some parents must concentrate their energies on making ends meet or securing adequate shelter and sustenance for their children. In all these cases, forging partnerships is difficult because of practical and relational factors (see the Barron case below). These parents are doing the best they can under extraordinary and complicated circumstances.

By and large, parents and caregivers are used to being told what to do by experts and authorities. It is understandable that they may not initially comprehend the need for their involvement in their children's therapy. They may not know what is expected of them or have faith in promises of collaboration and caring. Thus it is best to explicitly invite parents to engage in their children's therapy and to reinforce the value of their participation throughout the treatment relationship.

BUILDING AND STRENGTHENING
RELATIONSHIPS WITH PARENTS

Every interaction with parents and caregivers is an opportunity for workers to promote and model effective relationship. Even when the primary worker-parent task is service oriented, it is still relational. Parents benefit from emotional support from their first conversation to their last, no matter how brief. This is the case whether the conversation is in person or on the phone, by letter or through e-mail.

The quality of the earliest connections has significant impact. As one father stated, harsh words last a lifetime. Positive connections are also enduring, however, and frequently lead to good outcomes. In one mother's words: "[The pediatrician] made the time to listen to me. She wasn't in the door, out the door, see you later. She always seemed interested in how my child was doing and how I was doing" (Konrad, 2007).

How then are trusted and trustworthy relationships developed between practitioners and parents? Let's begin with some core principles.

- Children benefit from worker-parent relationships.
- Relationships are predicated on respect, open communication, commitment, and trustworthiness.
- Relationship is shaped by the circumstances and dynamics of its participants.
- Parents do the best they can.

Children Benefit from Worker-Parent Relationships

Parental investment in children's therapy is viewed as beneficial to children for many reasons. Parents who are listened to and have a voice in their children's treatment are more likely to implement and follow through on suggestions. When interventions succeed, children's therapeutic gains are reinforced and transferred reliably and sustainably to the home and community. As a result of positive and ongoing growth, parents experience increased feelings of competence and improvements in their parenting and caregiving relationships (Wilson & Ryan, 2001).

Understanding parents through the eyes of children provides further incentive for building strong worker-parent relationships. Children feel the sting when their parents are unacknowledged or disrespected. They see themselves as being made up of their parents' strengths, talents, and weaknesses. Indeed, we all inherit traits from our families that contribute both to our identities and to how we make meaning of the world. As an example, a young adolescent told me that every time his grandmother disparaged his father, he too felt criticized. He said, "Half my DNA belongs to my dad. So if Granny hates my dad, then she must hate me too."

Charise, a student in one of my classes, similarly brought home this point. "Don't get me wrong," she said. "I love my adoptive parents. They've given me a wonderful life." She then told about searching for and locating her biological mother, who, in the end, did not wish to continue their relationship. Yet even with this less than perfect outcome, Charise felt the search was well worth it. "Finding her," she said, "was necessary for me to feel whole." Charise's bonds with her adoptive parents coexisted with her desire to secure her biological mother's love and acceptance. Acknowledgment and validation of both these essential parental relationships would be critical if she were to become a client.

Relationships Are Predicated on Respect, Open Communication, Commitment, and Trustworthiness

Positive worker-parent relationships begin with identifying parents' strengths and recognizing vulnerabilities. Alliances should also aim to relieve feelings of isolation and loneliness brought about when dealing with children's problems. Parents look to professionals for validation that what they are feeling is normal. In some instances, as when children struggle with reactive attachment disorders or significant mental illnesses, parenting is extraordinarily challenging. Worker-parent relationships should address these feelings and never dismiss, judge, or minimize the struggles biological, foster, and adoptive parents face.

Parents most often describe competence in terms of human attributes such as attitudes of personal consideration and interest in the child and family's welfare, actions that are responsive to the child's needs and the family's desires, actions that go the extra mile, and investment in the child's health and well-being. Specific *qualities* that contribute to beneficial worker-parent relationships have been outlined in the child-centered literature across professions (Konrad & Browning, 2012; Turnbull, Turnbull, Erwin, & Soodak, 2006). These include respect, open communication, commitment, and trustworthiness.

Respect is conveyed by taking time to get to know parents rather than relying on the views of others. Acknowledging that parents know their children best implies respect for their role, whatever strengths, challenges, or vulnerabilities they may bring to child rearing. Respect also means accepting different family structures, cultures, and backgrounds and seeing the family as a whole. Parents also see respect when workers refer to their children as individuals, not as diagnoses or labels.

Respect in action requires being courteous, treating parents as one would want to be treated if the roles were reversed. Respect is expressed by calling parents by their last names unless invited to do otherwise, and being on time for meetings or informing parents of potential delays as soon as possible. Workers also act as advocates to ensure that all parties involved in children's care act respectfully toward parents (Blue-Banning, Summers, Frankland, Nelson, & Beegle, 2004). Respectful relationships are also characterized by worker-parent ability to agree to disagree on certain points.

Worker-parent communication should be candid, honest, and bidirectional. Particular attention should be paid to conveying difficult news, with time set aside to allow parents to respond. Parents' questions should be answered directly, using plain language free of professional jargon and acronyms. All forms of communication should be made accessible, and workers should translate professional rhetoric.

Workers should be tactful in discovering whether parents, especially nonreaders or non-English speakers, understand conversations and written reports. Feedback strategies are therefore important.

Attention should be paid to confidentiality and legal requirements such as HIPAA.[3] Workers should know their agency's policies about record keeping as well as whether there are fees for acquiring written documents.

Commitment is demonstrated, not merely stated. Workers express commitment through dedication to their work, following through on promises, and going the extra mile when necessary. An example of commitment is spending time researching parents' questions and supplying them with information in a timely manner. Persistence, patience, and perseverance are attributes of commitment.

Commitment shows parents that workers see them and their children as human beings, not cases. Invested workers advocate for children and families. They are committed to children's and families' rights beyond the door of their office, and combat injustice and inequities within broader systems.

Trust is an evolving quality that needs revision and retooling throughout the life of worker-parent relationships. Trust is established through actions that are responsible, reliable, and dependable. Trustworthiness means children are safe within practitioners' care. Safety in this context implies that workers protect children's physical and emotional interests, combat discrimination, and value human dignity. Lastly, trustworthiness includes the worker's discretion and protection of children's rights to confidentiality and privacy (Blue-Banning et al., 2004).

Relationship Is Shaped by the Circumstances and Dynamics of Its Participants

Milton Erickson, an American psychiatrist, captured the essence of effective worker-parent relationships when he taught that successful alliances result when clients and practitioners learn to work together in clever and harmonious ways. These ways of working together will be distinctive and dynamic. Positive outcomes are determined by attitudes and assets brought into the relationship and by the collective commitment made to invest in children's therapeutic success.

Workers must thus be prepared to work with a myriad of family circumstances and a wide range of parental expectations. Flexibility, adaptability, and confidence in the face of uncertainty are qualities well suited to working with parents and families. Furthermore, being open to a wide swath of opinions, customs, and beliefs helps build worker-parent alliances. At the same time, workers must not lose sight of who they are and the boundaries they must keep in this challenging work.

Often practitioners must balance wanting to do things *for* parents against working *with* them to do things for themselves. For example, there are parents who desperately want to know what to do; they desire guidance and support because they are not yet ready to take the lead in determining what's best for their child. The challenge for workers in this case is to respond to parents' need for direction while encouraging development of their confidence and skills. On one hand, reinforcement of dependency impedes parents from becoming active agents in their child's care. On the other hand, pushing too quickly for autonomy can cause parents to feel abandoned, inadequate, or afraid.

There are also parents who are self-determined from the get-go. They thrive when their decision making is supported. In this scenario, the practitioner's role is transformed to that of facilitator and coach.

Whatever the balance one seeks to achieve, the goal of any relational partnership is to ascertain what works best for parents, to optimize and support their functioning, and to foster skills that can be sustained once the formal relationship has ended.

PARENTS DO THE BEST THEY CAN

By and large, parents want nothing more than to raise healthy, happy children. When children's problems come to the attention of child-centered professionals, it is usually because parents have found their primary resources insufficient or because other variables, usually a life crisis or transition, have weakened their reserves.

An ethic underlying worker-parent partnerships is the belief that the vast majority of parents do the best they can. Webb (2003) reminds us that parents, like all human beings, are imperfect. Most parents provide children with "good enough" care. Some even provide extraordinary parenting in the face of highly challenging circumstances. Those who seek our help need knowledge, skills, support, and/or resources.

CAVEAT

A minority of people do not have children's best interests at heart, such as adults who sexually exploit children for personal gratification. Such people do not view their sexual desires and acts against children as distressing or inappropriate. It is disconcerting that approximately 50 percent of adults diagnosed with pedophilia (sexual exploitation of children) marry at some point and have children of their own or become parents to their partners' children (Blanchard et al., 2009). Such individuals should never be in a position of responsibility for children. It is sometimes the case, however, that workers come into contact with them in child-centered settings. Child-abuse reporting laws in America mandate that suspicion of child exploitation must be reported immediately to state child protection authorities.

There will inevitably be cases when parent-worker relationships are tested by workers' having to remove children from their primary homes due to physical or emotional abuse, family violence, or neglect. Building alliances should be attempted even with parents who may be unable to care for their children, and if possible, treatment should aim to strengthen parents' relational and child-rearing skills. This is especially important when children will be returning to their care.

DIVERSE PARENT POPULATIONS

The rest of this chapter briefly addresses the special knowledge that might be necessary to enhance worker-parent engagement. It discusses the complex situation of parents raising children with chronic health conditions; issues of multiculturalism that arise when workers and parents come from different racial, ethnic, and cultural groups; and relational, social, and political realities for same-sex and gender-nonconforming parents.

Parents of Children with Chronic Health Conditions

Child-centered workers are often the first to introduce parents to the unfamiliar world of childhood illness and disability. This can occur in intensive care units or after diagnoses that will affect children's lives. In some settings, workers deliver difficult diagnostic and prognostic information to parents. Parents may also ask workers or counselors to assist them with interpreting diagnostic reports. Guidance from social workers and counselors is also enlisted when parents need assistance coping with practical changes and emotions that accompany children's life-altering conditions.

It is not unusual for parents and family caregivers to be cautious when sharing information with outsiders. Many tell stories of feeling judged and blamed for their children's problems. Others have been dismissed in their efforts to communicate with practitioners. Parents report that they keep feelings to themselves in part because they do not want to appear selfish and weak or, worse, appear to put their needs before those of their vulnerable children. Parents also know when they are perceived as demanding and difficult. Most parents learn to cope with such views, because fighting for children's best interests will always trump popularity.

Like other vulnerable populations, parents of medically challenged children need workers to reflect upon what it might be like to be in their shoes. These families understand well the fragility of life. No one wants to be exposed to such life-changing circumstances, which force us to acknowledge that such things can happen to anyone. For the most part, we think of bad things happening to *other* people. Reflecting upon her daughter's fatal illness, wondering for years how such a tragedy could happen to her family, author Isabel Allende concluded, "Why *not* me?"

For the most part, parents who care for children with chronic health conditions appreciate the unavoidable gap between professionals' knowledge and parents' wisdom. They know that people who have not been in their circumstances cannot truly know their plight. It is inevitable that some parents feel frustrated by the discordance between their lived realities and professionals' perceptions. This mother's words convey such sentiments: "You know your kids, and sometimes people think you're overreacting. But so what? I feel bad about stepping on somebody's toes. But I don't care. This is my child and I'm his mother, and I really don't care if I hurt your feelings."

Reflexive practice urges workers to be curious and open to hearing parents' and children's stories, even when they are difficult to bear. Willingness to fully engage raises awareness of how parents become vigilant and sometimes demanding in pursuit of their children's care. Changing perceptions invite us to welcome these parents rather than criticize or avoid them. Learning from parents improves workers' insight about caring for a child with a serious illness or injury. Workers come to appreciate rather than judge the motivations and meanings of parents' views and behaviors and are therefore better prepared to work with them in true partnership.

Transcultural Worker-Parent Alliances

The rapidly changing multicultural landscape in America requires that workers be culturally responsive and prepared. Culture influences how parents care for, discipline, and guide their children's growth and development. In Oscar's case (chapter 3), being cared for by his mother's tribe was well within the norm of Micmac traditions. Even informed workers, however, must question their cultural knowledge. Though populations may share common beliefs and practices, there is also great diversity within any group. As with all relational situations, one must get to know the unique characteristics and customs of each individual and family.

Newcomers to America and those here without documented citizen status[4] are commonly skeptical of outsiders who seem eager to intrude into their families (see chapter 13). Many immigrate or seek refuge precisely because of injustices and violations perpetrated by state authorities in their original nations; some have lost loved ones as a result of genocide and war. Others are in the United States or Canada to find work; some enroll in schools, while others seek reconnection with extended family. In all of these situations, language barriers impede effective cross-cultural communication. Translators are scarce; emotional and relational content often gets lost in translation. Furthermore, people are understandably reluctant to reveal private information to translators and cultural brokers who are members of their family and cultural community. For undocumented immigrants, sharing personal information can jeopardize their safety or lead to deportation.

Parents from diverse backgrounds and circumstances may encounter discrimination, prejudice, and/or racism within medical and mental health systems, social service agencies, and educational institutions. Overt and covert racism and other forms of prejudice arise when workers are incurious about multicultural perspectives and meaning making. Culturally informed and responsive practice emphasizes the importance of examining our assumptions, naming them, and attending to how they influence the work we do. Stereotypes that reinforce discriminatory attitudes and lead to misjudgments impede our capacity to work effectively with parents.

Carole Beaulieu, a white, middle-class, fifty-year-old social worker employed in a culturally diverse middle school in a Montreal neighborhood, missed her opportunity to connect with the Lopez family.[5] Mrs. Lopez called her to complain about an incident involving Javiér, their thirteen-year-old son. She was upset because, the day before, Javiér was chastised by his teacher, Ms. Poulin, for not agreeing to participate in a multicultural celebration. Javiér and several other Latin American students were told that they needed to be role models for the black children in their school. When Javiér pointed out that he was from Mexico, not of African descent, he was reprimanded for being rude. When he tried to make a clarifying point about racial and ethnic difference, he was given detention.

Carole politely tried to smooth things over. She considered herself a person without prejudice and thus was surprised when Mrs. Lopez was unappeased. Carole went on to explain that Javiér's teacher was simply being enthusiastic about multicultural awareness. "You of all people should appreciate that," she chimed. Mrs. Lopez responded by saying that if Ms. Poulin was so enthusiastic about cultural awareness, she might want to learn that Mexicans are not African American, and hung up.

So what did Carole do wrong? First, she immediately defended her white colleague rather than inquire further into Mrs. Lopez's concerns. By doing so, she tacitly dismissed Mrs. Lopez's legitimacy and assumed that Javiér and his friends were in some way culpable.

Second, she missed an opportunity to directly address racism and how it might affect Javiér and other children and families at the school. The teacher may have good intentions, but she acted insensitively in a potentially volatile situation.

Third, Carole did nothing to assure Mrs. Lopez that she would meet with Javiér and his friends to hear their side of the story. As an immigrant and woman of color, Mrs. Lopez had likely encountered discrimination based on racial profiling. To ignore Javiér's perspective implies to his mother that the school does not care about her son's experience of racism.

Finally, Carole did not address how this incident might be used in a positive way to increase awareness of race, racism, and cultural diversity in the school. Acknowledging discrimination and talking openly about the differences between parents' racial and cultural identities and our own is important. Such dialogue sets the groundwork for building authentic relationship.

Same-Sex and Gender-Nonconforming Parents

More than a million children in the United States are being reared by lesbian or gay parents. In Canada same-sex parents represented less than 1 percent of all couples (married and common-law). Of these, 9 percent had children in the home (Statistics Canada, 2011). According to the American Academy of Pediatrics (Perrin, 2002), children raised by lesbian and gay parents develop in ways similar to those raised by heterosexual parents. In their position statement, the Child Welfare League of America (2002) affirms that lesbian, gay, and bisexual parents are as competent to raise children as their heterosexual counterparts.

Healthy growth and development is influenced by the quality and nature of children's relationships with their families and not by particular structural forms (single or married parents), gender makeup (same-sex or opposite-sex parents), or the parents' sexual orientation. Parenting studies show no apparent correlations between a parent's sexual orientation and children's antisocial or delinquent behaviors or the development of mental illness (Longres & Etnyre, 2004; Stacey & Biblarz, 2001). According to Ellen Perrin (2002), children do best when they have loving, responsible, and committed parents raising them. These parents can be heterosexual, homosexual, transgender, women or men: it doesn't matter.

Despite apparently growing tolerance for sexual orientation and gender diversity in America, same-sex or gender-nonconforming parents remain stigmatized. Gay and lesbian parents continue to experience rejection, disenfranchisement, and lack of recognition as parents. For example, a friend recounted the following story. He was shopping at the market one afternoon along with his three-year-old daughter, Jada, who was sitting in the child seat of the cart. Another shopper came along and remarked on Jada's chattiness. "She's adorable," she said. "Her mother is lucky to have you babysitting for her today." My friend took a breath and replied, "I am her mother." Awkward silence followed.

Heterosexism also causes many challenges for children of gays and lesbians. At its most destructive, it feeds into bullying, violence, and hate directed at children and their parents. Whether living in LGBT-identified families or families in which a parent has "come out" as lesbian or gay, children quickly learn about prejudice and may do their best not to be outed because of the dangers it might entail.

In Canada the Civil Marriage Act of 2005 made it legal nationwide for same-sex couples to marry. The law does not eliminate discrimination, but it legitimizes parenthood status for both partners. In the United States, marriage equality is a distant goal, and same-sex parents face legal inequities. Most states have no formal processes for same-sex parents to facilitate the ritual of becoming families (marriage) or of ending families (divorce). When parenting partnerships end, children's custody decisions are by necessity based upon decision makers' interpretations of legal statutes as well as their personal and moral values.

The consequences of subjective decision making can be tragic. For instance, children may unnecessarily be removed from parents who have no binding legal relationships to their children. For same-sex and gender-nonconforming parents, this constitutes uninformed and blatant injustice and social inequity.

Workers play dual roles with same-sex parents. First, they recognize that parenting struggles exist within a social context. Although worker-parent relationships are built on the foundations set forth above, they cannot be entirely separated from cultural effects. Second, workers must raise awareness of social injustices targeted at same-sex and gender-nonconforming parents. This should be done with peers, within agencies and institutions, and in broader political and social-action arenas.

Workers must also reflect upon their conscious and hidden heterosexism. For many years I worked in an urban clinical practice that served a broad range of children and families. One day I noticed someone in the waiting room who I assumed to be a man dressed in a beautiful, flowing dress. In group supervision later that day, a colleague requested consultation regarding this individual. I asked how this client identified—as transsexual, transgender, cross-dressing, queer, or third-gender. I did so because experience had taught me to ask rather than assume how people choose to identify themselves.

To my surprise my seasoned colleague stated that she simply ignored that this young father came to sessions dressed in stereotypically female clothes. "I thought it better not to mention it," she said. My colleague's response, though motivated in part by kindness, indicated her discomfort with gender-nonconforming identities and behaviors. Her choice *not to ask* led to erroneous assumptions and denied the client the opportunity to be fully known. Her choice in effect set the stage for the client *not to tell*.

When eventually asked, the client identified as third gender, neither male nor female. The good news was the relationship was good enough that the client felt safe to openly wear beautiful dresses to their appointments. The other positive outcome was that my colleague's dilemma got the entire group practice engaged in consciousness raising around gender diversity.

WORKING WITH DISENFRANCHISED PARENTS: THE BARRONS

Child-centered workers frequently find themselves in the position of delivering unwanted news or providing unsolicited services that elicit strong reactions from parents. You may recall that Linda Frost in chapter 5 was thrust rather unprepared into the difficult role of meeting with a family who knew she was there to investigate allegations of child neglect. She didn't quite know how to handle communicating with Mrs. Johnson, given the purpose of her visit with Kahlila.

Building positive and effective relationships with parents whose autonomy and parental authority have been overridden by outsiders is extremely challenging. How are relationships established when the worker is reinforcing decisions and actions that go against parents' desires and beliefs? How do attitudes of patience, flexibility, and respect collaborate or collide when parents' and workers' perspectives significantly diverge?

It is always the practitioner's responsibility to establish a foundation for positive and open communication. In some instances, constructing effective (and affective) rapport requires nurturing parents whose own relational needs have been historically unrecognized or unfulfilled. In these instances and others, setting the tone for alliances begins with acknowledging parents' reasons for mistrust and tolerating their understandably difficult feelings. It also involves enacting the qualities outlined above: being reliable, respectful, and honest in all communication, no matter how strenuous conveying information or reinforcing ground rules or boundaries may be. Maintaining positive relationships in difficult times further requires setting realistic expectations for yourself and knowing your limits. Workers must instigate a routine of self-care that provides ongoing, sustaining support.

The story of my work with the Barron family introduces an individualized method of relationship building with a family who was historically mistrustful of mental health outreach and social services. Although my time with them was in countless ways stressful for us all, I have no doubt that I learned as much, and maybe more, from them than they did from me. First and foremost they educated me about survival in the face of tremendous odds. They also solidified my belief in the strength of family ties. In the end they taught me a powerful lesson about the fragility of trust. From the Barrons

I learned that when families are battered by life, trust is established and reestablished one visit at a time.

I met the Barron family soon after their son Ben, thirteen, was sentenced to eighteen months in residential treatment in lieu of two years' incarceration at the juvenile detention center. The Barrons' participation in family treatment was a condition of this rehabilitative versus punitive treatment. Ben was assigned to Cascade Cottage, the residence for middle school boys at the Children's Home.

As the cottage social worker I was accustomed to working with challenging children and families. To prepare for meeting Ben and his parents, I combed through his thick case file to get a sense of the family's history. The Barrons had married young. Both had lived in foster care. According to the case files, Saul, Ben's father, age thirty-four, had severe cognitive disabilities due to brain injuries received as a young child. He dropped out of school in eleventh grade and since then had been an itinerant handyman.

Paula, age thirty-three, Ben's mother, earned a GED while pregnant with Wyatt, the Barrons' oldest child. At the time of Ben's admission to the Children's Home, she had a job as a part-time cashier for a big-box store.

Ben was the second of the five Barron children, ages three to fifteen. The youngest child, Maura, had Down syndrome. According to the records, Ben and Wyatt, fifteen, were both diagnosed with ADHD while in elementary school. The Barrons were firmly against having their children on stimulants and were skeptical about the validity of the boys' ADHD diagnoses.

A year before Ben's residential placement, the Barron family was evicted from their apartment. They could no longer pay rent and buy food with the limited money they earned, so they decided to try living in their car. From their perspective, they did so successfully: the children continued to attend school, and both parents worked as often as possible.

No one knew of their circumstances until a police officer saw the family asleep one night parked behind Walmart and reported them to CPS. With the aid of human services, the Barrons applied for and received subsidized housing, Medicaid, and food assistance. The children returned home from temporary foster-care placements to live with their parents. Saul enrolled in a job training program, hoping to become certified as a welder.

Overall I was impressed by the parents' ability to keep their family together despite the odds, and looked forward to meeting them. The Barrons, however, did not show up for their first two appointments at the Children's Home campus. Attempts to contact them failed because their phone was disconnected. Given that Ben's placement required the family's involvement in his treatment, I had no recourse but to do an unscheduled home visit.

On the way to the Barrons' home, I picked up doughnuts, thinking that perhaps they would soften the impact of an unanticipated visit. I knew the outcome of the meeting was iffy. If all else failed, I thought I'd have the doughnuts to soothe myself on the long ride home.

Paula answered the door. She seemed seriously perturbed to see me standing in the entrance. Saul was watching a small television in an almost empty living room. After several moments, I asked if I could come in. Saul yelled from the living room, "Let her in. She won't leave anyway." Paula turned away, and I followed. I had butterflies in my stomach.

It was early afternoon, and all the children except Maura were at school. She played contentedly with her toys, occasionally looking up and smiling at me. I handed Paula the box of doughnuts. "Congratulations on your new home," I said. "How's it working out?" Paula put the doughnuts on the small kitchen table. "Want coffee?" she asked. "Sure, thanks," I responded. Paula heated a kettle on the stove and spooned instant coffee into two mugs. Saul joined us at the table.

After some awkward small talk, I reminded them about the conditions of Ben's residency. Missing family therapy could jeopardize Ben's placement, I explained. I unfortunately had a legal obligation to report missed appointments to Ben's probation officer. "That's why I came to visit. It wasn't because I was checking up on you," I said.

Saul seemed suspicious of my explanation. He said that no one understood how hard it was for them to save money for gas and phone service. "People don't get it. They expect us to be at a million appointments a week," he said. "Our kids are in school, we have no child care, and Maura has in-home therapies three times every week. She can't miss that."

Saul went on to explain that he and Paula were working alternate hours so that the kids were never left alone. Paula interjected, "People don't care about how many responsibilities we have. They think we're screwups."

I sipped my coffee, trying to think of what to say next. "How can we make this work?" I asked with emphasis on the "we." Saul ate another doughnut. Paula spoke up. "If you judge us, we can't trust you," she said.

Her remark momentarily caught me by surprise—it was clear, simple, and deeply honest. I took a breath and responded, "I understand. It'll take time for you to trust me. No doubt we'll have our differences, and it's simply true that our relationship is not equal. But what we do have in common is we want Ben to succeed. So where do we start?"

Our dialogue had begun. By the end of that visit, we determined that for the short term I'd continue coming to their home. At the same time we'd both seek funding sources for gas reimbursement. We agreed to honor appointment times and let each other know when these needed to be rescheduled. When I left, the doughnuts were gone. As it turned out, I didn't need any for my trip home.

I visited weekly with the Barrons for nine months. Each time I brought doughnuts, played with Maura, and Paula made coffee. We spoke plainly and directly. Our time together had its moments, both good and challenging.

The parents shared stories about their upbringing and about the trials of raising five children. When conflicts occurred, it took time to restore the fragile trust we built.

But the Barrons were always available when I came to call. They gave honest consideration to my ideas, as I did to theirs. For my part, I showed up on time, called if I had to change anything, and followed up on all their requests for information.

Once Saul completed his training and got a welding job, the parents decided they could afford trips to the Children's Home. They took the initiative to set times that corresponded with Ben's free periods. Our meetings took place either before or after these visits.

When it came time for discharge planning, Paula and Saul informed me that they weren't yet prepared to handle Ben at home. Instead, they wanted to have him placed in a long-term therapeutic group home where he could get the supervision he needed. They didn't want him to backslide. This was not the outcome that I had initially hoped for; however, having come to know this family, I agreed that they knew best.

In retrospect Paula's statement "If you judge us, we can't trust you" served as a guidepost for our ongoing communication. When it came time for Ben's discharge, the parents knew themselves well enough to insist that he needed more structure than they could offer. They wanted what was best for Ben even if it meant having to be away from him longer. In a sense they advocated for Ben and for themselves and, in doing so, defined their own success as parents. They taught me about how love can be shown in many different ways and that relationship building, even when successful, doesn't always yield expected results.

SUMMARY

Establishing, strengthening, and maintaining relationships with parents regardless of culture, family structure, and circumstances is intrinsic to child-centered practice. Whether parents are ordinary, extraordinary, vulnerable, or challenged, their children's struggles are nevertheless deeply felt. Parents need us to believe in their abilities and the power of their love. When parents' abilities are not sufficient, efforts to support them should emanate from the knowledge that children do best when bonds to parents and family are acknowledged and respected.

Worker-parent relationships are built upon principles of respect, honesty, commitment, and trust, each of which is conveyed through mutual communication, transparency, and reliable action. The capacity to tolerate a range of strong emotions is vital when working to establish alliances with families, especially with those who have not yet experienced trusting relationships or who have been marginalized or mistreated by health, mental health, social service, and education authorities.

When parents feel respected, it is more likely that they will follow through on recommendations that will improve the lives of their children. When fully engaged in collaborative relationships, parents share in their children's success. Success builds confidence, and confidence helps parents offer children foundations for brighter futures.

Notes

1. Calvinism is a religion that held sway in the United States in the eighteenth century. It valued roles and expectations. The good child was characterized by compliance, gender-appropriate behaviors, and accomplishments. Social conformity and religious values, based in Christian traditions, set the standards for well-raised progeny.

2. The Fair Labor Standards Act regulating child labor was passed in the United States in 1938. By the early twentieth century most provinces in Canada had enacted labor legislation that restricted child employment. Although laws have been passed, child labor persists as an invisible social problem in both countries.

3. The US Health Insurance Portability and Accountability Act (HIPAA) of 1996 protects individuals' identifiable health information. The Health Information Protection Act (HIPA) of 2004 is Canada's version of HIPAA.

4. An undocumented (illegal) immigrant is a person who has entered the country without official authorization and has yet to become a naturalized citizen. Undocumented immigrants are subject to deportation. The term *person without status* may also be used to describe someone who has not been granted permission to stay in the country, has not attained citizenship, or has overstayed their visa.

5. This case study was developed from Feldman (2008).

References

Blanchard, R., Lykins, A. D., Wherrett, D., Kuban, M. E., Cantor, J. M., Blak, T., Dickey, R., & Klassen, P. E. (2009). Pedophilia, hebephilia, and the DSM-V. *Archives of Sexual Behavior, 38*, 335–350.

Blue-Banning, M. J., Summers, J. A., Frankland, H. C., Nelson, L. L., & Beegle, G. (2004). Dimensions of family and professional partnerships: Constructive guidelines for collaboration. *Exceptional Children, 70*(2), 167–184.

Brehony, K. J. (2009). Transforming theories of childhood and early-childhood education: Child study and the empirical assault of Froebelian rationalism. *Paedagogica Historica, 45*(4–5), 585–604.

Child Welfare League of America. (2002). *Position statement on parenting of children by lesbian, gay, and bisexual adults.* Washington, DC: CWLA.

Feldman, N. (2008). Exercising power from the bottom up: Co-creating the conditions for development with youth at an urban high school. *Families in Society, 89*(3), 438–446.

Jones, K. W. (1999). *Taming the troublesome child: American families, child guidance, and the limits of psychiatric authority.* Cambridge, MA: Harvard University Press.

Konrad, S. C. (2005). Mothers of children with acquired disabilities: Using the subjective voice to inform parent/professional partnerships. *Omega, 51*(1), 17–31.

Konrad, S. C. (2007). What parents of seriously ill children value: Parent-to-parent connection and mentorship. *Omega, 55*(2), 121–134.

Konrad, S. C., & Browning, D. M. (2012). Relational learning and interprofessional practice: Transforming health education for the 21st century. *Work, 41*(3), 247–251.

Longres, J. F., & Etnyre, W. S. (2004). Social work practice with gay and lesbian children and adolescents. In P. Allen-Meares & M. W. Fraser (Eds.), *Intervention with children and adolescents* (pp. 80–105). Boston: Pearson.

McAdoo, H. P. (2001). Parent and child relationships in African-American families. In N. B. Webb (Ed.), *Culturally diverse parent-child and family relationships: A guide for social workers and other practitioners* (pp. 89–106). New York: Columbia University Press.

Perrin, E. C. (2002). Technical report: Co-parent or second-parent adoption by same-sex parents. *Pediatrics, 109*(2), 341–344.

Richardson, T. R. (1989). *The century of the child: The mental hygiene movement and social policy in the United States and Canada.* Albany: State University of New York Press.

Stacey, J., & Biblarz, T. J. (2001). (How) does sexual orientation of parents matter? *American Sociological Review, 65*, 159–183.

Statistics Canada. (2011). *Gay Pride . . . by the numbers.* www.statcan.gc.ca

Turnbull, A., Turnbull, R., Erwin, E., & Soodak, L. (2006). *Families, professionals, and exceptionality: Positive outcomes through partnerships and trust* (5th ed.). Upper Saddle River, NJ: Pearson Education.

UN General Assembly. (1989, November 20). *Convention on the Rights of the Child* (United Nations, Treaty Series, 1577:3). Retrieved from http://www.unhcr.org/refworld/docid/3ae6b38f0.html

Webb, N. B. (2003). *Social work practice with children* (2nd ed.). New York: Guilford Press.

Wilson, K., & Ryan, V. (2001). Helping parents by working with their children in individual child therapy. *Child and Family Social Work, 6*, 209–217.

7

Play and Expressive Therapies

It is a happy talent to know how to play.

Ralph Waldo Emerson, *Emerson in His Journals*

THE RIGHT TO PLAY

Children across the world play. Though games, rituals, and toys may vary, play holds universal appeal and transcends cultures, nations, genders, and faith communities. Play is furthermore seen as critically important to early development. Evidence suggests that play and playfulness occupy pivotal roles in advancing the overall cognitive, emotional, and physical development of children of all ages and social environments (Bratton, Ray, Edwards, & Landreth, 2009; Schaefer, 2011). Lastly, play is a human right. No matter their circumstances, children have "the right to leisure, play and participation in cultural and artistic activities" (UN General Assembly, 1989).

To most adults, however, play is perceived as a luxury, not a necessity. For the most part its function is construed as recreational and seemingly aimless. However, children and child-centered practitioners would argue that play has many purposeful and powerful objectives. Benjamin Spock, noted pediatrician and author, observed that children love play not simply because it's easy, but also because it's such hard work. Children learn about the exigencies of life through play. They grapple with human relationship, master their fears, and contain their anxieties; they negotiate change; and when necessary, they use play to deal with expected transitions and unanticipated losses.

One has only to observe children in a day-care playground or playroom to see play at work. In the dress-up corner, you'll notice children of all genders playing the roles and responsibilities of caregivers and working through the meaning and functions of these relationships. Young children enjoy feeding baby dolls and changing their diapers. They are equally smitten with chastising them for making a mess or engaging in other activities that they themselves have been disciplined for at home. In another part of the playroom, preschoolers explore and release their normal aggression with dinosaurs and war toys, while others fantasize about being wizards and warriors, using wands and plastic swords to conduct their magical business.

Older children and youth channel unregulated energy into focused activities such as sports, theater, gaming, and martial arts. Intellectual competitions like debate and Odyssey of the Mind encourage children to use critical thinking and problem-solving skills in playful ways while teaching them how to collaborate and act respectfully toward one another.

Artful play provides boundless opportunities for children of all ages. It nurtures the creative spirit and cultivates imagination. Drawing and other visual arts legitimize the use of make believe giving children respite from their often trying lives. Art also affords children expressive outlets to convey difficult or silenced thoughts and emotions (figure 7.1). Worries and fears take on the shapes of monsters, snakes, and warriors; anxieties are portrayed as screaming bellies; and compartmentalized human figures reveal family tensions that might otherwise remain unacknowledged.

FIGURE 7.1   A four-year-old's scary monster

Play also fosters maturation, helping children integrate their inner and outer worlds. Children gain a sense of control and mastery over complicated and often incomprehensible experiences through playful activity. Play offers children opportunities to voice their views in their own ways and, at least for the moment, feel empowered in a disempowering, adult-focused world. One might say that, used wisely, play has the power to heal.

For child-centered practitioners, play offers opportunities to be both a participant and an observer in children's worlds. Child-worker relationships develop and grow through interactive play; whether actively involved or quietly watchful, practitioners are nevertheless always engaged in relational collaboration with children. Thus if play is children's work, then playfulness is an essential skill for those who work with children. Building relationship and communicating through play inevitably benefits and transforms both children and practitioners.

From the moment relationships begin, practitioners should inform parents that play is used as a therapeutic tool in their children's treatment. Explicit acknowledgment avoids the impression that children "do nothing but play" during their counseling or therapy sessions. This misinterpretation is akin to children's complaining that parents "just talk" in their meetings with workers. Child-centered practitioners frequently encounter criticism and skepticism from adults uninformed about play's therapeutic value and well-documented efficacy.

This chapter discusses the utility of play and expressive therapeutic approaches in child-centered practice. It explores the history of play therapy, its pioneers, and the principles that guide its use. A range of methods and applications for play therapy are discussed, and a detailed case illustrates how multiple methodologies can be effectively applied to a child-centered case.

The final section of the chapter addresses playroom design and toys, activities, and expressive devices used in play therapies. That section is not meant to be comprehensive: rather, it offers helpful ideas about tried-and-true therapeutic play materials for those working with children in their practices.

PIONEERS OF PLAY THERAPY

Most mental health practitioners are familiar with the legacies of Anna Freud, Melanie Klein, and Virginia Axline, but few are aware of the contributions of Austrian child psychoanalyst Hermine Hug-Hellmuth (also known by the name of Hug von Hugenstein), who introduced play into child psychoanalysis.

Hug-Hellmuth's contributions to the burgeoning child-therapy field were significant and varied (Plastow, 2011). She observed that play materials encouraged greater access to the inner workings and preoccupations of her child patients. These insights prompted Hug-Hellmuth to use play as a means of establishing relational connections with her young clients. She also instigated play as a method to enhance child assessment. Hug-Hellmuth also recognized the interdependency of child patients and their families and advocated the inclusion of parents in their children's psychoanalytic treatment.

Hug-Hellmuth's theories and practices are evident in the works of the child-centered clinicians that followed, most notably Melanie Klein, Anna Freud, and Virginia Axline. Klein and Freud were instrumental in distinguishing child-centered therapy as a separate field of psychoanalytic practice. This distinction was consistent with the emergence in America of child guidance as a psychiatric specialization.

Klein employed play to unearth and therefore better understand children's unconscious processes (Mason, 2003). In practice she observed child patients at play, assessed and interpreted these observations, and integrated her findings into therapeutic strategies used to help young patients work through their problems. Her style, though incorporating play, remained consistent with adult psychoanalysis, which insisted on the clinician's neutral and removed relational stance.

Unlike her colleague, Anna Freud viewed children's psychology as markedly different from that of adults. Freud appreciated play as a useful analytic tool and considered it a natural method for children to relate to the analyst. Through interactive play, children repaired inner conflicts and remediated problematic behaviors.

Freud also observed that children's play behaviors evolved and changed at expected developmental intervals, as did their symptoms. In 1933, after publicly stating his skepticism about child-centered analysis, Sigmund Freud, Anna's father, conceded, "The technique worked out for the adult must be largely altered for children. A child is psychologically different from an adult" (Donaldson, 1996, p. 169).

Against the trend of the times, Anna Freud took a somewhat relational approach in her work with children. She openly questioned the role of the neutral "opaque analyst" (Donaldson, 1996, p. 169), believing instead that child-centered work required engagement between children and clinicians. Like her mentor Hug-Hellmuth, Freud also sought to preserve, strengthen, and respect the integrity of the parent-child relationship. In the end, both Freuds agreed that child analysts played very different roles with child clients than with adults. In describing this conceptual change of heart, Sigmund Freud (cited in Donaldson, 1996) acknowledged that children greatly benefited when analysts and analysands were relationally connected.

Virginia Axline expanded the work of her child-centered mentors and colleagues. She was a student of Carl Rogers, who developed interpersonal therapies based on the concepts of person-centeredness and self-actualization (Rogers, 1942). Axline believed that children had natural propensities for play that could be used to solve problems and direct self-growth (Bratton et al., 2009). In Axline's view, play offered children opportunities to "play out" their feelings and problems in much the same way as adults in therapy "talk out" their difficulties (Axline, 1947, p. 9). Axline's theories of play in child-centered therapies are well illustrated by Oscar in chapter 4 and Abigail in chapter 5.

Play therapy is used today by a wide range of child-centered practitioners. It has been well evaluated and employs evidence-guided strategies to produce positive and enduring outcomes. Therapeutic play strategies are applied effectively to address an array of children's emotional, behavioral, relational, and social problems. Play therapy is conducted with individual child clients, in dyads, in groups, and with parents and families across settings.

EVIDENCE FOR THE ART OF PLAY

Engaging children in therapeutic work is important, given the increasing numbers of children in the United States and Canada who have mental health disorders. According to the US Public Health Service (Simpson, Cohen, Pastor, & Reuben, 2008), emotional and behavioral difficulties of children are among the leading health concerns of parents. In 2005–2006, nearly 18 percent of boys and 11 percent of girls had parents who sought out an educator or health-care provider regarding problems affecting their children's mental health (Simpson et al., 2008). In Canada one in five children and youth are identified with mental health disorders of enough severity to affect overall functioning and to warrant intervention (Waddell, McEwan, Hua, & Shepherd, 2002). Of this group the majority do not receive adequate and appropriate treatment.

Within the US group, approximately 50 percent of the children were prescribed medication, yet only 5 percent received directed therapeutic intervention. Problems inherent in medication-only protocols for children were identified more than a decade ago by the Office of the Surgeon General (US Public Health Service, 2000). Recommendations at that time suggested that access to nonmedication treatments be increased and that more research be focused on determining efficacious child-focused modalities for treating childhood mental illness.

Play therapy has been used for over six decades, and its variations are studied as a nonmedication or co-occurring child-centered therapy. Its utility is based on the premise that children are best understood from a developmental perspective (Wilson & Ryan, 2005), and that child-centered play therapies create optimal and empowering conditions for children to engage in their growth and healing (Bratton et al., 2009).

In 2005 Bratton and colleagues carried out a comprehensive meta-analysis investigating child-centered treatment modalities and their outcomes. They reviewed ninety-three controlled-outcome studies covering a span of fifty years. Their findings revealed that play therapy had overall benefits for children across ages and genders and that its gains were enhanced when used in tandem with other approaches, for example medication. Play therapies that included parents in child-centered treatments were seen as being particularly efficacious (Bratton et al., 2009).

Play therapy has mostly been investigated from the perspective of adults. Jo Carroll's (2002) study is one of a very few that used children to learn more about whether and how play therapy works. Carroll reviewed clinical case records and interviewed eighteen children (age nine to fourteen) and their play therapists. She found that children identified two factors as contributing to therapeutic success: having a positive relationship with a caring adult, and feeling a sense of control over the therapeutic process. Carroll also noted that having fun was central to children's perceived gains in therapy.

Play therapy has critics who say there is little evidence to validate its effectiveness. The studies that have been done are criticized for having methodological flaws, including small sample sizes. This critique could equally apply to studies of many clinical practice models, because qualities of human connection cannot easily be measured. Criticism, however, does not deter play therapy champions. Efforts to improve child-centered therapeutic outcomes will likely continue for another sixty years and beyond. For now, those practicing play therapy seem content to trust in its benefits and value the differences it can make in the lives of children and families.

GUIDING PRINCIPLES OF PLAY THERAPY

As noted throughout this chapter, play therapy occurs within the context of trusting relationships developed between children and workers and between workers and parents. What characteristics and attitudes do workers need to enlist the trust of children and their caregivers? How can workers build effective relationships with children who have been harmed by adults they know and love or by painful life circumstances beyond their control?

In her seminal work, Virginia Axline (1947) outlined eight guiding principles of play therapy that facilitate effective relationships with child clients. These principles have been expanded and personalized by experts in the play therapy field; however, the basic tenets have remained consistent.

- Genuine interest in the child, expressed in the context of a caring relationship
- Unconditional acceptance even when the child's behaviors are considered unacceptable

- Maintenance of a safe relational space that supports the child's ability to explore and express a range of feelings and behaviors
- Affective and cognitive responsiveness to the child's thoughts and feelings
- Recognition that children are resilient and active change agents
- Commitment to an individualized process that recognizes that children will at times direct conversations, while at other times workers guide the healing process
- Collaboration on rules for safety, with workers responsible for maintaining limits and structure
- Comfort with uncertainty, knowing that therapeutic work with children is an evolving process

These eight guiding principles focus on attitudes and behaviors generated and upheld by child-centered workers. They make up a set of intended standards, values, and practice principles and emphasize collaboration and respect as well as children's self-determination and agency.

APPROACHES TO PLAY THERAPY

Play therapy is recognized as a specialized treatment modality within the field of mental health.[1] Today the Association for Play Therapy in the United States, formed in 1982, lists over 4,500 mental health professionals who identify themselves as play therapists. The Canadian Association for Child and Play Therapy is the national play therapy organization for Canada.

Different approaches to play therapy have evolved throughout the years. These are often divided into nondirective approaches, directive or structured approaches, cognitive-behavioral play therapies, and sensorimotor approaches. Theories that guide these approaches vary, as do the purposes and goals of the interventions. However, play therapy approaches embrace common tenets and practices that are used by child-centered workers.

Nondirective Play Therapy

Psychoanalytic, nondirective play therapy was formally introduced in the writings and work of Anna Freud and Melanie Klein (see above). The earliest applications of psychoanalytic play therapy were similar to adult psychoanalysis in that they were not interactional. Psychoanalysts typically observed children's nondirected play activities, interpreted them, and classified what they symbolized. Children's perspectives were not considered in this interpretive process. Parents and other workers, for example social workers and psychologists, were also generally left out of assessment and treatment planning.

The goal of nondirective play therapy was to increase children's insights into their underlying conflicts. Psychoanalytic practitioners believed that greater understanding of children's inner lives would naturally lead to a reduction in maladaptive behaviors.

Nondirective play methods eventually expanded beyond psychoanalytic theories, embracing person-centered and interactional approaches. The therapeutic process shifted from one in which children were simply observed to one in which they were actively and relationally engaged. The value of children's perspectives also surfaced. Children were increasingly viewed as active agents in their change process. Those employing child-centered play therapy thus saw children's experience as a significant variable in sustainable and positive change (Bratton et al., 2009).

Adlerian play therapy (APT), an offshoot of nondirective play therapy, proposed that children's problems resulted from feelings of powerlessness and unworthiness rather than intrinsic pathologies. Alfred Adler suggested that the fundamental objectives of child therapy practice were to create a supportive relational environment where children feel accepted and therefore safe to experience, explore, and learn from their feelings (Porter, Hernandez-Reif, & Jessee, 2009). He envisioned that, once relational safety was established, children would rapidly gain insight into their previously unspoken thoughts and feelings. Similar to Anna Freud, Adler viewed child-centered play therapy as interactive and collaborative.

APT was one of the earliest models to integrate use of self and self-reflection into nondirective play therapy. Workers' ideas, feelings, and reflections were used to inform and provide insight into children's worlds. Empathetic connection was thought to prompt deeper inquiry, which in turn fostered richer understanding of issues confounding children's healthy functioning. Workers practicing with such reflexivity were also believed to be more in touch with how children's troubles affected their parents and families.

Nondirective play therapy approaches based in relational models are often criticized for their inapplicability to vulnerable and marginalized populations. Silin and Stewart (2003) argue that such models are not only compatible with the delivery of case management services but also enhance and sustain their effects. They contend that a reliable relational presence coupled with receipt of concrete sustenance and caring stimulates children's emotional and social growth, thus advancing the healing process.

Jemina's story reflects the benefits of using nondirective play with children from vulnerable and often misunderstood populations. I met Jemina, a thirteen-year-old, white youngster, while working in a residential treatment program. I was assigned to be her play therapist.

Jemina grew up in an isolated rural area where she lived with her father, brother, uncle, and two younger male cousins, all fishermen, in a large one-room cabin. Jemina's mother died when she was nine. Before coming into residence, Jemina left home only to attend school, and even that was sporadic. She had no known friends and few social skills. According to case records, Jemina's intellectual abilities were thought to be delayed, but she had never completed formal testing. In knowing her, I never questioned that she was deeply intelligent.

To say Jemina was initially mistrustful would be an understatement. For the first three months she refused to make eye contact or sit down in my presence. We made connection only when I brought her to the campus store to buy small necessities such as shampoo. Jemina seemed enchanted by these purchases. In conversations with her caseworker, I learned that she had little contact with women since her mother's death. Her dad, though caring, was not nurturing. Fortunately I had permission to take Jemina off grounds and was authorized to make necessary purchases. These weekly shopping trips became our relational ritual.

At thirteen Jemina was four inches taller than I and robustly framed. So when she began to run from me, it was difficult to catch her, let alone bring her back against her will. However, Jemina always paused and waited for me to catch up with her. I quickly realized that this pattern was not about leaving; it was about joining. Jemina ran because she wanted to be assured that I would run after her.

Our rituals to some degree fulfilled Jemina's need for tangible (buying small items at the campus store) as well as affective (running and joining rituals) evidence of caring. It took time, but the presence of a reliable relationship helped Jemina transform her beliefs about relational trust and worthiness. She became stronger, more connected, and though still equivocal, she came to appreciate that people cared for her.

Directive Play Therapy

Directive or structured play therapy is an active and goal-directed method that aims to help children release emotions and tensions brought about by negative early and ongoing experiences. In directive therapy, practitioners are "participant-observers" who facilitate play in a meaningful way. Gil (1991) emphasized that to be therapeutic, play must be guided, not random. Thus it is not the play itself that produces therapeutic change, but the therapist's management of the play.

Directive play therapy requires in-depth knowledge and understanding of the child's history and present problems. This is necessary so that the play therapist can connect themes or images in the child's play to real-life situations and, by doing so, help her enact and work through anxieties and problems. Strong and cohesive therapeutic alliances are required before engaging with children in therapeutic reenactments of traumatic events. Positive and safe relationships limit the likelihood of exacerbating or adding to the traumas children have already experienced.

The benefits of using directive play in work with traumatized children are well documented (Gil, 1991; Webb, 2007). It is not unusual for children to suppress memories of abuse; they work hard to avoid unbearable feelings in order to function in their day-to-day lives. The role of play therapists is first to gently help children unveil traumatic material and then to facilitate their retelling of the incident or events. Guided by workers, children then use specific play activities to work through feelings and responses associated with the trauma. These eventually reduce their emotionally disruptive impact and ultimately help children assimilate them into their lives in meaningful ways.

Cognitive-Behavioral Play Therapy

Cognitive-behavioral play therapy (CBPT) is based on the belief that changes in thinking lead to changes in feelings and behaviors. CBPT practitioners seek to understand the core beliefs that guide children's problematic actions. Then they work with children to develop strategies that will reduce and ultimately ameliorate behaviors through the use of positive reinforcements. Unlike nondirective and directive play therapies based in psychodynamic theories, CBPT therapists are typically unconcerned with the meaning or affect attached to behaviors. Instead interventions are aimed at extinguishing behaviors that interfere with children's day-to-day living. Play is thus a means to an end.

CBPT is particularly successful with children whose anxieties and fears hamper overall functioning. Children's anxieties can severely interfere with learning, impede social functioning, and disrupt family relations. Childhood anxiety disorders are manifestly different than those of adults, because of developmental differences. Techniques and language for CBPT are therefore modified to accommodate a child's age and maturational level.

Wagner (2003) provided an excellent example of CBPT designed for children diagnosed with obsessive-compulsive disorder (OCD). RIDE (R = rename the thought; I = insist that *you* are in charge; D = defy OCD; E = enjoy your success) up and down the Worry Hill uses an easy-to-visualize acronym to help play therapists explain CBPT to children in child-friendly language. Wagner describes the process to children in this way: "Learning how to stop OCD is like riding your bicycle up and down a hill. At first, facing your fears and stopping your rituals feels like riding up a big 'Worry Hill,' because it's tough and you have to work very hard. If you keep going and don't give up, you get to the top of the Worry Hill. Once you get to the top, it's easy to coast down the hill. But you can only coast down the hill if you first get to the top" (p. 294).

Using the RIDE model depicted in figure 7.2, practitioners encourage children to face their fears and use "self-talk" and other strategies to reduce and reshape negative and fearful thoughts. If children succeed, pride naturally follows. Self-confidence reinforces the use of similar strategies to manage other sources of anxiety and fear. Not only are referring problems addressed, but children and families also take home useful strategies.

Sensorimotor Approaches and Play

Sensorimotor approaches (SMA) focus on helping children gain control of their physical, cognitive, and emotional regulatory responses (Ogden & Minton, 2000). Problems in regulation affect children's abilities to control impulses, delay gratification, and tolerate frustration. SMA is effectively used with children who have experienced early and ongoing trauma, interfamilial violence, and attachment failures. SMA is also effective when working with

FIGURE 7.2   RIDE: up and down the Worry Hill (Wagner, 2003)

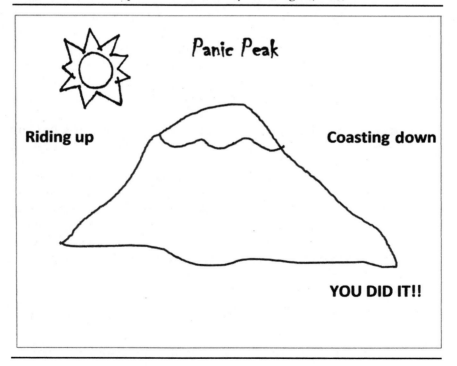

children who are predisposed to attentional difficulties and have neurological or developmental problems that affect their ability to manage impulsivity.

According to Ogden and Minton (2000), children who struggle with self-
regulation are triggered by everyday occurrences that remind them of previously traumatizing experiences. They are also easily disorganized and
distracted by these situations. Behaviors commonly seen include inattentiveness, hypervigilance, problems with redirection and change, and an inability
to self-soothe. Children with impulse or attentional difficulties but with no
trauma history may also express these behaviors.

A basic SMA used by child-centered workers is the "window of tolerance" (WOT; Ogden & Minton, 2000). The WOT focuses on helping children
modulate their hyper (high) or hypo (low) reactions to perceived or felt
danger. Johnny, age ten, offers an example of hypervigilance that disrupts
his regulation. Whenever he hears police sirens, clocks, or fire alarms, even
at a distance, Johnny becomes viscerally anxious and fearful. This is because
his body is recalling times when the police came to his home because of
family violence.

Although living in foster care and physically safe, Johnny still reacts
strongly to these images and sensory imprints. At school he is distracted and
unable to do his work because he is anticipating the next loud noise. As a
result, he may hide under his chair to avoid the sound, which causes flashbacks or visual memories of the violence he witnessed.

Kirree, age sixteen, supplies us with an illustration of hypoarousal.
Repeated sexual assaults by her mother's partner left Kirree highly mistrustful of the world. She responds to these feelings by self-medicating or sleeping whenever she can. When faced with unfamiliar social situations, Kirree
withdraws or tunes out. This is problematic for teachers and other adults
responsible for her education and socialization.

Using the WOT, youngsters are encouraged to identify feelings and
experiences that cause them to enter into states of hyper- or hypoarousal.
Together workers and children determine strategies, for example self-talk,
yogic breathing, or meditation, that might help reestablish affective equilibrium, returning them to a calmer state. Children are also taught methods to
identify situations or events that cause them to unravel. When able to predict
dysregulation, children are better prepared to keep themselves calm. Parents
and home caregivers are also taught strategies to help children moderate the
intensity of their responses. As in the case of DeShaun (chapter 5), modulation techniques are used, for example, drawing a thermometer that measures
mood and using it to name emotions and regulate them.

Games are increasingly being used as biofeedback mechanisms and
socializing agents aimed at helping children modulate and manage anxiety,
reactivity, and stress (Wilkinson, Ang, & Goh, 2008). Interactive video and
Internet games are effective in helping youth take charge of symptoms

resulting from conditions such as ADHD, ASD, anxiety, and other life-altering medical and psychiatric conditions.

Overall, SMA encourages youth to anticipate and prepare for emotionally challenging situations and cultivate self-efficacy by teaching skills for life. These approaches inspire hope for children and youth whose early lives and predispositions have left them without effective self-regulation and communication skills. One caveat to their usage is that workers must be specifically trained in sensorimotor models and other biofeedback approaches to use them responsibly.

Play Therapy Meets the Dodo Bird Verdict

The dodo bird verdict refers to the common-factors theory posited in 1936 by Saul Rosenzweig, a psychologist. It suggests that differing theories and approaches can result in equally successful treatment outcomes when therapeutic alliances are good and when clients are motivated. Rosenzweig got the title for his theory from Lewis Carroll's (1865) story *Alice in Wonderland*. At one point in the narrative, the Dodo observes multiple characters using different means to achieve the same ends. Being who he is, he makes the pronouncement, "Everybody has won, and all must have prizes."

Rosenzweig's (1936) theory suggests that several different therapeutic methods, when applied thoughtfully and strategically, achieve better outcomes than adherence to a single approach. The application of multiple approaches must be systematic, never random. Moreover, evidence-guided therapies should be integrated into the treatment plan to address conditions that are responsive to their implementation.

Lydia's unique situation illustrates a thoughtful integrative therapeutic process. Born in Vietnam, Lydia was adopted by the Taylors, a white, middle-class family, when she was sixteen months old. She was soon joined by an adoptive sister, Liah, just one month her junior. During her initial well-baby visit, the pediatrician noted that Lydia was malnourished, and X-rays further revealed previously broken bones. Despite her early disadvantages, Lydia rapidly grew to meet expected developmental milestones, and with the exception of being extremely shy, she seemed by all accounts to be doing well.

Lydia's musical talents developed early. By age ten, she was playing the violin in the youth symphony and composing music for her middle school orchestra. Her talents and intellectual precocity, however, served as a smoke screen for underlying anxieties and fears. Outside of her schooling and musical activities, Lydia spent most of her time at home in her room. She depended almost exclusively on her mother for social and emotional comfort. She avoided her father and sister altogether.

At first the Taylors explained Lydia's behaviors as a by-product of a difficult infancy. When Lydia was nine, however, Mrs. Taylor was diagnosed with progressive relapsing multiple sclerosis (MS). Her motor functions deteriorated rapidly, and she was hospitalized seven times in the first year of her diagnosis. Liah and Mr. Taylor rose to the occasion, but Lydia's functionality declined. She was afraid to leave the house, her sleep was fitful, and she stopped playing the violin.

Needless to say, it was hard for the Taylors to get Lydia, now eleven, to my office. There were several canceled appointments; Lydia simply refused to see a "nut doctor." She insisted that she was not crazy—just worried about her mother.

When I finally met Lydia, I was impressed by her poise and charm. In our early alliance-building sessions, I employed nondirective play therapy. Lydia selected the activity, which was most often drawing horses and rainbows. As we got to know each other better, she frequently chose modeling clay to sculpt small animals and human figures, which she always brought home. More often than not I would do an activity alongside her—sort of a parallel play activity. Lydia would ask me about my drawings and sculptures, which opened the door for me to ask about hers.

Let's for a moment step outside the case description and reflect upon the reasoning for choosing a nondirective therapeutic approach with Lydia. Children must be prepared for the hard work of change, and I was mindful that in Lydia's case her readiness would be predicated on whether a secure connection was made. Solidifying and strengthening this connection increased the likelihood that Lydia would find motivation to engage in the next therapeutic step.

Furthermore, nondirective play allowed me to be both an observer and participant in Lydia's therapy process. I became familiar with themes and patterns in her play and with the qualities and characteristics that made her uniquely Lydia. At the same time, I solicited from the Taylors as much information about Lydia's pre- and postadoption history as possible. Knowing past and current life stories prepared me with knowledge that we would later address in the treatment process.

As Lydia became comfortable in our relationship, I decided to approach her about doing a directive art exercise to relieve her anxiety. She was tentative at first, but as I explained my ideas, she became animated and engaged. Her assignment was to draw her worries. I felt secure asking her to do this because she had initially identified herself as worried, not crazy. She took to this task with an intensity I had not observed before in her play.

Her first drawing was a self-portrait, which filled a large (14 × 16-inch) sheet of white paper. Surrounding the portrait were words and phrases indicative of her worries, such as "Mom is too sick," "no one likes me," and "afraid to be alone." In another session I asked her to draw a picture to show me where her worries lived. She situated her worries in her belly, which didn't surprise me, as her father reported Lydia missed many days of school due to stomach pains. On her own, Lydia started making small clay figures of people, which she would then cut with a sculpting tool. When asked about this, Lydia said that her mother's body was "being taken away from her." She also felt that she was being "cut in half by her worries and fears."

Lydia's artwork and expressive activities provided language that we used to give voice to her worries and concerns. I asked her what it felt like being "cut up inside and out." Lydia responded by saying how afraid she was that MS would cause her to lose her adoptive mother. She had never been told what had happened to her biological mother but assumed the worst. Mostly she lived in fear of losing the only mother she had ever known.

Following this powerful exchange, Lydia built a heart out of red clay. She showed me the heart and then took the clay tool and cut it in half. She looked at me and said, "People who love me go away—it breaks my heart."

There was no doubt that Lydia's worries were valid; at the same time, she needed effective skills to manage life's realities, including her mother's increasing debility. Together Lydia and I developed a three-step treatment plan. The first step was based in cognitive-behavioral theory, the second employed narrative techniques, and the third was constructed from elements of social learning theory.

An underlying principle of CBPT is to concentrate attention and efforts on things that are within a person's control and to find acceptance for things that are not. The first step in Lydia's treatment plan was designed to effectively lower the volume of negative and fearful thoughts by using self-talk. Lydia chose to work on the core belief that she was unworthy of a mother's love. She made a pack of laminated cards, each with an affirming message that combated this powerful negative message (e.g., I am loveable). This method worked well because she had immediate access to alternative ways of thinking when she needed them.

The second step was for Lydia to name and then externalize her worries, a method used in narrative therapies. Lydia named her negative and fearful core beliefs "gloomy thoughts," and she identified ways in which she could lessen their impact (e.g., listen to music, draw a picture of them, talk to someone rather than keeping them inside). We put together a notebook, and every time she successfully pushed away "gloomy thoughts," she put in a sticker or affirming message (figure 7.3). Lydia and her parents developed a list of rewards, which she received upon successfully warding off gloominess.

The third step of the plan was informed by social learning theory. It posits that when people receive positive feedback about themselves from those they admire, change happens. Thus the final step for Lydia was to spend time with people whom she liked and respected, other than her mother. This was the hardest step yet, because she had to first push away

FIGURE 7.3 Lydia: "Here I come!"

"gloomy thoughts" (narrative) and remind herself (CBPT) that she was worthy even though she could not control her mother's health.

Gradually Lydia made positive connections with several peers as well as an adolescent mentor from the youth symphony. At the same time, she became closer with Liah, and they discovered that they both loved to cook. This in turn helped lessen some of the day-to-day pressures on Mrs. Taylor, and both girls felt empowered.

About nine months into the work, Lydia unexpectedly decided to end therapy. The precipitous ending illustrates that in real-life practice one does not typically have the luxury of meeting all desired goals. At first Lydia agreed to meet periodically, but after two such meetings, she reported that she was just too busy for therapy. In retrospect I chose to believe that this statement indicated a successful outcome.

The case described above illustrates the dodo bird verdict well. Positive outcomes in Lydia's case resulted from many factors. These included the establishment of a positive working alliance, Lydia's motivation to improve the quality of her life, and the use of varying approaches attuned to her evolving therapeutic needs. In the end, *everybody won, and we all got rewards.* Lydia's were perhaps most tangible. They included a growing community of friends, closer family ties, fewer stomachaches, and new skills to address present and future worries.

ENDINGS WITH CHILDREN

As is clear from Lydia's case, workers do not always get time to prepare for therapeutic endings or what is sometimes referred to as *termination.* Unlike family and friendship relationships, therapeutic relationships are meant to end. It is the worker's responsibility to anticipate and plan for endings when possible. This is to ensure that children understand why the relationship is coming to a close. It also allows enough time for children to feel some control over the ending process.

When endings are positive, they foster smooth transitions that highlight what children and families have accomplished. When they are unplanned or precipitous, children may believe that they have done something to cause the relationship to end, or they may altogether lose trust in the relational process. For children who have experienced hurtful and multiple relational losses, positive therapeutic endings are especially healing. Parents too benefit from termination that is anticipated, worked through, and constructively completed.

Having ample time to anticipate and plan for positive termination is ideal, though in reality endings may be planned or unplanned, precipitous, elongated, or simply unexpected (Walsh, 2007). Endings with children are affected by factors outside of the relationship. Children who work with school social workers or counselors expect that their time together will end according to the school calendar. On the other hand, children's therapeutic ties are sometimes precipitously disrupted. This occurs when foster placements unexpectedly change or when parents are relocated for reasons such as military service, job changes, or divorce.

Economic factors also affect termination timing. Reimbursement sources and agency policy often prescribe the number of sessions allotted for mental health treatment. Thus children may be deeply entrenched in therapeutic work when insurance or agency protocol cuts them off. Unemployment or other financial strains may also affect parents' ability to pay for services. Some agencies are flexible about sliding scales; others are not.

Workers prepare children for endings right from the beginning of the therapeutic relationship. When the length of intervention is predetermined, workers inform children and families of the time line ("I'll be coming for six weeks. I'll let you know each time how many meetings we have left"). If the therapeutic contract is open-ended, workers factor in set times to evaluate how things are going ("You've done really well managing your anxiety. Let's talk with your mom about meeting for another four weeks to make sure you've got these strategies squared away"). At these junctures, workers and parents estimate the next time frame and share it with children.

Joseph Walsh (2007) offers guidelines that help workers structure conversations in anticipation of endings. Although not specifically designed for children, they nonetheless provide a framework that can be developmentally informed and applied (see box 7.1).

In child-centered practice, workers solicit feedback from both children and families about what worked and what didn't. Workers' feedback should identify growth ("Remember when you got angry all the time? Now you have ways to quiet those angry feelings") and provide incentive to continue using proven methods ("You've done a wonderful job helping Josh structure his day. How are you going to continue with that?").

The feedback loop also includes what workers and children learned from each other. When wrapping up with Saul and Paula Barron (chapter 6), I was quite clear in telling them how much they taught me about family ties and strength in the face of adversity. They said that I had taught them that not all social workers are "bleeding hearts."

The range of emotions and behaviors experienced by children in preparation for endings is considerable. Workers inform parents and caregivers about what to expect and remind them that they too may have similar

---

BOX 7.1
Guidelines for Endings

- Share understanding that relationship is ending.
- Provide opportunities for child-worker-family feedback.
- Identify what children, families, and workers have learned from each other.
- Identify and name expected feelings.
- Plan for anticipated, expected responses.
- Plan and support ways to maintain change.
- Develop a plan in case problems resurface.
- Support investment in and transitions to new relationships.

Modified from Walsh, 2007, pp. 41–59.

responses. Avril, age thirteen, was definitely angry about ending our relationship. She didn't understand why we couldn't be friends after I stopped being her shrink. Conversely Vance, age eleven, was ecstatically happy when he found out he no longer had to come to appointments. In fact he and his foster family decided to end his sessions earlier than planned because his behaviors had improved. Sadness may also accompany endings. Claudia, age nine, tearfully told me that our relationship gave her faith that she could survive other losses.

Productive termination includes a plan in case children regress or lose skills gained through the counseling experience. In some instances I scheduled what I called "tune and lube" sessions, extending the ending process over a period of time and seeing the child every three weeks, then every six, and so on. When children continued to do well, families ended sessions before too long. The extended time period, however, allowed children to return without disruption if problematic behaviors resurfaced.

Sometimes endings occur because children are transitioning to new workers. This can result from an anticipated or unexpected change in residence. Transitions also take place because workers retire, are ill, move away, or take new jobs. Dissatisfaction over timely outcomes may also prompt parents to end treatment. Although reasons affect the meaning and process of termination, in the end workers must support transitions with positive handoffs and willingness to provide the next clinician or caseworker with whatever information they deem necessary.

TOOLS OF THE TRADE

Webb (2003, p. 149) defines play therapy as "caring and helping interventions with children that employ *play* techniques." Play therapy techniques are used in a variety of clinical, school, and community settings and complement a range of theoretical orientations. What they have in common is twofold: respect for the exigencies of childhood, and tools that can be used to enhance communication and help children build skills for life—tools of the trade.

The Playroom

A well-constructed play space promotes children's autonomy and problem solving. Workers should have enough toys and art materials to stimulate play activities but not so many that children are overwhelmed. Materials that have many parts or are messy should be out of sight. They can be brought out at supervised times or when children have exhibited self-mastery or are being rewarded for having achieved desired goals.

Once children choose their materials, workers allow time for play to evolve. Some give-and-take is expected. Spills and scattered toys are the norm. When play activities dissolve into chaos, however, it rests on the shoulders of workers to restructure and redirect ("Lyle, it's not OK to break the crayons. If you break them, we won't be able to use them. Let's try using just a few crayons at a time and see what happens").

Workers expect that children *will* lose emotional and behavioral control during therapy sessions. Observing problematic behaviors—knowing what triggers them and seeing firsthand what does and does not work—allows us to gain vital knowledge about children's real-life struggles. Parents and caregivers often apologize to workers when children exhibit their most difficult selves. I assure them that witnessing problems rather just reading or hearing about them is extremely instructive. It helps develop strategies that are more likely to fit children's individualized needs and produce better outcomes.

The therapeutic environment, like secure relational attachments, allows children to try out behaviors, fail, and try again within the confines of acceptance. Children may balk at redirection, but at the same time they appreciate structure. Workers do well to balance flexibility with clear, well-modulated, and enforceable boundaries ("I'm sorry you're angry. Being angry is OK. Breaking things is not. Let's find something softer you can throw that won't damage anything"). In the playroom, children can be themselves and gain pride in their growing ability to function productively in the world.

Playroom rules are established in the very first session. Rules apply to how play materials are used as well as to how people are expected to treat one another. Children may add to basic safety guidelines. They should be written and in plain sight so that children who are able to read can see them. Images can be used for nonreaders. For many youngsters it is necessary to restate the rules many times.

Workers provide specific materials for children to use when angry or distressed. Some child-centered settings have rooms where children can safely express strong feelings (see the Volcano Room, chapter 11). When Jake, age seven, had difficulty controlling his body and started hitting or banging up against the wall, I brought out the large inflated yoga ball. Initially I helped him roll on the ball while acknowledging his pent-up feelings. Over time Jake would let me know when he needed the yoga ball to let the anger out of his body.

Rules addressing behavior toward one another are particularly important when conducting child-centered groups. An undisputed rule is that hurting one another either physically or with words is not tolerated between group members. Ideally group members contribute to rule making and determine some of the consequences of rule breaking.

Tasha, age nine, lost her group privileges a number of times because she could not control her hurtful words or hands. Calling Kylee names and pinching Polly violated the group's established norms. Each week, however, members welcomed Tasha back and gave her a fresh start. Over time she came to understand the benefits of behavioral control and friendship. Positive feedback from the other girls was affirming to Tasha. When Polly complimented her on not swearing during group time, Tasha beamed with pride.

The following vignette offers an example of the effect of playroom rules on the behaviors and insights of one child. Vanessa, a petite Caucasian eight-year-old, came to our first session dressed from head to toe in pink. A recommendation for counseling had been made by her second-grade teachers, who described Vanessa as "a lot of work." Looking at this tiny youngster, it was initially hard to imagine what trouble she could cause.

Underestimating Vanessa's willfulness was my first mistake. My second was not establishing the playroom rules with her before she flew into action, and the third was leaving the glitter vials in her line of vision. Soon after entering the playroom, Vanessa noticed the glitter and glue sitting on the art-supply shelf. Without missing a beat she made a beeline for them, and within fifteen seconds she had emptied both on a pink sheet of 8 × 10-inch construction paper. Two more glitter dumps quickly followed.

I calmly commented on Vanessa's artwork, stating the obvious, "You seem to love glitter and glue."

"You're mad at me," she responded.

"Well, I'm not exactly mad," I said. "But I'm a little surprised by how fast you could use all that glitter and glue."

"I know," she replied. "I just can't help myself."

Here was the opening I was waiting for. "Let's start over," I said. "I promise that after we talk you can get back to your artwork."

Vanessa sat down, legs dangling from the couch. "Only for a minute," she complied.

I asked Vanessa what happened to her when she was unable to control herself at school and at home. She answered that she was always in trouble. "No one likes me," she said.

"Well," I replied, "it's our job then to figure out ways that you can learn to control yourself and keep trouble out of your life." I went on, "One of the first ways trouble is controlled is to know the rules of the playroom. If you know the rules, it will keep trouble away from our time together."

I asked Vanessa if she wanted to read the rules or if she'd rather I did. She read them competently: Do not hurt anyone with your hands or words; use appropriate language; be respectful toward others; listen when someone else is talking; do not break or destroy toys or playroom materials; remember supplies are here for everyone's use—make sure you leave some for others. "Now," I said. "Let's see how the rules might help you play with glitter and not make anyone mad." Vanessa jumped off the couch and proceeded to use the glitter and glue generously but not in the previously frenzied manner. I complimented Vanessa on her improved control and then helped her carry the seeping glitter works to the car where her mother was waiting for her.

Vanessa and I used playroom rules to keep trouble from finding her in the playroom. As you can see, I employed a narrative technique like that used with Lydia, that externalized "trouble" as something that found Vanessa, not something that defined her or that made her "a lot of work."

Vanessa keenly struggled with impulse control, so at least in the beginning, it was my job to keep the playroom activities structured and maintain clear limits and guidance. Glitter and other materials that were hard to control were kept in a locked cabinet for supervised use. She was permitted access to any and all other toys and supplies.

Most of the time Vanessa was responsive to reminders to check the rules, and we developed an additional strategy we called "rules of the road." These included receiving up to three warnings to stop a troublesome behavior before she was directed to put on the brakes. If she was unable to brake, then she lost glitter time. When she put on the brakes before getting out of control, "glitter time" was her reward.

At one point Vanessa decided that playroom rules might help stave off trouble at home. We invited her mother and grandmother, who lived with Vanessa and her two siblings, into the playroom. Together they designed a behavior plan using the brake metaphor and setting a goal of keeping "trouble" from visiting their apartment. Vanessa later reported that her little brothers needed to put on the brakes more than she did.

It took significant determination, but over six months, Vanessa managed to integrate playroom rules into everyday behaviors. Her tool kit for success included a three-step plan for deceleration (stop—breathe—brake) and a strong desire for affirmation and success. We also employed a modified WOT schema that helped Vanessa quiet her anxious feelings, which we learned triggered anger and impulsivity.

Vanessa did not transform from a feisty eight-year-old to a demure and perfectly regulated child. She did, however, learn skills to keep trouble at bay most of the time. She enjoyed being in control of her behaviors because as a result she made friends and, as she told me, they loved glitter too. Her family was pleased with her progress. Behavioral strategies learned in the playroom translated well to home and were appreciated by the adults caring for Vanessa and her boisterous brothers. Teachers now portrayed Vanessa as "an active and curious youngster who likes to follow the rules," a much kinder and gentler description than their earlier one, "a lot of work."

Play Materials

Toys, games, and expressive materials are vehicles to encourage meaningful interaction and conversation. They are a means to an end and thus should not be so complicated as to interfere with therapeutic goals. Intricate puzzles, for example, may be too absorbing for therapeutic utility. Games that have complex rules may take too long to be worthwhile tools. The following sections describe toys, games, and expressive materials that are commonly used in therapeutic playrooms.

Board Games

Board games are part of the culture of childhood, providing opportunities for adults and children to share playful and sometimes competitive experience. Early on in child-centered practice, D. W. Winnicott (cited in Oren, 2008) described game play as a ripe opportunity for children's emotions, thoughts, and attitudes to be expressed and received by adults.

Board games are sometimes used as informal mechanisms to assess children's developmental, regulatory, and relational strengths and challenges (Botha & Dunn, 2009). Workers observe the quality of children's play to evaluate how they tolerate frustration, enlist coping strategies, regulate disappointment, and respond to winning and losing.

Board games help children build adaptational skills. They facilitate and strengthen coping and foster cooperation and effective communication. Proficiency and confidence are enhanced as children acquire strategies to navigate a range of feelings and behaviors. Once developed, these are transferable to other situations in children's lives.

Board games are a natural mechanism to model how to parley natural tensions brought about by victory and defeat. Rules are followed unless the worker and child agree to extend their parameters. The emotional and behavioral consequences of game outcomes are managed within the context of reliable and mutual relationships.

Relational negotiations arose during games involving an eleven-year-old adjusting to residential care and his social work counselor. Antoine's counselor Steve observed that the youngster consistently miscounted the number of spaces advanced (always to his advantage) when they played the board game Sorry. Steve took the opportunity to reflect upon Antoine's strategy and asked him if he realized that he was breaking the rules. Antoine was defensive at first, called Steve out—"Man, are you accusing me of being a cheater?"—and got up to exit the playroom.

Steve calmly responded that if it was important for Antoine to win, he was more than willing to negotiate new rules—they just had to make this decision together. Antoine sat down. The two proceeded to discuss his overriding desire to win at games. Antoine admitted that the kids in the residential program refused to play with him. "They don't like that I throw the game right across the room if I'm losing," Antoine confessed. In the end they decided that when tensions surfaced during game playing, Antoine would let Steve know, and together they would determine what to do next.

There are a number of games designed to address common therapeutic issues such as divorce, illness, social communication, and behavior management. Perhaps the most well-known of these therapeutic games is the Talking, Feeling, and Doing Game (TFDG), designed by Richard Gardner, a child psychiatrist. The ostensible goal of TFDG is to earn more chips than your opponent. The therapeutic goal is for children to answer affect-related questions or engage in regulatory skill building or imaginative activities that lend insight into their worldview.

Child-centered workers disagree about the utility of therapeutically designed games. Some believe they prescribe children's responses to life situations. They would prefer nontherapeutic games that allow for children's feelings and behaviors to emerge within genuine, open-ended contexts. Other workers find therapeutically oriented games helpful because they normalize difficult situations for children and name feelings that they might otherwise not be able to articulate. In either case, workers have a wide variety of board games to select for their practice.

Imaginative Play

Dolls and puppets allow children to "play out" their experiences and concerns. Young children especially enjoy this form of play. Dolls and puppets encourage them to be candid, because they are telling their stories in the third person.

Toys used for expressive play should be durable, so that children can use them without restraint and workers aren't consumed with their maintenance. Gender-specific as well as gender-neutral toys should be on hand. It is common for children to use figures and puppets of people and animals to enact family and friendship dramas as well as traumatic events. A varied supply of characters and small toys stored on shelves or in bins is a good addition to the playroom.

Daria, age seven, used these types of toys well. She was referred for therapy because she was having nightmares stemming from an incident of sexual abuse when she was five. She particularly liked to play with the plastic dinosaurs that were kept in a large basket in the playroom.

About three months into play therapy, Daria took all the biggest dinosaurs and lined them up across the room. She then took all the small ones and did the same. She repeated this for several weeks until finally one day she shifted her ritual and used the small dinosaurs to get rid of all the big, bad dinosaurs.

For two months Daria systematically triumphed over the big dinosaurs, and as she did, her smile broadened. Her mother said that after these sessions, her daughter seemed lighter and less burdened. Daria never directly spoke about the abuse. However, dinosaur play seemed to have helped her work through some very difficult issues, leaving her feeling empowered and satisfied.

Many children enjoy playing with dollhouses. Dollhouses should be solid and furnished with inexpensive items because these often disappear from the playroom. Dollhouse people include racially and gender-diverse adults, babies, and children, as well as pets. The rooms should not be elaborately decorated, so that children can add their own objects and décor.

Children also love theater. As actors in their own productions, children reveal important emotional material and demonstrate how they make meaning of critical life events. Costumes and props add to role playing. Magic wands, wizards' hats, and crystal balls permit children to venture into their fantasies. Gear from professions, such as medical stethoscopes, firefighter boots, military and police paraphernalia, and other symbolic clothing, stimulates expression and allows children to reenact events from real-life crises.

Storytelling and Bookmaking

Children benefit from being the authors of their own stories. This is because all too many feel unheard and silenced in their lives. Some have disenfranchised stories to tell.

Books, blogs, scrapbooks, and oral storytelling make life histories tangible and are especially powerful for children who experienced early relational disruptions and losses. Foster and adopted children, for example, benefit from documenting the history of their prior and ongoing lives. Whether fictive or real, storytelling helps children and youth share their unique perspectives with important people in their lives. Bookmaking and writing are sometimes used with dying children to ensure they leave behind their legacies. They want to know that they will be remembered.

Children and families profit from telling stories together. Opportunities for adoptive parents to witness positive transformations in their children's negative inner stories are remarkably and mutually healing (Lacher, Nichols, & May, 2005). Alternatively, parents can retell their children's stories in ways that reshape their meaning.

Violet was abandoned by her mother when she was two years old. She went to live with a non–Native American foster family, where she was well cared for but did not flourish. When Ruthanne and Ben Francis from the Passamaquoddy tribe on the Maine/Canada border adopted Violet at age four, she was extremely withdrawn. Together the couple told Violet stories about how loons called for them many times to find her and give her a home. They taught Violet how to imitate the cry of the loon, so that whenever she needed them they would come. Loon stories became Violet's story of transition into the family who would be hers for life.

Sand Play Therapy

Sand play therapy is a complicated therapeutic approach that requires proper training to implement its best effects.[2] The following is a rudimentary description of its usage; you can learn more about sand play by participating in professional training sessions.

At its most basic, a sand tray is a box of fine sand where children arrange selected objects. The choice and placement of these objects are considered indicative of a problem or situation the child is attempting to make visible or bring to conscious awareness. Sand play therapy allows children to construct, deconstruct, and reconstruct their worlds by arranging and rearranging the figures in concert with play therapists (Russo, Vernam, & Wolbert, 2006; Turner, 2005).

Some children attach stories to their sand play, while others conduct their activities in silence. When invited, workers engage with children in putting together the sand tray display. While doing so, they might ask questions about children's choices and actions. They may also simply watch as the construction unfolds. Some children destroy their sand tray productions at the conclusion of each session; others request that their sand tray be saved or photographed so that they can pick up where they left off in subsequent sessions.

Sand play has also been used effectively to assist parent-child communication. In the play session, the practitioner might invite the child to describe his or her installation and solicit inquiry, feedback, or participation from the parents.

As with any expressive activity, workers must be careful not to rush to interpret children's sand tray installations. Instead they invite children to talk about why they chose to include and position their objects in certain ways. Specific questions are best ("I'm wondering about the knight you put in the corner. Can you tell me about why you put him there?"), or workers might ask children if their sand trays have stories to tell. Some children enjoy documenting their sand tray episodes in narrative form. Doing this helps keep a record of how children's designs transform over time.

Art Materials and Activities

Expressive activities promote opportunities for children and workers to engage in a process of creation and discovery. Children express difficult feelings and take risks in their paintings, drawings, sculptures, and comics. Making art reinforces children's mastery and sense of control over their emotions and impulses. Group art activities, such as mask making, provide opportunities for peer connection, reflection, and conversation. Within group settings, children can individually construct their masks, depicting their public personas on the outside and private selves on the inside (figure 7.4). Once the masks are completed, group members share them and reflect upon similarities and differences in the results.

Worry boxes, dolls, and cards help children manage strains and anxieties. Children decorate small wooden or cardboard boxes and then deposit their worries inside. These can be representational, written on paper, or symbolically inserted. Children can make worry dolls with a range of materials. They use them to self-soothe during trying times.

Affirming messages or behavioral guides can be made into laminated cards that accompany children during their day. They serve as tangible assurance that children can manage their feelings. Over time, card messages may

FIGURE 7.4 Mask from child-centered divorce group (courtesy of Kids First Center)

be internalized and integrated into adaptive behaviors. If you recall, Lydia carried laminated cards to help stave off negative self-thoughts and replace them with positive messages.

The terra-cotta pot exercise assists individuals with grief work. A clay pot is placed in a paper bag and gently hammered, and the broken pieces are saved for reconstruction. The pot is then reassembled and decorated (figure 7.5). Breaking the pot represents how losses leave us shattered. Reconstructing the pot reminds us that losses, though painful, nevertheless have the potential to transform us in unexpected and beautiful ways.

Interactive art activities are also used to communicate. The Squiggle game, for example, begins with drawing a squiggle line. The worker then invites the child to make something out of it. This can also happen in reverse, with the child drawing a squiggle for the worker to complete. This game promotes give-and-take, offers opportunities for children to be expressively playful, and occasionally yields insight into children's thoughts and feelings.

Artworks are employed for both formal and informal assessment. Family drawings are perhaps the most commonly used method to gain knowledge of a child's perspective. It is illuminating to observe who children include in their family drawings; what materials they use; and the shapes, sizes, and spacing of family members. In some instances, children use symbols rather than people to represent members of their family. One youngster I worked with chose snakes to convey the personalities of his family members.

FIGURE 7.5 Terra-cotta pot reconstructed by student in grief course

Understanding children's family drawings requires collaboration with child clients, to avoid the tendency to prejudge their meanings. Children's drawings are influenced by fine-motor coordination, developmental skills, and the materials that are supplied. Thus what seems meaningful—for example, leaving out a family member or using only a red crayon—might not be relevant.

However, children may share important information through their artwork that would otherwise not have been uncovered. What does figure 7.6 tell us? When I asked Robin, age twelve, to tell me about her drawing, she was circumspect. She said, "I'm not sure—but I just noticed that I didn't include myself. What do you think that means?" I responded, "Well, I don't exactly know, but you put a lot of detail into the people and things you did include. You're quite a good artist."

"Thank you," she said. "But you wouldn't know that if you talked to my parents." I waited a moment and then asked, "What do you mean?" We went on to have a long conversation about how being a creative person didn't count for much in Robin's high-functioning family. "Ray, my brother is a science nerd. He gets all the good attention," she told me.

I learned a considerable amount from talking with Robin about her family drawing. This knowledge, combined with other assessment tools, led to

FIGURE 7.6   Dinner with the Moreys

the development of an effective formulation of Robin's concerns and a useful intervention for Robin and her family.

Artwork also conveys children's inner struggles and pain. Lydia was able to depict debilitating worries through directed artwork exercises. DeShaun's radioactive plant conveyed the inner combustion he felt, which would likely never have been expressed in words. Drawings can also convey the depths of children's psychological suffering. The drawing in figure 7.7 is

FIGURE 7.7 A young child's world of conflict

by a seven-year-old child later diagnosed with a serious psychiatric condition. One can see worlds in conflict in this portrait of a flower—a beautiful and painful expression of this young child's distress.

SUMMARY

Play has innumerable functions for children. Children communicate through play, and they learn coping and adaptive skills by way of playful activities. Guided therapeutic play offers opportunities for children to candidly and uninhibitedly express themselves. Stories that were previously unspoken or silenced come to the surface in drawings and theatrical productions. Anxieties are quieted and contained in boxes or in the hearts of worry dolls. All of these expressive activities take place in a safe and accepting environment where children's perspectives are respected and workers genuinely attempt to make sure that they understand those perspectives.

Playfulness is requisite for relational child-centered practitioners. Through well-paced and informed playfulness, workers gain access to the inner lives of children. There are many tools of the trade to engage children in their healing process. Listening and responding, genuine engagement in playful endeavors, and responsiveness to spoken and nonverbal communication enhance the effectiveness of the play therapy experience. In the end, it is within these reliable and trusting child-worker exchanges that meaningful change takes place.

Notes

1. The link for the Association for Play Therapy in the United States is http://www.a4pt.org/. The Canadian Association for Child and Play Therapy can be found at http://www.cacpt.com/site/. Both organizations promote better understanding of play therapy and its utility for supporting children's emotional, social, and behavioral well-being.

2. Sandplay Therapists of America can be accessed at http://www.sandplay.org/.

References

Axline, V. (1947). *Play therapy*. New York: Ballantine Books.

Botha, E., & Dunn, M. (2009). A board game as Gestalt assessment tool for the child in middle childhood years. *South African Journal of Psychology, 39*(2), 253–262.

Bratton, S. C., Ray, D. C., Edwards, N. A., & Landreth, G. (2009). Child-centered play therapy (CCPT): Theory, research, and practice. *Person-Centered and Experiential Psychotherapies, 8*(4), 265–281.

Carroll, J. (2002). Play therapy: The children's views. *Child and Family Social Work,* 7, 177–187.

Carroll, L. B. (1865). *Alice in Wonderland*. London: Macmillan Press.

Donaldson, G. (1996). Between practice and theory: Melanie Klein, Anna Freud and the development of child analysis. *Journal of the History of the Behavioral Sciences, 32,* 160–176.

Gil, E. (1991). *The healing power of play: Working with abused children*. New York: Guilford Press.

Lacher, D., Nichols, T., & May, J. (2005). *Connecting with kids through stories*. London: Jessica Kingsley.

Mason, A. (2003). Melanie Klein, 1882–1960. *American Journal of Psychiatry, 160,* 241.

Ogden, P., & Minton, K. (2000). Sensorimotor psychotherapy: One method for processing traumatic memory. *Traumatology, 3*(3), 149–173.

Oren, A. (2008). The use of board games in child psychotherapy. *Journal of Child Psychotherapy, 34*(3), 364–383.

Plastow, M. (2011). Hermine Hug-Hellmuth, the first child psychoanalyst: Legacy and dilemmas. *Australasian Psychiatry, 19*(3), 206–210.

Porter, M., Hernandez-Reif, M., & Jessee, P. (2009). Play therapy: A review. *Early Child Development, 179*(8), 1025–1040.

Rogers, C. R. (1942). *Counseling and psychotherapy*. Boston, MA: Houghton Mifflin.

Rosenzweig, S. (1936). Some implicit common factors in diverse methods of psychotherapy. *American Journal of Orthopsychiatry, 6*(3), 412–415.

Russo, M. F., Vernam, J., & Wolbert, A. (2006). Sand play and storytelling: Social constructivism and cognitive development in child counseling. *Arts in Psychotherapy, 33,* 229–237.

Schaefer, C. E. (2011). *Foundations of play therapy*. Hoboken, NJ: John Wiley and Sons.

Silin, M. W., & Stewart, H. M. (2003). Mother Bear: A relational approach to child therapy. *Clinical Social Work Journal, 31*(3), 235–247.

Simpson, G. A., Cohen, R. A., Pastor, P. N., & Reuben, C. A. (2008, September). *Use of mental health services in the past 12 months by children aged 4–17 years: United States, 2005–2006* [Data brief]. Centers for Disease Control and Prevention, National Center for Health Statistics.

Turner, B. A. (2005). *The handbook of sand play therapy*. Cloverdale, CA: Temenos Press.

UN General Assembly. (1989, November 20). *Convention on the Rights of the Child* (United Nations, Treaty Series, 1577:3). Retrieved from http://www.unhcr.org/refworld/docid/3ae6b38f0.html

US Public Health Service. (2000). *Report of the Surgeon General's Conference on Children's Mental Health: A national action agenda*. Washington, DC: Department of Health and Human Services.

Waddell, C., McEwan, K., Hua, J., & Shepherd, C. (2002). *Child and youth mental health: Population health and clinical service considerations*. Vancouver: Mental Health Evaluation and Community Consultation Unit, University of British Columbia.

Wagner, A. P. (2003). Cognitive-behavioral therapy for children and adolescents with obsessive-compulsive disorder. *Brief Treatment and Crisis Intervention, 3*(3), 291–306.

Walsh, J. (2007). *Endings in social work practice*. Chicago: Lyceum Books.

Webb, N. B. (2003). *Social work practice with children* (2nd ed.). New York: Guilford Press.

Webb, N. B. (2007). *Play therapy with children in crisis: Individual, group, and family treatment.* New York: Guilford Press.

Wilkinson, N., Ang, R. P., & Goh, D. H. (2008). Online video game therapy for mental health concerns: A review. *International Journal of Social Psychiatry, 54*(4), 370–382.

Wilson, K., & Ryan, V. (2005). *Play therapy: A non-directive approach for children and adolescents* (2nd ed.). Toronto: Baillière Tindall Elsevier.

8

Working with Adolescents

Adolescents are not monsters. They are just people trying to learn how to make it among the adults in the world, who are probably not so sure themselves.

Virginia Satir, quoted in Louise Hart, *The Winning Family*

NO LONGER CHILDREN

Adolescence is characterized by both subtle and intense personal transformation. In American and European cultures, adolescence typically begins at twelve or thirteen years of age and ends between eighteen and twenty-one. Under certain circumstances and in non-Western cultures, adolescence can be longer or shorter than this.

During this developmental span, individuals are in flux as they gradually relinquish their childhood and take on tasks and expectations of adulthood. The term *autonomous relatedness* has been used to describe the dynamic tension that takes place when adolescents seek to differentiate themselves from others while remaining dependent on the adults who care for them (Bettmann & Jasperson, 2010). At the same time as adolescents seek autonomy from parents and caregivers, however, they seek connection and identification with peers and other adult role models.

As might be expected, adolescence is confusing and stressful because of the complex and interacting cognitive, physiological, relational, and psychological changes that naturally occur during this time of accelerated growth. Adolescents are vulnerable to a range of challenges, yet one should not assume that their struggles will necessarily lead to behavioral or mental health problems. For the most part, adolescents navigate their developmental transition with few if any significant problems. Moreover, despite popular stereotypes, most adolescents maintain positive and respectful connections with their biological, foster, or adoptive family and to their culture and community.

Some adolescents do come to the attention of mental health practitioners and other child-centered professionals. Depression, substance misuse, eating disorders, and self-harming behaviors are common mental health problems for teens. Some adolescents seek help for social and emotional distress caused by perceived failure to meet the expectations of their peer groups. The window of acceptance is often narrowly defined, yet acceptance is critically important to the development of adolescents' healthy identity. Youth who do not conform may be subjected to bullying and other forms of disenfranchisement. Gay, lesbian, and gender-nonconforming teens are frequent targets of bullying, as are overweight youth and those whose do not otherwise meet the standards of the popular culture.

Adolescents also look to supportive adults when their lives take sudden and unexpected turns. Such transitions occur for losses from death, divorce, or other family disruptions. Teen pregnancy also precipitates life-altering changes. These unanticipated life circumstances catapult adolescents from the known world of childhood into the unfamiliar territory and responsibilities of adulthood. Although most youth adapt to their revised life situation, it may be difficult for them to take full advantage of the benefits of this time of life.

One must be careful not to make assumptions about an adolescent based on age-related stereotypes. There is great variability in how youngsters negotiate adolescence and in the social expectations that confront them. Each possesses unique abilities, vulnerabilities, and temperamental proclivities; each has distinctive connections to family, cultural networks, and community resources.

This chapter brings up mental health and systemic issues pertinent to adolescents, as well as to their relational needs in the context of friendships, home, and community. It introduces a child-centered program that successfully reintroduces formerly disenfranchised youth to education through an experiential course on community-based sustainable agriculture. This program highlights how to build on adolescents' natural resilience and desire for relational connection.

GREAT EXPECTATIONS

Adolescence is an exciting time of high-velocity growth and exploration. It is a life stage of firsts: going to the mall with friends, getting a driver's license, luxuriating in that first kiss, getting a job, and feeling the agonies of heartbreak. Adolescents' brains absorb knowledge at a rapid pace; thus inspiration, creativity, and altruism flourish as young people gain insight into the beauty and perils of the world around them. Adolescents can be optimistic and view the possibilities with great expectations. They can also worry about the meaning of life.

While adolescence is seen as a time of increasing autonomy, self-awareness, and maturity, it can also be a time of poor decision making, risky behaviors, and psychological vulnerability. Like people of all ages, some adolescents are more resilient than others: while most adolescents cope sufficiently in the face of adversity, others find the rigors difficult to negotiate. Even when supports are available, some young people cannot effectively adapt to the stressors they face. Depression, anxiety, self-harming behaviors, suicidal thoughts, eating disorders, and addictions are some of the mental health problems adolescents experience when stress becomes too great. Antisocial behaviors may also ramp up in adolescence.

Rapid-fire biophysiological changes contribute to the internal and external upheavals of adolescence. Outside influences create uncertainty, and it is common for teens to receive both positive and negative messages from multiple and continuous forms of face-to-face and virtual communication. Direct input from parents, teachers, coaches, classmates, and siblings may foster adaptation or provoke disorientation, depending on the content and tone of the messages received. For example, setting a high performance standard can impel some young people to strive for academic and professional success whereas others can find these expectations overwhelming and discouraging.

It is important to recognize that even well-meaning adults can misinterpret young people's words and actions. Adolescents are often unpredictable, and adults' expectations can exceed their capacity to respond appropriately. As Geldard and Geldard (2010) aptly note, adolescents are in a process of growth and are more likely than not to make mistakes along the road to adulthood.

From a relational standpoint, adults too often assume that adolescents require less nurturance and support than younger children. This misperception is difficult for young people, because although they are moving toward independence, they still require the emotional and environmental safety nets that adults provide. Though parents need to gradually encourage opportunities for autonomy, they also need to maintain guidance and structure, knowing that the adolescent, though no longer a child, is not yet an adult (Geldard & Geldard, 2010).

It is sometimes difficult for parents to decide when to yield to adolescents' requests. Bob and Winne Spinner agonized over whether to let Micah, fifteen, call in sick on the day of his biology exam. Winne explained, "His anxiety was over the top. On the other hand, one can't always be excused when life gets too hard." The parents decided not to let Micah off the hook. "We held our breath all day waiting for the phone to ring with pleas to come home," said Bob. But in the end Micah took his exam, got a B-, was displeased with the outcome, and survived.

Relationships with family and other significant adults are instrumental during this transitional time. Reliable connections ensure that mistakes and false starts are met with understanding and guidance. Studies indicate that relationships with caring, reliable adults promote resiliency and predict psychological health in youngsters, including those who face adversities (Laursen & Birmingham, 2003; Spencer, Jordan, & Sazama, 2004). Given the preeminence of adult support in adolescents' lives, it is important for adults to be well informed about factors that underpin adolescent development and to be prepared for the ups and downs of their relationships.

PHYSICAL AND COGNITIVE CHANGES

Adolescence is perhaps best characterized by uneven and rapid growth in multiple developmental domains. *Puberty* is the term used for the physical changes that occur in adolescence. Such changes are most evident in the maturation of secondary sexual characteristics, such as breast development and the onset of menses in girls, and facial hair and ejaculation in boys. As in all areas of development, young people's physical maturation is variable. Some girls begin menstruation as early as nine years old, whereas others may not begin until their late teens. Boys may begin shaving in middle school or lack facial hair until well after high school.

Acceleration in hormone production during puberty stimulates adolescents' emerging awareness of sexual feelings. Some adolescents will experiment with their sexuality, while others explore the relational elements of intimacy through close ties with friends. During this time young people confront issues of sexual orientation and gender identity. Although younger children may have a sense of these, adolescents begin to seriously examine them.[1]

Youth who identify as heterosexual and gender conforming typically have fewer familial and social struggles than those who identify as gay, lesbian, bisexual, transgender, third gender, or questioning (GLBTQ). Although American and European cultures are generally becoming more tolerant of sexual and gender diversity, GLBTQ youth still face significant social and relational marginalization in schools and in the greater peer-group culture. Adults, including mental health practitioners, assume heterosexuality; most do not ask about sexual orientation or gender identity unless it is a referring question or the teen chooses to disclose. As one teen told me, "No one says to their counselor, I should probably tell you that I'm heterosexual." GLBTQ adolescents also fight for acceptance within their families. For some these battles lead to depression, and unfortunately GLBTQ youth have substantially higher suicide rates than heterosexual adolescents of the same age.

Puberty also has psychosocial repercussions for adolescents. Differences in physiological growth influence emotional, relational, and social development, especially when youth experience precocious puberty or when sexual maturation is significantly delayed. Either extreme can cause youth to be self-conscious. Sometimes maturational precocity, such as sudden changes in body shape and size, impacts adolescents' self-concepts. Pubescent girls may struggle with weight gain and become ashamed of their appearance. This can lead to problems with eating or other weight- or body-related issues. Boys also experience body insecurities, for instance, due to deepening but undependable voices and unpredictable arousal responses that cause them to have erections at highly awkward times. Like girls, they are concerned about how they look and, more importantly, how they are perceived.

Peer victimization is a significant risk factor for mental health problems. Approximately 10 to 20 percent of youth in the United States report frequent episodes of peer victimization; bullying is also seen as a major problem among Canadian youth (Pepler, Craig, Yuile, & Connolly, 2004). According to researchers, teens who are considered overweight or obese are less likely to have friends, are more susceptible to depression, and feel less worthy than their average-weight peers (Dave & Rashad, 2009). GLBTQ and gender-nonconforming youth are also subjected to bullying at higher rates than those assumed to be heterosexual.

At the same time that adolescents are contending with changing bodies, they are experiencing rapid cognitive growth. Positive aspects of the brain's newfound agility include increasing capacity for abstract thinking, which enhances the ability to consider multiple perspectives. This increasingly allows young people to anticipate the future and imagine a number of possible outcomes to situations they may face (Geldard & Geldard, 2010). Abstract thinking is also instrumental in the formation of empathy, which includes the capacity to reflect upon the views of others and envisage what it might feel like to be in their shoes. Advancements in cognitive sophistication, however, are unreliable at best. Adolescents' capacity for reason and abstraction fluctuate, which is a constant source of frustration to the adults who care for and work with them.

Adolescence is sometimes known as a period of existential contemplation. Deep reflection leads some youth to ponder profound concepts and the meaning of life. Acquisition of abstract thinking, however, is not necessarily accompanied by maturity in emotional development. Thus some young people may feel despair, anxiety, and fear as they consider their present and future prospects. Similarly, cognitive growth is not always consistent with other areas of adolescent physical, social, and emotional development. Teens are notorious for challenging adult authority while demanding to have their tangible needs met by the very same adults. They can be articulate, charming, and generous on some occasions and irrational, egocentric, and unyielding on others.

Such cognitive and behavioral inconsistencies are being explored in brain research. Neuroimaging reveals that the brain develops variably and, for some youth, is not fully formed until their midtwenties. In particular, the prefrontal cortex, the parts of the brain that mediate such functions as organization, anticipation, planning, working memory, impulse control, and mood modulation, grows at different rates. Because the brain is evolving, young people may seem to have more control over their thoughts and behaviors than they actually do. This can be explained in part by neurological immaturity.

This is not to say that all relational stresses and strains are the result of innocent brains; power struggles are generated from many sources. Neuroscience knowledge, however, helps some adults make sense of adolescents' bumpy developmental road. It leads to understanding that prepares them to have realistic behavioral expectations and to remember that adolescents are growing children and not immature adults.

Finally, some young people may be physically mature but have accelerated or delayed intellectual development. Some of these youngsters have permanent neurological differences (e.g., youth with Down syndrome or with ASD). Gifted youth experience highly advanced intellectual growth but may be immature in other developmental domains. Not unexpectedly, these adolescents have some difficult times because people assume that they are more reliable, capable, and autonomous than they are. As such they are judged by unreasonable social, emotional, and academic standards, many of which they can't possibly meet.

Jonah and Martha, both sixteen-year-olds, provide us with two very different examples of maturational inconsistencies leading to confusion in behavioral and social expectations. Both children advanced rapidly in their physical development; however, Jonah was intellectually precocious whereas Martha was cognitively delayed. Thus people would become impatient with Jonah because his verbal and intellectual skills made it appear that he was more capable of controlling his behaviors than an average youngster. As he got older, Jonah's regulatory system caught up with the advances in his intellectual development, and he was highly successful in high school.

Martha's cognitive and social abilities never caught up with her advanced physical maturation. At sixteen she looked to all intents and purposes like a young woman, but her intellectual and social understanding of the world lagged far behind. Teachers were frustrated by what they interpreted as her "resistance" to learning. Boys made advances she didn't quite understand. Unlike Jonah, Martha's high school experience was neither academically successful nor socially satisfying. Her parents ultimately homeschooled her, and she is now living successfully in a group home with other young adults.

PSYCHOLOGICAL DEVELOPMENT

Parallel to surges in physical maturity is the adolescent's developing sense of personal identity. Accordingly, teens and emerging adults are vigorously engaged in the process of figuring out who they are. They try on potential identities, learn about love and relationships, and grapple with what they hope to do with their futures. Ethnicity, race, sexual orientation, gender identity, family stability, faith, and culture are among the many factors that influence how youth negotiate their identity and life choices (Jensen, 2003).

Individuation refers to the adolescent drive to become relatively independent from the family. The growing ability to take on adult roles and responsibilities represents tangible proof of growing maturity. Adolescents are also keen to establish separate identities from their caregivers. Similar in many ways to rapprochement for toddlers, adolescents test out their individuality while simultaneously staying connected to those they love and trust. Though attracted to same-age relationships, youth continue to need reliable bonds with their parents and other significant adults. In fact, studies show that adolescents tend to go to biological, adoptive, and foster parents, not peers, when they need support, guidance, affection, and connection (Wilkinson, 2004).

The journey toward adulthood is varied, rich with stylistic and behavioral diversity. As young people mature, they discover what aspects of themselves are unique and what elements of self are formed from a sense of belonging to or identification with family, ethnic traditions, and community. As mentioned earlier, most adolescents traverse their teen years uneventfully; however, some are extreme in their need to individuate. They are rebellious and disagreeable, which contributes to friction and distress in their home and in their school and community relationships.

Adolescent uncertainties and culture clashes may also arise due to differences in social, economic, ethnic, and cultural norms and family expectations. For example, immigrant and refugee youth may be caught between the cultural expectations of their families and the pull of their new country's developmental rites of passage. Similarly, youth from socioeconomically disadvantaged groups or from families who need their physical or economic contributions may find themselves torn between their pursuit of personal identity and their obligations to family. Thus cultural and family values may be discordant for those adolescents trying to balance the desire to belong to peer groups with honoring religious and family commitments.

Hodge (2002) writes about this predicament for Muslim youth, noting that Muslim families do not generally presume that adolescents will seek independence, because of the value that is placed on family in their culture. Those working with Muslim adolescents as well as other culturally or religiously diverse populations should therefore investigate how adolescents in these cultures balance family ties with peer affiliations and outside commitments.

Theories developed in the context of primarily white, Western worldviews perceive children's separation from family as intrinsic to healthy development. Many well-adjusted youngsters, however, prefer to remain connected with their families and choose colleges or jobs that permit them to stay geographically close to their communities. Some also live within their original communities to contribute economic and social support to their family members. Other adolescents simply need more time than their peers to achieve a balance of autonomy and connectivity.

This was true for Althea, age seventeen, a star soccer player and gifted science student at her city high school in Baltimore, Maryland. To her teachers, coaches, and classmates, Althea, an African American teenager, seemed to have it all. She was bright, athletic, and popular across social groups. She received awards and recognition for her accomplishments.

Althea was also indispensable to her family. She helped around the house and was a faithful source of economic support. Althea's boss of four years sang her praises. He noted that she was responsible and cherished by the bodega's customers.

Yet Althea had never slept away from home and, according to her mother, crept into bed with her most nights. She didn't seem interested in obtaining a driver's license, explaining that she wasn't ready to take on the responsibilities of adulthood. Althea was being recruited by colleges across the country. Their letters and phone messages remained unanswered, however, as she wrestled with the concept of being away from her mother, brothers, extended family, and faith community.

Althea's mother and grandmother struggled with how to respond. Her mother urged Althea to be strong and assertive. She wanted better for her daughter than she had had for herself. On the other hand, she viewed the world as a dangerous place. In their neighborhood, six people had been killed in the past eight months as a result of gang violence. Thus she was understandably strict with her only daughter.

Althea's grandmother was of a different opinion. She cautioned Althea's mother to "let the child be." She believed that Althea's judgment was good; she had her feet on the ground and held Jesus in her heart, and that was enough for her. Mother and grandmother often argued about Althea's welfare, and this heightened Althea's anxiety and intensified loyalty conflicts in the family.

Althea's story brings up several important points. First, though bright, engaging, and talented, Althea's temperament was shy and reserved, perhaps even somewhat anxious. In effect she led a double life: in public she was viewed as capable and accomplished; in private she was seen by her family as vulnerable and dependent. It is likely that Althea will need to make peace with these equally valid parts of herself in the future. It would be important for someone working with Althea to appreciate her multidimensionality and the duality of the feelings she experiences.

Culture and context also play significant roles in Althea's world. She receives mixed messages from significant others about independence and interdependence, autonomy and safety, and assertiveness and vulnerability.

Culture is defined in Althea's case as traditions set forth by her family and by the ethos of her community and faith. It is also influenced by factors of racism and classism that exist in the broader society. As a result Althea faces tough decisions about how to differentiate her own beliefs, values, and desires from those that have been instilled in her by others.

Finally, Althea has experienced danger and death in her community. It is therefore not surprising that she has fears about moving on to a world without known comforts and protections. One cannot build an effective relationship with Althea unless one genuinely respects the context of her life.

PEER AND SOCIAL PRESSURES

Among many factors integral to identity formation is assessing how one measures up against others. This includes considering where one fits in relation to friends, families, and, increasingly, media images. The Internet and social networking offer seemingly endless options for adolescents to feel connected and communicate their thoughts and feelings to and about each other. Although mostly positive, technology can also lend itself to misuse. Cyberbullying, the act of harassing or stalking someone via social networks and texting, is one such inappropriate application. Because Internet and smart phones are so prevalent, they are ready tools for cyberbullies.

Unrelenting harassment erodes confidence in even stable youngsters. However, teens who already have emotional and social strains are particularly vulnerable to cyberpeer aggression. Some become so distressed that death becomes their only escape (Hinduja & Patchin, 2010).

Adolescents bump up against many other obstacles to healthy identity formation. When youngsters compare themselves to impossibly thin or airbrushed celebrity images, it's possible that their idealized self will fall short of their self-appraisal. Girls compete to eat the least and stay the thinnest. Some are tortured by inner voices telling them that they are fat, ugly, unloved, and undesirable. As experts say, eating disorders have little to do with weight management and everything to do with control. When young women feel that they have little control, staying thin may be the only way to exert their power. Unfortunately, some lose control rather than gain it. Eating disorders have the highest mortality rate of any mental illness and thus warrant immediate and directed intervention when detected.

Boys are not exempt from becoming dangerously obsessed with body image. An estimated 10 to 15 percent of people with anorexia or bulimia are males (South Carolina Department of Health & Human Services, 2006). Scott, a young man of thirty, recalled how as a teen he would exercise compulsively to stay fit. He toyed with steroids and at one point became so thin that he was hospitalized. Upon reflection, Scott acknowledged that he had something to prove as an adolescent. His father was absent. His brother was the apple of his mother's eye. Scott felt invisible most of his childhood, and building his body was the intended goal. Now a father himself, Scott recognized that his choices were unwise, and he was grateful for having survived his ordeal.

Similarly, acceleration of academic and athletic achievement in our culture has risen to significantly high levels. In some peer cultures the drive to excel above one's peers creates serious internal and external pressures. Micah (see above), whose parents insisted he take his exam on time, was one of those teens whose self-worth was highly reactive to whether he could keep up with his high-achieving peers. Such pressure subjects some youngsters to almost intolerable states of self-doubt. When harsh self-appraisal is reinforced by negative messages from peers and/or adults, it creates a perfect storm for internalized hatred, self-harm or suicidal ideation, and clinical depression.

MENTAL HEALTH PROBLEMS IN ADOLESCENCE

Risk for mental health problems escalates when young people lack adult support or have histories of relational disconnection, loss, and trauma. This section presents an overview of mental health conditions experienced by adolescents.[2] It is not within the scope of this book to cover all psychiatric conditions, nor is it possible to recommend a broad range of treatments. However, it is important for child-centered practitioners, who inevitably will assess, refer, and treat adolescents, to be familiar with common mental health conditions that they may face.

Like all people, adolescents experience both internal and external reactions when confronted with expected and unexpected life transitions. In most circumstances they experience transient symptoms of sadness, irritability, impulsivity, or lowered self-worth, which ameliorate with little or no intervention. However, there are cases when the stresses young people face are bigger than their capacity to deal with them. At these junctures school counselors, social workers, and other mental health practitioners are called upon to respond.

Depression

Depression is the most prevalent mental health concern for adolescents in America. Depression ranges from mild to severe and is characterized by mood impairment and loss of interest and enjoyment in life's activities. Adolescents express depression in a number of ways; for example, they may appear moody or sad, or they may be uncharacteristically irritable, impatient, or inattentive.

Depression may be precipitated by clear-cut circumstances, or it may emanate from internal sources. According to Dave and Rashad (2009), younger adolescents tend to show anxiety-like behaviors when depressed, including fearfulness, separation anxiety, and psychosomatic symptoms, whereas older adolescents are apt to isolate, self-medicate, and have difficulties with sleep and eating disorders. They may also become intensely existential. Negative and apocalyptic thinking is often expressed through poetry, music, and visual arts. Whatever its source and expression, depression significantly affects youths' overall well-being, impacts interpersonal relationships, and impairs academic performance.

Young people are good at camouflaging depression. Many of its manifestations coincide with what are considered normative adolescent behaviors. Teens are known to be feisty, moody, and withdrawn, but when such behaviors persist and interfere with everyday functioning, they may indicate depressive illness. Early intervention with depressed adolescents is critical: first to relieve their immediate suffering, and second to curb their use of alcohol, illicit drugs, or self-harming gestures that run the risk of becoming unhealthy lifelong coping devices.

Multiple modalities are used for treating depressive illness in adolescents. The cautious use of medication, along with positive therapeutic relationships, is helpful to adolescents struggling with depression (Dave & Rashad, 2009; McCarthy, Downes, & Sherman, 2008). Evidence-guided methodologies such as cognitive-behavioral and sensorimotor approaches have good results with youth whose depression is expressed by impulsivity, aggression, and negative rumination (Miller, Glinski, Woodberry, Mitchell, & Indik, 2002). Moreover, young people report that parents' involvement in any form of counseling and psychotherapy is instrumental to their recovery.

Anxiety and Panic Disorders

Many adolescents experience intermittent episodes of anxiety in response to the constant changes and challenges in their lives. When balanced with motivation and consistent with the demands of a given situation, anxiety can sometimes be useful, for example, when preparing for an exam or anticipating an athletic championship (Geldard & Geldard, 2010). Faced with unfamiliar tasks, many youth feel initial trepidation but find ways to get through transitional times.

As those suffering with an anxiety disorder can attest, however, it is a debilitating, discouraging, and demoralizing health condition. Anxiety and panic interfere with all aspects of daily life. Anxiety affects concentration and attentiveness, impeding academic and performance functioning. Because panic can arise without warning, teens avoid social and relational situations, fearful that they may embarrass themselves or not be able to cope. Anxiety's widespread and unpredictable effects often result in co-occurring bouts of depression because youngsters cannot meet expectations or lead normal lives. The risk of substance misuse also escalates, because alcohol and other drugs can provide temporary symptom relief.

Pierre, fifteen, recalls his struggles with an anxiety disorder in his freshman year of high school. Up until seventh grade, he would have described himself as outgoing and even mischievous. Teachers loved him even though he at times drove them crazy. In eighth grade, however, Pierre found that schoolwork became more difficult. At the same time Pierre's step-brother, Alphonse, joined the army and was deployed to Afghanistan. Pierre became obsessed with his brother's safety. He was unable to sleep and became inattentive at school. His mother and stepfather noticed that he was uncharacteristically irritable and edgy.

In fall of his freshman year, Pierre had his first panic attack while with friends at a movie. He thought he was dying. After that incident he avoided socializing altogether. He became distracted by anxiety and as a result lost ground in his coursework. Luckily the social worker at Pierre's school recognized symptoms of an anxiety disorder. She encouraged his parents to pursue treatment. Pierre was responsive to cognitive-behavioral and neurofeedback interventions.[3] Although he still had episodes of anxiety, Pierre gained tools to anticipate and manage his feelings.

Pierre was fortunate that his parents and school social worker identified anxiety as contributing to his distress. Often behaviors indicative of anxiety are misinterpreted as belligerence, recalcitrance, or other intentional behavioral maladaptions. Anxiety is a serious health condition that if unaddressed leads to other mental health problems and substance misuse. Thus it is important for child-centered practitioners to be aware of symptoms that can point to an anxiety or panic disorder and refer adolescents to mental health practitioners specifically trained to work in this area of practice.

Antisocial and Conduct Disorders

Although many adolescents deal with stress inwardly, others respond with antisocial behaviors or disorders of conduct that bring them to the attention of school principals, local authorities, law enforcement, and the court system. Antisocial behaviors can be triggered by anxiety or depression or can result from problems in physical and emotional regulation, leading to impulsivity.

Unfortunately, behaviors that were managed by family, school, and informal community resources when children were younger, in adolescence come to the attention of the court system. In the United States, over 2.4 million juveniles are arrested yearly, and over 125,000 convicted youth offenders reside in out-of-home care at any given time (Snyder & Sickmund,

2006). Youth crime in Canada is declining; however, it is still higher than a decade ago (Statistics Canada, 2009). In 2009, police identified nearly 165,000 youth in Canada accused of committing a crime.

Youth with behavioral disorders are perhaps the least understood and most vilified of any group of adolescents. This is especially true for those who come to the attention of the juvenile justice system. As a result, methods to effectively treat youngsters with behavioral difficulties are controversial. As Abrams (2006) argues, "In the past century, U.S. policy has oscillated between rehabilitation and punishment approaches to juvenile justice" (p. 62); however, neither of these approaches alone seems to be effective.

Youngsters with poor impulse control need equal portions of firm limits and guidance from adults. Such structure is not always available, however, because of concomitant problems such as insufficient parenting skills, material insecurities, domestic and community violence, and other problems affecting family stability. Attitudinal biases and social stigma also impede productive intervention efforts. Unfortunately, children with difficult temperaments typically escalate when parenting is ineffective and when they sense that they are being judged. At the same time, parents of children with behavioral disorders experience demoralization and shame when they are unable to control their children's behaviors. Thus treatment for these youngsters must come early and should, whenever possible, involve biological, adoptive, and foster families as well as other significant adults.

Self-Harm and Suicide

Self-harm and suicidal ideation and suicide attempts are risks to adolescents' mental health. Youth fifteen to nineteen years of age are among the highest-risk groups for suicidal behaviors. Adolescent boys and GLBTQ youth in particular have significant rates of suicidal ideation and action. As noted earlier, peer victimization is also associated with suicidality. More girls than boys attempt suicide, though rates for completed suicides are higher for boys. Since 2000, adolescent suicide rates seem to be on the decline; the reasons for this trend are yet unknown (Steele & Doey, 2007).

Risk factors for suicidal behaviors are similar to those for other mental health disorders in youth. They include poor self-worth, depression, isolation, being subjected to bullying, lack of familial and social supports, multiple relational losses, and family disruptions. Social forces such as oppression, discrimination, and social inequities also predict self-injurious, aggressive, and suicidal behaviors, particularly for GLBTQ and other marginalized youth (Crisp & McCave, 2007; Dave & Rashad, 2009). Finally, risk appears to accelerate when youth are exposed to the death of a peer from suicide (Poijula, Wahlberg, & Dyregrov, 2001). Suicide "contagion" is uncommon but is seen when youth are exposed to the suicide of a same-age peer or to learning from the media of the suicide of another (Davidson & Gould, 1989).

Risk assessments for youth suicide are mandated protocol in many schools, as is contracting for safety when youngsters have identified themselves as having suicidal thoughts and behaviors (Murray & Wright, 2006).[4] Unfortunately youth intent on suicide are less likely to seek counsel from friends and family or to pursue mental health or other professional assistance (Curtis, 2010). Youngsters who look for help tend to be more amenable to intervention than those who have already made up their minds (Curtis, 2010; Steele & Doey, 2007).

Youth report that their reluctance to seek help stems from shame and the desire to be perceived as self-reliant and not weak. However, recent studies find that those who make connections with mental health practitioners who take their suffering seriously have positive therapeutic outcomes. Understanding the importance of connection and context in working with these youth is instrumental to their care.

In recent years adolescent self-harming behaviors such as cutting and other injuries have received greater public attention. Though highly disturbing, self-injurious behaviors do not indicate suicidal intent. Rather, they are understood to be coping strategies used to allay extreme distress and inexpressibly painful feelings. Self-harming behaviors should nevertheless be recognized and taken seriously by adults, because they are likely signals of adolescent depression and/or anxiety. In some cases they may be symptoms of active, ongoing abuse or PTSD.

Left untreated, self-harm can develop into serious and incapacitating disorders that interfere with adolescent social, emotional, and cognitive functioning. As Murray and Wright (2006) aptly note, self-injuring behaviors warn us that adolescents are hurting and challenged by the troubles they face.

In summary, although adolescence as a life stage is characterized by temperamental and behavioral lability, persistent symptoms of emotional distress should be brought to the attention of mental health practitioners and other adolescent support agents who can assess, refer, and treat youngsters in need. Relational and cognitive therapies as well as medications can help young people regain their emotional and regulatory equilibrium. Family involvement is also requisite in creating safety and structure for those adolescents who cannot do it for themselves.

RESILIENCE AND THE CHARACTERISTICS OF CARING

Given the many transitions and obstacles adolescents face in the twenty-first century, how can adults circumvent stressors contributing to mental health problems and help young people grow and thrive? Let's begin by listening to researchers who have taken the time to learn from adolescents. What can they tell us about the needs of youth facing adversity? How can we apply this knowledge to effectively address the wishes and needs of the adolescents we serve?

Much has been written about risk and protective factors in adolescents' lives (Laursen & Birmingham, 2003; Masten, 2001; Spencer et al., 2004). Multiple losses and disruptions, exposure to family and community violence, chronic neglect and insufficient resources for living, parental mental illness and substance misuse, and isolation and rejection by peers, among other factors, have been noted to have serious implications for youth, especially those who lack reliable support from adults.

In the last two decades, resiliency research has demonstrated that adversity, though a formidable barrier to healthy adaptation, does not inevitably lead to poor adjustment (Laursen & Birmingham, 2003; Spencer et al., 2004). Then why is it that some adolescents thrive in the face of hardship and some do not? What fosters resilience?—that "ordinary magic" that Masten (2001) says is present, though sometimes dormant, in youth.

A prevalent factor in the lives of resilient youth is the presence of at least one caring, confiding, or good-enough relationship with an adult. Relational connection appears to mediate the impact of early and ongoing hardship and, though not a panacea, helps adolescents access their inherent potential to function successfully in a difficult world. Within this paradigm the troubles of youth are not dismissed or minimized, but validated. Problems are evaluated alongside and in conjunction with adolescents' strengths and resources; change comes about by using the resourcefulness and creativity of youth to address and remediate their challenges and struggles.

Qualities of relationship with adults found to be most helpful by adolescents include responsivity, mutual communication and exchange, respectful understanding, and reliability (Spencer et al., 2004). As noted by one adolescent, the merit of being genuinely cared for and respected "for who they were, rather than for how they were behaving or achieving in some particular way" (Spencer et al., 2004, p. 357) is a powerful incentive for healing. Conversely, adolescents report that disingenuous or punitive relationships discourage them from making alliances, and when forced to do so, they are apt to withhold information or simply shut down.

When youth have a voice in their treatment process, the likelihood of therapeutic success increases (Duncan, Miller, & Sparks, 2007). Collaborating with youth to develop interventions suited to their needs and desires promotes positive and enduring behavioral change. Working with their family system further ensures that recommendations are relevant and reinforced, and that growth is sustained.

Barry Duncan, a researcher, scholar, and practitioner who developed the Child Outcome Rating Scale (CORS) in collaboration with colleagues

Scott Miller and Jacqueline Sparks (Duncan, Miller, & Sparks, 2003), comments on the importance of developing responsive alliances with youth. These include ongoing feedback as a mechanism for increasing adolescents' investment in their own therapeutic success.

> The push for manualized treatments for youth is surely well-intentioned. In its most unfortunate interpretation, however, youth are reduced to a diagnosis and therapists defined by a treatment technology—interchangeable and insignificant to the procedure at hand. This "product view" is most empirically vacuous because the treatment itself accounts for so little of outcome variance, while the client and the therapist—and their relationship—account for so much more. Successful outcomes are more likely when services are youth and family driven—guided by their culture, worldview, and preferences—and tailored to their perspectives of the benefit and fit of treatment. (Barry Duncan, personal communication, August 28, 2010)

Not surprisingly then, when these elements of relationship and responsivity are present, young people describe positive motivation to change. Impetus is based upon increase in self-worth, desire for relational connection, ability to deal with conflict, and an overall sense of personal empowerment.

Equally important to youth is the perception that adults can relate to their experiences and are not wholly exempt from poor judgment or error. In a study by Spencer and colleagues (2004, p. 358), youth reported that "it was particularly helpful when adults indicated that they could relate to or understand the young person's struggle by drawing parallels to their own experience." An important counterbalance to this kind of sharing is adults' willingness to hold youth accountable for their behavior and to be authentic role models (Laursen & Birmingham, 2003). Being authentic implies walking the walk with the youth we serve. As Laursen and Birmingham (2003) found, "Authentic caring involves specific adult behaviors and beliefs that provide the foundation for reclaiming challenged youth. It is not enough for adults to *say* that they care; the task is to practically *demonstrate* caring behaviors to youth who often have encountered many adults not deserving of their trust" (p. 245, emphasis added). Thus when mutual and empowering relationships with caring adults are in place, adolescents may feel safe enough to reveal struggles, conflicts, and failures; work through their difficulties; and be guided toward a process of discovery.

PARENTING ADOLESCENTS

As discussed in chapter 3, when young children experience security in their primary attachments, they develop self-assurance that allows them to venture forth in the world. Adolescents also benefit from stable and caring attachments, but unlike their younger selves, they are actively engaged in a competing struggle between independence from and interdependence with their families.

Given the transitional uncertainties that adolescents face, it is to be expected that even competent parents wrestle with the constantly shifting needs of their maturing children. Parents thus need to provide teenagers with opportunities for change; at the same time, they must exert varying levels of parental control to help teens avoid the pitfalls of bad choices or negative associations (Geldard & Geldard, 2010).

What then are some of the essential qualities for parenting adolescents? Experts agree that successful parent-adolescent relationships require continual rebalancing of limits, love, and tolerance for the unique characteristics of youth. Qualities intrinsic to these relationships include flexibility, acceptance of difference, and open, responsive communication. Responsiveness requires being attuned to adolescents as well as anticipating and knowing the distinctive needs of one's child. At the same time, parents must be firm and authoritative. In other words, although young people need room to experiment with their growing skills, they need clear, consistent, and appropriate guidance and structure from their parents, perhaps more than ever before.

A number of factors help primary caregivers prepare to extend effective parenting to adolescents. First, parents must be open to and respectful of the many changes that adolescents experience and thus be prepared that they will make mistakes. Mistakes should be dealt with directly but without shaming. This stance conveys the message that positive connection exists even when there is conflict. It also represents respect for the culture of adolescents and projects parents' willingness to learn about their world, which may be very different from the one that parents experienced in their youth.

Second, parents should invite adolescents to participate in making decisions that affect their lives. This does not mean that they get the final say, but it does send a message that they are part of the decision.

Third, parents must be willing to have hard conversations with their teenagers involving risky behaviors, sexuality, substance use, and other relevant issues. How these conversations take place will depend on the adolescent's temperament and communication style, as well as the parent's interactional strategies and cultural beliefs. If there are two parents or parenting partners involved, living together or not, both should be on the same page about these conversations. It is important to convey consistent messages, because adolescents are skilled at divide and conquer. Parents must somehow agree to disagree in private and commit to consistency, coherency, and low conflict in their public conversations with their teenagers.

Finally, as mentioned above, adolescents benefit from relationships with adults other than their parents. Adolescents profit from relationships with a range of caring adults, including parents, grandparents, kin, teachers, school nurses, coaches, parents of friends, foster parents, members of faith-based groups, health professionals, and of course, social workers and other mental health practitioners. Parents should encourage these affiliations and not place obstacles to their children's developing positive relationships with trusted adults. These relationships are perhaps most important when environmental, situational, or family stresses impede adequate parent-child communication. They are also instrumental in collaboration with parents to prevent and circumvent social pressures that may create hazards, including negative peer influence, substance misuse, risky sexual behaviors, cyberbullying or inappropriate Internet relationships, and other potentially ill-advised or unsafe choices.

Some adolescents do not live with their biological parents and are therefore cared for by foster parents or kin, or live in residential settings where they are collectively parented. As Mallon and Hess (2005, p. xii) write, "Although family is the best place for children and youth to grow up, for some, their families of origin may not be safe and nurturing." As noted earlier in this chapter, resiliency in youth is promoted by having someone who will not give up on you. Accordingly, adolescents not living in their original families are more likely to sustain motivation and hopefulness if there are relational resources to assist them along the way (Fraser & Terzian, 2005).

While many youth in foster care and alternative living arrangements have adult champions, many do not. Moreover, child welfare staff and foster caregivers are often not sufficiently trained in resiliency models that best support youth development. Child-centered relational workers are in a good position to act as agents of change on behalf of these youth. We do this by advocating evidence-guided, high-quality systems of alternative family care that promote the well-being of all children, in all settings, being raised by a range of caregivers.

BOULDER TECH'S GREENHOUSE MANAGEMENT PROGRAM

In May 2010 I interviewed Heather Ridge, an innovative teacher and program developer for the Boulder Technical Education Center in Boulder, Colorado. Heather is the visionary behind the greenhouse management program (GMP), a two-semester course for high school students, many of whom are at risk for dropping out or have recently returned after leaving school for a period of time (see figure 8.1). GMP is an outgrowth of Boulder's vocational education system, designed as an alternative for students who do not maintain a level of academic achievement sufficient for college admission or who have interests outside of typical college curricula.

GMP is integrated into Boulder Tech's agriculture curriculum, a mainstay of their traditional programming. It introduces students to the plant sciences, genetics, and biotechnology and their application in the real world.

FIGURE 8.1 Heather Ridge in the GMP greenhouse, Boulder, Colorado

Heather's students develop community gardens at the elementary schools, a program called the Garden at the Table. The vegetables grown there are used in school lunchrooms and are sold at the biweekly farmers' market. Students help fund the program through plant sales on Valentine's Day and Mother's Day. The proceeds from these annual fund-raisers go directly into the next school year's budget and support students' memberships in local agriculture organizations. The objective of these hands-on activities is to help students witness connections between their learning and their capacity to succeed in work and community leadership.

In our conversation Heather reflected upon the changing culture of technical education and specifically the greenhouse management initiative: "The school's been around for almost fifty years now, but over the last fifteen years we've really started looking at not just preparing students for jobs but also for higher education. For that reason we've attracted a lot of students who are the first in their family to go to college." To improve the likelihood of success for those students, Boulder Tech forged a relationship with the Colorado Community College System. Thus participation in GMP nets students free college credits and provides a bridge to higher education for youth from economically strapped families.

Heather promotes student resilience by being an active role model for positive change. She's also adamant about setting clear structure and high expectations. Accordingly, she infuses competencies for leadership and professionalism into her curriculum and keeps her students on their toes. Students in her program must clock in and clock out and are permitted only two absences per semester, for any reason.

One of Heather's favorite assignments is based on conflict resolution. As she explains: "It's always the most colorful assignment—where they have to talk about a conflict you had at work—How did you resolve it? The exercise emphasizes leadership as a professional in the industry as well as personal professionalism—being on time, making up hours—so that's a big part, I think, of what makes this school stand out."

The benefits of such structure and discipline are many. Students graduate from GMP with a résumé, a cover letter, and at least one video-taped mock interview. The second-year students participate in internships, preferably paid; some work at research greenhouses, some work at local flower shops, and they're required to do assignments based on their work experience.

The GMP includes all students, in both traditional and special education programs. When not fully subscribed, GMP also accepts returning adults, some who have graduated and others who are coming back to complete their high school degrees. Although their individual education plans may vary, all students are treated as equals.

Heather firmly believes that highlighting choice, competency building, and empowerment motivates her students to graduate and go on to successful professional lives. She's seen it happen consistently and takes great pride in her students' accomplishments.

SUMMARY

This chapter examined the transitions and trials of adolescence with a particular focus on resilience and relationship as key factors in growth promotion and adaptation to life. Most individuals emerge relatively unscathed from their teenage years, as do their caregivers. However, the road to adulthood is inevitably full of bumps and pitfalls, especially for youngsters who do not have adults to nurture and guide them on their journey.

Knowledge of expected developmental hurtles and outcomes is critical for those working with adolescents. Surges in physiological, emotional, and social development understandably preoccupy adolescents, as do changes in their attachments. Adolescence is a transitional period of life when attachment bonds with parents are balanced with new attachments with peers, romantic partners, and the larger, broader world (Brandell & Ringel, 2007). These relational changes are both exciting and confusing and leave significant room for adolescent contemplation and rumination in brains that can now consider the past and the future, moral dilemmas, and existential concepts. They also leave teenagers ripe for emotional, social, and familial conflicts. Although adolescents continue to need nurturing connections to their adult caregivers, they also benefit from stable relationships with other adults, including social workers, school counselors, caseworkers, and mental health practitioners.

Notes

1. *Sexual orientation* refers to the object of a person's predominant sexual and affectional desires. *Gender identification* refers to a person's identification with anatomical gender.
2. For more comprehensive information see McKenzie (2008).
3. Neurofeedback is a form of biofeedback used to help control anxiety and other physiologically related regulatory conditions.
4. *Contracting for safety* means signing an agreement to not inflict harm on oneself or to contact an appropriate person should you have suicidal thoughts.

References

Abrams, L. S. (2006). Listening to juvenile offenders: Can residential treatment prevent recidivism? *Child and Adolescent Social Work Journal, 23*(1), 61–84.

Bettmann, J. E., & Jasperson, R. A. (2010). Anxiety in adolescence: The integration of attachment and neurobiological research into practice. *Clinical Social Work Journal, 38*(1), 98–106.

Brandell, J. R., & Ringel, S. (2007). *Attachment and dynamic practice: An integrative guide for social workers and other clinicians.* New York: Columbia University Press.

Crisp, C., & McCave, E. L. (2007). Gay affirmative practice: A model for social work practice with gay, lesbian and bisexual youth. *Child and Adolescent Social Work Journal, 24*(4), 403–421.

Curtis, C. (2010). Youth perceptions of suicide and help-seeking: "They'd think I was weak or 'mental.'" *Journal of Youth Studies, 13*(6), 699–715.

Dave, D., & Rashad, I. (2009). Overweight status, self-perception, and suicidal behaviors among adolescents. *Social Science and Medicine, 68,* 1685–1691.

Davidson, L. E., & Gould, M. S. (1989). Contagion as a risk factor for youth suicide. In Alcohol, Drug Abuse, and Mental Health Administration, *Report of the Secretary's Task Force on Youth Suicide: Vol. 2. Risk factors for youth suicide* (pp. 88–109, DHHS publication no. [ADM] 89–1622). Washington, DC: US Department of Health and Human Services, Public Health Service.

Duncan, B. L., Miller, S. D., & Sparks, J. A. (2003). *The child outcome rating scale.* Fort Lauderdale, FL: Authors.

Duncan, B. L., Miller, S. D. & Sparks, J. A. (2007). Common factors and the uncommon heroism of youth. *Psychotherapy in Australia, 13*(2), 34–43.

Fraser, M. W., & Terzian, M. A. (2005). Risk and resilience in child development: Practice principles and strategies. In G. P. Mallon & P. McCartt Hess (Eds.), *Child welfare for the twenty-first century: A handbook of practices, policies, & programs* (pp. 55–71). New York: Columbia University Press.

Geldard, K., & Geldard, D. (2010). *Counselling adolescents* (3rd ed.). London: Sage.

Hinduja, S., & Patchin, J. W. (2010). Bullying, cyberbullying, and suicide. *Archives of Suicide Research, 14*(3), 206–221.

Hodge, D. R. (2002). Working with Muslim youths: Understanding the values and beliefs of Islamic discourse. *Children and Schools, 24*(1), 6–20.

Jensen, L. A. (2003). Coming of age in a multicultural world: Globalization and adolescent cultural identity formation. *Applied Developmental Science, 7*, 188–195.

Laursen, E. K., & Birmingham, S. M. (2003). Caring relationships as protective factors for at-risk youth: An ethnographic study. *Families in Society, 84*(2): 240–246.

Mallon, G. P., & Hess, P. M. (Eds.). (2005). *Child welfare for the twenty-first century: A handbook of practices, policies, & programs.* New York: Columbia University Press.

Masten, A. S. (2001). Ordinary magic: Resilience processes in development. *American Psychologist, 56*(3), 227–238.

McCarthy, J., Downes, E. J., & Sherman, C. A. (2008). Looking back at adolescent depression: A qualitative study. *Journal of Mental Health Counseling, 30*(1), 49–68.

McKenzie, F. R. (2008). *Theory and practice with adolescents: An applied approach.* Chicago: Lyceum Books.

Miller, A. L., Glinski, J., Woodberry, K. A., Mitchell, A. G., & Indik, J. (2002). Family therapy and dialectical behavior therapy with adolescents: Part 1. Proposing a clinical synthesis. *American Journal of Psychotherapy, 54*(4), 568–582.

Murray, B. L., & Wright, K. (2006). Integration of suicide risk assessment and intervention approach: The perspective of youth. *Journal of Psychiatric and Mental Health Nursing, 13*, 157–164.

Pepler, D., Craig, W. M., Yuile, A., & Connolly, J. (2004). Girls who bully: A developmental and relational perspective. In M. Putallaz & J. Kupersmidt (Eds.), *Aggression, antisocial behavior, and violence among girls* (pp. 90–109). New York: Guilford Press.

Poijula, S., Wahlberg, K., & Dyregrov, A. (2001). Adolescent suicide and suicide contagion in three secondary schools. *International Journal of Emergency Mental Health, 3*(3), 163–168.

Snyder, H. N., & Sickmund, M. (2006). *Juvenile offenders and victims: 2006 national report.* Washington, DC: US Department of Justice, Office of Justice Programs, Office of Juvenile Justice and Delinquency Prevention.

South Carolina Department of Health and Human Services. (2006). *Eating disorders statistics.* Retrieved from http://www.state.sc.us/dmh/anorexia/statistics.htm

Spencer, R., Jordan, J. V., & Sazama, J. (2004) Growth-promoting relationships between youth and adults: A focus group study. *Families in Society, 85*(3), 354–362.

Statistics Canada, Canadian Centre for Justice Statistics. (2009). *Uniform Crime Reporting Survey* (UCR 2.0). Ottawa: Author.

Steele, M. M., & Doey, T. (2007). Suicidal behaviour in children and adolescents: Part 1. Etiology and risk factors. *Canadian Journal of Psychiatry, 52*(1), 21S–33S.

Wilkinson, R. B. (2004). The role of parental and peer attachment in the psychological health and self-esteem of adolescents. *Journal of Youth and Adolescents, 33*(6), 479–493.

9

Neurodiversity and Other Developmental Disabilities of Childhood

And we all need to feel accepted, protected, and respected; but most of all we need to be loved.

Rory Hoy, quoted in E. Sellman, review of *Autism and Me*

ALL KINDS OF MINDS

Neurodiversity is a broad term used to describe atypical or divergent neurological development. Diagnostic classifications such as autism spectrum disorders (ASD) and Tourette's syndrome (TS) fall under this description. Learning differences, developmental disabilities (e.g., Down syndrome), and a range of conditions that contribute to intellectual disabilities are included in the spectrum of human neurodevelopmental variability.

Every society includes "many kinds of minds" (Levine, 2002, p. 13). Fostering acceptance for children and adults with different cognitive abilities, intellectual capabilities, and communication styles inevitably leads to a stronger and more cohesive human community. Understanding how individuals with neuro-atypicality see and interact with their world reduces misunderstanding that leads to stigma and hopelessness.

Such knowledge is increasingly important for child-centered practitioners, as diagnoses of ASD and other developmental disorders are on the rise. Explanations for this increase are speculative and varied. Some attribute it to advances in early assessment measures. Others believe that definitions of mental health and special needs have changed over the years, leading to a narrower range of children considered to be adjusting normally. Some think ASD and other cognitive and communicative disorders are environmentally caused.

While scientists and sociologists seek to make sense of the current trends, it is left to child-centered practitioners to aid children with neurodiversity and to support their families as they work to keep pace with life's complicated demands. Workers must be prepared with practice knowledge and relational skills to work directly with children with learning differences and to collaborate with parents who will make critical life decisions on their behalf.

Caring, compassion, and acceptance are central to working effectively with parents who are raising children with disabilities (see chapter 6). Open and caring attitudes are important to building trust, as these parents frequently encounter medical, educational, and mental health professionals who misunderstand and judge them. At the same time, parents learn to live with criticism because their children's best interests always come before their own. Thus effective practice with these families requires recognition that parents are vigilant advocates and experts in their children's care.

This chapter presents multiple perspectives on the experiences of childhood neurodiversity and developmental and intellectual disability. It begins by examining criteria for conditions such as ASD and TS. It explores the evolution of public understanding of these conditions, and the impact of faulty science and misunderstanding on families, especially mothers.

The chapter addresses a number of factors that influence child and family adaptation and quality of life. Why is it that some families find benefit in caring for their children while others feel unmitigated despair? What common and disparate effects do children's intellectual and functional differences have on parents, partners, siblings, and extended family? How can a child-centered practitioner provide support, aid adaptation, and interact with children, families, and the multiple systems that they need in their day-to-day lives?

The chapter also describes two exemplary programs serving children and youth: the TEACCH program, designed for people with diagnoses of autism across the life course; and the Adaptive Dance Program, a collaboration between Boston Children's Hospital and the Boston Ballet for youngsters with Down syndrome.

OVERVIEW OF AUTISM SPECTRUM DISORDERS

Leo Kanner's seminal paper *Autistic Disturbances of Affective Contact*, published in 1943, was one of the first scholarly works describing children "whose condition differs so markedly and uniquely from anything reported so far, that each case merits—and I hope, will eventually receive—a detailed consideration of its fascinating peculiarities" (p. 217). These youngsters would likely now be identified as having social communication disorders and ASD. Outstanding characteristics that were consistent in each of the eleven cases documented by Kanner included "inability to relate to themselves," "failure to assume at any time an anticipatory posture," and "extreme *autistic* aloneness" (p. 242).

Kanner was struck by these children's early and unremitting disregard for relational contact. Like many early child psychiatrists and researchers, he initially thought that insufficient parental attachments contributed to these extraordinary relational and communication disabilities. Over time, however, Kanner rejected the idea that parents caused autism. Instead he came to believe that its etiology was likely congenital; that children were born "with innate inability to form the usual, biologically provided affective contact with people, just as other children come into the world with innate physical or intellectual handicaps" (1943, p. 250). This shift in Kanner's focus led to a more compassionate view of parents, especially mothers, whose seeming relational disconnectedness likely originated from their children's social incapacity rather than from their lack of love.

Unfortunately the diagnosis of autism is still encumbered by a legacy of blame rooted in theories of the 1950s and 1960s that saw cold, disinterested mothers as causing their children's distress. Bruno Bettelheim (1967), a major proponent of this theory, coined the term "refrigerator mothers," proposing that children could be cured of autism if removed from the toxicity of their emotionally impoverished caregivers. Although Bettelheim later discredited his own theories, fallout from this perspective still pervades public understanding of autism.

Contemporary science and clinical evidence lends significant support to Kanner's early assumptions. Research points to ASD being a continuum of neurologically based developmental disabilities of unknown etiology (Mesibov & Shea, 2011; Turnbull, Turnbull, Erwin, & Soodak, 2006).[1] Behaviors characteristic of ASD vary in composition and severity from individual to individual; however, they all result in conduct that qualitatively impairs relationships, social interaction, and verbal and nonverbal communication. Youngsters with ASD may be intellectually high functioning with impairments only in social communication. However, nearly 70 percent have co-occurring cognitive disabilities and/or mood disorders. In some instances, children with ASD display significant psychiatric impairment (Mesibov & Shea, 2011).

Common among children with ASD is their inability to understand the give-and-take of relationships. If verbal, they are apt to talk without awareness of how or whether others are engaged in the discussion. When at play, they are likely to participate in parallel, not shared, activities. Preoccupation and special interests as well as repetitive motor mannerisms are behavioral capstones of ASD.

As a result of these behaviors, typical friendships for these children are nearly impossible. Sean Barron (Barron & Barron, 2002, p. 15) offers an insider's view of living with ASD: "I was fascinated by the holes in the registers as well as by the darkness of the holes themselves. I'd throw a crayon down the hole and listen to the sound it made when it hit bottom. Sometimes I'd just love looking through the register, so I'd stick my finger through the metal covering as far as I could reach . . . I loved repetition."

Children with ASD rely heavily on structure and become agitated when routines are altered. Transitional difficulties significantly affect the overall quality of daily life. Even routine activities, however, such as waking, eating a meal, going to school, taking a bath, and going to bed, can be accompanied by behavioral meltdowns. Siblings are especially affected by ASD in the family. It's not unusual for their needs to be ignored because of a brother's or sister's behavior. Parents too find it difficult to spend time together, exhausted by the demands of their vulnerable children.

Approximately 1 in 150 children in the United States and Canada are annually diagnosed with ASD before the age of four (Harrington, Patrick, Edwards, & Brand, 2006). Manifestations of ASD typically appear before the age of three. Parents may notice that their child avoids eye contact or is especially reactive to physical, auditory, or visual stimuli tolerated by other children.

Bloch and Weinstein (2010) observed that atypical development may not be noticed by family members because of its gradual onset. In retrospect parents describe a healthy and normal child who slowly began to lose skills and never got back on track. On the other hand, some parents report that they were aware of their children's atypical development yet had to plead with pediatricians or family doctors to take their concerns seriously. Unlike those whose early recollections are of a normally developing child, these parents offer documented histories of their children's awkward communication and unusual motor patterns. For such families the ASD diagnosis is validating and comes as a relief, in spite of their loss.

Doris, the mother of three youngsters diagnosed with varying degrees of ASD, spoke of such trials with her youngest son, Eben. She recalled that during one well-baby visit, Eben's pediatrician gently implied that she was overreacting to his behaviors because she was overtaxed by her older children. "He suggested that Eben was imitating his siblings and that I was just not used to raising a 'normal' child," she said. Soon after, Doris brought Eben to see a new developmental pediatrician for assessment. The practitioner took one look at Eben and asked Doris if she was familiar with ASD.

Gary Mesibov (personal communication, October 2009) suggests that an important first step in ASD awareness is recognizing that autism is a culture. Within this culture are general characteristics that children share and characteristics that caregivers and helpers must possess in order to be invited into their worlds. Such characteristics include willingness to get to know each child and family as individuals and being open to the fact that no one educational or therapeutic approach fits all children.

Missy Hendrick (personal communication, October 16, 2009), who teaches preschoolers with ASD, gave me a short course on how the culture of autism translates day-to-day with the children (see the section "TEACCH" below). She said that teachers and parents don't view behaviors as "good" or "bad." Instead they notice what isn't working and look for ways to "translate the world for them so that they can spend more time in our world and understand it."

From Missy's perspective, "translating the world" involves recognizing that each child is different. One mother's comment reveals a similar view. She told me, "If you've met one child with autism, you've met *one* child with autism." Optimizing children's distinctive skills is the goal of therapeutic and educational intervention, so they can live the best, most functional life possible.

TREATMENT APPROACHES

An array of valid educational theories and therapeutic strategies are available for working with children with ASD (Cosden, Koegel, Koegel, Greenwell, & Klein, 2006; Duncan & Klinger, 2010; Renna, 2004; Mesibov & Shea, 2011; Prizant, Wetherby, Rubin, Laurent, & Rydell, 2006; Wieder & Greenspan, 2003). Some have powerful proponents who believe that their particular strategy uniquely offers a cure or answers the mysteries of ASD. However, it is more useful to children and families when child-centered professionals are open to diverse educational and therapeutic approaches that have had good results.

Eric Schopler, a psychologist and founder of the TEACCH program,[2] advised that regardless of approach, treatment for ASD must occur within the context of caring, consistent, and accepting relationships. Wieder and Greenspan (2003) found that children with ASD can establish positive and accepting relationships within their individual level of functioning. Their approach—the developmental, individual-difference, relationship-based model (DIR)—uses play to facilitate social and communicative development. TEACCH and DIR proponents refute the notion that children with ASD are incapable of forming relational attachments.

Cosden and colleagues (2006) highlight the benefits of conducting assessments and implementing treatment approaches focused on the strengths of children with ASD and their families. Concentrating on successes rather than on deficits creates a foundation of hope. Such hope is augmented by the increasing success of strengths-focused intervention protocols. It is also reinforced by stories of children diagnosed with ASD who are doing well within mainstream society (Cosden et al., 2006).

Advancements in our understanding of ASD have led to more effective treatments and, to varying extents, have lessened the stigma attached to the diagnosis. Structure, routine, visual cues, and patience are hallmarks of interventions that work best for children. Presently there is no known cure for ASD, but even in the most severe instances, workers must focus on developing strengths that will enable each child with ASD "to function as meaningfully and as independently as possible" in their home and in their community (TEACCH Mission Statement, 2012).

UNEXPECTED LIVES

ASD are complex and severe behavioral disorders that present daily challenges to family functioning. Parents raising children with ASD live with uncertainty. Most experience higher levels of stress than parents of children who do not have ASD (Altiere & Von Kluge, 2009). This is especially the case for those whose youngsters have particularly severe behavioral and communication impediments. Finally, most parents must at some point revise their hopes and dreams for their youngster's future.

How families conceptualize or cognitively appraise raising a child with ASD influences their coping mechanisms and capacities. For example, family adaptation to ASD may be difficult when parents dwell only on negative aspects or continually struggle to make sense of their child's disability. For these parents, recurring feelings of fault, blame, and hopelessness pervade their thoughts and affect their ability to cope.

On the other hand, some parents describe improved family connectedness, increased compassion, and greater acceptance of human variability as unanticipated benefits of raising a child with ASD. Such gains, however, do not minimize ASD's global impact, and the same parents who acknowledge positive experiences do not dismiss accompanying struggles and strains. Successful coping seems predicated on parents' ability to be realistic about their children's challenges while finding positive ways to integrate ASD into their family system and worldview.

Childhood diagnoses of ASD reverberate throughout family systems. Parents and family members revise priorities and adapt strategies to manage the child's newly defined needs. Established roles shift as families determine how best to redistribute responsibilities for the foreseeable future.

How an ASD diagnosis is understood and accepted within a family's community of care has powerful implications. Sometimes parents are at odds over the diagnosis, one embracing it while the other questions or rejects the notion that his or her child has a permanent, life-affecting condition. As an example, Sam's father insisted to everyone that his son was just like him and would grow out of his awkwardness. Sam's mother was instead relieved to finally have a label that explained her child's struggles. Such basic differences often disrupt parenting and the partnership relationship.

The opinions of extended family, friends, and community resources also matter to parents and children. Parents feel most strongly supported when family, kin, teachers, coaches, and members of their faith community share a common, nonjudgmental view of their children. Raising children with ASD never should be done in isolation. It is a family and community process. It took Doris's father (see the case above) considerable time to use the word *autism* in reference to his grandchildren. The family's pastor also questioned the diagnosis. Doris's persistence eventually helped Eben's grandfather and the pastor understand and accept his diagnosis.

While most families find ways to favorably manage the rigors that accompany a diagnosis of ASD, it is not uncommon for even those functioning well to describe a grieving process. The following is an abridged version of an essay written by a grandmother who had just learned of her grandson's diagnosis of ASD:

> For our family the news came on Valentine's Day. It was not totally unexpected, but it certainly was not what we had hoped for. Jennifer and Robert learned that day that Ben, 18 months, had autism. The diagnosis came after months spent telling the pediatrician that something was wrong with Ben. The first pediatrician minimized their concerns, implying that they were just young parents and compared Ben's development too closely to his precocious five-year-old brother, Evan. But Jennifer knew shortly after her second son's birth that something was different about him. Her hopes were pinned on getting Ben help as early as possible. Better yet, maybe therapy could fix the problem if not help him to function as normally as he could. Her brother had learning problems and he did okay. Why not Ben?
>
> That day the neurologist bluntly told Jennifer and Robert that their beautiful child had autism. Autism. Autism was not a death sentence . . . but it was devastating to our family. The dreams Robert and Jennifer had for their son were gone—the possibilities for his future were now limited by a label that would mark his life forever. And even worse, Robert and Jennifer would have to handle the blame that would come. Jennifer said that even her most supportive friends seemed to think that autism was somehow their fault.
>
> I've read about chronic sorrow and in the past I've dismissed it as self-absorbed. People should just get over their problems and move on. As a soldier in Afghanistan I witnessed tragedy and managed to cope. Yet now I look at my daughter, her husband and my grandsons, and I fully believe that we will all probably feel sadness forever—it's a logical response to autism.
>
> So Ben has autism, now what? Robert and Jennifer need my ongoing support. I can provide love and encouragement, and I can also provide respite for Ben and give Evan special time away from the demands of his little brother. We will handle this crisis in different ways. Jennifer and I will learn everything we can, and the men will take it one-day-at-a-time, knowing that at the end of the

day, *Ben is still Ben.* Nothing has really changed. Ben is still the perfect, best-looking baby there ever was. There will be good days and bad days and there will be love, laughter and a lot of tears.

This grandmother's musings vividly illustrate the complicated feelings experienced by families. She makes eminently clear that she is concerned with both the health and welfare of her grandchild and the well-being of her parenting children and older grandson. Her story reveals the profoundly multilayered and dynamic features ASD brings to a family. It emphasizes the inter- and intrafamilial aspects that practitioners must explore and address in similar cases.

Well-prepared child-centered workers support families as they come to terms with their changed life circumstances. They recognize that parents respond variably to an ASD diagnosis. Some draw inward to harness their resources, while others isolate to avoid judgment and blame. Some become vocal advocates and find benefit in a larger cause, while others show a vigilance that belies deep-seated feelings of loss and despair. Workers need to work *with* parents, even those who initially seem inflexible or opinionated. The ultimate goal is to deepen relationships and become useful allies to parents, acting as advocates and liaisons within schools, health-care systems, and social service programs.

Opportunities for mentorship with other parents in similar circumstances can ease the burden of isolation that all too often befalls families of children with ASD and other intellectual and developmental disabilities (Bloch & Weinstein, 2010; Konrad, 2007). Parent-to-parent mentorship takes many forms, including in-person, peer-facilitated support groups; one-on-one mentorship; community-based parent networks; and websites and chat rooms. Learning with, from, and about other parents' shared experiences offers parents of newly diagnosed children a safe environment in which to air concerns (Konrad, 2007).

An often overlooked aspect of an ASD diagnosis is its differential impact on siblings. Factors including age, developmental maturation, temperament, sibling relationships, and family dynamics determine how siblings are affected by ASD in the family. Some siblings focus on the benefits of having a brother or sister with ASD. Advantages include enhancement of maturity, coping skills, and resilience. These youngsters are often viewed by adults as intensely loyal, insightful, kind, and more tolerant of diversity than their peers. Other siblings experience undue pressure to be mature beyond their years. These youngsters may not be emotionally or developmentally ready to assume increased caregiving burdens and household responsibilities. Some reel from the impact their affected sibling has on their parents. They experience anger and abandonment because their parents' time is often consumed with the needs of their autistic sibling.

Some children experience strain because they are expected to somehow compensate or make up for their sibling's deficits. It is not uncommon for these youngsters to feel neglected or forgotten or to believe that their worries are minimized because of the extraordinary demands their autistic sibling places on the family (Bloch & Weinstein, 2010). Finally, youth report being embarrassed by their siblings' ASD behaviors. Whether on the bus or in the playground, they feel the stigma associated with childhood disability. Surprisingly, these same youngsters are quick to defend their siblings from the teasing of classmates and peers.

Marla, twelve, the older child in a family of intergenerational lobstermen, was an expert when it came to teaching me about the rigors of having a brother with ASD. She was referred to my practice after being thrown off the school bus for hitting a classmate and breaking his nose. Although the assault was in defense of her brother, she nonetheless lost bus privileges and was on a seven-day school suspension. I knew from her parents that Marla's younger brother, Albert, eight, was diagnosed with Asperger's syndrome,[3] a condition on the ASD spectrum characterized by strong intelligence and intense special interests. His was chess. At the time of the assault, Albert was having a meltdown after being mercilessly teased by the alleged victim, a fourteen-year-old boy named Billy.

I can only describe Marla as one tough girl. She made no excuses for her behavior, nor did she pardon anyone else's. She explained that she hated her brother and was angry at her parents virtually all the time. She felt ignored and neglected and thus didn't feel it was worth trying to be smart or being a good kid. She simply got through her day. On the other hand, it was against her code of ethics and island culture to allow people to harm family. Though she thought Albert was a complete *turd*, she would defend him to the end.

Marla's parents acknowledged that they expected her to consistently "be the better person" when it came to her brother. This translated into allowing him to go into her room uninvited, to use her computer, or for that matter, to do anything he wished, just to maintain peace in the household. Marla felt her parents' expectations were unreasonable, yet on some level she understood their desperation.

Marla benefited from having a place to "dump her feelings," in her words. She used our time to strategize and develop methods to communicate with her parents. Fortunately they were open to hearing Marla's distress, and over time the family dynamics improved, as did Marla's choices and judgments. She still complained bitterly about Albert's behaviors, but she realized that she had a positive future to look forward to if she took the time to invest in it.

Sibling support groups and one-on-one counseling with a person knowledgeable about ASD are helpful to siblings. One resource for youth is Sibshop, an outgrowth of the Sibling Support Project (http://www.sibling support.org). Developed by Meyer and Vadasy (1996), Sibshops provide much-needed peer-led support.

A solid relationship with a trusted adult is also foundational to sibling well-being. As described in Marla's case and noted in chapter 8, a reliable relationship with at least one caring adult often promotes resilience in siblings and reroutes potentially negative behaviors. Important as well to siblings' health and well-being is to alert parents to their desires and need for family connection.

CHILDREN WITH TOURETTE'S SYNDROME

Tourette's syndrome (TS) is an often misunderstood neurodevelopmental condition characterized by motor and vocal tics.[4] Prevalence estimates range from 0.1 to 1 percent in children between the ages of six and seventeen (Piacentini et al., 2010). Boys are more often diagnosed with TS than girls, and its symptoms seem to diminish with age. Coprolalia, the blurting out of obscene comments, is the symptom most often associated with TS, although it is quite rare. More commonly, motor tics include eye blinking, mouth movements, facial grimacing, and jaw stretching. Vocal tics may be expressed by sniffing, coughing, throat clearing, and grunting. Motor and vocal tics can occur in combination and can be internally felt and therefore not visible or acknowledged by others. Youngsters report that tics are preceded by unpleasant and sometimes painful urges or sensations that can be relieved only by completion of the tic.

Tics typically appear in early childhood, peak in adolescence, and decline in early adulthood. Their occurrence is associated with considerable impairment in children's daily activities. Young people report that tics are particularly difficult to manage and control while at school, in part because of stress caused by the desire to fit in with peers and meet adult expectations (Cutler, Murphy, Gilmour, & Heyman, 2009). TS-related behaviors are also correlated with negative social outcomes such as isolation, ostracism, and bullying. Youngsters able to separate out the behavioral repercussions of TS from their sense of self as a whole seem better able to cope with the disorder. Those who focus on the negative impact of TS report more emotional distress than their otherwise well-adjusted counterparts (Cutler et al., 2009).

Youngsters in the HBO film *I Have Tourettes, but Tourettes Doesn't Have Me* (http://www.tsa-usa.org/news/HBO_Release_apr06_update.htm) reinforce many of the points highlighted by social science and behavioral researchers. One young boy describes the contradictory experience of tics in this way: "You can't think of anything except holding them back, and you can't think of anything else except doing them." He advises that children with TS alert their classmates to fend off discrimination: "OK, note to you. Before you go to school, you need to tell people that you have Tourette's or else it will be a big, big bad time for you." This youngster's concluding remark sums up what children with TS need us to know: "Kids with Tourette's are just like any other kid—just with a few disabilities. But really we're just like you."

TS has been linked to co-occurring neurocognitive and mental health conditions, for instance ADHD, learning disabilities, obsessive-compulsive disorder, and depression (Collins, 2005; Piacentini et al., 2010). It is not always clear whether these coexisting conditions emanate from true neurobiological, mood, or cognitive disorders or whether they result from children's distractibility and helplessness associated with uncontrollable tics and behaviors. It is evident, however, that these psychosocial and learning issues exacerbate children's already compromised emotional and social well-being.

Although children with TS are reported to have intelligence comparable to children without it, they have greater problems with school performance. Academic problems include difficulty with organizing work and playing quietly, excessive talking and interrupting others, distractibility, and not anticipating the consequences of risky behaviors (Collins, 2005). Psychological distress is represented by disturbances of mood and self-worth, while anger, frustration, and irritability are common responses to difficulties with behavioral regulation. Medications are sometimes prescribed to help children control their mood-related symptoms. Cognitive-behavioral therapy is the treatment method of choice for helping children with TS manage their daily lives and emotions.

Perhaps most relevant to child-centered practitioners is the fact that TS often goes unrecognized or misdiagnosed because of lack of awareness and training. TS is underreported in part because its criteria are not seen in combination but rather as separate indicators of such conditions as PTSD, mood disorders, and attentional or behavioral disabilities (Collins, 2005). When improperly diagnosed or insufficiently addressed, children with TS and their families do not receive the recognition, acknowledgment, and care they need. As a result youngsters suffer unnecessarily and are unfairly blamed for being *unwilling* to control their behaviors.

Parents of children with TS may be perceived as inadequate or unresponsive to their children's dysregulated behaviors. Like their youngsters, they become victims of incurious misunderstanding. Knowledge of TS is a first step in reaching appropriate diagnosis and treatment. Although there is no cure or foolproof pharmaceutical intervention, a number of strategies are helpful to reduce stresses associated with TS, for example, cognitive-behavioral techniques, narrative strategies, and relational therapies.

The circumstances of Gabriel Ortiz, nine years old, a charming, well-mannered youngster whose parents immigrated from the Dominican Republic, illustrate the unnecessary strains and tensions caused when TS is neither recognized nor diagnosed. I got to know Gabriel at the beginning of the school year because retained students had to meet with the school social worker. He was clearly discouraged by having to repeat second grade. He assured me that he was not "retarded"; he just couldn't pay attention because of "everything that was going on inside of him."

Gabriel said that he was taunted by peers and was "sick to death of being teased." He described "losing it" more often than he liked because the kids relentlessly called him "tripper." He explained that this was because his "urges" caused him to trip himself while walking down the hallway.

I knew from the records that Gabriel's pediatrician had tried stimulants to help with what she assumed was ADHD. But the medication failed to work, and Gabriel's parents, educators, and health providers couldn't make sense of what they called his "continuous antics." These included rubbing his genitals and tripping himself to "get attention." Gabriel's parents blamed themselves for spoiling him and speculated that their relocation and subsequent economic hardships might be triggering his distress. Their relatives in the Dominican Republic suggested they send Gabriel back home or that the Ortizes employ harsher punishments to curb his behaviors.

Gabriel was sensitive to the fact that his behaviors caused distress to those he loved. However, he couldn't quell his urges. He said sensations were like "bees buzzing inside my body that had to be pushed away" or he would go crazy. Indeed, teachers, peers, and family members thought that Gabriel might be mentally ill, though psychological testing did not bear this out.

In collaboration with Gabriel's parents, I referred him to a neurologist. The diagnosis of TS was initially devastating to the family, but it provided them with a rationale for their son's behaviors. Moreover, learning that his symptoms would lessen as he matured gave them hope for the future.

Following his diagnosis, Mrs. Ortiz organized a TS information session for his teachers and then for his classmates. Knowing about TS helped them and school staff respond appropriately to Gabriel's needs. Mrs. Ortiz's efforts inspired school personnel to address broader issues of diversity, which led to the development of zero tolerance for bullying within their school district.

Gabriel's story supports the value of learning about TS and other forms of neurodiversity and developmental differences and bringing this knowledge to child-centered settings. Maintaining open dialogue with teachers, school counselors, coaches, school nurses, and other staff members heightens awareness and invites others in schools and institutional systems to combat discrimination.

SPECIAL EDUCATION

Prevalence of neurodevelopmental and chromosomal abnormalities, among other conditions contributing to childhood disabilities, has increased in the twenty-first century. Trends indicate that one in six children currently living in the United States will receive a disability diagnosis (Boyle et al., 2011).

Approximately six million children in 2012 received special education services, and one in ten children in the United States has a physical or cognitive disability, chronic health problem, or life-threatening illness (Lin, 2012). In Canada the Participation and Activity Limitation Survey indicates that approximately 4 percent of all children ages five to fourteen have a diagnosed disability of some sort (Landsman, 2003), and most of these are learning disabilities.

As noted earlier, explanations for these growing numbers are varied and mostly theoretical. Lack of rationale does not, however, erase the reality that more and more children require early and ongoing special education. Disparities in access to appropriate intervention are particularly salient for low-income, uninsured, and minority children (Boyle et al., 2011). These inequities are a major public health concern.

Although compulsory education laws have been in existence in the United States since 1918, before the 1950s children with disabilities frequently did not attend public school or dropped out early because the system was not designed to meet their complicated and diverse needs. Similarly, students with mild to moderate cognitive differences who enrolled in public school typically left before graduation because they could not pass state-mandated educational requirements (Pardini, 2002). Parents were thus faced with limited options: educate their children at home or, in the case of more severely affected youngsters, place them in state-run institutions.

The success of the civil rights movement and the 1954 decision in *Brown v. Board of Education*, which extended equal protection under the law to minorities, served as inspiration and impetus to parents of children with disabilities as well as to sympathetic educators (Pardini, 2002). It paved the way for parents to advocate equal protection under the law for their children, including the right to appropriate educational opportunities.

In 1975 as a result of this advocacy, the US Congress passed PL 94–142 to promote appropriate education for children with disabilities. The law was designed to ensure that youngsters between the ages of three and twenty-one who were diagnosed with developmental and learning disabilities received free and appropriate education in all public schools. The Individuals with Disabilities Education Act (IDEA), passed in 1990 and revised in 1997 and 2004, expanded services for children with disabilities to include physical, speech, and occupational therapy and educational program accommodation.

Concurrently, the Americans with Disabilities Act (ADA) of 1990, though not specific to children, reinforced the US Congress's position that people with physical, cognitive, or mental impairment deserved the same civil rights and protections against discrimination as those without disabilities. In 2009, ADA was amended to include people of all ages with disabilities, including those with a range of impairments affecting activities of daily living and livelihood.

Legislation affecting disability rights and entitlement to special education in Canada was enacted in 1982. The Canadian Charter of Rights and Freedoms guarantees that people with disabilities have rights equal to those of other citizens. Substantial educational reforms have taken place since the passage of the charter. Canadian provinces are required by law to integrate children with learning and other disabilities into schools where they receive free and appropriate education. As in the United States, how educational institutions interpret what is appropriate for children's needs varies, and more research is needed to determine whether children are indeed receiving the education and services necessary to meet their optimal development (Uppal, Kohen, & Khan, 2008).

These sweeping legislative acts enhanced public awareness of the needs and rights of children with disabilities. They also recognized and affirmed the importance of parents as educational partners "in making decisions about their children and thereby holding educators accountable for benefiting the child" (Turnbull et al., 2006, p. 43).

FAMILY QUALITY OF LIFE

Legislative changes in the 1970s and 1980s opened the door to revised attitudes toward mental retardation and neurocognitive disabilities. Parents and educators turned their attention toward what was possible for children, rather than assuming limitations and preconceiving futures. Child- and family-centered models emerged that promoted not only education but a broader view of quality of life for previously underserved populations (Park, Turnbull, & Turnbull, 2002).

The family quality of life (FQL) paradigm is a well-researched, resiliency-based model for working with families of children with disabilities. It was developed by researchers at the University of Kansas and expanded upon by other disability scholars (Brown, Schalock, & Brown, 2009; Poston et al., 2003). FQL is defined as the capacity of families to meet the needs of their members, to partake of enjoyable times together both at home and in the community, and to do the things that bring meaning and value to family life. Quality of life for children and families relies on family resilience as well as on the supports and services that families receive and on the partnerships with caring professionals that they have (Beach Center on Disability, http://www.beachcenter.org). Turnbull et al. (2006) characterize partnerships as consisting of seven essential principles: communication, professional competence, respect, commitment, equality, advocacy, and trust, with trust being the "keystone" or base on which all other principles depend. These qualities appear throughout the chapters of this book as being highly relevant to relational child-centered practice.

Let's now consider FQL in conjunction with one family's journey. Myrna was forty-two when she learned she was pregnant for the seventh time. Her youngest child was five, and she and her husband, Mike, were excited about the prospect of no more diapers. When Myrna's pregnancy test came back positive, she was shocked and disappointed that she had somehow conceived again, even with birth control. But she and Mike never hesitated about going through with the pregnancy, and decided against any genetic testing because, regardless of its results, they were going to have this baby.

Early on February 18, 2000, Phoebe Anna Fleming was born. When Myrna looked at her daughter, she knew immediately that she had Down syndrome; no one, however, not even the pediatrician, said a word. She felt anxious and frightened and strangely disconnected from her tiny newborn. The day after Phoebe's birth, Myrna was visited by a woman who introduced herself as the mother of a child with Down syndrome. Myrna was appalled by the intrusion and asked the woman to leave.

Myrna and Mike brought their baby home two days after her birth. Before leaving the hospital, their pediatrician confirmed the diagnosis—Phoebe had Down syndrome, also known as trisomy 21, a condition resulting in mental and physical symptoms that could range from mild to severe. What he could guarantee was that Phoebe would be slower in her development than a youngster without Down syndrome. Yet he couldn't say how much slower or specify what other development symptoms might evolve. He did tell the Flemings that Phoebe had mild heart abnormalities that would need to be closely monitored over her lifetime.

For the first few months of Phoebe's life, Myrna kept hoping that the doctor was wrong about her diagnosis. "I kept looking at her and thinking that she would suddenly be normal. But then I'd see her too large tongue, her short little fingers, and those almond-shaped eyes, and I knew there was no going back."

When Phoebe was five months old, Myrna contacted the woman who had come to the hospital. They gradually became close friends as well as vocal advocates for kids with disabilities in their school district. Phoebe's siblings were also helpful to Myrna, except for Gregory, the five-year-old, who was very jealous of his baby sister and the time she took away from him.

As she got older, Phoebe's engaging personality earned her many friends and advocates. The Flemings were lucky that Mike's insurance provider covered most of her added health expenses. This was especially important because shortly after birth Phoebe was diagnosed with an intestinal malformation that required two surgeries. However, the family had to pay for many of her therapies out of pocket; for example, occupational and physical therapies were not considered medical necessities. Because the school did not recommend these treatments, they too were not required to pay for them. To make ends meet, Myrna opened a small day care in their home to supplement Mike's income.

Myrna candidly talks about the exhaustion she felt and admits that at times she was resentful of Phoebe. But this resentment was easily quelled when Phoebe danced into the living room wearing her bear slippers and made everyone's day a little brighter. Both Mike and Myrna worry about what the future will hold for their now ten-year-old daughter. "She's advancing far beyond what we expected," Myrna said. "But her deficits will likely prevent her from living on her own, and we don't know yet what that means for her and for us."

Both parents acknowledge that waves of grief still encompass them when they think about their little girl and the prospects lost. They describe moments of overwhelming sorrow that hits at unexpected times—like when their oldest daughter graduated from college and when their son got engaged. Myrna reflected, "Phoebe will never experience those things, and though she will not grieve those losses, I will."

At the same time, both parents affirm that they wouldn't want Phoebe to be anyone but who she is. "She's brought into our family an amazing perspective on life. She always sees the positive. She's always in the present. She's always hopeful. And even when she's uncompromisingly stubborn, she does it in a way that reminds us to slow life down—just like the doctor said, she would take things slower, and now we do, too."

The Flemings have achieved a positive quality of life within their family and across community ties. Their story resembles those of other parents of children born with Down syndrome as well as those who raise children with a number of life-affecting disabilities: some have adapted well and some have not.

Skotko (2005) reports that most parents who have a baby with Down syndrome learn of the diagnosis after birth, because for a number of reasons there was no prenatal testing. Most are initially shocked, then frightened about what the diagnosis means. Many leave the hospital with very little useful information about what it will be like to care for their child, especially when it is difficult to predict how physical and cognitive symptoms will manifest.

Parents are even less aware of the range of emotions they will experience in response to having a child with disabilities. Shock, disappointment, guilt, grief, and anger are common yet disenfranchised emotions reported by parents. Describing the myriad of emotions parents feel, Maria Lin (2012), the mother of Jacob, age three, born with a rare chromosomal disorder, writes: "I have been challenged and pushed beyond my limits in raising my son. I've grown tremendously as a person, and developed a soft heart and empathy for others in a way I never would without him. But I'm just like the next mom in some ways. Sometimes I get cranky, my son irritates me, and sometimes I want to flee to the spa or go shopping."

Lin (2012) also speaks to the jealousy parents experience when watching typically developing children. She writes, "I can even feel jealous of other special needs kids who seem to have an easier time than Jacob." Difficult feelings often coexist with powerful emotions such as love, pride, and awe at what children are able to accomplish, given their struggles. Worries for the future are particularly poignant, and faith often guides parents when reason and certainty are in short supply.

Practitioners working with families such as Jacob's and Phoebe's do well to recognize that no matter how knowledgeable, skilled, or seasoned they might be, they can never truly know what it's like to raise a child with special needs unless they have done so themselves. Indeed, studies of parental perspectives find that professionals overlook or underestimate the complex emotional needs of these families (Konrad, 2008; Perrin, Lewkowiez, & Young, 2000).

With these findings in mind, I asked Myrna to describe how social workers and other health, mental health, and education professionals could be most helpful to parents of children with disabilities. Here's what she had to share:

- Honesty is important—tell the truth no matter how hard the truth may be.
- Know that at any given time you are only hearing part of our story.
- Don't expect me to be candid with you if you don't share information with me.
- Don't minimize the reality of the situation, but at the same time don't diminish my hope.
- Don't set arbitrary limits on my child's potential—she may surprise us all.
- Respect that our lives are complicated.
- Always remember that parents know their children best.
- Remember that my child is more than a diagnosis.

Lin (2012) adds to Myrna's list by reminding us that parents are tired, sometimes lonely, scared, and upset by insensitive remarks, even when people are trying to be supportive. She comments that parents are eminently human and that, though it's often hard to talk about their children's struggles, they desperately want to do so.

Myrna's and Maria's suggestions speak for many parents raising children with disabilities and other chronic health conditions. They echo not only the evidence-guided research findings of esteemed disability researchers but also the sentiments offered by Rory Hoy, the youngster who introduced this chapter. What do parents want? They want to be accepted, respected, and from time to time, protected. But most of all they want the opportunity to love and be loved by their children.

TEACCH

I happened to visit the TEACCH offices and preschool in Carrboro, North Carolina, the week of Halloween. The final learning activity for the day was practicing trick-or-treat skills. The teachers and students practiced putting on Halloween costumes. There was a robot, a monster, a lion, a pirate, and one costume I couldn't quite decipher.

This was followed by an activity designed to prepare these little ones for door-to-door encounters on Halloween eve. I was given candy and asked to wait behind a closed door in anticipation of the young costumers. Each in their turn knocked, waited, greeted; said "trick or treat"; accepted the candy; and graciously said "thank you." The children carried out this exercise well. All in all it was a very successful learning day.

As this activity exemplifies, the preschool teachers creatively and intentionally integrate TEACCH's educational philosophy into their daily lesson plans. Structured learning activities occur within a consistent and reliable environment where even their youngest students gain skills to function meaningfully and independently in their community. As one of the preschool TEACCH instructors puts it, "Anything from sorting colors to getting dressed—if we know that skill will eventually foster independence, even from the beginning we're working to promote it and not have them be dependent on us" (figure 9.1). Gary Mesibov, the former director of TEACCH, agrees about the objectives of the TEACCH program. "We want the world to be meaningful and to make sense," he told me. Most of the time, life in the neurotypical world simply doesn't make much sense to children with ASD.

TEACCH's approach does not focus on changing the child's brain but on altering the environment to fit his or her learning style. Thus some children are included in the classroom setting, while home-teaching methods may fit better with others' strengths and disabilities. Some youth will go on to work traditional jobs, while others will have more success living and working in structured group residences and job placements.

Those using the TEACCH model aim to balance what children with ASD have in common with what makes each child unique. As mentioned earlier, Mesibov ascribes to a "culture of autism." While he believes in individualizing education and treatment for children, he also feels strongly that people with ASD share some general characteristics. For example, they tend to be visual learners and to have narrow or specialized interests that are highly intense. Thus one of TEACCH's goals is to find *the* thing that the autistic child is really interested in and capitalize on it. TEACCH methods begin by

FIGURE 9.1 Preschool instructors in the TEACCH classroom

respecting differences and then work within those differences to advance common skills that will help children function within their family, community, and the broader society.

The TEACCH model also builds on the expertise and strengths of parents. Eric Schopler, the founder of TEACCH, broke away from the parent-blaming models that were pervasive when he first came into the field. Instead of analyzing parents, he invited their perspectives and partnered with them in decision making. According to Gary Mesibov (personal communication, October 16, 2009), seeing parents as part of the team was revolutionary for the times: "Eric's whole model was that the parents watch everything, you teach them how to work with their children, and you listen to the parents—that was unheard of in mental health back then. You took the kids away, and then you brought them back. Now it's all right there, and you're working together."

Gary also commented on the growing population of children diagnosed with ASD over the last three decades, many of whom enroll in the TEACCH program in North Carolina. I asked him what factors he thought contributed to this puzzling growth rate. He reflected that ASD is relative to the demands of a given society: "the biggest change in the field is identifying autism as a continuous rather than a categorical variant . . . so basically we all have autism. It's just a matter of how much we have it and when it crosses the line to become impairment or something that interferes with everyday life. Today school is much faster, there's more stress, there are many more tests, and there's much, much more multitasking. So I think the place where we draw the line in the sand about autism has moved—it's a much broader group. We don't refer to kids like Bill Gates as autistic because they're able to succeed. Rather we refer to kids who can't make it."

TEACCH continues to actively engage parents in every aspect of its programming. Linda Varblow, a psychoeducational therapist for TEACCH, believes that parents' involvement is pivotal to the success of the TEACCH model. She reflected upon how the complementary expertise of parents and professionals is basic to TEACCH's success. "We always tell parents, you're the expert on your child, but we're the expert on autism. We have to collaborate because neither one of us can help this child alone."

The nine regional TEACCH centers in North Carolina serve preschoolers to young adults. TEACCH also has strong partnerships with local organizations such as the Autism Society of North Carolina (ASNC). Thus the last stop in my whirlwind TEACCH visit was in Durham to talk with Maureen Morrell, director of government relations, and Anne Palmer, director of advocacy and chapter support for ASNC. Both women are mothers of grown children with ASD, and both have strong connections to TEACCH.

Their focus during our meeting was on the importance of parent-to-parent mentorship. Anne described how the TEACCH mothers' group was a lifeline for her. "We met other parents there, and we still are friends with all these women—our kids are now adults—but personally for me, that was my survival, that was my therapy."

ASNC has been instrumental in developing parent advocacy programs that help families navigate the complex educational and social service systems associated with ASD. Advocates are primarily parents of children with ASD; some have several children who have been diagnosed with ASD. Anne described the advocate's role as "the in-your-community experts on autism." As such they provide information, locate resources, offer workshops and training, and listen to parents wanting to talk with someone about what they're going through.

Autism is a lifelong struggle, and according to Mesibov the next hurdle for researchers and educators is to develop evidence-guided models that can meet the diverse and growing needs of young adults. His hope and that of everyone I spoke with is to develop programs based on TEACCH principles that will enable people of all ages with ASD to function meaningfully and independently up to their highest level of ability.

THE ADAPTIVE DANCE PROGRAM

Since 2002, the Adaptive Dance Program in Boston's South End has hosted a cadre of young dancers with Down syndrome. They meet at the Boston Ballet studios on Clarendon Street, where they learn about ballet, rhythmic dance, and friendship. Classes are taught Saturday mornings by professional dance instructors and physical therapists.

Michelina Cassella, program founder and a physical therapist by training, allowed me to observe the classes in the ballet studio. She told me that adaptive dance's goals are to ensure that participants will feel successful no matter what. Its mission statement highlights the program's objectives: "Adaptive dance class provides a fun-filled experience for children with special needs by providing a positive environment to enrich their lives with movement, music, friendships, and a personal sense of accomplishment" (Michelina Cassella, personal communication, April 11, 2012).

Mickey explained to me that children with Down syndrome are often excluded from traditional extracurricular programs; thus opportunity for social learning outside of school is difficult to find. She noted that adaptive dance is designed to model cooperation and to help these youngsters develop skills such as following directions and getting along with others, both of which readily translate into other social aspects of their lives.

Learning to set appropriate personal boundaries is another skill taught in the dance studio. According to Mickey, children with Down syndrome are characteristically affectionate and friendly toward others, even strangers. During class time children are taught to regulate and channel their naturally loving inclinations. Hugs are not entirely discouraged, however; they're used to demonstrate appropriate displays of caring. As Mickey described it, "This class is very effective because we said no hugging in class, but we'll have a group hug after. And that's worked beautifully" (figure 9.2).

Instructors also work with the children to help them manage more difficult feelings, such as frustration, extreme shyness, and anger. Children in the class are invited, but never forced, into activities. Some watch on the perimeter while others dive right in. Once engaged, children's energies are directed toward the instructor, in this case, Gianni Di Marco, who skillfully leads them through structured dance exercises. At one point I watched the young dancers form a line, dance across the room, and execute their own improvisational moves.

While the children are in class, parents gather in an adjacent room to watch them through a one-way mirror. Many of them spoke with admiration about Di Marco's teaching style. They described his impressive ability to balance discipline and structure with respect for the individualized needs of the children. A professional dancer now retired from the Boston Ballet, Di Marco never imagined that he would someday teach dance to children with special needs. Yet he clearly knows how to motivate and guide these youngsters and is obviously proud of their accomplishments.

FIGURE 9.2   Group hug with adaptive dancers and instructors

The positive outcomes of the adaptive dance classes are sometimes surprising even to parents. As one mother said, "Adam didn't start until he was thirteen. He loved music and everything but couldn't follow directions. Now he's so focused—whatever Gianni says, Adam does. Adam's so comfortable with him. And so the ability to follow instructions and move and just stay with the teacher—it's made a big difference in his life."

Like the children, parents have benefited from being part of the adaptive dance experience. Some spoke about the value of spending time with other parents who share common child-rearing experiences. Others identified the value of making enduring connections and establishing social networks. As one mother told me, "It's also great for the parents cause we can talk. What works, what school is best . . . Even to keep the parents notified of what's going on outside of ballet. That's been great."

All in all, the Adaptive Dance Program exemplifies what creative community-based partnership can accomplish. When we met in 2009, Mickey was excited about the attention the adaptive dance model was garnering around the country. She attributed its success to the common commitment shared by the Boston Ballet, Boston Children's Hospital, and the community of children and parents that adaptive dance serves each year. From my vantage point, its success also relies on Mickey's enduring vision and her tenacity in maintaining the integrity of the mission statement.

Summary

This chapter has two important take-home messages. First, the relationships established between families and professionals are extremely important. How well or how poorly families fare has much to do with the support they do or do not receive and the partnerships they do or do not have with professionals. This is true for all families of children with special needs, because even those who seem to be doing well experience underlying struggles in their day-to-day functioning. As one mother stated, "Every day, every day is different. I mean, we're doing well right now, but it's hard because you never know when you're going to be kicked off your ass" (Konrad, 2006).

Positive worker-parent alliances are even more essential for families with fewer means and resources and for those who have otherwise experienced social disenfranchisement. These are the children and families who require workers to go the extra mile and find empathy and hope in the face of adversity.

The second take-home message has to do with the strength and joy that exceptional children bring. We tend to recognize and prepare families for the inevitable challenges and losses of raising children with differences. What often surprises us is that these children have so much to offer and do so with all their heart.

Notes

1. Changes in the ASD classification are expected in the revised *Diagnostic and Statistical Manual of Mental Disorders* (DSM-5), due out in spring 2013.

2. Treatment and Education of Autistic and Communication-Related Handicapped Children (TEACCH) is an education, treatment, and research program in the University of North Carolina School of Medicine.

3. Asperger's syndrome was first described in 1944 and was entered into the DSM-IV in 1994. It is a severe developmental disorder characterized by impairments in social interaction and by restricted and unusual patterns of interest. There is some question as to whether Asperger's syndrome will be subsumed under the category of ASD in the DSM-5.

4. TS is referenced in several ways by different experts. I have chosen to use the term *neurodevelopmental* to describe the condition, but *neuropsychiatric* and *neurobehavioral* are alternative terms used to describe the disorder.

References

Altiere, M. J., & Von Kluge, S. (2009). Searching for acceptance: Challenges encountered while raising a child with autism. *Journal of Intellectual and Developmental Disability, 34*(2), 142–152.

Barron, J., & Barron, S. (2002). *There's a boy in here: Emerging from the bonds of autism.* Arlington, TX: Future Horizons.

Bettelheim, B. (1967). *The empty fortress: Infantile autism and the birth of the self.* New York: Free Press.

Bloch, J. S., & Weinstein, J. D. (2010). Families of young children with autism. *Social Work in Mental Health, 8,* 23–40.

Boyle, C. A., Boulet, S., Schieve, L. A., Cohen, R. A., Blumberg, S. J., Yeargin-Allsopp, M., Visser, S., & Kogan, M. D. (2011). Trends in the prevalence of developmental disabilities in US children, 1997–2008. *Pediatrics, 127*(6), 1034–1042.

Brown, R. I., Schalock, R. L., & Brown, I. (2009). Quality of life: Its application to persons with intellectual disabilities and their families; Introduction and overview. *Journal of Policy and Practice in Intellectual Disabilities, 6,* 2–6.

Collins, K. S. (2005). Using a biopsychosocial paradigm in social work practice with children who have Tourette syndrome. *Child and Adolescent Social Work Journal, 22,* 477–495.

Cosden, M., Koegel, L. K., Koegel, R. L., Greenwell, A., & Klein, E. (2006). A strength-based approach to parent education for children with autism. *Journal of Positive Behavior Interventions, 31*(2), 134–143.

Cutler, D., Murphy, T., Gilmour, J., & Heyman, I. (2009). The quality of life of young people with Tourette syndrome. *Child: Care, Health, and Development, 35*(4), 496–504.

Duncan, A., & Klinger, L. G. (2010). Autism spectrum disorders: Building social skills in group, school, and community settings. *Social Work with Groups, 33*(2), 175–193.

Harrington, J. W., Patrick, P. A., Edwards, K. S., & Brand, D. A. (2006). Parental beliefs about autism: Implications for the treating physician. *Autism, 10*(5), 452–462.

Kanner, L. (1943). Autistic disturbances of affective contact. *Nervous Child, 2,* 217–250.

Kiely, M. C. (2000, September/October). What is perfect? A former Rhodes scholar reexamines the value of intelligence with a little help from her 5-year-old. *Dartmouth Alumni Magazine,* 30–31.

Konrad, S. C. (2006). Posttraumatic growth in mothers of children with acquired disabilities. *Journal of Loss and Trauma, 11*(1), 101–113.

Konrad, S. C. (2007). What parents of seriously ill children value: Parent-to-parent connection and mentorship. *Omega, 55*(2), 121–134.

Konrad, S. C. (2008). Mothers' perspectives on qualities of care in their relationships with health care professionals: The influence of relational and communicative competencies. *Journal of Social Work in End-of-Life and Palliative Care, 4*(1), 19–53.

Landsman, G. (2003). Emplotting children's lives: Developmental delay vs. disability. *Social Science and Medicine, 56*(9), 1947–1960.

Levine, M. (2002). *A mind at a time.* New York: Simon and Schuster.

Lin, M. (2012). 7 things you don't know about a special needs parent. Retrieved at http://www.huffingtonpost.com/maria-lin/special-needs-parenting_b_1314348.html

Mesibov, G. B., & Shea, V. (2011). Evidence-based practices and autism. *Autism, 15,* 114–133.

Meyer, D. J., & Vadasy, P. F. (1996). *Living with a brother or sister with special needs: A book for sibs* (2nd ed.). Seattle: University of Washington Press.

Pardini, P. (2002). The history of special education. *Rethinking Schools, 16*. Retrieved at http://rethinkingschools.org/archive/16_03/Hist163.shtml

Park, J., Turnbull, A. P., & Turnbull, R. (2002). Quality indicators of professionals who work with children with problem behavior. *Journal of Positive Behavior Interventions, 4*(2), 118.

Perrin, E. C., Lewkowiez, C., & Young, M. H. (2000). Shared visions: Concordance among fathers, mothers, and pediatricians about unmet needs of children with chronic health conditions. *Pediatrics, 105*(1), 277–285.

Piacentini, J., Woods, D. W., Scahill, L., Wilhelm, S., Peterson, A. L., Chang, S., . . . & Walkup, J. T. (2010). Behavior therapy for children with Tourette disorder: A randomized controlled trial. *Journal of American Medical Association, 303*, 1929–1937.

Poston D., Turnbull A., Park J., Mannan H., Marquis J., & Wang M. (2003). Family quality of life outcomes: A qualitative inquiry launching a long-term research program. *Mental Retardation, 41*, 313–328.

Prizant, B., Wetherby, A., Rubin, E., Laurent, A., & Rydell, P. (2006). *The SCERTS model: A comprehensive educational approach for children with autism spectrum disorders*. Baltimore: Paul H. Brookes.

Renna, R. (2004). Autism spectrum disorders. *International Journal of Reality Therapy, 23*(2), 17–22.

Sellman, E. (2007). [Review of *Autism and Me*, produced/directed by Rory Hoy]. *Pastoral Care in Education, 25*, 50–51.

Skotko, B. (2005). Mothers of children with Down syndrome reflect on their postnatal support. *Pediatrics, 115*, 64–77.

TEACCH Mission Statement. 2012. Retrieved at http://teacch.com/about-us-1

Turnbull, A., Turnbull, R., Erwin, E., & Soodak, L. (2006). *Families, professionals, and exceptionality: Positive outcomes through partnerships and trust* (5th ed.). Upper Saddle River, NJ: Pearson Education.

Turnbull, A., Zuna, N., Hong, J. Y., Hu, X., Kyzar, K., Obremski, S., . . . & Stowe, M. J. (2010). Knowledge-to-Action Guides: Preparing families to be partners in making educational decisions. *Teaching Exceptional Children, 42*(3), 42–63.

Uppal, S., Kohen, D., & Khan, S. (2008). *Educational services and the disabled child*. Health Analysis and Measurement Group, Statistics Canada. Retrieved at http://www.statcan.gc.ca/pub/81-004-x/2006005/9588-eng.htm

Wieder, S., & Greenspan, S. I. (2003). Climbing the symbolic ladder in the DIR model through floor time/interactive play. *Autism, 7*, 425–435.

10

Family Disruption and Ambiguous Losses

> One of the pitfalls of childhood is that one doesn't have to under-
> stand something to feel it. By the time the mind is able to compre-
> hend what has happened, the wounds of the heart are already too
> deep.
>
> Carlos Ruiz Zafón, *The Shadow of the Wind*

WOUNDS OF THE HEART

Relational separations and transitional life events are part of the ever-
changing landscape of childhood. The birth or adoption of a sibling, moving
on to middle school, and relocating to a new neighborhood, to name a few,
are expected transitions for youth. Unexpected changes also take place. The
death of a loved person is an unforeseen yet common loss experienced by
children. (Chapter 11 specifically addresses death and grief in the lives of
children.)

Death-related losses generally prompt sympathy and support from children's inner circle and their community of care. Other unanticipated relational separations in childhood may be less recognized and therefore
underacknowledged. Separations from parents are instigated by divorce,
military deployment, incarceration, and hospitalization. These separations
can result in temporary or permanent realignments in families. Youngsters
experience significant emotional instability in response to family changes,
and for some, such uncertainty brings about feelings of undefined and often
unrecognized grief.

Less obvious yet powerfully felt are losses experienced by children
when parents, family members, or caregivers are physically present yet emotionally and relationally inaccessible. Pauline Boss (1999) described such
losses as ambiguous because the lost person is alive yet not the same as
before. Ambiguous losses occur for children in families where there is

223

domestic or intimate-partner violence (see chapter 12). They occur when family members are emotionally unreliable due to addiction, mental illness, or chronic and disabling health conditions. Although most parents don't choose to be remote, their struggles disengage them from parenting and relational responsibilities. Such disconnections cause children to feel a range of insecurities and, in some cases, grief.

Child-centered workers and other helping professionals respond to the myriad ways children express and react to relational separations and transitions. They handle situations for which there are clear-cut guidelines and tangible solutions, such as finding safe havens in cases of family violence or identifying housing options when families unexpectedly need to relocate. When divorce takes place, practitioners advise adults about what their children need to know and what is best left unsaid. They also help children and families adapt to changes in roles and responsibilities precipitated by parental deployment, incarceration, and extended work-related separations.

Well-intentioned social institutions may inadvertently trigger children's feelings of parental separation and loss. Young children of incarcerated parents, for example, feel the sting of their loss when they're asked to make a card for Mother's or Father's Day. Father-daughter dances will likely stir up complicated reactions for girls with combat-deployed fathers. Youth whose parents are impaired due to mental illness or addiction may not know what to say to well-meaning teachers who "can't wait" to meet their parents at the next parent-teacher conference. Workers can help negotiate these situations.

This chapter covers a few of the many kinds of separations, disruptions, and transitions experienced in childhood. It focuses first on the effects of divorce and the common responses seen in children from early childhood through adolescence. It covers different options for parenting after a divorce and some pitfalls that result from chronic discord between parents. It also offers children's views of separation and divorce.

The chapter then examines three less-recognized separations and disruptions experienced by children and parents: parental deployment, parental incarceration, and serious illness or disability. Case examples bring children's situations into focus and remind us of the importance of the tools we have: evidence-guided knowledge, a well-worn tool kit, compassion, and caring.

IMPACT OF DIVORCE

Every year, approximately one million children under the age of eighteen are newly affected by parental divorce. The term *divorce* refers to the legal dissolution of a marriage, while *parenting-partner separation* describes the formal split-up of parenting partners, for example, same-sex couples in states where they cannot legally wed. Legal divorce occurs in 47 percent to

51 percent of all first marriages and 60 percent to 72 percent of second marriages in the United States and Canada, respectively. According to the 2010 US census, divorce rates may be on a slightly upward trend from those of the previous decade.

These general percentages and trends, however, reflect only legal marriages. Parenting-partner separations are not represented in US census metrics.[1] Yet children are equally affected by parenting disruptions in a range of nonmarried and therefore untracked family systems. These include same-sex parents, heterosexual and GLBT partners who choose not to marry, and grandparents or other kin who serve as primary caregivers.

An extensive literature describes common factors that influence outcomes for children of all ages who have experienced parental separation and divorce (Amato & Afifi, 2006; Neale & Flowerdew, 2003; Kelly & Ward, 2002; Saywitz, Camparo, & Romanoff, 2010; Smart, 2006; Warshak, 2003). Factors affecting children include chronic parental conflict, economic strains and disadvantages, repartnering of one or both parents, introduction of same-sex partners, transitions into stepfamily life, and parental relocations (Neale & Flowerdew, 2003; Kelly & Ward, 2002; Smart, 2006). Characteristics that influence a child's adaptation include age at time of divorce, cognitive level and ability, temperament and social adjustment, history of trauma or abuse, and extent of previous losses (Kot & Shoemaker, 1999).

As with other family-based problems, the quality of family functioning before, during, and after divorce affects children. Not all parents have insight and good-enough postseparation relationships to help children negotiate changes in family makeup and structure. Indeed, in the midst of the separation process, some parents find themselves so distracted by their own feelings of distress and loss that family routines and disciplinary strategies become disorganized or entirely ignored. Although such occurrences are understandable, these tumultuous times call for parents to be somewhat extraordinary and to model authority, reliability, and self-regulation.

Studies conducted over the last thirty years consistently affirm that enduring parental conflict is the single most deleterious factor affecting children's postdivorce adaptation (Amato & Afifi, 2006; Kelly & Emery, 2003; Saywitz et al., 2010). Chronic conflict is especially toxic when children are witness to or placed in the middle of their parents' battleground. Unrelenting parental conflict results in a range of adjustment and behavioral problems, which may evolve into serious relational problems as children become adults (Amato & Afifi, 2006). Another common consequence of postdivorce contentiousness is seen in a child's decision to choose one parent over the other in order to reduce ongoing tensions and deflect damage. This was the case for Ariana, an articulate six-year-old. As she explained, "It's just too hard to love my mama and papa at the same time. So I pretend to myself that I don't love my mama because if I did it would be too sad to be away from her to live in my papa's house. When I'm with my mama, I stay quiet because I'm just gonna have to leave."

As one can see, Ariana developed a well-reasoned rationale to help make sense of her fractured life. She knew that she could love only the parent she was with in order to survive the loyalty conflicts she felt. This adaptational process is what some mental health experts call *compartmentalizing*. It permitted Ariana to simplify things by seeing her life with each parent as distinct, not as a whole system of which she was a part. So when she first began living in two homes, Ariana refused to have photos of her mother at her father's home and vice versa. She simply did not want to think about the absent parent when she was with the other one.

Fortunately Ariana's parents understood that she needed explicit permission to love them both. Once this was established, transitions between their homes went more smoothly and were less stressful for all concerned. Like many other parents, Ariana's benefited from a parenting education program that provided guidance about what to expect from children in her age group and helped them deal more effectively with family changes (see "The Kids First Center" below; Sigal, Sandler, Wolchik, & Braver, 2011).

Economic loss and disparity in incomes between postdivorce coparenting households also affect children's functioning. Children are exquisitely aware of material inequities and view such financial differences as patently unfair. Internal and external tensions arise when one parent can clearly offer more tangible goods to the children than the other. In some cases children play parents off each other to garner material gain. Similarly, sparring parents may use material goods to lure children into spending more time at their residences. In the best of situations, parents ensure that their children's basic needs are met regardless of residential times or the status of the adults' relationship.

Introduction of new partners and remarriage can also cause disharmony between former spouses and with the children from both former relationships. Children's earlier feelings of loss and relational insecurity may reemerge when new parental relationships form and stepsiblings appear. In many respects new relationships are powerful reminders that parents will never be reunited, thus spoiling a common fantasy of divorced children.

Ironically, the reunification fantasy can be unintentionally reinforced when parents do a good job of maintaining positive postdivorce relationships. This was true for nine-year-old Pammy, whose parents legally divorced when she was four. They had worked hard to sustain a positive and loving coparenting experience for their children, which included Pammy; her sister Zoe, age seven; and her brother, Zach, age twelve. The parents spent holidays together with the children and provided child care for each other when necessary. They made joint parenting decisions without much conflict, and for all intents and purposes they cared for their children exactly the same way they had when they were legally married.

It wasn't until John, Pammy's father, moved in with his partner, Vernon, that Pammy experienced a renewed sense of grief for the family she once knew and lost. Like other children whose parents repartner, Pammy had to now weave many new relationships into her conceptualization of family. The fact that John's partner was a man created an added dimension to integrating the new relationship. With the support of her parents and a family counselor, however, Pammy eventually worked through her sorrow and came to accept and love the two families she now had.

As the cases of Ariana and Pammy illustrate, and studies confirm, most postdivorce parents reconcile or adjust to their differences and go on to parent effectively. For some it becomes a matter of conflict management based on "loving our children more than we hate our ex-partners," as one parent put it. Respect for children's attachments to parents and stepparents is critical if children are to successfully navigate the relational losses brought about by divorce.

It is regrettably the case, however, that some children are passively or actively encouraged by one or both parents to take sides. *Parental alienation syndrome* (PAS) is a term used by mental health and legal professionals to describe situations where children experience such loyalty conflicts that they refuse to be in the presence or household of one of their parents. The impetus and prevalence of PAS is poorly understood and fraught with controversy as to whether it constitutes a psychiatric syndrome or represents an act of intended domestic abuse (Bow, Gould, & Flens, 2009; Warshak, 2003).

It is certain, however, that some children respond to extreme parental conflict by choosing to have a relationship with only one parent, while letting go of their relationship with the other. One has only to look through the eyes of the child to imagine the effect of such dissention. In effect these youngsters endure a triple loss: first they watch their known family dissolve, and then they lose connection not only to one of their parents but also to the family and community systems that make up the context of that parent's life. Many children cannot identify why they refuse to be with the rejected parent; they only know that for some reason they feel unsafe. Some are so strongly allied with one parent that they unquestioningly accept his or her perceptions and fears.

There can be legitimate reasons to protect children from a parent, as in the case of a substantiated history of child abuse, sexual abuse, or family violence. Protection may also be appropriate when a parent is severely impaired as a result of addiction or mental illness. Such caution does not constitute intent to alienate and should not be construed as such.

Even in these circumstances, children need opportunities to safely and candidly express their feelings about the unavailable parent and if possible maintain some form of safe, ongoing contact. Contact might involve supervised visits or other forms of thoughtful communication, for example, supervised letter writing, e-mails, or journal exchanges. Planned interactions aim to prevent the child from either experiencing an unexplained sense of parental abandonment or blaming himself or herself for causing disconnection.

If no parental contact is recommended by the court or other authorities, the rationale for this decision should be carefully explained so that children do not harbor unhelpful thoughts or fantasies about why contact has been prohibited. As in all cases, custodial parents must support children's desire for connection with the other parent or, at the very least, remain neutral.

CHILDREN'S NEEDS AFTER DIVORCE

This section is a brief overview of developmental needs and potential problems for children after a divorce. It offers insights for parents and child-centered practitioners about how to effectively respond to the needs of youngsters during transitional times.

Early Childhood (up to Three Years)

As you learned in chapter 3, parents and infants or toddlers are focused on developing relational attachments. Positive parent-child attachments contribute to children's emotional security as well as to their capacity for physical and affective regulation. The ability to self-regulate is a cornerstone of well-being, and as such it influences other areas of development, including learning, socialization, and mental health.

When parents divorce during children's earliest years, attachments and family ties are at least temporarily destabilized. Parents should do their best to avoid expressing overt disharmony in the presence of their infants, in order to cement secure relationships and not disrupt the child's developing regulatory skills. It is not unusual for infants to express increased distress (e.g., crying, fussiness, clinginess) and be more difficult to soothe during and immediately following parental separations. These behaviors should decrease with the reestablishment of reliable parenting routines.

In addition to lowering the volume on conflict, parents of infants and toddlers must determine residency schedules that give children quality time with both parents. Children under the age of three do not have stable relational memories and thus need routine reinforcement to secure their bonds. Scheduling is often difficult, however, given parental employment and babies' complicated sleep and feeding routines. Thus parents should focus on when they are indeed available to care for their infants and not base contact schedules solely on equal division of hours in the day or days in the week. The goal for parents is to optimize time with their children, to maintain secure and reliable relationships, and to help them grow and flourish.

Young Children (Ages Three to Eight)

Children from three to eight years old will vary in their responses to learning about their parents' divorce. Some may react with sorrow and anger while others take the news in stride. Some children exhibit behavioral difficulties while others of the same age withdraw. Young children don't necessarily absorb the reality of family change until it actually happens. For example, parents may tell their young child about the impending divorce, but he or she may not react until the moving trucks arrive (see Pammy's story above). Young children will mimic what their parents tell them ("Mommy and Daddy have a divorce"), but they do not really understand the reality of these words until they live with the separation on a daily basis. This can be seen, for instance, in repeated and distressed inquiries about why the other parent isn't there to kiss the child goodnight.

Explaining family changes to younger children should be well planned and age appropriate. As noted by the Kids First Center (2008, p. 19), "Parents have only one opportunity to make a first good impression." Although young children may be aware of their parents' troubles, most do not anticipate change in their parenting situation. When directly speaking about divorce, parents must assure their children that they are not at fault. Children are by nature egocentric and relate to life based on limited experience. It is therefore natural for them to assume that something they did, or even thought, might have contributed to their parents' split.

If feelings associated with fault for the divorce are not addressed, they can have enduring ramifications. I learned this firsthand from Marcia, age seven. She told me that her parents divorced when she was five. When I asked about what her parents had told her, she said that they never said anything. "Dad just left one morning. He never lived with us again."

When I inquired about why he left, she told me this story: "One day Daddy had to get us ready for school 'cause Mom was late for work. I just got new party shoes and really, really wanted to wear them. Daddy said no because it was snowy on the ground. But then he let me. When I came home, Mom got mad at me for wearing my new shoes. She and Daddy had a big fight that night, and that's when he left. So I know they got divorced because Dad made a bad decision and Mom got mad at him because he let me wear my party shoes."

Children also require reassurance that there is nothing they can do to change the situation. After learning of the divorce, children may attempt to be extra "good" or extra "bad" to draw their parents' attentions away from thoughts of separation. Take Wally, for example. Wally was a model pupil in first grade until his parents announced their divorce to him and his little brother. Shortly thereafter, Wally's parents started receiving e-mails from his teacher, reporting that his grades were slipping and that he was involved in inappropriate behavior.

Such actions were so out of character for Wally that his parents connected him with the school guidance counselor, fearing that he had developed a psychological disorder. The counselor quickly surmised the method in Wally's madness. She advised his parents to let Wally know that his behaviors would not change their adult decision to divorce. Wally got the message quickly and for the most part resumed his previously positive attitude at school and at home.

If possible, both parents should tell young children that their needs will be taken care of and that their secure attachments will remain intact. When parents are living in two locations, it is important that they support residency transitions and not interfere with children's relationship with the other parent. If parents cannot reliably keep strain out of their encounters, they can make alternative options for transitions and decision making. These include transitions that occur away from the home (e.g., school, day care, and extracurricular activities), communicating only when children aren't present, and avoiding face-to-face decision making whenever possible.

Older Children (Ages Nine to Twelve)

Older children (nine to twelve years old) deeply feel the changes and losses of parental separation. Although they are developing interests of their own, they still depend on parents and adults for security, nurturance, and limits. At this age, children may be embarrassed by their parents' actions and may not tell their friends or other significant adults (e.g., teachers, coaches) about what is happening in their family. Keeping secrets can take a toll on children and affect their overall well-being.

Because children of this age lack abstract thinking skills, they tend to view divorce as one parent's fault and may ally with one parent against the other. This is a slippery slope for the parent with whom the child has allied. It is easy to feel bolstered by such loyalty, but parents must remember that children do best when their relationships with both parents are strong and enduring.

Behaviors seen in children of this age before, during, and after divorce range from regression to aggression, from being overly solicitous to noncompliant and hostile. Like younger children, older ones need direction, clear limits, reliability, and love. They flourish when parents take the time to do things that both parents and children enjoy. They also need to be encouraged to continue their favored activities and develop relationships with peers and other trusted adults. Most youngsters in this age bracket navigate the transition well if their parents and extended family keep them on track and out of the middle of the adults' frays.

Adolescents

Because adolescents are undergoing significant developmental growth and change, their relationships with the adults in their lives are constantly being revised and renewed. Adolescents seek to differentiate themselves from their parents by asserting independence and seeking autonomy. At the same time, however, they rely on parents to provide shelter, safety, and reassurance, knowing that at the end of the day they can come home and be cared for.

More than their younger counterparts, adolescents possess sufficient cognitive maturity to understand the reasons that precipitate parental divorce. They may therefore be disappointed by their parents' behaviors and choices or relieved that their struggles might be ending.

Frankie, fourteen, reported that because his parents fought all the time he didn't get too attached to the idea of their being together forever. He described waking up in the middle of the night because he could hear doors slamming and his parents arguing. Frankie avoided talking about the fights, and so did his parents. He wanted to keep the peace and stay out of the way. Thus when his father told him that he was moving to a new apartment, Frankie wasn't happy but neither was he surprised.

The appearance of maturity may lead divorcing parents and other adults to expect adolescents to take on adult responsibilities and to offer parents advice and support. Some youth cope with family changes by overfunctioning to compensate for the tensions that are felt. Either way, adolescents can feel caught in the middle of their parents' difficulties and burdened by pressure (real or imagined) to take on practical and emotional responsibilities that exceed their capacity to meet them.

Such pressures, along with feelings of loss associated with the dissolution of the family, have both long- and short-term effects. These include increased risk for depression, lowered academic achievement, social isolation, antisocial behavior, substance misuse, and wariness about the value of intimate relationships (Kot & Shoemaker, 1999). When adolescents have good friends, outside interests, and hobbies, and feel cared for by their parents and other adults, they will likely rebound from the strains of divorce without enduring effects. Like children of any age, however, adolescents are deeply affected by ongoing parental conflict and other divorce disruptions. Parents must be reminded that even though their adolescents may look mature, they are still and will always be their children.

MODELS OF POSTSEPARATION PARENTING

Parenting roles and responsibilities undergo many revisions when parents separate and in some cases go on to new partner relationships. As discussed above, children do best when their parents can move past their differences and resume stable parenting routines. Most postdivorce families manage to establish good-enough coparenting structures that support their children's growth and development. These relationships, however, may look very different as a result of the parents' inter- and intrarelational capacities. The continuum of parenting strategies may vary somewhat from place to place and household to household.

Coparenting partnerships assume that parents can collaborate effectively and maintain a child-centered perspective. In day-to-day practice, coparenting involves ongoing and authentic communication that focuses on the immediate physical, material, relational, emotional, educational, spiritual, and social needs of children. Effective coparenting requires that parents can solve problems and make decisions when challenges and transitions arise. Such challenges might involve common situations such as sleepovers, dating, getting a license, and summer camps. They may at times concern more complex and potentially divisive decision making about religious education, changing residency schedules, or major changes brought about by a parent's geographic relocation.

Of course, effective coparents are committed to keeping children out of the center of their conflicts. Thus even the most proficient coparents may need an outside party (counselor, mediator, parent coordinator, or court-appointed guardian ad litem [GAL][2]) to help them make these tough calls without unnecessarily disrupting children's lives or relationships.

Parallel parenting is a strategy recommended for parents who are unable to maintain cordial postdivorce communication and are at risk of exposing children to relational conflicts. Many couples end relationships because of communication difficulties. Thus some parents may wisely choose to use a parenting strategy that reduces the likelihood that they will replicate these unhelpful interactional patterns with their children.

Parallel parenting plans are most often determined through mediation or court procedures. Parents determine an outline of the responsibilities that each will carry, to avoid areas that might have required negotiation. For example, one parent may be responsible for dental visits while the other is responsible for buying sports equipment. Typically, parallel parenting plans include strategies for communicating when parents must make collective decisions (e.g., health decisions) or convey unexpected information (e.g., death in the family). Sometimes mental health and legal professionals are engaged by families to help resolve impasses.

A parallel parenting plan works only when both parents remain focused and child-centered and when there is no *known* risk of abuse to children or to either parent. Indeed, some parents may begin with a parallel parenting plan and, when initial postdivorce conflicts subside, move to cooperative coparenting. Conversely, parents may begin with coparenting arrangements but find that a parallel parenting plan reduces ongoing conflicts between households.

Sole parental custody has become a relatively rare postdivorce parenting arrangement. It's legally enacted when a parent is determined to be abusive or sufficiently negligent, to have engaged in a pattern of intimate-partner violence, or to suffer from serious mental illness or other condition that is harmful to children (Hardesty & Chung, 2006). Sole custody is divided into two categories: physical and legal. Sole physical custody establishes that children live with and are supervised by one parent. The other parent is entitled to reasonable visitation, however, unless it's determined by the courts that such visitation would not be in children's best interests.

Sole legal custody allots to one parent legal rights and decision-making responsibilities, including those pertaining to health, mental health, education, and religion. This legal arrangement is established when one parent actively denies, rejects, or abandons parenting obligations or is incapable of caring for children. Mothers are more commonly awarded sole legal custody of children, but there are circumstances when fathers or other caregiving adults become sole legal parents (Kelly & Emery, 2003).

Joel Finnegan-Smith was awarded sole legal custody of his six-year-old twins, Fern and Holly. The court's decision was based on their mother's ongoing struggles with heroin addiction. Although Joel made all decisions regarding the children's care and welfare, he ran these by Sandra, his ex-wife, when she was stable. When she was unwell or homeless, Joel made decisions without her. They both agreed that this arrangement made sense. The twins got to see their mother when she was actively engaged in recovery. At times, Sandra disputed the arrangement, and legal wrangling took place. Given the circumstances, however, the parents did the best they could, considering the exigencies of addiction and postdivorce disagreements.

Stepparenting takes place when parents remarry or establish new same-sex partnerships with someone who may eventually be responsible for the children's care. Stepparents must never interfere or intentionally try to take the place of a biological parent, even when that parent is absent or unable to fulfill a parenting role. As noted in chapter 3, children are fiercely loyal to even the most neglectful parents.

Introducing children to new partners is a delicate matter that requires careful thought, timing, and planning. It is best that children have sufficient time to adjust to the divorce before new partners are permanently established in their lives. If possible, the other parent should attempt to support or remain neutral toward the new relationship.

Over time the newly formed couple should determine what role the stepparent will play in parenting. Some stepparents take an active role in caring for children, while others function more like adult friends. It is important for adults to understand that accepting stepparents into their lives is a difficult process for children, one that may involve a spectrum of ongoing challenges and conflicts. Finally, children should never be pressured to "love" the stepparent; indeed, there is no requirement for children to even like their parents' partners. However, children are responsible for being respectful toward their parents' partners, as for any adult.

CHILDREN'S BEST INTERESTS AND VOICES

The *best interest of the child* standard is used by most courts in the United States "to determine a wide range of issues related to the well-being of children after divorce, including which parent children will reside with, the extent of contact or visitation with the nonresident parent, and child support" (Hardesty & Chung, 2006, pp. 201–202). It is difficult at times even for the most seasoned professionals to determine whether parents are acting in their children's best interests, especially during highly volatile and conflict-laden times. It is thus difficult to actualize the standard of the best interest of the child when vulnerable adults are making the decisions and when affected children are not permitted to articulate what it is that they feel, need, or want.

Some have argued that children involved in contested divorces have already been deprived of their best interests. Social scientists have explored the psychosocial impact of divorce, and most conclude that at least in the short term, children experience a variety of adjustment and adaptational problems generated by both normative and unexpected hurdles. These transitional changes usually abate as parental contention lessens, new family structures get established and stabilized, and parents settle into adaptive coparenting relationships. Problems persist, however, when parental discord is prolonged after divorce and children continue to be put in the middle of their parents' conflicts.

Canadian best-interest standards recognize that children want a say in legal matters that affect their lives. "Having a voice does not mean making final decisions; but it does mean serious consideration is given to the views of children" (Canadian Coalition for the Rights of Children, 2009, p. 24). Some divorce researchers share similar views, finding that children want their perspectives known but do not want to be responsible for final legal determinations (Cashmore & Parkinson, 2008; Saywitz et al., 2010). Proponents of this view assert that children are expert witnesses to their own experiences and as such are instrumental to informing successful residency and custodial arrangements. Furthermore, they speculate that engagement in the decision-making process is beneficial to children on multiple levels: first because it helps them feel some sense of control over difficult, life-altering changes; and second because children invest in recommendations when they feel they have been heard.

Carol Smart (2006) is one of a small contingent of researchers who have systematically interviewed children postdivorce. She found that children clearly have preconceptions of appropriate parental responsibilities and hold strong opinions about what a proper childhood, even after divorce, should be like. The children Smart interviewed were also able to distinguish between the immediate effects of family change and the often disruptive subsequent behaviors of their parents. For instance, some children in the study described feeling damaged by their parents' behaviors but not by the divorce itself. Conversely, youngsters who said they were consistently cared for seemed to navigate family changes with relatively few adverse effects. These children also reported that new family structures were mostly positive because they extended the circle of people who supported them.

Kathleen Clark (personal communication, April 1999) heard similar themes in the stories of children who participated in her study. These youngsters agreed that once conflicts simmered down, most divorces had positive overall outcomes. Clark shared with me the comments of a sixth grader who explained how she adapted to the postdivorce family structure: "Getting used to your parents' divorce is like wearing an old pair of shoes that hurt your feet but you have to wear them because that's all you have. Getting over your parents' divorce is like getting a new pair of shoes."

On the other end of the spectrum, there are those who believe that children are placed at risk when asked to articulate any choices that could jeopardize their relationships with parents (Warshak, 2003). Warshak contends that methods for soliciting children's preferences are unreliable and therefore "do not give children a meaningful voice in decision-making" but rather place them in the position of taking sides "in their parents' disputes" (p. 373). One can appreciate how children can be in double jeopardy in such instances; they have already lost the family they've known and don't want to risk losing the love of either of their parents.

As can be seen, there is substantive disagreement between knowledgeable and child-focused scholars about the role children should play in legal proceedings. Yet within this climate of mixed findings, child-centered social workers and other mental health professionals are increasingly being asked to help parents and representatives of the court make residency, timesharing, and custodial decisions. Fortunately there is some agreement about the attitudes and skills necessary to assess children's positions without placing them in harm's way.

Saywitz and colleagues (2010) reviewed the literature on interviewing children of divorce and developed a list of principles for practice (box 10.1). First and foremost they advised that practitioners meet children where they are in their emotional and cognitive understanding of the divorce process. For instance, some children may be stunned and numbed by the information they've received, while others may be dealing with angry feelings toward one or both of their parents.

Attending to children's ages, developmental levels, and temperamental styles further sets the context for productive conversations. When practitioners use a multilayered approach rather than a cookie cutter, it increases

BOX 10.1
Principles for Interviewing Children in
Cases of Parental Dissolution

- Provide an age-appropriate environment with minimal distractions.

- Prepare children with age-appropriate explanations of the interview's purpose, the child's role, and the function of the professionals.

- Create an objective, nonjudgmental atmosphere where children's perspectives are explored and respected. Demonstrate a willingness to hear all sides without pressure.

- Make an effort to establish rapport through nonsuggestive means.

- Promote a supportive, welcoming, nonthreatening atmosphere.

- Match the demands of the interview to the child's developmental capability. Use language that the child understands.

- Collectively establish ground rules and shared expectations.

- Engage children in conversation on a wide range of topics relevant to the decision-making process. Do not ask the children where or with whom they prefer to live.

- Use open-ended, nonleading questions. Invite children to elaborate in their own words.

- Avoid suggestive or coercive techniques that introduce bias or reinforce one perspective over another.

Modified from Saywitz, Camparo, & Romanoff, 2010, pp. 549–556.

the likelihood that information will be both relevant and useful to youngsters and to their reconstituted families. Box 10.2 has age-related conversation starters geared for youngsters whose parents are divorcing.

Interviews with children are conversational. Practitioners should keep the information simple and should invite children's feedback. The context for these conversations is nonjudgmental, the environment one in which children feel comfortable enough to share difficult feelings.

Genuine assurance about what might happen is tricky if not impossible, as practitioners can't predict what parents will actually do. Children do best, however, when apprised of upcoming alterations in routines, schedules, and living arrangements whenever possible. Helping children anticipate such changes should be done in such a way as to calm them ("When parents get divorced, they have to make a lot of decisions. So when we can, we'll let you know when things are changing"). Moreover, confidentiality cannot be guaranteed when workers are required to report to the court or the court's

---

BOX 10.2
Conversation Starters for Youngsters
Whose Parents Are Divorcing

An explanation of divorce that is appropriate for young children might sound like this: "Your mom and dad have decided not to live in the same house anymore. This is called getting a divorce, and it means Mom and Dad are no longer married. But they are still your parents, and they will always take care of you."

School-age children might understand more about divorce, but they don't want all the details. An interview might begin this way: "Your parents told me that they're getting divorced. What do you know about what's happening?" (The child gives some details.) "Are there things you want to know that would help you deal with your feelings and thoughts?"

Adolescents are likely to know more detail, may appear less interested in the divorce, and may minimize or deny its effects. It's important to check in, however, and to acknowledge that a range of feelings and worries may occur even for the most sophisticated youth: "So you're here to see me because your parents are getting a divorce and want to make sure that you and your brothers are all right." If there's no response, you proceed. "Would you be willing to talk about how it's affecting you or your brothers?" Allow time for a response. "It's a hard time for everyone, and it's not unusual to feel distracted or worried about how everything will play out. Do you have any specific questions?"

Similar conversation starters could be used with a range of children in separating and divorcing families, using different words and contexts appropriate to same-sex or never-married partners.

---

representative vis-à-vis the GAL. Workers thus let children know what information must be shared with parents and authorities.

As illustrated above, the starting point for effective child-centered conversation is to put oneself in children's shoes. Open-ended questions and gentle prompts aim to discover *what* divorce might be like for this particular child and *how* to accommodate alterations in residency and time spent with each parent.

These critical points are well illustrated by the seemingly identical circumstances of two five-year-olds being evaluated by the same GAL. Both Joshua's and Ezra's parents were legally married and seeking divorces. According to the GAL, Joshua could be described as a buoyant youngster. He loved being at school and enjoyed spending time away from his parents with friends and relatives. When asked what life was like for him since his mother moved out, Joshua stated that it was fun because he got to have two cats instead of just one. When asked if anything made him sad, he replied that he wanted time with his parents to be "even steven" because he didn't want to hurt either of their feelings.

Ezra, on the other hand, took a long time to warm up to the GAL. His parents described him as shy and socially inexperienced. This was borne out by his awkward interactions and limited verbal exchanges. The GAL learned that Ezra's mother worked from home and that he had never been in preschool or group child care. When asked what life was like since his father moved out, Ezra said he was sad but got to talk to his dad on his cell phone every day. When asked if anything else made him sad, he said that he didn't want to leave his toys, his neighborhood, or his mother.

The GAL recommended that Joshua spend alternating weeks with his parents and be allowed to call either one whenever he felt the need. She recommended that Ezra remain in his mother's home during the week and spend weekends with his father. Six months after accepting the GAL's recommendations, Joshua's parents reported that he readily adjusted to his new living circumstances and was thriving. Ezra, on the other hand, was having difficulty making transitions between households. His father reluctantly agreed to temporarily delay overnights until Ezra had more experience being away from his mother. At first these alterations increased the tension between the former partners. With ongoing and patient support from a coparenting counselor, the parents were eventually able to agree upon a slowed-down version of the original plan and keep Ezra's needs at the forefront of their decisions.

One caveat should be noted before concluding this section on divorce. Working with children and families before, during, and after divorce is a complicated endeavor made more difficult by the emotional turmoil typically present when family systems fall apart. Engaging with children and parents therefore requires an informed balancing act for all those working with children and families.

Perhaps the best advice one can offer is to remain aware that there is no single story in any situation. Each member of the family, each professional involved, has a unique take on what may be in the best interests of children. It is easy to get caught up in tensions, but one must studiously avoid taking sides except in cases of substantiated abuse. The appropriate position is to consider the needs of developing children and, if there are no clear-cut solutions, to advocate the least detrimental options.

Workers must consistently be reflexive in their approaches, making certain that their personal relational histories do not get in the way of fair and evidence-guided practice. It's a worker's job to remain anchored especially when conflict is high and children and families are most vulnerable.

THE KIDS FIRST CENTER

The Kids First Center (KFC) is a community-based, nonprofit, low-barrier program for children and parents from separating or divorcing families.[3]

Established in 1998 in Portland, Maine, KFC was one of the earliest programs to recognize the importance of interprofessional practice in divorce work. Andrew Schepard, director of Hofstra University's Center for Children, Families, and the Law, describes KFC in this way: "Kids First is an interdisciplinary volunteer effort of divorce lawyers, mental health professionals and the courts to give parents and children tools to turn away from conflict during family reorganization and move towards growth and healing" (Kids First, 2008, p. xi).

As noted throughout this chapter, ongoing conflict between parents is the number one factor associated with emotional and social problems seen in children postdivorce. Furthermore, research indicates that chronic tensions between parents contribute to difficulties for young adults that frequently interfere with secure attachments in their intimate adult relationships. KFC seeks to prevent these problems through timely education for children, parents, and professionals. They also provide ongoing resources that intervene at critical junctures while the family changes.

KFC endorses education for divorcing parents as early as possible, so that they can learn how to navigate the often thorny and always complex circumstances of family disruption and prevent unnecessary distress for their children. Staff and facilitators know that when parents struggle, children are hurt. KFC's "flagship" program is a four-hour educational presentation facilitated by a team of men and women in mental health and legal professions. This education explicitly speaks to both fathers and mothers, and while conflict is acknowledged as an expected response to divorce, methods to address it encourage and exemplify collaboration.

Programmatic decisions and instructional methods at KFC are co-designed by mental health and legal professionals and by community stakeholders. This interprofessional, community-sensitive method prescribes cooperation in the household as well as in the courtroom. KFC programs are educational, not therapeutic. If children or adults require therapeutic intervention, however, KFC has an extensive resource and referral list, and staff are trained to help families find professionals who fit their needs.

Theories and practices underlying KFC programming are child-focused and family-centered, no matter what the family constellation. For example, KFC offers groups for gay, lesbian, bisexual, and transgender (GLBT) parents; provides specialized workshops for parents who have experienced domestic violence; and runs dedicated educational programs for stepparents. KFC operates on a sliding scale for fees, and no one is ever turned away because of inability to pay. The KFC board of trustees and community stakeholders tirelessly raise revenue to provide scholarships for children and parents and to ensure that all costs are met without burden to KFC clients.

Support groups for children (ages six to eighteen) are developmentally designed. Therefore the goals and objectives of each group as well as their format are determined with cognitive, social, and emotional factors in mind.

As an example, younger children may engage in art and play activities, while adolescents may use film or media to express common themes in their divorce experiences (figure 10.1).

KFC's reach is cross-disciplinary because they recognize that divorce and family change affect youth and adults across settings and throughout the life course. As one school principal stated, "One of the most difficult situations we have in schools is when parents use the school as a battleground" (Kids First, 2008, p. iv). KFC's professional education provides knowledge and skills for effective practice in areas of mediation, conflict resolution, and nonadversarial dispute approaches. At the same time, divorce professionals, including lawyers, mental health practitioners, child-care workers, school counselors, teachers, clergy, law enforcement, and family-violence workers come together to demystify the professional divide, building attitudes of trust and collaboration along the way.

FIGURE 10.1 Art project from Kids First group for nine- to twelve-year-olds

AMBIGUOUS AND DISENFRANCHISED LOSSES IN CHILDHOOD

Pauline Boss coined the term *ambiguous loss* in 1975 to refer to two types of loss that often go unrecognized: loss that takes place when a family member is physically present yet psychologically unavailable, and when a family member is missing.

Over the years the concept of ambiguous loss has broadened to include other types of uncertain changes, many of which are considered unresolvable or, at the very least, hard to define and thereby difficult to manage (Bocknek, Sanderson, & Britner, 2009; Huebner, Mancini, Wilcox, Grass, & Grass, 2007; Lee & Whiting, 2007). In the lives of children, ambiguous losses occur when parents are inconsistently available, as in substance-abusing families, or when a formerly reliable parent becomes incapacitated due to illness or disability and is no longer readily accessible or present. Grief related to ambiguous loss is also felt by children whose military parents are deployed, sometimes multiple times, and by those who lose parents for extended incarceration, hospitalization, or other types of separation. The words of this youth illustrate the deep uncertainty children feel when families are disrupted, in this instance by parental deployment: "I just didn't know how long they would be gone and when they would come back, because plans change a lot. And we just don't know like how long we would have to go without our parent" (Huebner et al., 2007).

According to Boss (2004), when loss is ambiguous, grief is understandably complex and episodic. She has written about ambiguous loss in relation to the September 11, 2001, attacks on the World Trade Center in New York: "Since 9/11, my greatest learning is that closure is a myth, yet highly touted by professionals who view closure after loss as a criterion of normalcy and evidence of their successful clinical work" (2004, p. 560). She advises mental health professionals, educators, and researchers to concentrate on meaning making and tolerance for uncertainty as measures to enhance clients' resilience and adaptation to ambiguous and often inexplicable situations.

The following sections provide snapshots of situations that provoke ambiguous yet powerfully felt experiences of anxiety, loss, and grief in children. Although highly different in composition and context, such family disruptions may have common effects of triggering insecurity and children's worries and fears about more permanent parental losses.

Parental Deployment

We live in a time when children are exposed to terrorism and war almost daily by way of media and social networks. Thus it is not surprising that for children in military families, the experience of uncertainty and anticipation of loss is powerfully interwoven into all aspects of everyday life. Such inse-curities often begin for children even before their parent's actual deploy-ment. According to Huebner and colleagues (2007, p. 113), "This feeling of uncertainty may begin when families wonder about what if—or when—their husband/father's or wife/mother's unit will be mobilized and then de-ployed." It continues after deployment and is often exacerbated by unex-pected changes in return dates and unanticipated redeployments.

In many cases when parents return, they are often changed. Children observe visible changes as a consequence of physical injury and disability and/or invisible changes as in cases of traumatic brain injuries or post-traumatic stress disorder (PTSD). Most, if not all, veterans return from active combat changed in some way or other by having witnessed death and envi-ronmental destruction. Many live with the exigencies of having been under pressure in unremitting conflict for long and repeated stays.

Many factors affect children's functioning when parents are absent due to military service. Active-duty military families live on military bases and thus share values as well as common experiences within their community. Under these conditions, children and nondeployed parents have relatively easy access to social and practical resources (Weiss, Coll, Gerbauer, Smi-ley, & Carillo, 2010). Proximity to similar families provides nondeployed par-ents with knowledgeable support, which helps them be more available to their children when separated from deployed parents. These supports are especially needed when active-duty parents return home from combat and reintegrate into their families. When parents return with visible or invisible disabilities, these human resources are invaluable (Everson, Darling, & Her-zog, 2012).

National Guard and Reserve (NGR) families live in civilian or nonmili-tary communities. Thus traditional active-duty supports are less accessible, and families sometimes find themselves socially isolated from the kinds of support and services needed when active-duty parents return home (Echter-ling, Stewart, & Budash, 2010). These families often lack sources of support attuned to military culture. NGR parents may thus experience well-intended but uninformed guidance and intervention to help them with their children's adjustments during reintegration and in response to physical and psycholog-ical changes in the returning parent.

All military families face a host of ongoing stressors related to children's separation from parents. These include multiple deployments and therefore frequent separations from family members. Moreover, although military culture is slowly changing, families and children still feel the effects of the military's ambivalence about mental illness, which culminates in general re-luctance toward instigating mental health services even for their children (Keen, 2012).

Other factors that influence children's adaptation to separation from deployed parents include age, gender, and ability of children; the quality of predeployment family functioning; whether the family has experienced other periods of separation; the extent of known danger that the deployed individual may be exposed to; and how effectively the home-based parent functions (Faber, Willerton, Clymer, MacDermid, & Weiss, 2008; Huebner et al., 2007).

Perceptions and appraisals of deployed parents' military role also makes a difference. For example, when children see their parents as taking on a noble effort, separations are mitigated by feelings of pride and purpose. But if youngsters feel the strains of multiple redeployments or they have lost faith in the purpose of their parent's service, they may experience stress beyond their capacity to cope. Children stretched beyond their adaptational abilities can develop emotional and behavioral symptoms such as depression, antisocial behaviors, withdrawal, lowered academic performance, and irritability (Huebner et al., 2007; Webb, 2005).

Parental absence due to deployment in and of itself creates shifts in family structure, routines, and tasks. Family tensions increase and children's reactions to them intensify when a parent or caregiver is deployed (Echterling, Stewart, & Budash, 2010). It is not unusual in these circumstances for children to direct their anger and aggression toward the nondeployed parent. Or children may be highly protective of their available parent and lash out at siblings and peers. And some youngsters hold back their emotions and cope in silence.

Researchers strongly suggest that mental health professionals become familiar with the stresses that result from both parental deployment and reintegration (Echterling, Stewart, & Budash, 2010; Huebner et al., 2007). Constantly changing family roles and responsibilities contribute to tensions between children and parents as well as between siblings. For some youngsters, increased responsibility builds pride and strength, while for others, added tasks and revolving roles cause emotional and behavioral problems.

Boss (2006) constructed a framework for helping children manage ambiguous losses, including children living in military families. It involves this process:

1. Finding meaning

2. Tempering mastery

3. Reconstructing identity

4. Normalizing ambivalence

5. Revising attachment

6. Discovering hope

Suggestions guide children as to what they can and cannot control. The framework helps develop positive coping strategies that externalize blame and helps children adapt to expected and unanticipated separations.

Boss (2006) also suggests that healthy adaptation is more likely to occur when children miss their loved one yet stay emotionally connected to available and caring others. Compared to adolescents, younger children seem to have an easier time being open and willing to engage with adults outside the family. Adolescents tend to isolate themselves rather than seeking support. Building relationships with youth therefore requires intentionality, concerted effort, and time (Huebner et al., 2007).

Acknowledging that children in military families face turmoil normalizes their realities. Knowing that others respond similarly alleviates pressure and may allow these youngsters to accept their feelings. Acceptance does not minimize children's stressful circumstances; however, it lets them know that their feelings are understandable and expected, and that they are not weak or "crazy."

Specific training in the culture, values, and circumstances of active military and veterans' families prepares child-centered professionals for effective practice with this population. In times of war, we must think on our feet and not dwell in uncertainties. Contemporary trends in the military, however, recognize the powerful and sometimes enduring emotional repercussions that combat service can have on personnel and on their spouses, partners, and children. Thus practitioners who are aware of military culture are in the best position to use language and convey attitudes that will encourage youngsters to express their feelings within a context of secure understanding.

Parental Incarceration

Disenfranchised grief was first described by Kenneth Doka (1989). It occurs when people experience losses that are neither acknowledged nor publicly mourned. This definition applies to the undefined and unrecognized losses experienced by children separated from incarcerated parents or family members. Unlike children of deployed military parents who receive praise and sympathy for their plight, children of incarcerated parents remain secretive about their parental separations. This is due to anticipated stigma or social disapproval when others learn of their parents' crimes. In many respects children of incarcerated parents experience ostracism and judgments similar to those projected on their parents.

It is not surprising that children of incarcerated parents "are forced to 'go underground'" (Sack, Seidler, & Thomas, cited in Lowenstein, 1986, p. 83). Indeed, we know very little about this population of children because of limited access to their perceptions and circumstances. What we do know is that an estimated 1.5–2 million children in America have incarcerated parents during some point in their formative years (Bocknek et al., 2009) and up to 10 million youth at any given time have mothers and fathers involved to some extent with the criminal justice system (Arditti, 2005).

Children with incarcerated parents exhibit insecurity and disruption in their attachment patterns, making it all the more difficult for them to establish trusting relationships with other available adults (Bocknek et al., 2009). Internalizing behaviors such as sadness, guilt, shame, and anxiety are evident, as are externalizing behaviors such as anger, aggressiveness, and poor impulse control. Several studies indicate that trauma and loss are persistent themes in the lives of these children (Ruchkin, Henrich, Jones, Vermeiren, & Schwab-Stone, 2007), while PTSD is a common diagnosis. Symptomatic behaviors associated with PTSD include hypervigilance, somatic reactivity, impulsivity, apathy, and guilt. These behaviors result from exposure to trauma associated with parents' criminal actions and are common responses to children's interaction with the harshness of the prison system itself (Bocknek et al., 2009; Jones & Beck, 2007).

Many of these youngsters live in nontraditional family structures, and some experience multiple disruptions in caregiving. Family financial insecurity and living instability are common, and children frequently lose contact not only with their incarcerated parent but also with other significant caregiving adults, due to relocations. Inevitably children learn to cope with relational separations through denial and avoidance. They become all too familiar with uncertainty. Some idealize and conflate their relationship in order to stay emotionally bonded with an incarcerated parent, regardless of whether there is reciprocity or indeed any relationship at all (Bocknek et al., 2009).

Even when caregivers want children to maintain family ties with incarcerated parents, they are wary of exposing children to prison life. Restrictions and protocols associated with parent-child visitations in prisons are undermining and even traumatizing rather than helpful and therapeutic: "On a typical visitation, children and their caregivers could expect to wait for 30–60 minutes before getting called to have their turn for a 20-minute, no-contact visit with their family member. During the wait in the visiting area, children were bored, restless, and had little to do but hang on to their mothers or lie down between the bolted plastic seats on the hard linoleum floor. Upon being called by the deputies to line up, the family then passed through a locked door, a metal detector, an elevator, and another locked door that eventually led to a row of small cubicles to visit the incarcerated parent" (Arditti, 2005, p. 255).

Like all children, those of incarcerated parents require consistency, coherency, security, and a sense of being cared for. Barriers to establishing security and trust are often staggering. To work effectively with this population, child-centered workers and other helping professionals must respect the complexity of these children's lives and the resilience that gets them through each day. Critical as well is identifying family, kin, or other caregivers and mentors who can provide foundational support while children remain separated from their parents.

Ambiguous loss is one of the many risk factors affecting this population of children. Boss's (2006) framework translates well to helping children of incarcerated parents adjust and adapt to their circumstances. Adaptation begins with fostering resilience, supporting mastery of purposeful skills, and finding meaning through activities and achievements. Relationships with reliable adults willing to hang in through the good times and the bad increase children's resilience. These significant others help children see themselves as separate from, yet connected to, their incarcerated parent: separate in that they are neither responsible for their parent's choices nor destined to make the same mistakes; connected because they can love and be loved by their parent even though they may disapprove of the decisions their parent made. As children embody these positive qualities, they see hope for their future.

Children of Parents with Chronic Physical and Mental Health Conditions

When Hedy was ten, her mother had a mountain-biking accident that permanently damaged her brain. Years later Hedy described her experience this way: "My real mother left for the mountains that morning, and a different mother returned. I never saw my real mother again."

Rahmin, twelve, and Sonya, eleven, miss their mother although they visit her weekly. She lives in a small apartment in a halfway house. Their father reluctantly allows the kids to visit her. Both children know that it's hard for him not to say negative things about their mother. Since his mother moved out, Rahmin has been alternately sullen and aggressive. Sonya does her best to make everyone happy. She's captain of the middle school soccer team and gets A's and B's in all her classes. She's preoccupied, however, with religious deliberation. Every night she prays that her mother will stay sober, that her father will find steady work and a nice girlfriend, and that Rahmin won't end up in jail like their uncle.

Phil's girlfriend, Tess, is sure she is the only one who knows about his secret life. They'd been dating for three months when she insisted on meeting his mother. Phil avoided her request, but she gave him an ultimatum—if she wasn't good enough to meet his mother, then their relationship was over. In hindsight Tess wishes she hadn't put Phil in this position. On the outside, his house looked like any other on the street: a little rundown but neat with a tiny grass patch and a few flowers along the fence. Inside though, it was packed tight with boxes and garbage bags. It smelled of cat pee, and the television was on a shopping channel with no sound. Mrs. Poundstone,

Phil's mom, greeted Tess warmly, but there was something off about her smile. Later he told her that his mother suffered from bipolar disorder and was not taking her medications. Until he could cajole her into taking them again, packages of stuff would show up at their house for weeks on end. Tess thinks she loves Phil, but she isn't sure she wants to be with someone who has so many problems.

These youngsters have frequent if not daily contact with their parents; however, their relationships are marked by uncertainty, love, and distress. Children whose parents live with cognitive disabilities, life-altering physical illness, chronic mental illness, addictions, or intimate-partner violence may experience ambiguous loss. Their parent is physically present but relationally and psychologically unavailable (Boss, 2006). Hedy, for example, endured a confusing dual loss. The mother with whom she had formed her primary attachment is forever lost; the mother she now lives with is in many respects unrecognizable and incapable of caregiving.

How children respond to these situations is of course influenced by many factors, including their age, extent of their parent's impairment or disability, their relationships and attachments to both parents, their parents' relationship to each other, and availability of at least one consistent nurturing adult. Young children whose loved ones are chronically fragile may experience insecurity and anxiety about their own survival and that of their well parent and siblings (Webb, 2003). Such worries are understandable, given that young children rely on adults to meet their basic needs.

School-age children are more apt to experience shame and anger in response to their parents' difficulties. This is particularly true of children whose parents struggle with less apparent or invisible chronic conditions such as mental illness or addiction. These disabilities are also veiled by stigma, family secrecy, and denial.

Children are well aware that the needs of their affected parents take priority, but they may not understand why. What they do know is that "the household revolves around something other than themselves but they are not allowed to know what it is and they are not allowed to ask what it is" (Barnard & Barlow, cited in Kroll, 2004, p. 132). When children are not directly informed, they are likely to become confused or resentful, or feel culpable for their parents' distress. Thus children like Rahmin and Sonya are reluctant to reach out for help because they do not want to betray their family and risk embarrassing or angering their parents. Being a devout Christian, Sonya seeks daily help from God but secretly wishes she could directly confide feelings to her pastor.

Youth like Phil are accustomed to living a dual existence. He's been quietly caring for his mother since he was eight, after his father left with his younger brother. They support themselves with his mother's social security checks and occasional child support sent by his father. Phil has also been working at Walmart four nights a week since he turned fourteen. He's now seventeen and concerned about what will happen to his mother when he goes to college.

Phil's situation is similar to those illustrated in Robinson and Rhoden's work (cited in Kroll, 2004) with children of alcoholics. As one youngster stated, "I was already, at nine years old, used to covering up, pretending that life inside our house was as pretty as the outside" (p. 132). Some children, like Phil, take on caregiving roles that require skills and responsibilities well beyond their age or maturational level. *Young caregivers* are under eighteen and have had to assume extraordinary household and caretaking responsibilities for their siblings and their vulnerable parents (Mechling, 2011). Although young caregivers are often considered at greater risk for emotional, social, and academic problems than children of healthy, functioning parents, some later find benefit from their experiences. Maggie Jarry (2009, p. 1588), whose mother was diagnosed with bipolar disorder in 1974, writes: "People often ask me what factors contributed to my resilience. I credit my mother. Despite 30 years of struggling with mental illness, she never insulted me and believed strongly in reinforcing children's self esteem."

Carol Rambo Ronai (1997) describes her early experiences as fostering both love and hate for her disabled mother. Ronai wrote a candid account of her childhood. She begins her story "I am never sure how to speak of this to others. When I am asked, 'Is your mother still alive?' or 'What does your mother do for a living?' or 'Where does your mother live?' I am filled with dread. As I contemplate the inevitable, resignation cancels out the dread and I know I will enact this script once again. I could choose to evade or lie in an attempt to spare the inquirer embarrassment. This approach usually backfires, forcing me into a situation where I must 'fess up' inside the context of having told a lie I got caught in, thus exacerbating the individual's discomfort. It is better to tell the truth up front: My mother is mentally retarded" (p. 417).

As is immediately apparent, Ronai does not sugarcoat her childhood or idealize the reality of having a mother with significant cognitive limitations and impeccably poor and often hurtful judgment. She loved her mother and knew that her mother loved her. At times she realized that she was ashamed of her love for this woman, who was clearly disenfranchised by family and society. Ronai wanted a mother she could not have.

In the end, Ronai speaks of her mother as her salvation. She was secure in her mother's love and took strength from her mother's faith in her. Ronai challenges theorists who predict that children of parents with developmental disabilities or other frailties will never reach their potential or lead satisfying lives. She asks us to see her and those with similar childhoods as individuals. She does not see herself as special or particularly strong, but as someone who was loved.

SUMMARY

Boss's (1999) groundbreaking work on ambiguous loss encourages practitioners to understand that even the strongest, most functional people may live with irresolvable, ambiguous separation experiences. When these impair caregivers, even the most resilient of children and families may require support in managing their stresses.

The first step in implementing support is recognizing the many situations that separate children from their parents. Second, practitioners need to educate children and families about the emotional highs and lows that such circumstances create, and treat them as normal responses to predictable and unpredictable strains and losses.

Even though individuals may react very differently, it is best for families to work together and support one another if possible. Strategies for support may vary, depending on individual and collective needs. Thus practitioners may suggest psychoeducation, social networks, therapeutic interventions, or alternative therapies such as yoga and meditation to help children and families cope with ongoing tensions and manage decision making.

Those providing support and intervention must have faith in children's resilience and capacity to grow in the presence of adversity. As Ronai (1997) cautions, we must be wary of prescriptive outcomes that focus only on pathologies. Instead we must balance hopelessness with hope, loss with benefit, and grief with gratitude to help children and families use their skills to manage their lives productively and to find strength in the present and promise in the future.

Notes

1. In 2005 the Canadian Civil Marriage Act legalized same-sex marriage.

2. A guardian ad litem (GAL) is an adult selected by a court order to oversee the rights and well-being of minors for the duration of a legal proceeding. A GAL may be a lawyer, mental health professional, or paralegal trained to represent children's interests.

3. KFC reaches families and children throughout Maine and beyond, using their on-site resources; their collaboratively written book, *Kids First: What Kids Want Grown-ups to Know about Separation and Divorce* (2008); and their website, www.kidsfirstcenter.org.

References

Amato, P. R., & Afifi, T. D. (2006). Feeling caught between parents: Adult children's relations with parents and subjective well-being. *Journal of Marriage and Family,* 68(1), 222–235.

Arditti, J. A. (2005). Families and incarceration: An ecological approach. *Families in Society, 86*(2), 251–260.

Bocknek, E. L., Sanderson, J., & Britner, P. A. (2009). Ambiguous loss and posttraumatic stress in school-age children of prisoners. *Journal of Child and Family Studies, 18*(3), 323–333.

Boss, P. (1999). *Ambiguous loss: Learning to live with unresolved grief.* Cambridge, MA: Harvard University Press.

Boss, P. (2004). Ambiguous loss research, theory, and practice: Reflections after 9/11. *Journal of Marriage and Family, 66*(3), 551–566.

Boss, P. (2006). *Loss, trauma, and resilience: Therapeutic work with ambiguous loss.* New York: W. W. Norton.

Bow, J. N., Gould, J. W., & Flens, J. R. (2009). Examining parental alienation in child custody cases: A survey of mental health and legal professionals. *American Journal of Family Therapy, 37*(2), 127–145.

Canadian Coalition for the Rights of Children. (2009). *Best interests of the child: Meaning and application.* Retrieved from rightsofchildren.ca/wp-content/uploads/bic-report-eng-web.pdf

Cashmore, J., & Parkinson, P. (2008). Children's and parents' perceptions on children's participation in decision making after parental separation and divorce. *Family Court Review, 46*(1), 91–104.

Doka, K. J. (1989). *Disenfranchised grief: Recognizing hidden sorrow.* New York: Lexington Books.

Echterling, L., Stewart, A., & Budash, D. (2010). Suddenly military: Play-based interventions for deployed National Guard and Reserve families. Retrieved from http://counselingoutfitters.com/vistas/vistas10/Article_19.pdf

Everson, R. B., Darling, C. A., & Herzog, J. R. (2012). Parenting stress among US Army spouses during combat-related deployments: The role of sense of coherence. *Child and Family Social Work.* doi:10.1111/j.1365-2206.2011.00818.x

Faber, A., Willerton, E., Clymer, S. R., MacDermid, S. M., & Weiss, H. M. (2008). Ambiguous absence, ambiguous presence: A longitudinal study of military families in war time. *Journal of Family Psychology, 22*, 222–230.

Hardesty, J. L., & Chung, G. H. (2006). Intimate partner violence, parental divorce, and child custody: Directions for intervention and future research. *Family Relations, 55*(2), 200–210.

Huebner, A. J., Mancini, J. A., Wilcox, R. M., Grass, S. R., & Grass, G. A. (2007, April). Parental deployment and youth in military families: Exploring uncertainty and ambiguous loss. *Family Relations, 56*, 112–122.

Jarry, M. (2009). Personal accounts: A peer saplings story: Lifting the veil on parents with mental illness and their daughters and sons. *Psychiatric Services, 60*(12), 1587–1588.

Jones, S. J., & Beck, E. (2007). Disenfranchised grief and nonfinite loss as experienced by the families of death row inmates. *Omega, 54*(4), 281–299.

Keen, M. T. (2012). *Coping with post-combat injury: Responses from a media presentation with military and civilian families* (Unpublished doctoral dissertation). Smith College, Northampton, MA.

Kelly, J. B., & Emery, R. E. (2003). Children's adjustment following divorce: Risk and resilience perspectives. *Family Relations, 52*(4), 352.

Kelly, R. E., & Ward, S. L. (2002). Allocating custodial responsibilities at divorce: Social science research and the American Law Institute's approximation rule. *Family Court Review, 40*(3), 350–370.

Kids First. (2008). *What kids want grown-ups to know about separation and divorce.* Standish, ME: Tower.

Kot, L., & Shoemaker, H. M. (1999). Children of divorce: An investigation of the developmental effects from infancy through adulthood. *Journal of Divorce and Remarriage, 31*(1/2), 161–178.

Kroll, B. (2004). Living with an elephant: Growing up with parental substance misuse. *Child and Family Social Work, 9,* 129–140.

Laybourn, A., Brown, J., & Hill, M. (1996). *Hurting on the inside: Children's experiences of parental alcohol misuse.* Aldershot, UK: Avebury.

Lee, R. E., & Whiting, J. B. (2007). Foster children's expressions of ambiguous loss. *American Journal of Family Therapy, 35*(5), 417–428.

Lowenstein, A. (1986). Temporary single parenthood: The case of prisoners' families. *Family Relations, 35,* 79–85.

Mechling, B. M. (2011). The experiences of youth serving as caregivers for mentally ill parents: A background review of the literature. *Journal of Psychosocial Nursing Mental Health Services, 49*(3) 28–33.

Neale, B. A., & Flowerdew, J. J. (2003). Time texture and childhood: The contours of qualitative longitudinal research. *International Journal of Social Research Methodology, 6*(3), 189–199.

Ronai, C. R. (1997). On loving and hating my mentally retarded mother. *Mental Retardation, 35*(6), 417–432.

Ruchkin, V., Henrich, C. C., Jones, S. M., Vermeiren, R., & Schwab-Stone, M. (2007). Violence exposure and psychopathology in urban youth: The mediating role of posttraumatic stress. *Journal of Abnormal Child Psychology, 35*(4), 578–593.

Saywitz, K. S., Camparo, L. B., & Romanoff, A. (2010). Interviewing children in custody cases: Implications of research and policy. *Behavioral Sciences and the Law, 28,* 542–562.

Sigal, A., Sandler, I., Wolchik, S., & Braver, S. (2011). Do parent education programs promote healthy post divorce parenting? Critical distinctions and a review of the evidence. *Family Court Review, 49*(1), 120–139.

Smart, C. (2006). Children's narratives of post-divorce family life: From individual experience to an ethical disposition. *Sociological Review, 54*(1), 155–170.

Warshak, R. A. (2003). Payoffs and pitfalls of listening to children. *Family Relations, 52*(4), 373–384.

Webb, N. B. (2003). *Social work practice with children* (2nd ed.). New York: Guilford Press.

Webb, N. B. (2005). Groups for children traumatically bereaved by the attacks of September 11, 2001. *International Journal of Group Psychotherapy, 55*(3), 355–374.

Weiss, E., Coll, J., Gerbauer, J., Smiley, K., & Carillo, E. (2010). The military genogram: A solution-focused approach for resiliency building in service members and their families. *Family Journal, 18*(4), 395–406.

Zafón, C. L. (2001). *The shadow of the wind.* London: Penguin Books.

11

Death and Grief in Childhood

When you die you can float through walls and doors and stuff you can't do now. Even Libby. When she was alive her bones were mixed up. She couldn't even hug anyone or crawl anywhere. But now she can even float through the walls.

Jack Simon, *This Book Is for All Kids*

MAKING SENSE OF DEATH

Children process death in ways that fit their understanding of the world. They are curious and ponder where the goldfish goes after it's flushed down the toilet. They wonder whether Uncle Charley is a star in heaven, and they speculate what it might be like to hang out with the angels. Though their responses might appear entirely different than those of adults, children's grief is no less real. As Wolfelt (1991) reminds us, "Anyone old enough to love is old enough to grieve."

Children try to make sense of death's aftermath. At five, Jack's musings about Libby's death are fixated on the functional and the fantastic. He wants to be assured that his baby sister's life in heaven will be better than the one she had on earth. His questions are sometimes concrete: "Will Libby have the same face and clothes when we see her as an angel?" He worries, "How will we recognize her?" His inquiries are also relational, and because Jack remains connected to his little sister, he wants to know "How much does she love and miss us?" (Simon, 2001).

Death also touches children directly. Approximately 55,000 children in America die each year from illness and disability. There are children born with serious health problems who never know a life outside of their illness. There are also youngsters who lead normal, active lives until terminal disease or acquired disability causes premature death.

Even when children do not personally experience deaths, most are passive witnesses to them in the media. Reports of deaths caused by war and natural disasters, as well as those of public figures and murder victims, flood the airways and Internet. Older children engage with violent and graphic cartooning and gaming, which exposes them to previously unimaginable forms of death and destruction.

In the twenty-first century it is much more difficult than in less networked times to shield children from death's realities. Some speculate that children can separate everyday circumstances from what they see on screens. Rather than prepare children for loss, however, frequent media exposure may heighten their fears. This is especially true for young children, who have difficulty distinguishing between what they see on television and what happens in real life.

Overexposure to media violence has the unintended effect of numbing children's responses. Where community violence is prevalent, being inured to death sets youth up for high-risk and potentially lethal behaviors. Taking chances is part of the developmental landscape, but youngsters witnessing daily violence may seek danger, rather than gaining respect for it. Grief in these children may also be attenuated. Emotional survival becomes dependent on avoiding or denying the overwhelming feelings that lay dormant under the surface.

Whether children feel understood in their grief depends to a large extent on how parents and other significant adults respond to their feelings and inquiries. It is not unusual for adults, particularly those steeped in their own grief, to want to protect children from sorrow. Although this instinct is understandable, it is not particularly helpful. Rather than protecting children from unnecessary suffering, avoiding discussions about death may exacerbate and prolong children's grief. Luckily for Jack, his parents were open to talking about Libby's illness and death, and invited his questions. Thus he was able to process Libby's death while going on with his life as a typical five-year-old boy.

Indeed, most children are best comforted when provided with age-appropriate and timely information that conveys that the adults around them can handle their feelings and fears. With people there to support them, children and youth manage their losses and make meaning of them in ways that enrich their understanding of the world. As in so many transitional situations, they will be changed by death but not unduly harmed.

This chapter considers developmental factors that influence children's perceptions of and responses to death and how these inform strategies that support their adaptations to loss. It examines the differential impacts of parental and sibling death, and considers how parents manage the death of a child. It also explores the roles practitioners play in supporting families through these most painful transitions.

How children navigate living while dying is discussed, as is how child-centered workers can help this process. The chapter concludes with an exemplary program, the Center for Grieving Children (CGC) in Portland, Maine. It provides volunteer-facilitated and peer-support programs for child grievers and outreach to families and communities affected by loss.

GRIEF IN INFANTS AND PRESCHOOLERS

Infants and toddlers respond to the affective expressions of their grieving parents and primary caregivers. As with divorce and other separations, very young children suffer distress related to distracted caregiving. They also feel the effect of prolonged absences while adults manage the aftermath of loss. On the other hand, infants can be unanticipated sources of comfort to adult grievers. Their unconditional love and the joy it brings is soothing and reassuring to adults who are in mourning.

Preschoolers also react to caregivers' bereavement. They have individualized grief responses as they learn to understand the world from their evolving perspectives. When death occurs, they may recognize it but not be able to name the relational void that unsettles them. As a result, they may behave in puzzling ways that are efforts to communicate to adults about the struggle to make sense of their losses.

For example, when four-year-old Avery's grandmother died, she insisted on bringing a plastic shovel to the graveside in case Grammy Mae wanted to "wake up" from being dead. Children of Avery's age do not appreciate death's permanency. They assume that they can do something that will reverse or undo their losses. Avery employed magical thinking as a means of making right a situation that caused her distress. Such behavior is representative of young children's age-related understanding of death.

It is also not uncommon for young children to ask blunt and probing questions because they want to understand what it means to be alive and what happens when someone is dead. Upon learning that his little brother died of a brain tumor, Ian, age five, asked, "Did they take out his brain? Can I keep it?" To grief-stricken adults these questions may appear insensitive; adults often assume that children have a more mature understanding of death and bereavement than they do.

Children naturally experiment with life and death concepts by stomping on ants and wondering why they don't return to life. First encounters with meaningful loss often occur when a family pet dies. When people close to children die, some will blame themselves for the death, unable yet to distinguish between thought and action. For instance Floyd's Tia Marietta died unexpectedly while he was at day care. When his mother informed him of her passing, Floyd, age four and a half, broke down sobbing and fled to his room. It took quite some time for his mother to determine that Floyd blamed himself for causing Tia's "broken heart" because he had called her a "bad name" at breakfast that morning.

Some young children understand the ramifications of death earlier than others, particularly if they've had direct encounters with the loss of close family members, friends, or beloved pets (Pomeroy & Garcia, 2011). Five-year-old Jack (quoted above) was confronted by death early in his young life. Because his family dealt directly and openly with Libby's death, he processed the loss in developmentally appropriate ways.

Unlike Jack, three-year-old Alec was left to his own devices. When Papa Mel died, Alec was told that "Papa went away." But this didn't make any sense to Alec. He knew that Papa always came back, even after his long hunting trips. Alec was especially suspicious because Papa's truck was in the garage and he knew that it didn't belong there. "Where's Papa Mel," he kept asking. Alec's questions were left unanswered, and for a long time he felt angry and abandoned by his beloved Papa.

GRIEF IN SCHOOL-AGE CHILDREN (SIX TO TWELVE)

Maturing cognitive capacities and increasing social and emotional awareness enhance school-age (six to eleven) children's appreciation for the universality of death and its irreversibility. At these ages children have some experience in the world. They also are developing the capacity for empathy and ability to appreciate others' perspectives. They understand the logic of cause and effect, and as a result they know that bad things happen that cannot be changed. Although children of all ages tend to assume that death is a reality for the old and infirm, it is during the early school years that children comprehend that everyone, including them and their parents, will die.

Awareness of death's inevitability precipitates anxiety and separation difficulties in some youngsters. Ingrid's parents described to me how she suddenly went from being an eight-year-old child who loved sleepovers to one who couldn't fall asleep in her own bed without ruminating over their possible deaths. They depicted sleepless nights holding their daughter and repeatedly convincing her that they wouldn't leave her. Her fears diminished during the day but reliably returned at bedtime.

Ingrid's developmental anxiety was apparently unrelated to actual events; rather, it was based on growing existential awareness that everybody eventually dies. Ingrid ultimately benefited from cognitive-behavioral play therapy (see chapter 7) that gave her skills to manage intrusive thoughts, reduce anxiety, and get to sleep.

By the time children enter the preteen years (nine to twelve), they have a solid understanding of what causes death and appreciate its irrevocability. Advancing cognitive development permits them to synthesize what they know and to reflect on situations. For example, Desirée, age eleven, was philosophical when her young uncle Alan, sixteen, died from an overdose. In her speech at his memorial service, she brought mourners to tears when she spoke about how Alan had taught them all about courage: "He tried to face his problems. Now God will help him find his much needed sobriety."

Desirée's earnest sentiments are not unusual for children her age. Older school-age children can articulate feelings associated with grief, and some, like Desirée, have started to tentatively explore existential and spiritual dimensions, including life after death (Webb, 2005b). Conversely, some children this age need concrete explanations in order to process and manage their grief. This was the case for Edgar, age twelve, whose mother died unexpectedly from a fatal aortic aneurysm. The emergency department medical resident assured Edgar that his mother's death could not have been anticipated; the fatal condition happens without warning.

Edgar found great solace in the physician's words; there was nothing he or his father could have done to prevent his mother's death. To express his feelings, Edgar carved a heart out of wood, then placed it at the base of a forsythia bush that his family planted to honor his mother's memory. He said that the heart symbolized his mother's life, and when he looked at it, he felt at peace.

Because older school-age children understand what death means, their grief is deeply felt. They tend to experience a range of emotional responses that include mood and behavioral distress. Sorrow is an expected grief response, as are anxiety, anger, poor concentration, and in some cases irritability and hyperreactivity. Children respond to loss in the same ways they respond to other life stresses. Adults should therefore be alert when youngsters express uncharacteristic moods or behaviors, for example, aggression in a typically even-tempered child or extended periods of isolation in a socially active youth. These may signal deep-seated rather than transient reactions to loss.

Other factors that affect children's grief are temperament and their relationship with the deceased. Bram, age nine, was described by his father as a "tender" boy who insisted that his beloved dog, Slumber, would never die because he had special "genes." Though well aware of death's permanence, Bram was shocked when told by his parents that Slumber had passed. For weeks he searched the woods, looking for his beloved dog, certain that he was merely lost and would eventually return. His younger sister's response was quite different. Norah wasn't as bonded with the family pet, and the matter-of-fact eight-year-old impatiently reminded her brother, "Slumber's in heaven—he's dead and gone."

Young and school-age children have what might be described as intermittent grief responses. Without apparent effort they transition from sorrow to playfulness. Adults are baffled by this chameleon-like behavior, and some question the sincerity of children's bereavement. Children are by nature egocentric, however; they live in the moment and are bereft when contemplating their losses and joyful when distracted by or engaged in activities they enjoy. The episodic manner in which they express grief does not mean that they are any less affected by their losses.

Youngsters this age are capable of expressing sincere compassion and heightened levels of support, especially in group situations. This is seen in classroom settings and groups when children are brought together to deal with shared grief. Compassion may be short-lived, however, and targeted toward only those directly affected by loss. Children are children, and especially in middle school it is not uncommon to witness youngsters showing compassion to a bereaved classmate and moments later being called out for mercilessly teasing peers on the playground.

ADOLESCENT GRIEF

Adolescents (thirteen to twenty-one) are in extraordinary developmental flux. Their overall momentum is aimed at growth, not loss. They are immersed in discovering who they are and where they fit into their worlds. It is not surprising then that emotional and functional variability is reflected in their attitudes and responses to death.

The primary concern of most adolescents is to be accepted, especially by their peers. As a consequence, talking about or expressing grief is suppressed because teens fear reprisals for showing weakness and for losing control over their emotions. Maintaining emotional status quo taxes the coping skills of even well-adjusted, bereaved adolescents. Furthermore, efforts to forestall, disguise, or blunt grief often have unfortunate by-products. For example, some adolescents misuse alcohol or drugs or embark on risky behaviors as methods to avoid difficult feelings (Pomeroy & Garcia, 2011).

When Brittany died as a result of a brain tumor at age seventeen, her friends conducted rituals to honor her passing. Winston, however, chose not to participate. This surprised her friends, because she and Britt had been inseparable. Instead Winston spent evenings alone, smoking pot and trying to forget. When she started missing school, Winston's teacher e-mailed her grandmother, who was unaware of the absences.

When asked, Winston denied that anything was wrong. "I knew all along that Britt was dying. We talked about it and everything. So I was ready." But Winston clearly wasn't prepared for the power of her grief. She was ashamed that she couldn't be strong in front of her friends, so pot became her sole ally.

Grieving adolescents may also take to their screens. Preoccupation with gaming and the Internet immerses teens in activities that disconnect them from difficult feelings and isolate them from the sorrow of others. It should be said that, used appropriately, time spent with games, chat, and other social networking may provide a necessary reprieve from hard to absorb, painful emotions.

Christ, Siegel, and Christ (2002) observe that adolescents, like older grievers, can feel grief in the moment and recall distressing memories that bring up previous feelings of sorrow and despair. The enduring nature of adolescent grief, however, is seen by researchers as variable. Some suggest that adolescents' grief is powerfully felt but less enduring than that of adults (Christ, Siegel, & Christ, 2002). Other scholars propose that grief in adolescence is surprisingly intense and that rather than being short-lived, it becomes permanently woven into long-term identity (Balk, 1996). One might offer that both perspectives are true, depending upon the individual adolescent and his or her circumstances.

When grief is unrecognized or dismissed, it is more likely to precipitate depression that undermines healthy growth and development. In some families adolescents take on adultlike roles during the illness and after the death of a parent, caregiver, grandparent, or sibling. Many experience enhanced self-esteem when such responsibilities are balanced with encouragement to participate in normative life activities (Jones & Tesh, 2011). However, some adolescents feel that they lost their childhood. Such responses occur particularly when youth take on roles abdicated by grieving parents and assume responsibility for household and caregiving tasks.

Sarah Gold-Bromberg, twenty-eight, described such a lost childhood to her therapist. Sarah was the oldest child of four in a busy household. Her two younger siblings were adopted as infants, and her biological brother is eighteen months her junior. Just two years after her little brother's adoption, Sarah's mother was diagnosed with amyotrophic lateral sclerosis (ALS), a progressive and degenerative disease of the brain and spinal cord. Sarah was told that her mother's disease would progress slowly, but in fact it took a rapid course. Because her father traveled for business, Sarah quickly assumed responsibility for her mother's physical care. She also handled much of the child-care responsibilities for the younger children.

Sarah's mother died approximately thirty-six months after diagnosis. Sarah deferred acceptance to a top-tier university and instead took courses at the local state university while caring for her siblings. Two years after her mother's death, Sarah's father married a woman he met at a business conference. He soon moved to another state with his new wife and the younger children. Sarah was invited to join them, but she chose to stay put and complete her education.

Now in her late twenties, Sarah finds herself revisiting the choices she made, as well as those that were made for her when her mother became ill and died. Sarah still feels the unfairness of having carried much of her family's burdens. "They've moved on, and I'm still so angry," she tells her counselor. "I'm disappointed in myself. I want to have a relationship, but honestly I can't trust in anyone." Sarah is hopeful that therapy will help resolve what seems to be endless grief associated with the many losses she's experienced.

Christ, Siegel, and Christ (2002) offer useful recommendations for working with grieving adolescents and for those dealing with serious illnesses of family members. Their recommendations have been modified and are highlighted in box 11.1.

Youth are more likely than younger children to be exposed to and affected by the death of people outside of the family, including classmates and friends. As Balk (1996, p. 368) aptly notes, adolescents are by no means "innocent when it comes to encounters with death and bereavement." Such deaths occur as a consequence of motor vehicle crashes and other accidents.

Youth living in violent neighborhoods experience death firsthand, including those of same-age friends and relatives. In America these youngsters are for the most part disproportionately African American and male. Nancy Boyd-Franklin and A. J. Franklin (2000, p. 2) outline the causes of death for black youth: "Homicide is the primary cause of death for black males between the ages of thirteen and twenty-five. The threat of death comes from many sources: crime within the black community, mistaken identity, drug-related incidents, gang activity, police brutality, and a host of others." Parents of these youngsters live in fear of the possibilities, as do most of the adults in their extended communities. Boyd-Franklin and Franklin (2000) suggest that African American parents prepare their children early on to protect themselves, avoid trouble, and survive to adulthood.

As mentioned in chapter 8, adolescents are in a period of life marked by an increased incidence of suicide. Although suicide rates have declined since the 1990s, it remains the third leading cause of death among youth between fifteen and twenty-four (Miniño, Xu, & Kochanek, 2010). Boys of fifteen to nineteen are four times more likely than girls to commit suicide and eight times more likely to be involved in a firearm-related death. Although rates are hard to determine because youth are reluctant to speak of their sexual orientation or gender identity, GLBT youth are seen to be at high risk for suicidal thoughts and actions.

Motor vehicle accidents are a leading cause of death for teens ages sixteen to nineteen (Miniño, Xu, & Kochanek, 2010), and some of these are single-vehicle accidents that might be disguised suicides. National death surveys also find that male children in this age bracket are six times more likely to be victims of homicide than males and females in other age brackets (American Foundation for Suicide Prevention, 2012; Miniño, Xu, & Kochanek, 2010).

Grief and loss associated with suicide are complicated by its unexpected and intentional nature and by perceptions of its untimeliness and unfairness. Youth experience the frailty of life that comes with unanticipated loss as well as a decreased sense of trust in themselves and the world. They also feel responsible and powerless for not having foreseen the suicide of a family member or friend.

BOX 11.1
Recommendations for Working with Grieving Adolescents

DURING THE ILLNESS

- Provide information in a factual and age-appropriate way.
- Facilitate discussions about feelings and concerns.
- Understand adolescents' age-appropriate reactions.
- Encourage peer-to-peer connections.
- Limit household responsibilities and child-care tasks.
- Understand that adolescents may be ambivalent about hospital visitation.

DEATH AND FAMILY RITUALS

- Minimize and manage conflict, which naturally intensifies at end of life.
- Keep adolescents aware of the end-of-life process.
- Encourage adolescents to have a final good-bye.
- Support adolescents' return to school and other activities.
- Encourage adolescents to select mementos belonging to the deceased parent.
- Encourage adolescents to express grief in meaningful and tangible ways.

BEREAVEMENT AND RECONSTITUTION

- Recognize that adolescent grief is expressed in many different ways.
- Educate parents and adolescents that grief is a process.
- Balance grief's expression with pleasurable family activities.
- Maintain consistency and structure.
- Encourage adolescents to participate in meaningful and purposeful activities.
- Access natural supports and those provided by community resources (religious organizations, schools, counseling agencies).
- Refer adolescents to counseling if they exhibit uncharacteristic behaviors.
- Encourage family counseling if systemic conflict or distress persists.

Christ, Siegel, & Christ, 2002.

Shame complicates suicide, particularly in response to parental death. Finding meaning is difficult for children who can't accept that their parent has chosen death over them. Webb (2005a) comments that professionals must be able to skillfully facilitate child and adolescent grief in response to suicide, particularly because evidence suggests increased vulnerability for future suicidal behaviors in these youngsters.

Despite myths to the contrary, adolescents appreciate being listened to and acknowledged in their grief (Christ, Siegel, & Christ, 2002; Pomeroy & Garcia, 2011). Respect and patience are essential qualities for facilitation of grief conversations with adolescents, because they are likely to withhold their feelings to protect significant others from their pain and because they fear being seen as vulnerable. Thus silence should not be interpreted as resistance. Rather, it is simply a first step toward relational connection. Being available and open to the variable ways that youth express their loss opens the door to helping them transition from grieving to healing.

THE DEATH OF A PARENT

The death of a parent is considered a highly stressful, life-changing event for people of every age, but it is especially felt in childhood. Parents are primary caregivers, and children depend on them for security, sustenance, stability, and nurture. For young children a parent's death is particularly devastating, because they invest so much of themselves in their primary attachment relationships (Webb, 2005a).

Older children also experience intense feelings of loss when a parent dies. These feelings are associated with ongoing ties and relationships as well as with grief over lost opportunities. The grief of older children is also complicated by their developmental drive toward differentiation and independence. Thus adolescents may struggle with perplexing feelings at having lost the person that they were so desperately trying to separate from.

Approximately 2.5 million children under eighteen years of age in America (3.5 percent) will lose a parent to death each year (Newcomb, 2003/ 2004). In developing countries, the rate of early parental death is significantly higher, due to higher incidence of AIDS, insect- and water-borne infectious disease, and maternal death in childbirth (*Preventing chronic diseases*, 2005). Although children in developing countries may experience parental loss with greater frequency than those in westernized nations, their losses are no less painful. National and global statistics underscore the critical importance of being prepared to work with children of all ages and cultures who have experienced parental losses (see chapter 13).

The impact of parental death depends on many intersecting factors, some of which have been described above. What makes parental death in childhood especially heartfelt is the reverberating effects it has on the past, present, and future relational bonds that parents and children share. As Masur (cited in Webb, 2005a, p. 56) movingly states, "Only in childhood can death deprive an individual of so much opportunity to love and be loved."

When parental death is anticipated, most children will experience anxiety about who will care for them and how their daily life will be affected without one or sometimes both of their parents (Pomeroy & Garcia, 2011). Responses to parental loss are additionally tempered by whether the loss was anticipated or unexpected and whether it was shared and discussed with the child. Optimally, when death is expected, children are encouraged to remain engaged with their parent throughout his or her illness and dying process. Following the parent's death, children should be engaged in developmentally informed rituals of mourning. Children of all ages do best when they know what's going on and what to expect.

For people of all ages, grief following suicide is likely to last longer than that resulting from other deaths. Survivors tend to feel a range of complicated feelings, including anger, guilt, and responsibility for not having thwarted what they perceive to be a preventable death. Finding meaning in the aftermath of suicide is seen as critical to recovery, although for many it is difficult to locate.

Children have an especially difficult time adjusting to loss after the suicide of a parent or close family member. Being left behind because of an intentional death hits children hard and at least temporarily destabilizes their attachments. According to Ratnarajah and Schofield (2007), suicide-bereaved children exhibit higher levels of depression than those whose parents died from illnesses or from accidental causes. Moreover, these youngsters have symptoms of post-traumatic stress, including prolonged periods of distractedness and confusion.

Adults are often ambivalent about whether to disclose that suicide was the cause of death. Sharing this news with children is a judgment call, but it's always best to be as honest as possible. Moreover, children tend to know the truth even if adults have not directly told them.

I recall one time discussing with an acquaintance whether her seven-year-old nephew should be told that his beloved uncle had died from a self-inflicted gunshot wound. The family was leaning toward telling the boy that Uncle Wes had died in his sleep. They worried that he would think less of Wes and therefore have a more difficult time recovering from the loss.

A short time later I bumped into this acquaintance again and asked her what the family had decided to tell her young nephew. She said that the boy had preempted the family's decision by stating out of the blue, "I wonder where Uncle Wes got the gun to shoot himself?" He already knew the circumstances. Now he needed the surviving family members to help him make sense of them.

As always, availability of the surviving parent or close adults to support suicide-bereaved children is essential to recovery and healing. Equally important is for adults to help children construct a developmentally appropriate understanding of parental suicide. "The messages from the surviving parent, wider family, and community about the event can either foster resilience and self-worth in the child or result in feelings of isolation and hopelessness" (Ratnarajah & Schofield, 2007, p. 90). In the instance of the seven-year-old above, the family encouraged him to ask questions and did their best to assure him that nothing could have been done to prevent Uncle Wes's actions. They emphasized that his death was not the boy's fault. This was followed by creating a way to say good-bye to his uncle and begin to appropriately grieve his loss.

Most children find ways to cope with and adapt to parental losses stemming from many causes. They continue to learn, grow, play, and hopefully thrive. They adjust to the reconstituted family structure, relearn the world, and settle into a new sense of normal (Worden, 2009). Like people of all ages, children assimilate their parents' deaths in their own ways and at their own pace. As Silverman (2000, p. 94) writes, "[It] may take a long time of traveling on a bumpy road for them to live comfortably in a single-parent family and build a comfortable relationship with their surviving parent and the deceased." Silverman's statement implies that a child's bonds to a parent endure beyond death and that for most children these ties are everlasting. How children make sense of parental losses, however, changes over time and with experience, and for some, "the loss will remain a part of their lives forever" (Jones & Tesh, 2011, p. 125).

SIBLING DEATH

Siblings share a common history that transcends time. At best, brothers and sister are friends for life. Even when they're not, relationships with siblings leave lifelong impressions. Thus the grief that occurs when a sibling dies in childhood is significant and powerful. In retrospect, adults describe without equivocation that the death of a sibling was the hardest loss of their lives, one from which they never fully recovered. It is therefore disturbing to note that youth who are grieving a sibling are often viewed as forgotten survivors (MADD Victim Services, 2011).

Children's reactions to sibling loss are influenced by multiple variables, including age at time of sibling death, quality of parental functioning, the closeness and attachment between siblings, and whether sibling rivalry was a factor in the relationship (Jones & Tesh, 2011). Gender is also viewed by some researchers as contributing to adaptation to a sibling's death, with girls seeming more affected than boys by the loss (Worden, 2009).

Studies examining the psychological aftermath of sibling loss offer mixed findings. Some contend that children whose siblings have died are at higher risk for behavioral and emotional problems than nonbereaved youth

(Paris, Carter, Day, & Armsworth, 2009). Children who lose a brother or sister exhibit heightened vulnerability and concerns about their own mortality, having experienced the death of someone who is relationally close and similar in age. Some may also feel guilt at simply being alive or, in the case of accident or suicide, at not having prevented their sibling's death.

Harry, age seven, felt extremely guilty for having survived the car accident that took the life of his older brother, Axel. Harry admitted that before the accident he sometimes wished Axel would just disappear, so that he could get all his parents' love. Six months after the funeral, Harry's mother first noticed he wasn't himself. It took another three months before teachers sat down with Harry's parents and told them that he cried at school every day over "nothing."

In retrospect, the adults in Harry's life felt terrible for having missed the signs of his deepening depression. As for Harry, he didn't blame them. He had tried his best to remain as invisible as possible. He didn't want to worsen his parents' sadness, nor did he wish to distract attention from Axel. Being ignored seemed to be minimal punishment for what he really felt: he didn't deserve to be alive.

Research also suggests that for the most part, children adapt to sibling loss with no apparent long-term pathology (Davies, 2005). Indeed, in some instances youth develop enhanced compassion and maturity in the aftermath of a sibling's death (Davies, 2005).

Davies (2005), one of the earliest researchers to investigate sibling grief, identified four general responses to this distinctive loss: I hurt inside; I do not understand; I do not belong; and I am not enough. In some ways Harry's story illustrates these themes. He couldn't make sense of why Axel died and why he didn't; he felt tremendous guilt and pain; and he was certain he could not replace Axel's goodness in his parents' hearts.

Davies's themes provide guidance to child-centered practitioners who work with siblings' grief. They offer a framework for beginning conversations enlightened by possible reactions these youngsters may be experiencing. Thus when children acknowledge that they hurt inside, practitioners can offer a range of approaches to express and externalize that hurt. In Harry's case, a worker might ask him what hurt looks and feels like. He could then illustrate, act out, or tell a story about his hurt, helping the worker understand his experience. Together they might determine how to normalize or transform hurtful feelings, so that they don't interfere with his self-worth or functionality. Harry might also be a perfect candidate for a grief support group (see "The Center for Grieving Children" below). There he could talk about his feelings with other children who have been in his shoes.

Children who *do not understand* may be conveying two separate but related messages. On one hand, they may need more information to fill in the gaps about their sibling's death and what will happen in its wake. On the other hand, they may be expressing an existential lack of understanding, as in why did this happen to their sibling and family.

In Harry's family there was no explaining away Axel's death. Harry's worker might therefore choose to convene a family meeting, when they could collectively express feelings about Axel's death. Perhaps each could draw a picture of their current family constellation and share these with each other. This could be followed by identifying that which they could control—for example, ways they could honor Axel's memory and establish new family rituals that promoted mastery over helplessness and transformation toward a new normal.

For children who feel they *no longer belong* or describe feelings of being overwhelmed or displaced, family therapy may help families reconfigure relations and work toward common goals. When using a narrative approach, family therapy allows grieving siblings to externalize sorrow and guilt by providing metaphors that the family collectively selects to combat distress and engage in problem solving. Thus Harry's family might find a name for the survivor guilt he feels and notice when it affects his mood and behavior.

Finally, surviving siblings may believe that they cannot fill the shoes of the child who has died. This was definitely true in Harry's case, and in many respects his predeath reality bore this out. Directed play therapy and group work separately or in combination help children like Harry understand that no one can ever replace anyone else. Even so, people are valued for who they are, not for who they're not. Family work reinvigorates and reinforces attachments between surviving family members. Harry needed to know that even though they all grieved for Axel, he was "enough" for his parents and that they were glad he survived.

There is no doubt that surviving children get lost in the shuffle when parents are grieving. As was said earlier, those who are grieving siblings are often the forgotten survivors. When a child's illness and dying has been protracted, healthy siblings may carry legacies of feeling ignored—sometimes for extended periods of time (figure 11.1). They've watched as their seriously ill brother or sister was given gifts and special attention. They've struggled with jealousy and feelings of abandonment colored with guilt and shame. As one youngster hesitantly said, "I watched as Davey got all these presents. He knew I wanted them and I knew he wouldn't play with them . . . but he wouldn't share them with me and I was really, really angry at him. Now that he's died I feel so bad."

Parents recognize losses endured by their other children but sometimes feel helpless and overwhelmed by the burdens of caring for their seriously ill child. As one mother explained, "It's the whole family, not just the sick child; it's everybody who's affected. The day-to-day struggles that we have as a family are huge, and it takes a lot for our family just to stay together" (Konrad, 2005). It is difficult, however, for children to be assured of their

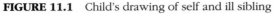

FIGURE 11.1 Child's drawing of self and ill sibling

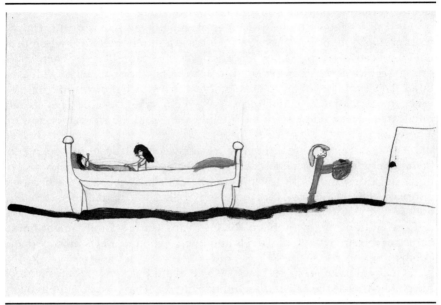

parents' love, and sometimes healthy children may harbor feelings of abandonment or resentment for having been pushed aside by the needs of their
brothers or sisters (Jones & Tesh, 2011). Indeed, Davies (2005) found that
such feelings have strong long-term effects that can lead to dynamic tensions
within families as well as complicated grief for the surviving sibling.

Ryna had few positive memories of her older sister, Gina, who died
from complications of spina bifida when she was nine. Her mother could
see that Ryna, now a young teen, suffered the effects of being neglected
because of her older sister's medical demands. "She doesn't talk about it
much, but we can see it all the time," says her mother, Kellyjo. "She needed
me and her other mother, my partner, and we essentially left her on her
own. Now she really wants very little to do with us. Her loss is another form
of grief for us."

Clearly, parents do not intentionally ignore the needs of their healthy
children, and many try desperately to make retrospective amends. One
mother offered this insight, having tried to atone to her surviving son for the
time they lost during his younger sister's illness and death: "I think out of
necessity I tried to make it up to him after Lily died. But what you realize
when all is said and done is that you can't. I think Derek missed a great deal
of his childhood and I'm sorry for that" (Konrad, 2005).

In much the same way, siblings of children who die unexpectedly can take a back seat to the grief of their family and community. Thus they may suffer dual losses: that of a brother or sister and, at least for a period of time, the loss of their parents and other reliable adult supports. Such losses are compounded when, like Harry, they survive the incident that caused a sibling's death.

Sibling loss is powerfully felt by children, yet it has received surprisingly little attention compared to other family losses. What we do know is that surviving children need to be recognized and consoled in a timely fashion. If this is done, they will likely grieve, adapt, and heal but never lose the memories of their siblings. Those whose grief remains unacknowledged may struggle with lifelong unresolved and complicated grief. In the end, the best outcomes are when bereaved siblings can integrate their losses in meaningful, relational, and regenerative ways (Davies, 2005).

PARENTAL PERSPECTIVES

The death of a child is one of life's saddest and most stressful events. It defies the natural order of things. Life-course expectations dictate that children should outlive their parents. In this respect the death of a child is perceived to be unfair, and it is seen as all the more tragic.

Adding to this sense of unfairness is what is often called the conspiracy of silence around child death, especially in Western cultures. It is understandable that parents, health and mental health professionals, friends, and family wish for miracles or seek out every option to extend children's lives. Hope is a necessary element of resilience, and parents have every right to hope for another day or to pray for a cure.

It is therefore a reasonable assumption that no parent is ever prepared for a child's death. To "contemplate the death of one's child is to imagine the unthinkable" (Konrad, 2008, p. 19). Anticipating a child's death imposes complicated and profound burdens on parents and family systems. Enduring the unexpected death of a child launches families into unimaginable pain and suffering. For most parents, feelings of loss and grief begin when they first become aware of their children's life-limiting diagnoses, whether congenital or acquired. Periods of grief abate and resurge as parents watch and wait. They experience seemingly contradictory emotions—balancing hope with disappointment, triumph with sorrow—and grapple with this emotional balancing act throughout the remainder of their child's life.

Olshansky (1962) first coined the term *chronic sorrow* to explain feelings of grief described by parents whose children were born with birth defects and other disabling, potentially life-shortening health conditions. Bruce and Schultz (2002, p. 7) identified a similar process, what they termed *nonfinite grief*, associated with parents' sadness about lost futures and "a lack of synchrony with hopes, wishes, ideals, and expectations."

In line with these descriptions, Blaska (1998) observed a pattern of intermittent and recurring grief felt by parents of children with chronic health problems throughout the child's lifetime. These feelings arise at significant transitions or developmental junctures, such as holidays, birthdays, graduations, and other age-related rituals. Difficult emotions also resurface at unexpected moments, stimulated by unanticipated memories or sensory experiences. Cyclical grief has been noted by parents of children living with debilitating and terminal conditions and for those whose children have died.

The following exchange with one mother illustrates the concepts of recurring grief highlighted above. The mother of Tim, a youngster born with a terminal, neurodegenerative illness, told me that every spring the smell of lilacs revived her sorrow. "It's not that I'm not happy that Tim is still with us," she said. "It's just that my other sons play Little League in the spring and Tim never will. I can't help but feel sad for that."

Tim's mother said it helped that I understood her feelings were normal, because when she mentioned them to some people, they would quickly remind her how lucky she was that Tim was still alive. When Tim died at age ten, I noticed that his mother placed lilacs on his casket during the memorial service. When I asked her about them, she said, "I wanted spring to be with him forever."

Every family makes meaning of child loss in dramatically different ways. For some parents, everyday life after the death of a child includes remembrance rituals and celebrations. For others, especially those with strong faith or belief in an afterlife, acceptance of a child's loss means letting go while being consoled by anticipated reunion after death. And for some families the death of a child is seen as a closed chapter of their life, and they move on (Konrad, 2009).

So how can child-centered workers and other caring professionals apply relational practices in their work with grieving parents and others whose histories contain the experience of a child's death? Should death be mentioned, or will acknowledging it unnecessarily precipitate painful feelings? And in the end, can anyone truly ease the pain of losing a child?

Most parents navigate the grief process without assistance from a professional counselor or therapist. Grief is a normal process, and for the most part people find ways to assimilate their losses, adapt to life without the deceased child, and move ahead. Moving on does not imply, however, that the pain of loss goes away; rather, it implies that feelings connected to the child's death diminish and become manageable but not forgotten.

In some instances, however, people seek the support of someone outside the family system so as not to further burden family members and friends who are also mourning. These grievers find that they are inhibited or constricted by their sorrow in ways that interfere with desired functioning.

As a consequence they seek out or are encouraged to pursue formal counseling relationships focused on grief work. Conversations with these parents and caregivers must not avoid direct questions about the deceased child. Asking questions acknowledges that the child remains alive in people's hearts and minds.

As with all therapeutic relationships, grief work calls upon the worker to suspend preconceived assumptions about what grief will look like and to be fully and emotionally present as parents' stories unfold. Although parents may grieve together, they do not necessarily share the same perspective or express their grief in the same way (Gilbert, 2001). Differences in parental grief can follow gender lines as well as personal styles (Doka & Martin, 2007). It is not uncommon, for example, for women to express themselves verbally or emotively, whereas men may work through their sorrow through actions, not words.

This was the case with Harry's parents (see above). Though both of them unexpectedly lost a child, the mother found comfort in talking about Axel with her pastor, while the father built a new shed adjacent to their home, rarely mentioning Axel to anyone. It was hard for Harry's mother to perceive that her husband was indeed grieving: "He hasn't cried," she told the pastor.

Their different grieving styles eventually caused enough friction in the marriage that the couple pursued grief work for Harry's sake. The bereavement counselor facilitated healing conversations that helped them accept, process, and integrate memories of Axel into their concept of family.

Adapting to life without their older son required environmental as well as existential changes for everyone concerned. Harry and his father decided to build a train layout in his bedroom in honor of Axel's love of railroads. His mother determined that when people asked how many children she had, she would continue to say "two" and if necessary explain about Axel's death.

Grief scholars note that families generally experience a transformational process as a consequence of accepting their loss. Of course, families make their transition in variable ways and with divergent outcomes. Robert Neimeyer (2001) suggests that practitioners shy away from determining what a normal grief process should look like or how it should proceed. He submits that although death is universal, there is no "right" way to grieve. Thus child-centered workers will come to understand that there are as many stories of loss to be told as there are parents to tell them.

Indeed, parents want to talk about their deceased children to those willing to listen. People refrain from asking parents about their children's deaths, afraid that they will cause undue suffering. Rather than being harmed by such conversations, however, parents crave opportunities to say their child's name out loud and tell their child's life story regardless of how limited the life might have been.

This was true for Lorraine, whose daughter Tessa died shortly after birth. One afternoon Lorraine shared mementos of Tessa's brief life, which she kept hidden in a wooden box. She carefully and thoughtfully showed me each of Tessa's tiny sweaters and swaddling blankets, all wrapped in soft cloth. At the end of our conversation, Lorraine thanked me. She said that there were very few people in her life who could truly hear her story. Yet she loved to talk about Tessa. "It keeps her memory alive," she said.

THE DYING CHILD

Children living with serious and terminal illnesses frequently acquire a maturity that transcends their years (Beale, Baile, & Aaron, 2005; Cincotta, 2004; Sourkes, Frankel, Brown, & Contro, 2005). People who get to know these children observe that they intuitively grasp when they are close to death. Yet some will share this inner knowledge only with practitioners because they do not want to upset the ones they love.

Indeed, seriously ill and dying children sometimes go to great lengths to protect their parents from grief and sadness, having witnessed their family's pain and knowing that there is little they can do about it. This seventeen-year-old youngster's comment reflects common sentiments experienced by these youth: "When I think back on my experience, what strikes me most is not my pain; after all, having lived through it once, I know I could do it again (though of course I'd rather not). It is my parents and sister who I grieved for most, knowing how much emotional trauma they were forced through on my part. They couldn't feel my pain, certainly, but they could see mine, . . . and even worse . . . they could do nothing about it."

Some children express inner knowledge of death's course through art, play, or other expressive modalities. Elisabeth Kübler-Ross described a moving example of a progressive drawing done by a dying five-year-old. The child initially drew a bouquet of seven flowers in the lower quadrant of a blank piece of paper, each with a stem and flower head. As the child progressed in her illustration, one flower at a time was eliminated from the bunch until only a single, flowerless stem remained. She was letting Kübler-Ross know that there would soon be an empty page. She was gently telling her that death was near.

Although children become progressively aware that their options are diminishing, not all will want to talk about or express their feelings about dying. Supportive adults must take care not to impose or pressure children to speak of their death if they prefer to focus instead on other things. Certain youngsters, however, are intensely curious about what the end of life means and what it might look like. They ask questions; for example, What if this drug doesn't work? What if there are no more treatments? (Sourkes, 1995). One rather precocious child, age nine, asked his social worker whether there were golf courses in heaven. He wanted to know if there'd be occasions to partake of his favorite sport once he made the transition.

Children may become exhausted by curative efforts before their families and medical team are prepared to end treatments. Tired of being subjected to frequently intrusive interventions and difficult side effects, some children request that treatments stop. Parents, health-care teams, and guardians usually make treatment determinations for minor children. Most take into account the child's view as well as variables such as the child's age, aims of treatment, progression of the disease, and its prognosis. Some parents prolong treatments until the very end, whereas others heed children's wishes, knowing that there is no restorative solution and wanting their young one to have the best possible quality of life until their death.

Margaret's parents made the decision to end treatments at her request when she was about twelve years old. Diagnosed as a toddler with cystic fibrosis, a chronic debilitating lung disease, Margaret's health progressively declined until she could no longer breathe on her own. A number of circumstances made her a poor candidate for lung transplant. From the start her parents rigorously followed medical protocols and investigated alternative treatments. Over time, however, they observed that rather than benefiting from increasingly intrusive treatments, Margaret became weaker.

In her last year of life, Margaret let her family know that she was all done with treatments and prepared to move on to a peaceful death. It took every ounce of her parents' strength and humanity to acquiesce to her wishes. According to her father, "We had to decide whether life alone was worth it for our daughter and we decided that no, it wasn't. She needed to have a quality of life no matter how brief it was going to be and no matter how emotionally painful it felt to us." After Margaret's death, her mother told me that she died peacefully with her family around her.

According to pediatric end-of-life scholars, the present is all that matters for seriously ill children (Cincotta, 2004; Sourkes, 1995). Barbara Sourkes (1995) explains that "[t]he 'now' becomes paramount" to dying children. The future holds no promise, so quality of life in the present is essential. Parents and practitioners are thus faced with urgent incentives to make each day as good as possible, while remaining emotionally available and authentic. This is no small feat, given the often overwhelming daily caregiving burdens that parents of dying children manage while coping with powerful and difficult feelings. On the other hand, parents report benefiting from the lessons they learn from their fragile children. Three years after Margaret's death, her mother confided that her daughter taught everyone about living in the moment and appreciating the little things in life.

There is no doubt that children need an enormous amount of parental and family support throughout the dying process. As with all matters, children cope best when they know what is going on and are given developmentally informed, clear, and honest information. Cincotta (2004) advises that being candid about difficult news, rather than frightening children, actually eases suffering. Half truths or withholding information typically invalidates children's lived experiences. Moreover, when left uninformed, children create their own stories or fill in the gaps, using information found on the Internet. Either of these options can lead to unnecessary anxiety and uncertainty.

Children old enough to communicate and connect with others want to be remembered. Older children are more likely than younger children to consider the legacy they wish to leave behind. Some will create scrapbooks, blogs, or videos as tangible mementoes of their lives. Older children and adolescents also wonder about life's meaning and question what they might find in life hereafter. Some have religious convictions that mark their journeys, while others may be comforted by the thought of reunion with lost family members, pets, and friends.

It is not unusual for parents to prefer that professionals familiar with end-of-life issues be the ones to share much of the difficult news with children or be at their sides when such painful information is conveyed. In fact, families as a whole benefit from the ongoing presence of people willing to listen, who neither minimize nor dramatize their life circumstances. They also value information and guidance that helps reduce uncertainty in already unsettling circumstances. Families are comforted knowing that there are people who have been there before who can help them manage and master unfamiliar tasks and frightening realities (Cincotta, 2004).

THE CENTER FOR GRIEVING CHILDREN

Since 1987 the Center for Grieving Children (CGC) in Portland, Maine, has offered support to grieving children, adolescents, and their families through peer support, outreach, and education (figure 11.2). The founding philosophy behind CGC is that children's experiences of grief are both commonly felt and "as different as fingerprints" (Maasdorp & Martin, 2000, p. 53). Children participating at CGC attend developmentally designed programs that foster healing and strengthen their inherent resilience and resourcefulness.

Valerie Jones, program coordinator and social worker at CGC, outlined for me its very personal history. CGC was founded by Bill Hemmons after the death of his sister, who left a nine-year-old daughter behind. Soon after this loss, Bill learned that there was a startling lack of resources in the United States dedicated to serving grieving children and families. Determined to create opportunities for bereaved children, Bill ventured out to Portland, Oregon, where he visited the Dougy Center. There he observed volunteers facilitating peer-support groups that encouraged grieving children to express their losses in the company of others who had lost family members.[1]

FIGURE 11.2   The Center for Grieving Children in Portland, Maine

Bill returned to Maine and soon after opened CGC. To this day, its programming is guided by these five basic principles (St. Thomas & Johnson, 2007, p. 49):

- Grieving is a natural response to change, loss, and the death of a loved one.
- Grief is individual and has its own time and duration.
- Within each individual, child or adult, is the natural ability to heal oneself.
- Caring and acceptance assist in the healing process.
- We honor the diverse cultural and spiritual beliefs of all who come to the center.

CGC serves approximately 150 families per year and has over 200 volunteers functioning in various capacities. "Families come to us sometimes shortly after a death, and sometimes not until a year or up to eighteen months afterward," says Valerie. "There are no limits on how long a family may attend CGC programs; most come for about a year; some longer; it's up to the family to determine their own needs."

Program volunteers are required to complete rigorous training in bereavement facilitation. Valerie makes the distinction between the types of groups offered at CGC and those that are more therapeutically oriented: "If families and children are going to access our services, they need to be able to own their feelings and hear others' stories. Not everyone is ready to do this right after a death. However, we always keep the door open for people whenever they feel ready for what we have to offer." She adds that CGC has a broad network of community partners; thus when and if a child or family member requests mental health services, there is a relatively seamless referral process connecting them to community programs that provide professional counseling.

CGC also offers several other programs for related populations. The Tender Love and Care Program helps family members deal with issues that arise when a loved one has a life-affecting illness. For the last decade CGC has also collaborated with the Portland public schools and other citywide support agencies in offering multicultural children's groups. The city's growing immigrant, refugee, and asylum-seeking populations and awareness of the many losses they face was the impetus for this program (see chapter 13).

Though ostensibly facilitated by two adult volunteers, the multicultural groups are guided more or less by the children's needs and desires "to creatively express and socially explore some of the losses associated with their movement from other world communities and their omnipresent acculturation process" (St. Thomas & Johnson, 2007, p. 51). The philosophy that underlies group process is that once children feel safe and trusting, they find their own paths to healing.

Another resource available at CGC is the Volcano Room (figure 11.3). The Volcano Room is designed to give children opportunities to physically and emotionally express powerful feelings within a safe and protected environment. Padding covers all four walls, and a punching bag hangs in the middle of the room. Valerie comments that the room was designed for youth "to vent some of the larger feelings that they might otherwise not be able to express." The room is equipped with soft blocks and bats and other materials that allow for a range of movements. The room is also soundproofed, so that children can yell and scream and release their feelings. There are hard and fast rules that must be followed in the Volcano Room. First and foremost,

FIGURE 11.3   Valerie Jones in CGC's Volcano Room

you cannot hurt anyone, including yourself. As Valerie says, it's a place to express big emotions, within a safety net of care.

CGC is well known for its community outreach programs. These programs respond to community losses as well as to national losses that affect children and families, as was seen after the World Trade Center tragedy. Support services are tailored to meet the needs of the agency requesting intervention. For example, some schools have CGC volunteers train teachers how to respond to bereaved children; others ask volunteers to talk to whole classrooms about a death. In some instances CGC sets up a "quiet room" where youth gather of their own accord to support one another after a shared loss. CGC staff are also available to offer guidance and information to parents about how to talk with children about death.

CGC is a long-standing, well-respected, and sought-after program that is an invaluable resource for grieving children in Maine and across the nation. Its peer-support structure and rigorously trained volunteers provide authentic and creative avenues for children and their families to communicate and express their grief within the context of a safe, trustworthy, and caring community.

SUMMARY

Children and their families view death from a range of perspectives and experience their losses in diverse and distinctive ways. Workers translate these losses across ages, situations, and cultures. Listening to and delivering hard news requires both skill and compassion. Practitioners who are prepared to witness sadness, loss, and grief with openness and empathy can tolerate a range of difficult feelings without being overwhelmed by them.

Child-focused counselors are likely first or secondary responders when there is a death in the family or when a local or national disaster occurs. Learning how to address death and other difficult subjects is an essential skill for child-centered relational practice. Evidence suggests that harsh or insensitive words may not be life-threatening, but they are life-affecting and have long-term consequences for many families (Konrad, 2010). Such thoughtlessness, intended or not, causes unnecessary suffering to those already mired in distress and grief. Conversely, kind and sympathetic words may not be curative, but they can be healing.

Consistent with other themes in this book, relational practice principles apply when it comes to working with children and families facing life-limiting illnesses and end-of-life realities. They are consistent with standards outlined by health policy organizations such as the Institute of Medicine and the World Health Organization that call for all health and health-related professionals to be mindful of the individual needs of children and families as well as of the multifaceted perspectives that they bring to their experiences of illness, death, and grief.

Note

1. The Seasons Centre for Grieving Children in Barrie, Ontario, is similarly designed to meet the needs of bereaved children and families in Canada. The center is founded on the belief that every child deserves an opportunity to grieve in a supportive and understanding environment.

References

American Foundation for Suicide Prevention. (2012). *Facts and figures: National statistics.* Retrieved from http://www.afsp.org/index

Balk, D. (1996). Attachment and the reactions of bereaved college students: A longitudinal study. In D. Klass & P. Silverman (Eds.), *Continuing bonds: New understandings of grief* (pp. 367–387). Washington, DC: Taylor and Francis.

Beale, E. A., Baile, W. F., & Aaron, J. (2005). Silence is not golden: Communicating with children dying from cancer. *Journal of Clinical Oncology, 23*(15), 3629–3631.

Blaska, J. K. (1998). Cyclical grieving: Reoccurring emotions experienced by parents who have children with disabilities. ERIC ED419349.

Boyd-Franklin, N., & Franklin, A. J. (2000). *Boys into men: Raising our African-American teenage sons.* New York: Plume Books.

Bruce, E., & Schultz, C. (2002). Non-finite loss and challenges to communication between parents and professionals. *British Journal of Special Education, 29*(1), 9–13.

Christ, G. H., Siegal, K., & Christ, A. C. (2002). Adolescent grief: It never really hit me . . . until it actually happened. *Journal of the American Medical Association, 288*(10), 1269–1278.

Cincotta, N. (2004). The end of life at the beginning of life: Working with dying children and their families. In J. Berzoff & P. R. Silverman (Eds.), *Living with dying: A handbook for end-of-life practitioners* (pp. 318–347). New York: Columbia University Press.

Davies, B. (2005). The grief of siblings. In N. B. Webb (Ed.), *Helping bereaved children: A handbook for practitioners* (2nd ed., pp. 94–127). New York: Guilford Press.

Doka, K. J., & Martin, T. L. (2007). *Men don't cry—women do: Transcending gender stereotypes of grief.* New York: Brunner/Mazel.

Gilbert, K. R. (2001). "We've had the same loss, why don't we have the same grief?" Loss and differential grief in families. *Death Studies, 20,* 269–283.

Jones, B. L., & Tesh, M. (2011). Children, adolescents, and grief in medical settings. In E. C. Pomerory & R. B. Garcia (Eds.), *Children and loss: A practical handbook for professionals* (pp. 120–144). Chicago: Lyceum Books.

Konrad, S. C. (2005). Mothers of children with acquired disabilities: Using the subjective voice to inform parent/professional partnerships. *Omega, 51*(1), 17–31.

Konrad, S. C. (2008). Mothers' perspectives on qualities of care in their relationships with health care professionals: The influence of relational and communicative competencies. *Journal of Social Work in End-of-Life and Palliative Care, 4*(1), 19–53.

Konrad, S. C. (2009). Loss in translation: A model for therapeutic engagement and intervention with grieving clients. *Families in Society, 90*(4), 407–412.

Konrad, S. C. (2010). Relational learning in social work education: Transformative education for teaching a course on grief, death and loss. *Journal of Teaching in Social Work, 30*(1), 15–28.

Maasdorp, V., & Martin, R. H. (2000). Grief and bereavement. In E. Bruera, L. De Lima, R. Wenk, & W. Farr (Eds.), *Principles of palliative care in the developing world* (pp. 53–66). Houston, TX: International Association for Hospice and Palliative Care Press.

MADD Victim Services. (2011). Victim Services. Retrieved from http://www.madd .org/victim-services/

Miniño, A. M., Xu, J., & Kochanek, K. D. (2010, December 9). Deaths: Preliminary data for 2008. *National Vital Statistics Reports, 59*(2), 1–52.

Neimeyer, R. A. (2001). *Meaning construction and the experience of loss.* Washington, DC: American Psychological Association.

Newcomb, C. (2003/2004). Demographic and economic characteristics of children in families receiving social security. *Social Security Bulletin, 65*(2). Retrieved from http://www.ssa.gov/policy/docs/ssb/v65n2/v65n2p28.html

Olshansky, S. (1962, April). Chronic sorrow: Responses to a mentally defective child. *Casework,* 190–193.

Paris, M. M., Carter, B. L., Day, S. X., & Armsworth, M. W. (2009). Grief and trauma in children after the death of a sibling. *Journal of Child and Adolescent Trauma, 2*(2), 71–80.

Pomerory, E. C., & Garcia, R. B. (2011). Children and grief. In E. C. Pomeroy & R. B. Garcia (Eds.), *Children and loss: A practical handbook for professionals* (pp. 17–38). Chicago: Lyceum Books.

Preventing chronic diseases: A vital investment. (2005). *WHO* Global Report. Geneva: World Health Organization.

Ratnarajah, D., & Schofield, M. J. (2007) . Parental suicide and its aftermath: A review. *Journal of Family Studies, 13*(1), 78–93.

St. Thomas, B., & Johnson, P. (2007). *Empowering children through art and expression: Culturally sensitive ways of healing trauma and grief.* London: Jessica Kingsley.

Silverman, P. R. (2000). *Never too young to know: Death in children's lives.* New York: Oxford University Press.

Simon, J. (2001). *"This book is for all kids, but especially for my sister Libby. Libby died."* Kansas City, MO: Mighty Max.

Sourkes, B. (1995). *Armfuls of time: The psychological experience of the child with a life-threatening illness.* Pittsburgh: University of Pittsburgh Press.

Sourkes, B., Frankel, L., Brown, M., & Contro, N. (2005). Food, toys, and love: Pediatric palliative care. *Current Problems in Pediatric and Adolescent Health Care, 35*(9), 345–392.

Webb, N. B. (2005a). Assessment of the bereaved child. In N. B. Webb (Ed.), *Helping bereaved children: A handbook for practitioners* (2nd ed., pp. 45–69). New York: Guilford Press.

Webb, N. B. (2005b). The child and death. In N. B. Webb (Ed.), *Helping bereaved children: A handbook for practitioners* (2nd ed., pp. 3–18). New York: Guilford Press.

Wolfelt, A. (Writer). (1991). *A child's view of grief* [Video]. Fort Collins, CO: Center for Loss and Life Transition.

Worden, J. W. (2009). *Grief counseling and grief therapy* (4th ed.). New York: Springer.

12

The Impact of Violence on Children

Violence is the most extreme form of communication.

A. Edwardson, *Frozen Tracks*

WITNESSING VIOLENCE

Children's exposure to interpersonal and community violence is a significant concern for public health, social service, and mental health practice. *Interpersonal violence*, also referred to as *domestic violence, intimate-partner violence*, or in broader terms, *family violence*,[1] is a pattern in which the offender intentionally harms his or her partner physically, emotionally, sexually, psychologically, economically, or in other ways. In some instances both partners engage in abusive behavior, causing harm to one another. Violence is used as a means of control, and although it is often reactive, it is motivated by a driving need to wield power over the victim (Postmus, 2005). Added to the roster of victims are the children who passively witness or become unwilling participants in family violence.

It is estimated that 15.5 million children in the United States are exposed to intimate-partner violence every year, and approximately 7 million reside in homes where it's chronic and severe (DeBoard-Lucas & Grych, 2011; McDonald, Jouriles, Ramisetty-Mikler, Caetano, & Green, 2006). Similarly, the Canadian Incidence Study of Reported Child Abuse and Neglect (Black et al., 2005) found that children in Canadian homes were exposed to domestic violence at a rate of 10.51 per 1,000 children.

Interpersonal violence occurs across age groups and in a range of relationships that involve close, ongoing, and intimate contact, such as marriage and postdivorce, dating, and nonmarriage committed relationships. It takes place between family members and friends who might be temporarily or permanently sharing shelter and caring for others, including children. Both women and men are targets of violence; however, women are far more often the victims (Postmus, 2005). The offender will be assumed to be male unless otherwise specified. This does not imply that violence against men is any less serious than that against women.

Over the last two decades, attention has also focused on the effect of community violence on children, vis-à-vis violent street crime, bullying, school shootings, and other public displays of aggression (Goldner, Peters, Richards, & Pearce, 2011; Groves, 2002; Mrug, Loosier, & Windle, 2008). Groves (2002, p. 27) describes "*community violence* as those incidents that occur in the streets, in neighborhoods and in the schools." Demographics bear out the growing rate of community violence in America. It pervades the lives of some children more than others: males more than females, urban and minority youth more frequently than their rural counterparts. Prevalence rates of violent victimization during adolescence is estimated to be between 50 percent and 68 percent (Mrug et al., 2008), and approximately 90 percent of children witness violence in their schools. These rates suggest that most children in the United States and Canada are aware of, witness to, or victims of violent acts.

Children in the twenty-first century are also increasingly exposed to media violence. Unlike any other time in history, children witness and become victims of violence through virtual and passive media such as television, computer screens, e-mail, and smart phones and by way of films and music lyrics. Studies suggest that for children in these media-centric times, "the effects of media violence are both real and strong" (Murray, 2008, p. 1212).

So what questions can we ask to elicit children's narratives of violence? How does one create safety in relationship when there is violence in the home and on the street? And what can be done to prevent interpersonal and community violence and its devastating effects on children?

This chapter examines family, community, and virtual violence in the lives of children across ages, locations, and circumstances. As always, we will explore this subject from multiple perspectives: of researchers, of parents who are or were intended victims, and of children and youth. The chapter highlights programs, practices, and policies that seek to prevent, intervene in, and raise awareness about violence in children's lives. It concludes with suggestions for helping children and families find resilience and hope, so as to break the cycle of violence in their homes and communities.

LIVING WITH INTERPERSONAL VIOLENCE

Bella's earliest memories of violence go back to when she was seven. She remembers her mother running into her bedroom late at night, waking her, and screaming for help. Bella recalls feeling frightened, but nonetheless comforted her mother into the early morning hours. She can't explain these instinctively protective gestures. She can only say that they happened.

Bella, a Caucasian woman of Italian heritage now in her thirties, still has vivid flashbacks of her mother's blackened eyes, broken bones, and hidden bruises. She thinks that she, her brother, and her father are the only ones to have ever seen the brutal effects of these assaults. The day after the beatings, her mother would typically minimize their effect. In fact, most times she would chastise Bella for even mentioning them. "Your father works hard," she'd say. "I overreacted and he had every right to get angry at me. Now leave it alone."

Bella's father was assistant principal in an urban school system. He never spoke of the violence, and neither did her brother, Leon, two years her junior. Even worse, her parents did nothing when Leon began to beat Bella. When Bella was twelve, she approached her priest about the violence. He called her parents, who dismissed the complaints. "You know how girls are at this age," they said. He skeptically agreed and avoided Bella on Sundays when her family came to worship.

Bella's high school guidance counselor became aware of her plight from friends who were concerned about her noticeable weight loss and frequent absences. At sixteen, Bella had learned how to deal with the craziness. The day after a violent episode was followed by denying herself food, skipping school, and shoplifting. The thrill she got from risky behaviors helped her forget the fear from the night before. This coping method worked for Bella until the day she passed out during tennis practice. The guidance counselor called Bella into her office after hearing about what happened. She directly asked Bella about family violence.

Bella contemplated the option of telling. She couldn't bear to be dismissed again. On the other hand, her brother, now fourteen, had started coming into her room at night and insisting that she perform sexual acts or risk being "punched out." Sometimes he hit her even when she acquiesced to his demands. In the end Bella opted to keep silent; the guidance counselor just couldn't be trusted.

Bella's story powerfully illustrates that children are the unrecognized victims of domestic violence. An estimated 7 million children live in families where severe and ongoing intimate-partner violence takes place (McDonald et al., 2006). Mothers in caregiving roles are subjected to 2 million injuries from intimate-partner violence each year (Centers for Disease Control and Prevention, 2008). Many of these assaults are observed by children. According to Osofsky (2003), given the powerful secrecy associated with domestic violence, it is likely that traditional surveys underestimate the true prevalence of children's exposure.

Children's experiences of domestic violence are variable. Some live in chronically violent homes, while others witness episodic physical and verbal assaults. Many children escape violence only to return to live with previous or new perpetrators. Others leave their homes, never to return, after the first serious incident of intimate-partner violence (Mullender et al., 2002). Resources available to these children typically correspond to their socioeconomic circumstances. Victims with financial means can disguise their abuse and seek private treatment. Those without material resources may come to the attention of law enforcement or seek help in emergency departments or family-violence shelters. Despite the range of circumstances, there is little doubt that all children living with domestic violence experience considerable insecurity, disruptions, and hopelessness.

Children and youth are exposed to violence in a number of ways. They report watching or hearing violent events, never being detected by adults. They are directly involved in the abuse when they break up fights or try to protect their parents. Like Bella, they experience the aftermath of violence and are positioned as their parents' caregiver and confidante. Such violence can occur daily or intermittently for children across social class, race, ethnicity, religion, gender, geographic setting, parenting relationship, and age groups. Diversity is also seen in how children, even within the same household, make meaning of their experiences. Some accept violence as part of family life; others wonder what they did to cause it and how they can prevent it.

Common to children exposed to family violence, whether as bystanders or participants, are risks for a range of short- and long-term emotional, relational, and behavioral difficulties (DeBoard-Lucas & Grych, 2011; Goldner et al., 2011; Hamby, Finkelhor, Turner, & Ormrod, 2010). Symptoms such as anxiety and depression and behaviors associated with PTSD (e.g., hypervigilance, reactivity, and inattentiveness) are observed in children living in violent homes and neighborhoods. Salloum and Overstreet (2008) note that, along with recognizable psychiatric and behavioral symptoms, children experience grief for the losses brought about by family violence.

Given the known life-affecting risks of family violence, it is essential that child-centered workers routinely and repeatedly ask questions about its prevalence. This should be done as part of initial assessment interviews and throughout the therapeutic or case work they do with their child clients. Naming violence sets a tone. It implies that workers are aware that even within seemingly stable families, abuse might be taking place. An open approach assures children that the worker is willing to have a conversation if violence is part of their lives. Although some children will maintain silence, others will see these questions as opportunities to safely disclose their experiences.

Family violence can coexist with a range of childhood mental health problems. It can be camouflaged by behaviors like those common to psychiatric problems or conditions. Diannah Stone, an African American youngster, age nine, was referred to the school social worker because of complicated grief following the sudden death of her beloved grandmother. Nana Mills took care of Diannah and her sister, Francie, seven, after their mother died. Diannah's father and grandmother were known in their community as kind and gentle people. They were active in the Abyssinian Church, and Nana Mills cooked for the community food kitchen. Mr. Stone was seen as an exceptional parent who despite harsh economic circumstances had raised his daughters after the loss of their mother.

Soon after Nana Mills's death, Mr. Stone and the girls moved in with his girlfriend and her two boys, ages ten and thirteen. During a routine parent-teacher conference, Diannah's teachers said that her grades were declining and that she seemed preoccupied. Mr. Stone was greatly concerned and immediately agreed to have Diannah see the school's social worker.

During intake, the social worker observed Diannah's nonverbal reactions to questions about family violence. When asked about her feelings, Diannah responded by saying she was sad. When asked why, she shrugged her shoulders, and her eyes went blank. However, the social worker noted that Diannah's artwork was rife with violent images.

Slowly and thoughtfully the social worker inquired into Diannah's experiences. "You know, I've met a lot of kids who have tough times at home," she said. "Sometimes they don't like to talk about them." Diannah stared at her drawing. "But when they do they seem to feel better—like they've let go of a big secret that they needed to tell somebody about for a very long time." Diannah listened attentively but did not offer much in the way of personal information in their first month of meetings.

The social worker was gently persistent. She made it clear that she could tolerate whatever feelings and thoughts Diannah wanted to share. Eventually Diannah revealed that her father's new girlfriend beat him up regularly and called him "bad names." "He doesn't want anyone to know," Diannah said. "He's embarrassed cause he's a man and not supposed to let a woman beat him down." Diannah told the worker that she also witnessed the girlfriend hitting and screaming at her boys. They, in turn, took their frustration out on Diannah and Francie. "Nothing we can't handle," she reported to the social worker. Diannah, however, reluctantly admitted she was terrified about her father's and sister's safety.

With Diannah's consent, the social worker brought Mr. Stone into a session. He acknowledged the family violence but didn't realize the repercussions it was having on Diannah. "I thought she was still grieving for her grandmother and mother," he said. "I didn't even think about how Bonnie's actions were hurting the girls." It took a while, but Diannah's father finally left his girlfriend's home. Additionally, he and the social worker reported the boys' abuse to CPS.

Diannah's reactions to witnessing and experiencing domestic abuse are typical of children in violent homes. Such psychosocial outcomes include lowered academic performance, absenteeism and school withdrawal, and antisocial or aggressive behaviors, which can lead to involvement with the juvenile justice system (DeBoard-Lucas & Grych, 2011; Goldner et al., 2011).

Long-term repercussions of witnessing family violence are represented by violent and antisocial behaviors in adulthood and unwillingness or incapacity to engage in fulfilling, nonabusive relationships (Osofsky, 2003). In other words, "children learn from what they observe" (Osofsky, 2003, p. 164), and for some, violent behaviors are expected and justifiable aspects of life.

Gender is another mediating factor in violence's long-term effects (Osofsky, 2003). For example, boys exposed to domestic violence are more likely to view it as an acceptable component of intimate relationship than those who come from nonviolent families. Girls who have seen their mothers consistently abused may either avoid intimacy altogether or believe that they inevitably will be abused by a partner or spouse. Furthermore, propensity toward intimate-partner violence seems to cross generations. Children who have witnessed domestic violence frequently have parents who experienced the same (Osofsky, 2003).

Researchers have identified a strong link between domestic violence and child abuse, noting in an estimated 66 percent of cases, children are affected by more than one form of violence (Turner, Finkelhor, & Ormrod, 2010) and in some instances, offenders are guilty of both partner and child assault (Hamby et al., 2010). Research on violence in childhood identifies the phenomenon of polyvictimization, or patterns of ongoing and multiple traumatizing events (Finkelhor, Shattuck, Turner, Ormrod, & Hamby, 2011). Child welfare rosters reveal a robust association between reports of child abuse and domestic violence, as illustrated in the case of Diannah (Postmus, 2005). Accordingly, more attention has been directed to children who are doubly victimized, as abuse victims themselves and as witnesses to the abuse of their parents (Hamby et al., 2010). Similarly, intimate-partner violence, child abuse, and community violence share an unfortunate synchrony.

CHILD DEVELOPMENT AND FAMILY VIOLENCE

Age and other developmental factors influence children's responses to family violence. Studies find that children in the United States are present in 81 percent of households where domestic abuse has occurred, and in 48 percent of these households, children under the age of five witnessed the violence (Kelly & Johnson, 2001). In Canada 52 percent of domestic-violence victims with children reported that their children witnessed assaults on them (Statistics Canada, 2012). This was up from 43 percent in 2004, the last time the General Social Survey on Victimization was conducted. Interpersonal violence is particularly damaging to younger children, because it harms people they love and depend upon. Moreover, young children can neither understand nor adequately defend against the effects of violence. The earlier family violence appears in a child's life, the longer the exposure lasts, unless the offender leaves the household (Groves, 2002; Jaffe & Geffner, 1998).

Although parents may believe that they protect children from violent episodes, studies suggest otherwise. According to Jaffe and Geffner (1998), between 80 and 90 percent of children are well aware of the violence that takes place in their homes, even when parents believe them to be asleep or occupied.

As emphasized in chapter 3, the quality of children's early attachments affects many developmental domains. When these bonds are ill-formed or disrupted by violence, children's overall well-being is negatively affected. Infants and toddlers exposed to violence may exhibit excessive irritability, sleep and eating disturbances, inconsolability, separation anxieties, and developmental and social delays (Kelly & Johnson, 2001; Osofsky, 2003).

Moreover, mothers of young children cannot guarantee their own safety, let alone that of their infants. Some batterers resent the attention devoted to dependent infants, which puts mothers in a relational bind. They are compelled to focus attention on the needs and whims of the batterer while keeping their dependent children as safe as possible. As a consequence of having to choose the batterer over their babies, abuse victims feel shame, frustration, and helplessness about their caregiving capacity. Such feelings set up a vicious cycle of detachment, despair, and loss of relational opportunities for both infants and parents.

As children mature, they become increasingly cognizant of the harm family violence imposes. Some feel robbed of the love and protection of both their parents (Groves, 2002), their loyalties torn by a conflict without apparent resolution. School-age children (ages seven to twelve) may blame themselves for causing the violence or for being unable to prevent it. Furthermore, children quickly become aware of power and control as elements of interpersonal violence. As one ten-year-old girl explained, "Dad was jealous because Mum was having a good time and I don't think that he liked it" (Mullender et al., 2002, p. 95). Such comments *confirm* children's instinctive understanding of the control issues that prompt domestic violence.

While school-age children have increased insight into their parents' violent conflicts, they are nonetheless confused, anxious, afraid, and uncertain. "Do you want to know how I feel about it? It gets me all confused and muddled up" (eight-year-old boy, quoted in Mullender et al., 2002, p. 95). Some children express anger or act upon aggressive impulses. Others are possessive of the abused parent and become anxious upon separation. Some children try to protect their mothers and siblings even though such actions could lead to their own victimization. Other youngsters experience their mother's powerlessness as tacit abandonment of her rightful parenting role; they are apt to identify with the batterer and direct their anger and disempowerment toward their mother rather than the offender.

Such was the case with Jamie, age eleven. Jamie witnessed vicious verbal and occasional physical assaults on his mother by her longtime boyfriend, Ralph. He pleaded with his mother to stop the fights and move out. She promised Jamie they would leave, maybe go to a shelter or find an apartment. But she never followed through. Jamie didn't understand why his mother stayed with Ralph, and over time he became frustrated by too many broken promises. He began to emulate Ralph's abusive language and refused to comply with his mother's requests. When asked, he said he was sick and tired of putting up with his mother and her "stupid" decisions.

For school-age children and adolescents, mistrust and shame affect friendships and contribute to social isolation and loneliness. Some become skilled at making excuses for not inviting friends over and at maintaining an illusion of normalcy. "The fear of their friends and others finding out, linked with a sense that they will cease to be considered worthy of care and support, silences many children and makes them discount the fact that others often know more than they admit" (Mullender et al., 2002, p. 114).

In adolescence, family violence confounds lives already fraught with normative turmoil. The effects of cumulative stress and witnessing violence hits adolescents hard, resulting in behaviors consistent with those seen in PTSD, antisocial behaviors, and conduct disorders. Symptoms observed in teens include distractibility, intrusive thoughts, hypervigilance, fearfulness, depression, aggression, reactivity, risk-taking behaviors, and social withdrawal. The extent and chronicity of exposure adds to its negative impact (Mrug et al., 2008).

Older children seem capable of recognizing how domestic violence affects their younger siblings and parents. However, they typically minimize or altogether deny the effects it has on themselves. In a study conducted with high school youth, 20 percent speculated that younger children who witnessed partner violence could potentially become violent, whereas only 2 percent could see this as a possibility for people their age (Mullender et al., 2002). This discrepancy may be explained by the bravado of youth or by their self-perceived invincibility. Other studies found that youth exposed to ongoing violence become desensitized and seemingly inured to its effects (Mrug et al., 2008; Mullender et al., 2002).

PARENTAL RESPONSES TO DOMESTIC VIOLENCE

Parents, and in particular mothers, who stay in abusive relationships are harshly judged by public opinion and by those closest to them. Most people do not understand why they do not leave their abusers, thereby placing their children at risk. So why *do* parents stay with consistently abusive partners? Why don't they just leave? Perhaps the most condemning question is, Why would any parent *choose* a violent partner over the welfare of their children?

Although leaving an abusive partner may seem logical to outsiders, victims see it very differently. Often they are physically, economically, and/or psychologically compromised and therefore unable to leave safely. According to feminist theorists and domestic-violence researchers, offenders are highly skilled in psychological control, instilling fear and helplessness in their partners and thereby systematically destroying their confidence and self-efficacy (Raghunandan & Leschied, 2010). Moreover, it is not uncommon for offenders to intentionally undermine and destroy their victims' relational attachments, including those with their extended families, friends, and children. Given these conditions, it is understandable that victims experience depression, suicidal ideation, social isolation, addictive behaviors, and PTSD (Raghunandan & Leschied, 2010).

In some instances, offenders manipulate children or directly threaten their welfare to control their partners' behaviors. The result of such calculating actions is that mothers urge children to comply with offenders against their better judgment, in order to keep them safe. Victims of intimate-partner violence learn that "every action will be watched, that most actions will be thwarted" (Raghunandan and Leschied, 2010, p. 53).

Another less-recognized but common strategy used by batterers is withholding and controlling family finances. These abusive partners take charge of bank and credit accounts. They dole out income, demanding that every dollar be accounted for. Physical and/or verbal abuse may follow when abusers consider their partner's spending unjustified. This strategy not only holds victims economically hostage but also deprives them of financial resources if they decide to leave.

Pat Moore, a white, middle-class mother of three, was caught in this economic bind. When they were first married, the couple agreed that as soon as they had children, Pat would leave her job. For fourteen years of marriage, she was a home-centered mother. When she separated from her husband after years of emotional abuse, he insisted on maintaining control over the family's financial holdings. Everything was solely in his name, and Pat was desperate to leave, so she decided not to dispute the matter.

Without savings of her own, Pat had to manage with what her husband gave her. She worked seasonally as a chambermaid and was taking online courses to get her master's degree in social work. As might be imagined, the children preferred being with their father because he bought them things and took them to restaurants and on vacations. When they were with their mother, the girls had to share a bedroom, while she slept on the couch in their tiny apartment. Pat had no income to spare for special activities.

When the girls asked their mother about the economic disparities, she assured them that it was something that Mom and Dad would eventually work out. She was looking for a better job and believed their fiscal circumstances would improve once she had her MSW. When they asked their father, he told them that their mother had plenty of money and just didn't know how to manage it. Pat eventually initiated a divorce, but many victims in these circumstances stay married to abusive partners to ensure their children's economic security.

Most people who batter their partners are similarly authoritarian and controlling with their children (Osofsky, 2003). As in their intimate partnerships, offenders' parental affection is conditional, inconsistent, and unreliable. On any given day they may be indulgent or denigrating, playful or sadistic. As a consequence, their children do not know what to expect from them. They feel confused and mistrustful—they never know which daddy will show up.

Some people, however, can separate their parenting and partnering roles. They may be attentive and kind to their children while they are denigrating or physically hurtful to their partners. One can argue that partner mistreatment constitutes child abuse, regardless of the quality of the relationships offenders have with their children. The best interests of children require that parents treat each other with respect. Children have difficulty making sense of these disparate relational behaviors and often feel caught in the middle because they love both parents and do not want to see them harmed.

LEAVING VIOLENT RELATIONSHIPS

Family, friends, and professionals are often baffled by and unsupportive of an individual's decision to remain in a violent relationship. Victims, however, recognize that there are significant risks in leaving, and believe that by staying they are acting in their children's best interests (Block, 2003). Indeed, the choice to leave abusers precipitates escalation of violence and intensifies potential dangers for both victims and children. Block (2003) reports that women who seek help or try to leave are more likely to experience severe abuse upon return to their partner. There is also a strong association between acts of seeking safety and domestic-violence fatalities (Block, 2003; Sillito & Salari, 2011).

Supporting children's growth and development and protecting them from harm are the most basic functions of parenting. It is not surprising that parents who are aware that they cannot protect their children from violent partners feel despair and powerlessness (Osofsky, 2003). Abused parents are preoccupied with their own trauma and have difficulty ensuring their children's safety. For these dependent youngsters, vital relational attachments with their parents are compromised, and short- and long-term risks to their welfare are ever present. But there is evidence to suggest that strong ties with other caring adults can be a significant protective factor that mediates harm and fosters resilience in children from violent homes (Groves, 2002; Osofsky, 2003).

Close relatives or kin can provide important safety nets for children who may need to leave their homes because of violence. Kinship placements are usually preferred because they ensure continuity of ties between children, their culture, and their community. Continuity of family ties is seen as highly important to mothers, whether they stay with or attempt to leave their abusers. Mothers living with violent partners face the ultimate dilemma: they want to keep their children safe, but they also want to keep their families together.

Abuse survivors undeniably face enormous internal and external turmoil when it comes to making life-affecting decisions, including seeking help, keeping their families together, and finding alternative living arrangements for their children. They hope to protect their children from multiple sources of potential harm: the offender, the police and legal system, and CPS, with whom many have already had unprofitable and painful encounters (Raghunandan & Leschied, 2010). As will be discussed below, domestic violence and child welfare have a complex and ambivalent relationship with one another, which further complicates the choices abused parents have to make.

CHILDREN OF MURDERED FAMILY MEMBERS

Children who witness and survive the murder of family members are an underrecognized population. Sillito and Salari (2011, p. 286) contend that bearing witness to violent death is "more common than childhood leukemia" and "one of the most traumatic events a child can observe." Furthermore, experts note that direct observation occurs with more frequency than expected; for example, one study found that 10 percent of the callers to 911 to report a murder were children (Fantuzzo et al., cited in Sillito & Salari, 2011). Another study estimated that children witness their mother's murder in approximately 25 percent of reported cases (Jaffe & Geffner, 1998).

Thousands of children in the United States and Canada are affected by the murders of loved ones. Over the past three decades there has been a general decline in the rate of domestic-violence homicides in Canada, decreasing 32 percent from 1980 to 2010. This is attributed to many factors, including improvements in women's socioeconomic status and increased availability of resources for victims of violence (Statistics Canada, 2012). In the United States, violent crimes by intimate partners totaled 509,230 in 2010 and accounted for 13.36 percent of all violent crimes committed (Bureau of Justice Statistics, 2011). It is estimated that a third of female homicide victims that are reported in police records are killed by an intimate partner (Federal Bureau of Investigation, 2000).

Murder is both unexpected and violent; when it occurs, child survivors are faced not only with grief but also with post-traumatic stress due to its brutal nature (Salloum & Overstreet, 2008). Children who witness a parent's violent death may initially appear numb or dissociated from actual events. Over time, as feelings of safety resume, children may become able to articulate details of the event and feel its emotional consequences.

Some children, however, are so overwhelmed by witnessing murder that it invades every aspect of their young lives. Groves (2002) tells the story of Daquan, who was with his mother when she was shot and killed by her boyfriend. After the murder and without hesitation, the preschooler could recite the details of his mother's death and even enact how she fell to the ground after being shot. However, what appeared at first to be articulation was in fact rumination. As Groves (2002, p. 14) observed, "My initial worry about how to help him to talk about the trauma was groundless . . . What I should have worried about was how to help him stop talking and thinking about it. I learned that this event was utterly overwhelming to him and pervaded every aspect of his being."

Young children like Daquan may also have witnessed multiple threats of violent death toward their loved ones (Sillito & Salari, 2011). Preoccupation with the possibility of violence and death affects attention, learning, and social functioning.

In addition to the horrors of the homicide itself, children are psychologically affected by ongoing criminal justice proceedings, public media coverage, and family changes that take place in murder's wake. Children of murder victims may be marginalized simply by their proximity to violent death, and in the end they become members of a "forgotten victim population" (Salloum & Overstreet, 2008, p. 499).

CHILDREN'S PERSPECTIVES

Few studies have investigated interpersonal violence directly from the perspective of child witnesses. Although adults certainly lend vital perspectives, they cannot accurately speak for children. Only child witnesses themselves can give true voice to their experiences. As Mullender and colleagues (2002, p. 3) summarize, "We now understand that adult representations and interpretations of children's lives might say more about the observer than the observed and, to avoid this, it has come to be seen as essential to convey children's own accounts first hand—to include their voices."

Children's capacities to speak about and make meaning of their experiences are variable. Recounting the violence may be challenging if not impossible for some; for others, telling their story may be validating and ultimately healing. Fear of not being believed or, worse, being ignored, as in the case of Bella, seems to be the primary inhibitor of disclosure (Georgsson, Almqvist, & Broberg, 2011).

When able to speak of violence, youngsters state first and foremost that they desperately want to find safety for themselves and their family. They also want to be listened to by adults who care. As a nine-year-old child put it, "[I]f they were like me, sometimes I'm really sad and I need someone to talk to" (Mullender et al., 2002, p. 107).

Children also describe a range of coping strategies used to manage family violence; for example, some youngsters consciously or unconsciously avoid thinking at all about the violence by immersing themselves in activities, blanking out to screens, or dissociating from their feelings. Others seek comfort from friends and pets; younger children may choose a stuffed animal or transitional object to self-soothe (Georgsson et al., 2011).

Children in Mullender and colleagues' (2002, p. 120) study had this to say about how they survived and managed difficult and violent circumstances: "We all cope in all sorts of ways . . . Children don't necessarily get upset and in a state about it. They can do fine with it. Some do get upset and they need support and caring because it is such a big thing."

Perhaps the most powerful lesson learned directly from children is that they need to be taken seriously by significant adults in their lives. They want to be heard and not forgotten (Mullender et al., 2002). Children understand that their parents are in pain, but at the same time they want their distress to be recognized as on a par with that of the adults in their lives. As one youngster reported, "Grown-ups don't realize sometimes because they are always going on about *their* stuff and they forget that the children might be hurting, too" (p. 121).

Protective factors identified by children in violent homes include accessible and ongoing relationships with at least one caring adult and availability of safe and protective resources, for example, safe houses or family-violence shelters. Personality characteristics and resources that aid children's resilience are intelligence, self-worth, self-efficacy, good health, positive social relationships, faith-based beliefs and resources, strong regulatory skills, and socioeconomic stability (Georgsson et al., 2011; Mullender et al., 2002). All too often, however, childhood protective factors that might have been accessed for coping are precisely those that are eroded and damaged by ongoing domestic abuse (Mullender et al., 2002). Thus finding ways to build relationships with these understandably untrusting children is foundational to beginning what may be one of the most important conversations of their lives.

DOMESTIC VIOLENCE AND CHILD PROTECTION

It would seem that the needs and goals of abused parents and their children would be, if not identical, at least synchronous. Abuse victims and children are often set at odds, however, because of differences in the ways CPS and domestic-violence workers view the best interests of their clients. For example, CPS workers focus on the safety and well-being of children. If children's exposure to domestic violence is considered a form of neglect or abuse, then failure to protect children from bearing witness is viewed as maltreatment. Logically then, abused women who do not intervene to protect their children from exposure to violence may be judged by CPS workers as neglectful rather than as victims of systemic family and societal dysfunction (Edelson, Gassman-Pines, & Hill, 2006).

Conversely, domestic-violence workers seek to empower women and support them in their decision-making process. Those who work with abused women understand that mothers who stay with their partner may be doing so to control and redirect the level of violence aimed toward their children. In some instances, domestic-violence workers may seek to protect abuse victims from CPS workers because they fear that child-centered practitioners will misinterpret their decisions and actions (Edelson et al., 2006).

Attempts to address these complex issues have mixed results. Some state laws have defined child exposure to violence as a form of child neglect and have subjected it to mandated reporting laws (Edelson et al., 2006; Postmus, 2005). Defining exposure as child abuse has resulted in some unintended outcomes, the most problematic of which is that women who are battered become doubly victimized: first by their abusive partners, and then by CPS, which blames them for not protecting their children (Edelson et al., 2006; Postmus, 2005). Moreover, children of battered women are likely to be removed from their homes (Postmus, 2005). This practice of removing the children rather than protecting the family as a whole from the batterer has been widely criticized.

Other states have initiated domestic-violence screening and services as part of their child welfare and dependency court systems (Postmus, 2005; Rivers, Maze, Hannah, & Lederman, 2007). These measures seek to engage adult victims early in the legal or social service process under the premise that "if approached by a skilled and understanding social worker asking appropriate questions in a voluntary, nonthreatening manner, a mother may be willing to discuss her experiences" (Rivers et al., 2007, p. 128). Willingness to disclose experiences of abuse opens many possibilities. These include safely separating mother and children from the batterer, providing protection and locating shelter, and supporting the renewed family through legal channels, such as helping the abused parent file for protection from abuse (Postmus, 2005).

It is important to remember that abused mothers, like any population, are not all the same. As McKay (1994, p. 29) observed, parent victims of abuse "range from women of great strength and coping capacity to women who experience a wide spectrum of mental health difficulties." Thus each parent-child situation warrants unique consideration and individualized safety planning. Successful programs must therefore be multilevel, culturally proficient, and coordinated, and must effectively address the needs of all affected family members.

COMMUNITY VIOLENCE AND CHILDREN

Children are exposed to and victimized by violence that occurs in their communities, neighborhoods, and schools. Mrug and colleagues (2008) report that up to 90 percent of youth in urban neighborhoods have witnessed violent incidents in their schools, while nearly 80 percent have seen or experienced violence in their neighborhoods. One study conducted at Boston City Hospital found that 10 percent of children under six reported witnessing a violent crime (Zeanah & Scheeringa, 1998).

Researchers estimate that community violence occurs most often in low-income urban areas, affecting African American and Hispanic youth appreciably more than their European, Caucasian counterparts (Goldner et al., 2011; Mrug et al., 2008). Boyd-Franklin and Franklin (2000) suggest that violence toward African American male children profoundly affects their lives as well as their family and neighborhood. To personalize these effects, Boyd-Franklin (personal communication, March 16, 2012) related the story of a mother whose son was killed in a neighborhood shooting. Addressing the crowd at his funeral, the mother pleaded, "Please stop the violence for my son's sake."

Violence perpetrated in schools in both the United States and Canada is not as restricted to troubled city neighborhoods or to a single race, ethnicity, or socioeconomic class as are gang-related and other forms of community violence (CBCnews, 2008; Groves, 2002). Violent incidents are increasingly taking place in middle- and upper-income suburban and rural schools. Furthermore, school-related violence is frequently underreported, due to staff and student fears of retribution.

Exposure to community-based violence affects children's adjustment in areas of social, emotional, and cognitive functioning. Health and functional risks include heightened anxiety, depressive symptoms, hypervigilance, and other responses like those seen in PTSD; academic failure; antisocial behavior and aggression; and relational difficulties. Violence and its impacts may not be comprehensible to younger children, but they feel the repercussions it has on their families. Older children may be terrified of neighborhood violence (see Althea in chapter 8), while some minimize, dismiss, or deny its impact. Perhaps most disturbing is when youth proactively join in the violence to defend themselves and their families.

Vincent (2009) comments that family factors can exacerbate or mediate children's capacity to manage and adapt following exposure to community violence. Community violence distracts most parents and caregivers, but those with resources and supports maintain structure, security, and stability for their children. Vulnerable families are particularly negatively affected when violence takes place. Vincent (2009) found that community-violence victims and their families do not receive the material resources, mental health services, or community supports they need.

Support groups for children have shown promise in remediating the effects of violence exposure. One example, Project LAST (Loss and Survival Team), supported by the Children's Bureau of New Orleans, was developed in the 1990s to help children address the emotional fallout resulting from violent crimes in their city.[2] In the group sessions (twelve to fourteen weeks), facilitators work with children to address issues of trauma, grief, and loss, using developmentally informed approaches such as storytelling, games, theater, and artwork. Cognitive-behavioral strategies are used to reduce the effect of feelings of fault or self-blame for violent events. Children in the group identify the violent events, name their effects, and by doing so, decrease symptoms of PTSD and other stress-related disturbances (Salloum & Overstreet, 2008). Hope for the future is another goal of the group process.

Salloum and Overstreet (2008) found that children affected by violence who completed LAST groups expressed fewer symptoms of PTSD than their counterparts who did not participate. Symptom reduction was most noticeable in areas of avoidance and reexperiencing symptoms or flashbacks.

Yet even children who participated in LAST reported continuing symptoms associated with trauma, the legacy of violence having far-reaching implications. More research is needed to learn why some children adapt despite being exposed to violence, while others are significantly affected. More study is also needed to determine interventions that are effective in reducing children's anguish and supporting parents' efficacy.

IMPACT OF TELEVISION AND OTHER MEDIA VIOLENCE

Fifty years of research suggests that children's perceptions of violence are influenced by what they see on television and other screen devices (Christakas, Zimmerman, DiGuiseppe, & McCarty, 2004; Groves, 2002; Murray, 2008). Watching televised violence heightens children's tolerance for physical conflict and increases their use of aggression as a means to resolve disagreements or manage frustration (Murray, 2008). Youngsters who have had personal experiences with violence are thought to be at greater risk for being adversely affected. Consequently, real-life violence combined with exposure to media violence "may have a synergistic effect" (Groves, 2002, p. 25) resulting in episodes of intensified anxiety, fear, and aggression in children who have themselves borne its impact.

Two-thirds of children ages six months to six years are tuned into screens for at least two hours a day (Christakas et al., 2004). Children from eight through adolescence spend more than four hours a day watching programming on television or computers and two hours or more playing video games or surfing the web. Anyone who lives or works with children in contemporary America might not be surprised by these findings, and as screens become more portable, it is hard to estimate how much more time youth will spend tuned into media and social networking.

Children are also passively exposed to media violence. Twenty-four-hour news often forms the background of children's day-to-day lives. They are thus subconsciously tuned into an array of programming that displays violent crime, war, argumentative exchanges, and graphic crime depictions. The American Academy of Pediatrics is especially concerned about the amount of time children and youth spend watching media. They recommend that children under two years of age watch no media at all and that those over two be restricted to one to two hours a day watching age-appropriate, high-quality programming (Christakas et al., 2004).

There is no doubt that children and youth are highly vulnerable to being swayed by television violence. Young children already blur what is real with what is not. As technology becomes more realistic and "reality shows" ubiquitous, little ones will find it harder and harder to distinguish entertainment from real life. Older children are enamored of celebrities and seek to emulate their favorite actors or reality stars. It is understandable then that without capable monitoring, children can readily see the world through the eyes of their favorite action heroes, rock stars, or video-game fantasy characters.

Xander, a Caucasian youngster of six, illustrates the stressful impact that televised violence can have on children. He was referred for counseling because of repeatedly stating to anyone who would listen that he wanted to kill himself. His parents and teachers were baffled. Xander was precocious, curious, and intense but had never expressed these qualities in negative or self-harming ways. The family had its share of struggles; however, Xander had never been exposed to known abuse or neglect, nor had he experienced any immediate losses. So what was going on with him?

Puppet and sand play helped Xander map out his concerns. He enacted large buildings collapsing, people dying, and children and pets crying and feeling scared. He threw puppets across the playroom and piled large pillows and cardboard blocks on top of dolls and stuffed animals. When asked about his play, Xander looked at me quizzically and said, "Don't you know these terrible things happen every day."

As you might already suspect, Xander's distress began in late September 2001, right after the attacks on the World Trade Center. His parents, like many Americans, had their television constantly turned on, and so Xander witnessed the planes hit the Twin Towers over and over again. He assumed, however, that each replay was a new event. From his perspective the world was likely to end, his parents would be killed, and he would rather be dead by his own hands than be alone and afraid. Xander had no prior experience with violence. Once aware of the cause of his distress, his parents shut off their television and monitored his television exposure. They explained what had happened on 9/11 in developmentally appropriate terms and assured him that they were safe. The threats of self-harm gradually stopped.

Social networks (e.g., Facebook, Twitter), e-mails, and texting, though wonderful for connecting people to one another, are also used as opportunities for stalking, bullying, and other forms of emotional, verbal, and psychological abuse. For bullied youth, these negative messages are nearly inescapable and leave lasting scars.

A survey conducted by the American Osteopathic Association (2011) found that more than 85 percent of parents with teenagers ages thirteen to seventeen reported that their children had social media accounts, and of that group more than half voiced concern about cyberbullying and social media harassment. Of the parents surveyed, one in six knew of at least one instance of their children being cyberbullied or harassed. In extreme cases, some youth become so distressed that they end their own lives rather than be unremittingly badgered by emotional and relational violence.

The American Psychological Association (APA) has called for increased health promotion to eradicate the explosion of media and social-networking violence and its growing negative outcomes (Murray, 2008). Their evidence suggests that children's increased media watching contributes to health problems such as obesity, learning problems (e.g., lowered school performance and inattentiveness), and social problems (e.g., decreased time spent in creative or relational activities).

The APA encourages adults to curb children's access to television and to limit and monitor their use of video games, social networks, the Internet, and smart phones. They also challenge those who produce violent media to reflect upon the effects of its content and the social consequences (Murray, 2008). Finally, the APA recommends that children be instructed in media literacy so they can make better choices about what they watch and how they use the rapidly expanding technology available to them.

HOPE AND INTERVENTION

Children's experience with violence is vast, and much of the research has been dedicated to identifying its negative and pathological outcomes. Yet a review of children's perspectives shows hope emerging among the adversity. For example, Mullender and colleagues (2002) found that children who were eventually able to leave violent households expressed joy in possibilities for the future. Reflecting upon the changes brought about by leaving a violent past, one teenage boy stated: "I'm not seeing the things I used to see that I didn't want to. I hated those things. And I'm seeing Mum being happy instead and laughing. Seeing Mum happy—every day. I get up every day. I have friends. I'm happy, Mum is happy" (pp. 115–116).

Themes of emerging hope also appear in the drawings of children who witness community violence (Lewis, Osofsky, & Moore, 1998). Symbols of hope are represented by religious images such as churches, depictions of joyful rainbows, and drawings of smiling parents and happy children. Not surprisingly, as violence decreases in children's lives, hopefulness increases; when children feel safe, hope revives. Children's drawings send a clear and imperative message that child-centered practitioners, public health authorities, community organizers and activists, and policy makers must translate children's hope into safe and secure homes, violence-free neighborhoods, and healthy communities.

Successful interventions include formal domestic-violence services that permit children, perhaps for the first time, to speak of their experiences without fear of judgment or retribution. Such services may involve building stable relationships with adult counselors trained in family violence, or participating in groups with other youngsters who have lived in violent families and/or communities. For young children like Xander, play therapy is a perfect format for expressing and mastering difficult feelings and giving voice to emotions associated with the violence (see chapter 7).

Because children live within family systems, parents and extended family need solid and supportive interventions if they are to keep their children and themselves safe. Like their youngsters, parents who experience violence need to work with specialists attuned to their circumstances and needs. Interventions for people who experience domestic violence will be different from those designed for families and children exposed to community violence. The first line of intervention in interpersonal violence is keeping victims and children safe from the abusing partner/parent. Safety may require either temporary or permanent separation of family members. Such separations are necessary losses in the service of physical and emotional safety and the eventual elimination of violence from children's lives.

As mentioned earlier, evidence suggests that victims of community violence often do not receive necessary services. Vincent (2009) argues that traditional, office-based services do not adequately meet the needs of these family systems. Instead, intervention services should be home-based or offered through accessible community venues, including churches and schools. Outreach efforts convey to victims that workers are willing to go the extra mile to build collaborative, family-centered, and safe relationships.

Family-driven collaborative relationships are the first step in developing a comprehensive intervention plan. Community violence is a public health problem. It does not occur in isolation; environmental factors such as living in low-income, chronically troubled neighborhoods make it more difficult for families to stem the violence (Goldner et al., 2011; Vincent, 2009). Thus broader-based issues such as employment, education, and health care also need to be addressed in order to reduce the multilevel impact of community violence.

First and foremost, parents must establish safety for themselves. As flight attendants tell their passengers, air masks go on adults first, then children. Once parents know that they are safe, they can counteract the helplessness that children feel and do whatever it takes to secure and maintain their ongoing safety and build hope for the future.

Groves (2002) offers these suggestions to parents for helping children counteract the effects of violence.

- Help your children reestablish a sense of order, routine, and trust.
- Provide age-appropriate explanations for the violent events.
- Assure children that violence is not their fault.
- Respond to children's fears and anxieties with authenticity, honesty, and reassurance.

These tasks can be adjusted to fit the ages of children, the circumstances, and the goals for each family. Although parents want to assure children that they will always be protected, this is not necessarily true, especially for those who continue to live in dangerous communities or who may choose to return to abusive partners. The best parents can do is to offer realistic assurances and to model hopefulness. Groves (2002, p. 85) recommends that "[c]hildren need to hear that we, as adults, are doing everything we can to make the world safe for our children."

SUMMARY

Children are exposed to and victimized by violence in their homes, in their communities, in their neighborhoods, and with increasing frequency, in their schools. Violent assault is both physical and psychological; it is seen in actions, threats, and words that destroy the lives and dreams of children and their victimized parents. Violence also invades children's lives through technology, social networking, and public media.

Children are affected by violence in a variety of ways; some grow from the adversity they faced; some succumb to mental health and substance problems; others repeat patterns of violence witnessed in their youth. Children who feel the effects of violence also experience grief. Regardless of the form violence takes, children need acknowledgment, validation, and the support of caring adults.

Often the conflicting needs of parent victims and their children create dilemmas for workers and social service systems. Eradication of all forms of violence therefore requires respectful collaboration between professionals, public health, and community resources. Dedicated collaboration avoids exacerbating already existing contention, while capitalizing on the strengths and resources of individuals, programs, and agencies. It prioritizes family systems, recognizing the interdependent relational needs of parents and children. Programmatic decisions and policy development improve when the needs of those affected by violence are viewed collectively.

Collaborative efforts start with encouraging those who witness violence to name it and report it to authorities. Asking about the presence of violence should be a routine part of screening in *all* mental health assessments and medical intakes. Social work and other mental health and health practitioners must be proactive in addressing and dismantling violence at all intersections of practice. We must be unafraid to persist when our inquiries, as in the case of Diannah, are initially met with denial. We must remember that those who commit intimate-partner and other forms of family and community violence are skilled at keeping their victims silent. We must be just as skilled in building trust with those who have perhaps never felt safe in their own homes and communities. Hope lies in the struggle to ameliorate violence in homes and communities, and as Nancy Boyd-Franklin reminds us, every aspect of the struggle is worth our time and energy (personal communication, March 16, 2012).

Notes

1. These terms will be used interchangeably throughout the chapter.
2. In 2005 Project LAST expanded its scope to working with children in New Orleans affected by Hurricane Katrina. See Salloum and Overstreet (2008).

References

American Osteopathic Association. (2011, July 11). Parents fearful of cyberbullying: American Osteopathic Association survey shows more than 85% of teenagers are on social media. Retrieved from http://www.osteopathic.org

Black, T., Trocmé, N., Fallon, B., MacLaurin, B., Roy, C., & LaJoie, J. (2005). *Children's exposure to domestic violence in Canada* (CESW Information Sheet 28E). Montreal: McGill University, School of Social Work.

Block, C. R. (2003). How can practitioners help an abused woman lower her risk of death? *National Institute of Justice Journal, 250,* 4–7.

Boyd-Franklin, N., & Franklin, A. J. (2000). *Boys into men: Raising our African-American teenage sons.* New York: Plume Books.

Bureau of Justice Statistics. (2011). *Criminal victimization, 2010* (table 5). Washington, DC: US Department of Justice. Retrieved from http://bjs.ojp.usdoj.gov/content/pub/pdf/cv10.pdf

CBCnews. (2008, January 10). Violence in Toronto's schools is citywide: Report. Retrieved from http://www.cbc.ca/news/canada/toronto/story/2008/01/10/toronto-schools.html

Centers for Disease Control and Prevention. (2008, February 8). Adverse health conditions and health risk behaviors associated with intimate partner violence: United

States, 2005. *Morbidity and Mortality Weekly Report.* Retrieved from http://www.cdc.gov/mmwr/preview/mmwrhtml/mm5705a1.htm

Christakas, D. A., Zimmerman, F. J., DiGuiseppe, D. L., & McCarty, C. A. (2004). Early television exposure and subsequent attentional problems in children. *Pediatrics, 113*(4), 708–713.

DeBoard-Lucas, R. L., & Grych, J. H. (2011). The effects of intimate partner violence on school-age children. In S. A. Graham-Bermann & A. A. Levendosky (Eds.), *How intimate partner violence affects children: Developmental research, case studies, and evidence-based intervention* (pp. 155–177). Washington, DC: American Psychological Association.

Edelson, J. L., Gassman-Pines, J., & Hill, M. B. (2006). Defining child exposure to domestic violence as neglect: Minnesota's difficult experience. *Social Work, 51*(2), 167–174.

Edwardson, A. (2001). *Frozen tracks.* London: Harvil.

Federal Bureau of Investigation, Uniform Crime Reports. (2001). *Crime in the United States, 2000.* Washington, DC: Federal Bureau of Investigation.

Finkelhor, D., Shattuck, A., Turner, H. A., Ormrod, R. K., & Hamby, S. L. (2011). Polyvictimization in developmental context. *Journal of Child and Adolescent Trauma, 4*(4), 291–300.

Georgsson, A., Almqvist, K., & Broberg, A. (2011). Naming the unmentionable: How children exposed to intimate partner violence articulate their experiences. *Journal of Family Violence, 26*(2), 117–129.

Goldner, J., Peters, T. L., Richards, M. H., & Pearce, S. (2011). Exposure to community violence and protective and risky contexts among low income urban African American adolescents. *Journal of Youth and Adolescence, 40*(2), 174–186.

Groves, B. M. (2002). *Children who see too much.* Boston: Beacon Press.

Hamby, S., Finkelhor, D., Turner, H., & Ormrod, R. (2010). The overlap of witnessing partner violence and child maltreatment and other victimizations in a nationally representative survey of youth. *Child Abuse and Neglect, 34,* 734–741.

Jaffe, P. G., & Geffner, R. (1998). Child custody disputes and domestic violence: Critical issues for mental health, social service and legal professionals. In G. W. Holden, R. A. Geffner, & E. N. Jouriles (Eds.), *Children exposed to marital violence: Theory, research, and applied issues* (pp. 371–408). Washington, DC: American Psychological Association.

Kelly, J., & Johnson, M. P. (2001). Differentiation among types of intimate partner violence: Research update and implications of interventions. *Family Court Review, 46,* 476–499.

Lewis, M., Osofsky, J. D., & Moore, M. (1998). *Violent cities, violent streets.* Washington, DC: American Psychiatric Press.

McDonald, R., Jouriles, E. N., Ramisetty-Mikler, S., Caetano, R., & Green, C. E. (2006). Estimating the number of American children living in partner-violent families. *Journal of Family Psychology, 20*(1), 137–142.

McKay, M. M. (1994). The link between domestic violence and child abuse: Assessment and treatment considerations. *Child Welfare, 73*(1), 29–39.

Mrug, S., Loosier, P. S., & Windle, M. (2008). Violence exposure across multiple contexts: Individual and joint effects on adjustment. *American Journal of Orthopsychiatry, 78*(1), 70–84.

Mullender, A., Hague, G., Iman, U., Kelly, L., Malos, E., & Regan, L. (2002). *Children's perspectives on domestic violence.* London: Sage.

Murray, J. (2008). Media violence: The effects are both real and strong. *American Behavioral Scientist, 51*(8), 1212–1230.

Osofsky, J. (2003). Prevalence of children's exposure to domestic violence and child maltreatment: Implications for prevention and intervention. *Clinical Child and Family Psychology Review, 6*(3), 161–170.

Postmus, J. (2005). Domestic violence in child welfare. In G. P. Mallon & P. M. Hess (Eds.), *Child welfare for the twenty-first century: A handbook of practices, policies, and programs* (pp. 355–372). New York: Columbia University Press.

Raghunandan, S., & Leschied, A. (2010). The effectiveness of kinship services with children exposed to partner violence: Exploring a dual victim treatment approach. *Families in Society, 91,* 52–59.

Rivers, J. E., Maze, C. L., Hannah, S. A., & Lederman, C. S. (2007). Domestic violence screening and service acceptance among adult victims in a dependency court setting. *Child Welfare, 86*(1), 123–144.

Salloum, A., & Overstreet, S. (2008). Evaluation of individual and group grief and trauma interventions for children post disaster. *Journal of Clinical Child and Adolescent Psychology, 37*(3), 495–507.

Sillito, C. L., & Salari, S. (2011). Child outcomes and risk factors in U.S. homicide-suicide cases, 1999. *Journal of Family Violence, 26*(4), 285–297.

Statistics Canada. (2012). *Family Violence in Canada: A Statistical Profile, 2010.* Retrieved from http://www.statcan.gc.ca/daily-quotidien/120522/dq120522a-eng.htm

Turner, H. A., Finkelhor, D., & Ormrod, R. (2010). Poly-victimization in a national sample of children and youth. *American Journal of Preventive Medicine, 38*(3), 323–330.

Vincent, N. J. (2009). Exposure to community violence in the family: Disruptions in functioning and relationships. *Families in Society, 90*(2), 137–143.

Zeanah, C., & Scheeringa, M. (1998). The experience and effects of violence in infancy. In J. D. Osofsky (Ed.), *Children in a violent society* (pp. 97–123). New York: Guilford Press.

13

Children of the World

Children's hopes, dreams and wishes cross all geographic, ethnic,
cultural and racial boundaries.

> B. St. Thomas & P. E. Johnson, *Empowering*
> *Children through Art and Expression*

THE FACES OF CHILDREN

When I first moved to Maine in the 1980s, it had the dubious distinction of
being the least racially and ethnically diverse state in the nation. Over the
three decades that have followed, racial and ethnic diversity, particularly in
the urban areas of the state, has grown exponentially. The 2010 census
revealed that the nonwhite population increased 37 percent, with a 135.3
percent increase in Maine's African American population and an 80.9 percent
increase in its Hispanic residents (US Census, 2010).

Portland's multilingual community has also seen substantial growth. In
2012 the school districts in Portland, the largest city in Maine (population
about 63,000), reportedly had over 1,800 students living in households
where, cumulatively, over fifty languages were spoken. Now 40 percent of
students in the elementary schools come from families where English is a
second, third, or fourth language, and Khmer, Vietnamese, Somali, Spanish,
Arabic, Acholi, Russian, and Serbo-Croatian, among other languages, are
spoken in the hallways of Portland's schools (St. Thomas & Johnson, 2007).

The increasing ethnic and racial diversity of Maine is attributable in part
to its robust refugee resettlement program, orchestrated through Catholic
Charities, a nonprofit human services agency that serves children, adults,
and families from a variety of nations, who have come to this large, relatively
underpopulated state because of its reputation for good quality of life (St.
Thomas & Johnson, 2007). According to St. Thomas and Johnson (2007,
p. 51), "A large percentage of immigrants who first settle elsewhere in the
United States often choose Maine as a second or third home because of its
'peaceful, quiet' reputation." They also come because it's known as a safe
place to raise and educate children. Much of the cultural diversity in Maine
is reflected in the faces of children.

The increasing diversity of Maine may not impress those of you living in New York, Los Angeles, Miami, Montreal, Toronto, or other cities rich with multiculturalism. I cite Maine's demographics to demonstrate that even the least diverse state in the United States has broadened its cultural diversity. It is not surprising then that the populations who come to the attention of clinical practitioners, social service providers, guidance counselors, social workers, and other mental health practitioners mirror this societal change. Indeed, Walker (2005) points out that in the next fifty years ethnic-minority children under the age of eighteen will become the majority in the United States.

Developing cultural knowledge and sensitivity is essential for direct practice with children and families. There are many strains and potential pitfalls. Over a decade ago Webb (2001, p. 3) described the intricacies of developing helping relationships with clients from diverse cultures. She noted that a "meeting of the minds and feelings" is always complicated, even with children and families whose lives appear similar to our own. When that work involves unfamiliar cultures and circumstances, the relational roadmap becomes even more complex. This is partly due to language and communication barriers and partly due to different perceptions of health and helpers, problems and solutions. Moreover, many immigrant and refugee children and families who come to the attention of helping professionals in America have experienced unimaginable trauma, forced relocation, and multiple losses. The emotional toll of such events adds to the cultural obstacles faced in trying to respond appropriately to the intensity of such human suffering (Walker, 2005).

For relational connections to be effective, workers must be culturally prepared and open to learning directly from child clients and families about their unique and collective experiences (Airhihenbuwa, 2007). This standpoint conforms to professional values that elevate client self-determination, diversity, and human dignity while appreciating that cultural identities are constantly evolving and changing (Laird, 1998). As Adichie (2009) reminds us, we should reject a "single story" about any culture or cultural group, remaining open to the diversity within. Airhihenbuwa (2007, p. 4) cautions professionals to neither marginalize nor romanticize a person's culture, recognizing instead that within any set of values and customs live possibilities for "positives that should be promoted" and "negatives that should be overcome."

Also important to culturally informed practice is workers' commitment to continually reflect upon their own cultural assumptions and identity. The concept of cultural humility emphasizes interrogating our own beliefs: naming them and attending to their influence. Such factors as race, language, customs, faith, and beliefs shape our estimations of people from unfamiliar nations, religions, and cultures. Previous relationships and experiences also color how we approach people and whether we feel safe to do so. We must be aware that as we attempt to understand others' perspectives, they too are trying to understand us. Developing relationships is always bidirectional.

A cultural encounter from my early days in practice comes to mind. I was working in the 1970s with a feminist-based mental health collaborative located in the basement of a church. It is safe to say that back then all of us felt a spirit of solidarity with our women clients and their children. The times were rife with openness to differences and acceptance for diverse life choices.

Within this context of what I assumed to be openness, I met Alana, a twenty-one-year-old Latina, and her nine-month-old baby, Tigress. Alana was sent to our counseling practice by the local free clinic because Tigress was not successfully gaining weight, a serious problem for infants. In the first moments of our interaction, Alana presented me with a challenge. She asked, "How can someone like you possibly help someone like me?" I was struck silent by her directness. What did she mean by "someone like you"? Too quickly I assumed she was referring to my youth, or perhaps she was simply overwrought because of what I presumed to be difficult circumstances. I responded enthusiastically by saying "Of course I can help you."

This was the first and last culturally misaligned comment I would make in this case, because shortly after it, Alana stood up and said, "I can't work with an educated, privileged white girl like you. You don't know anything about me," and she left. I had missed the point entirely. Her question wasn't about *her* problems and *our* resources. Rather it was about *me*; she was questioning whether someone from my background and culture could truly understand her. And she was right to do so.

In the forty years since that exchange, I've often revisited it. What could I have done differently? Perhaps simply saying "I'm not sure what you mean—but I'd like to know more" would have opened up conversation rather than shutting it down. At the very least I could have been more attuned to the power differentials we faced by virtue of our different ethnicities and socioeconomic circumstances. Indeed, Alana had every right to be concerned about sharing her personal story with a young, white, and apparently culturally ill-informed social worker. I now understand her reluctance not as resistance but as strength; her departure protected her from the harsh judgments she expected to receive. Her life had clearly taught her a lot more about disparities, racism, classism, sexism, and cultural humility than had mine at that time in my career.

Immigrant and refugee children and families are increasingly using mental health and social services in their newly established countries. Workers must be prepared with knowledge, skills, and attitudes that increase the likelihood that these clients will receive relevant services based in culturally attuned relationships. St. Thomas and Johnson (2007, p. 69) say it well: "Our task as clinicians is to sift through and sort out different impressions, layers of meanings and awareness as we concurrently learn about ourselves and others." It is unrealistic, however, to expect that anyone can attain complete knowledge about any culture or cultural group. Indeed, the best time to question one's knowledge is when one believes there is nothing more to learn.

How do we become culturally proficient and combine humility with professional knowledge, responsivity with health promotion? What is the optimal balance between cultural knowledge and "informed not-knowing" (Dean, 2001)? What gaps exist between evidence-guided knowledge and culturally guided values? How can workers guarantee that discrimination is sufficiently addressed in their encounters with people who become their clients?

This chapter examines culturally informed and responsive practice with children and families from diverse backgrounds, circumstances, and ethnicities who come to the attention of practitioners in child-care settings, schools, health-care facilities, social service agencies, and other child-centered care sites. Although much of the discussion focuses on cultural differences embodied in clients, we should remember that workers also come from divergent cultures.

The chapter begins by exploring definitions of culture and how they shape perceptions and cultural beliefs that professionals carry into their work. It considers the distinctive experiences of refugee and immigrant children and parents, as well as the risk and protective factors that contribute to their capacity to adjust, acculturate, and excel in their surroundings. Factors such as migration and illegal status are discussed, as are ethical considerations that commonly surface in working with diverse family practices and perceptions. The chapter concludes with a discussion of the attitudes and approaches that contribute to culturally responsive child-centered practice.

CULTURAL KNOWING

One's cultural identity is informed by knowledge and customs that are passed on in families. Culture shapes behaviors, communication patterns, and worldviews and is expressed through formal and informal laws and the arts (Vasquez, 2010). Cultural groups share a collective consciousness that influences the perceptions and expectations of its people, including present and intergenerational experiences of oppression and power. According to the Convention on the Rights of the Child (UN General Assembly, 1989), children have the right to embrace their cultural identities and to be protected from all forms of discrimination and oppression.

Ethnicity and race interact with culture, and there is considerable overlap between these two terms. The concept of ethnicity embraces a people's common experiences and connectivity, based on such factors as nationality, religion, history, ancestry, language, and political experiences and memories

(Johnson & Munch, 2009; Vasquez, 2010). Political memories represent collective experiences and histories of genocide, persecution, and forced migration. Discrimination based on citizen status and religion also affects cultural identity. On the positive side, ethnic traditions such as celebrations, foods, and rituals are intergenerational. Cultural traditions are especially important to those who, through no fault of their own, are geographically disconnected from their family and community.

Race is a biological descriptor that characterizes people who share similar skin color and other physical characteristics (Miville, 2010; Webb, 2001). Opinions differ about whether a person's race should be considered truly biological (Miville, 2010). This is because race and other cultural identities don't have clear boundaries. Yet those of us working with children and families must consider race part of diversity, because of its social, political, economic, and psychological realities. As Miville (2010) points out, one's ethnicity can be assimilated into a broader cultural identity, whereas race cannot be transcended. McIntosh's (1989) seminal article on white privilege elucidates how in the United States, race, rather than other factors such as class, ethnicity, gender, and faith, is targeted for discrimination.

Race is an important aspect of identity in childhood. As Webb (2001, p. 5) observes, "Preschoolers are aware of skin color and other physical features long before they have the ability to engage in the more mature abstract thinking that is necessary for identification with a culture." Race is observable, and children compare their own skin color to that of other people. Many children are proud of their racial identity, whereas others instinctively feel racism's negative effects. According to Boyd-Franklin (2006), African American parents strive to instill pride in their children's racial identity. At the same time, they educate them about the realities of racism and prepare them to encounter potential discrimination.

Children respond differently to their racial identity, as do adults, even within the same families. This is true for biological families who share racial and biracial identities as well as for adoptive families whose children are from another racial or ethnic group. Some examples of children's racial awareness come to mind. Adopted at birth by a white couple, Laramie, a four-year-old African American child, was brought to my office because he was trying to rub off his skin. He told his parents that his skin was always "dirty" and he was trying to clean it so that he would look like his friends. Laramie's adoptive parents explained that his birth parents also had dark skin and that he should be proud of his racial heritage. But Laramie still saw mostly white people around him, and though he stopped rubbing his skin, he continued to struggle with being different from his family and peers.

On the other hand, Toby, age sixteen, was proud of his race and First Nation heritage. Unlike many of his friends who couldn't wait to flee the reservation, he made a point of learning the Passamaquoddy language and practicing the ceremonies and rituals of his tribe. Toby told family and teachers that he intended to carry on the traditions of his respected elders. He hoped to attend medical school off the reservation, but would return to share his skills with his tribal cousins, aunts, and uncles.

CULTURAL COMPETENCE AND PROFESSIONAL STANDARDS

In America we live and work in an increasingly multicultural, multiracial, and global society. Standards for cross-cultural practice encourage social work and mental health practitioners to seek knowledge and skills that are relevant to the people they serve. Many professional organizations have broadened their definition of cultural competence. For example, the National Association of Social Workers (NASW) includes in its elaboration of cultural diversity the "sociocultural experiences of people of different genders, social classes, religious and spiritual beliefs, sexual orientations, ages, and physical and mental abilities" in their professional standards document (NASW, 2001, p. 8).

The American Counseling Association's Code of Ethics and the American Psychological Association's Ethical Principles of Psychologists urge practitioners to "be aware enough not to engage in unfair, discriminatory, and harassing or demeaning behaviors" and "maintain evidence-based knowledge about the groups with whom we work" (cited in Vasquez, 2010, p. 128). Acquiring cultural knowledge aims to reduce practice errors and avoid misinterpreting cultural behaviors and beliefs that may lead to inappropriate and perhaps unsafe practice choices. Cultural knowledge includes recognition of inequities and disparities that exist for different racial and ethnic groups. Starting points for best practice are respecting rather than challenging difference, finding commonalities, addressing discrimination, and "moving forward in partnership and cooperation" (Walker, 2005, p. 51).

Terminology reflects how professionals both perceive and act on their responsibilities. The term *cultural competence* has been criticized for implying a one-dimensional rather than multilayered conceptualization of culture. Indeed, over the past thirty years globalization, increasing migration, and the blending of cultures and religions through marriages and partnerships have contributed to rapidly changing distinctions between and across cultures. Current vernacular suggests that terms such as *cultural humility* or *being culturally attuned* rather than *cultural competence* are more appropriate for today's real-world practice.

No matter how culture is framed, we can't escape the reality that systemic health disparities and inequities affect minority groups and immigrants in the United States and Canada. Minority children and families experience a disproportionate share of chronic disease, infant mortality, and death across the life span. Disparities in access to health care in America also exist, particularly for migrant, immigrant, and minority children and families. As we consider the impact of culture on attitudes and practices, we must not forget the larger issues of bias and discrimination that influence the health and welfare of a growing part of our nation.

IMMIGRANT AND REFUGEE CHILDREN AND FAMILIES

Multiple and interacting factors such as country of origin, race, ethnicity, religion, impetus for immigration, and life-course stage affect children's immigration experience. Influential as well is the political climate of the *receiving* country and the immigration policies that reflect attitudes and opportunities that arriving immigrants and refugees will likely run into (Trask, Thompson, Qiu, & Radnai-Griffin, 2009). To most Americans these children are seen as a homogeneous group; however, this is far from true. Each child's immigration journey is unique, even for those who come from the same country or who practice the same faith. Recognition of such diversity is essential to understanding how children make meaning of their experiences and reconstruct their lives once settled in their newfound homes.

Immigrant youth may come from war-torn countries, and some have experienced dramatic losses (Luster, Qin, Bates, Rana, & Lee, 2010; St. Thomas & Johnson, 2001; Walker, 2005). Some left their homelands knowing they can never return, because of racial, political, and religious persecution (Yohani & Larsen, 2009). Some child immigrants and refugees arrive in the United States and Canada with their families, while those considered more vulnerable come as unaccompanied minors who are resettled with foster families or previously relocated family members (Luster et al., 2010; Walker, 2005).

Some children and families come voluntarily to the United States and Canada to seek a different or better future. Some become citizens, while others remain undocumented or illegal residents of their host country. As can be seen, many factors influence how well or how poorly children in these circumstances fare, with socioeconomics, employment, educational opportunities, and immigration status being perhaps the most powerful factors.

Approximately 1.7 million children who have been living in the United States most or all of their lives are undocumented (Suárez-Orozco, Suárez-Orozco, & Sattin-Bajaj, 2010). These children live in fear of deportation, without a country to call their home. Furthermore, an estimated 5 million children who are citizens of the United States have at least one undocumented parent. For these youngsters, worries about being separated from or losing a parent pervade daily life (Suárez-Orozco et al., 2010). Children in these families must keep secrets that if revealed could lead to deportation of their parents or other family members. Indeed, many families with undocumented members are disrupted and reunified multiple times,[1] a reality that affects the quality of children's family ties and their overall sense of security in the world.

Regardless of the circumstances of their arrival and entry, children who immigrate to the United States and Canada[2] face many challenges, not the least of which are adapting to an unfamiliar culture, learning a new language, adjusting to new social norms and peer-group rules, and assimilating into foreign school systems. Not surprisingly, such challenges, combined with elements of poverty, racism, uncertainty, trauma histories, and fears of deportation or separation from family, take a substantial toll on children's well-being.

Research on the mental health of immigrant and refugee children has focused extensively on problematic outcomes of their experiences. Bronstein and Montgomery's (2011) systematic overview outlines the types of mental health problems that practitioners might encounter in schools and child-centered mental health and social service settings. They found that many refugee children were at risk for mental health problems because of cumulative and interacting stressors, including forced migration and traumatic displacement during naturally tumultuous periods of growth and development. Older children expressed internalizing and externalizing problems more often than younger children; girls were apt to experience depression and internalizing behaviors, whereas boys had conduct problems.

PTSD and depression were the most common diagnoses. Not surprisingly, separation from or loss of one or both parents was correlated with high PTSD scores. Unaccompanied minors as well as those who experienced a violent death in the family displayed intense symptoms of PTSD (Bronstein & Montgomery, 2011).

Repeated separations from parents have significant and lasting effects on children. One study found that more than three-quarters of youth surveyed ($n = 400$) had been separated from their parents for periods from six months to ten years (Suárez-Orozco et al., 2010). Many had been relocated to kin or foster placements and then reunited with biological families several times. In some of these situations, family ties as well as parent-child attachments were tenuous, if not permanently severed. According to one Haitian-born teenager, "I didn't know who I was going to live with or how my life was going to be. I knew of my father, but I did not know him" (Suárez-Orozco et al., 2010). Such problems were made worse by housing and food insecurities.

The enduring effect of traumatic parent-child separation is a significant theme in Luster, Qin, Bates, Johnson, and Rana's (2009) study with Sudanese youngsters (sometimes referred to as the lost boys of Sudan). These youngsters were torn from their families by civil war and relocated to displacement camps in other countries. Some witnessed the death of their parents, while others remain uncertain of their parents' whereabouts or whether they are alive or dead. Worry about lost family members exacerbated feelings of sadness, insecurity, anxiety, and depression. The researchers identified ambiguous loss as a key element of these boys' experiences. (As noted before, ambiguous loss occurs when a loved one is physically absent and his or her status is unknown.)

FOUND HOPE

Although much of the research with child immigrants and refugees has focused on mental health problems, attention has also been directed to those who exhibit positive social adjustment despite the many stressors they have faced (Huemer & Vostanis, 2010; St. Thomas & Johnson, 2007; Yohani & Larsen, 2009). In light of the trauma experienced by this cohort, it is surprising that they survive, let alone prosper. Yet according to Bronstein and Montgomery's (2011, p. 52) review, a common message found in studies with child immigrants and refugees was that "despite their experiences, a large number of refugee children appear to be resilient to adversity."

In their group work with child refugees, St. Thomas and Johnson (2001) observed that children expressed hope in spite of harsh circumstances and multiple losses. Yohani and Larsen's (2009) study similarly found that hope bolstered children's coping capacity and allowed them to manage seemingly insurmountable life challenges. Factors contributing to children's hopefulness and resilience include collectivity and peer support, emotion-focused coping strategies, and suppression of difficult feelings in order to move forward. Strong religious faith supported adaptation in the aftermath of traumatic, life-changing events. It also fostered children's gratitude in having survived.

Researchers suggest that family and community support is instrumental to children's positive adaptation. In the absence of biological family, adults who act as "alternative" family members and kin help children transcend the horrors of their experiences (Huemer & Vostanis, 2010; Luster et al., 2009). Cultural beliefs reinforce adults' collective responsibilities for not only their own children, but for all children. These values cemented adults' ties to homeless refugee and asylum-seeking youth. Other adult caregivers included family members already established in host countries, foster parents, and older peers who had been through the refugee journey themselves (Goodman, 2004; Luster et al., 2009). In Luster and colleagues' study (2009), adults living in the displacement camps served as surrogate caregivers for youth.

Resilient youth seemed to accept that bad things had happened that they could not control. This reflection about such experiences is typical: "It happened. I did not have any control over it. I just think I wish it did not happen. But it did and I could do nothing about it" (Luster et al., 2009,

p. 209). Thus the capacity to embrace uncertainty and to focus on what one can control was another protective factor noted in refugee children. Goodman (2004) observed that the Sudanese youngsters she interviewed seemed to impose some level of closure on their experiences, not questioning why they had suffered. Rather, they concentrated on moving on and taking advantage of future opportunities. Getting an education was consistently identified as a way to rebuild their lives.

Finally, the role of peer support for refugee children, especially those separated from their parents, was noted in several studies (Goodman, 2004; Luster et al., 2009; St. Thomas & Johnson, 2007). Therapeutic group work described by St. Thomas and Johnson (2007) highlighted the power of peers to support transformational healing. According to the authors, telling life stories in the company of others who understood their experiences was growth promoting. St. Thomas and Johnson (2007, p. 143) described the group process: "Throughout the 12-week program participants not only get to tell their life stories and be heard, but more importantly get to re-discover the roots of their own resiliency."

Whether focused on pathology or protective factors, those who serve refugee and immigrant youngsters agree that there has been insufficient research focused on their needs. Suggestions for future research include determining factors that contribute to the coping skills necessary for children to survive and achieve posttraumatic growth. Given the importance of adult caregivers in children's coping, future studies should also examine qualities of relational attachments. They could explore methods that support continuing bonds and that mend both active relationships and relational images disrupted by relocation and trauma (Huemer & Vostanis, 2010; Luster et al., 2009).

Further investigation is also necessary to improve culturally informed service delivery. Recommendations include employing ethnic minorities in planning and evaluating service provision, training practitioners and advocates in empowerment and nondiscrimination practices, engaging community health workers in service programs, and integrating indigenous healing practices with evidence-guided mental health interventions (Walker, 2005).

PARENTS OF REFUGEE AND IMMIGRANT CHILDREN

Children of immigrant parents form one of the fastest-growing demographics in the United States and Canada. In 2001 approximately 1.8 million people living in Canada were immigrants, and of these, 17 percent, or close to 310,000, were children between the ages of five and sixteen living with at least one parent (Statistics Canada, 2012). In 2009 it was estimated that one in seven families in the United States was headed by a foreign-born adult

(Piedra & Engstrom, 2009). Given current trends, these numbers are expected to grow.

Relocation to the United States and Canada begins with parents' great hopes for their children's futures (Perreira, Chapman, & Stein, 2006). Stresses and strains of adapting to new and unfamiliar environments, however, quickly unfold. Relocation means leaving one world behind and entering into a new and unfamiliar culture. For example, Latino immigrant parents interviewed in Perreira, Chapman, and Stein's (2006) study reported tremendous hurdles in adapting to parenting in their new communities. Not the least of these was dealing with language barriers and unfamiliar cultural and social norms. As one mother in their study explained, "In Mexico, I knew all the families of my son's friends . . . Here it's different. I don't know the families of his friends" (p. 1396).

Racial and ethnic prejudice also affects newcomers. Many are targets of discrimination, and families feel the sting of growing intolerance caused by heated controversies in US immigration policies. Parents who find themselves targets of hostility live in fear that their children will experience the same. According to Dogra, Karim, and Ronzoni (2011, p. 200), many "find their parenting compromised as they struggle to make sense of a perhaps more threatening environment." Additionally, newcomers are often exposed to racial groups and populations previously unfamiliar to them (Perreira et al., 2006).

Researchers agree that children's well-being is closely tied to how well their parents adjust. If parents have difficulties settling into their new environment, it is likely that the children will, too (Dogra, Karim, & Ronzoni, 2011; Huemer & Vostanis, 2010). Accordingly, children of parents who struggle with their own mental health and adaptational problems seem to do less well unless they possess extraordinary resilience. Immigrant children in households where child abuse, intimate-partner violence, and substance abuse take place are at even greater risk for poor mental health outcomes.

This was the situation for Hakim, age five, who was referred to an urban counseling center because of aggressive behaviors at home and at preschool. His mother was pregnant with her third child. Mr. Yaqob, the children's father, was separated from his wife and children because of intimate-partner violence. He was temporarily living with another Ethiopian family in the neighborhood, and CPS had been called into the family home on numerous occasions.

Hakim's counselor firmly believed that Hakim's aggression was a consequence of seeing his mother repeatedly beaten by his father. His play enacted violence, as did his drawings. Yet there were many obstacles to engaging Mrs. Yaqob in discussions about family violence, not the least of which was the language barrier and the fact that the translator was Mr. Yaqob's cousin. Mrs. Yaqob would not speak of her husband's behavior in front of her cousin-in-law because she would be shaming his family.[3] This would likely result in her being shunned by the only people she knew in her new country.

Cultural customs and perceptions of helpers were equally powerful factors. When the counselor met alone with Hakim's mother, she was politely yet firmly told to mind her own business. Mrs. Yaqob was committed to a lifelong relationship with her husband to ensure a better future for her children. She didn't expect to be happy in an arranged marriage, only to make the best of it. Living separately was their agreed-upon solution to stem the violence and keep CPS at bay.

Although the counselor wished to be sensitive to cultural differences, she felt strongly that she couldn't use it as a rationale for family violence. Hakim was clearly struggling and heading for more troubles at school. The counselor sought guidance from community leaders she knew well, many of whom were from Ethiopia. They advised her to continue seeing Hakim and to the best of her ability develop trust with Mrs. Yaqob. They made it clear, though, that it would ultimately be the father's determination whether counseling continued. Over six weeks Mrs. Yaqob brought Hakim to counseling less and less often. The worker received a final voice message from Mr. Yaqob stating that his son would no longer be coming to his appointments. The counselor's follow-up call to CPS yielded little comfort. They could do nothing unless someone reported evidence of child abuse or domestic violence to their offices.

Parents are affected by protective and vulnerability factors similar to those of their children. Along with bearing witness to trauma, many have themselves been subjected to political persecution and torture. PTSD is a commonly diagnosed condition in adults who have been forced to relocate to escape further harm. These parents are apparently at risk for having their parenting compromised by mental health and functional problems (Huemer & Vostanis, 2010).

Immigrants and refugee families often experience economic disadvantage. Many left lucrative jobs or steady employment only to find themselves unemployed or underemployed in America. Those who were at home raising children must now seek jobs. A mother employed outside of the home is unheard-of in many cultures. Given these involuntary shifts in roles and responsibilities, parents are challenged to find personal meaning and identity in their new homelands. As one mother reported, "Adjusting to what we don't have any more is still difficult" (Perreira et al., p. 1399).

Tensions in parenting roles and responsibilities may also surface as families acclimate to their new community and society. Children typically acculturate more quickly to the language and behavioral norms of their new homeland. In some families, youth act as translators for their parents and other family members. When this occurs, children appear to have more power than their parents, as they are better situated to interact with the community at large. This transfer of authority is not well received back home:

parent-child tensions may emerge, and intergenerational conflicts between parents and family elders can intensify.

Parents who choose or are forced to leave their country also experience a loss in their connection to extended family members, friends, lifestyle, and community. Changes brought about by these losses are apparent in families who have come from collective societies where child-rearing responsibilities are shared within the community. Going outside the family for assistance is antithetical to them. Transition to the use of formal support systems for child care and other family-related services may cause confusion and stress for those accustomed to informal caring networks. This is possibly most deeply felt by parents who have moved their children from remote rural areas to cities.

Like all parents, immigrant and refugee parents worry about their children. They want them to have academic success, but many cannot support their children's education because of language and work-related barriers. Parents want their children to adjust well to their new homeland but are also concerned that they will be exposed to values in conflict with the family's culture and traditions.

Some families become more cohesive as a consequence of the struggles they have shared before, during, and after they have migrated to a new country (Dogra, Karim, & Ronzoni, 2011). Strong religious faith helps many parents make meaning and transcend adversity. Children in these families are well nurtured by parents who can meet their needs. Furthermore, these households appear to balance between the family's ties to traditional values and the parents' willingness to be more flexible and philosophical in the face of innumerable cultural differences.

Parents, like children, profit from relationships with helping professionals and community resources committed to culturally informed practice and culturally relevant service delivery. Prepared workers avoid potentially relationship-ending errors, such as labeling an unfamiliar parenting pattern abnormal when it may be appropriate to that family's culture (Goldenberg & Goldenberg, 2004; Hess & Hess, 2001). Steering clear of cross-cultural misunderstandings is important because their repercussions often go beyond the affected family and produce wariness toward the community in general. Practitioners must be equally careful not to dismiss or disregard problematic child or parenting behaviors in the name of cultural attunement.

THE FORGOTTEN PEOPLE

Migrant or seasonal workers are defined as "transient or temporary workers whose employment and residence in any locale is of limited duration" (Waldman, Cannella, & Perlman, 2010, p. 53). Temporary living situations and undocumented status make it difficult to track the whereabouts of these parents, children, and families and nearly impossible to enforce laws designed to protect their safety and welfare.

An estimated 3 to 5 million migrant laborers are working in America at any given time (Waldman et al., 2010). This population is made up of husbands, wives, children, and extended family members, who for the most part blend invisibly into the rural landscapes of the United States and Canada. About two-thirds travel between their homeland and work opportunities, mostly in agriculture. The remaining third follow seasonal crop patterns, working under hazardous conditions and living with constant uncertainty, disruption, and extraordinary disadvantage. Migrant workers and their families are ripe for exploitation by people aware of their economic vulnerabilities and lack of legal status. It is not unusual for employment recruiters to illegally charge workers thousands of dollars for transportation across a border. As a consequence, many spend their first year or more paying off debts and warding off retribution (Edwards, 2002).

This migrant population includes more than 400,000 children. By law, children are permitted to accompany their parents to work at age twelve. At fourteen they can work during nonschool hours. According to the US Department of Labor, children under the age of sixteen are not allowed to perform labor that is dangerous. However, the National Farm Worker Ministry reports that children as young as six have been observed toiling in fields, exposed to toxic materials and other hazardous conditions (Waldman et al., 2010).

Children and migrant-worker families face tremendous economic and health disparities as well as injustices perpetuated by a thorough lack of understanding of the exigencies of their lives. Waldman and colleagues (2010) compare the plight of migrant farm workers with that faced in the past by people with intellectual disabilities and mental illnesses who were "out of sight and out of mind," forgotten by the vast majority. According to some surveys, up to 60 percent of migrant children meet criteria for mental health diagnoses (Waldman et al., 2010). Trauma is also common in their lives. Few if any of these children receive appropriate mental health or medical care.

When in school, migrant children are frequently identified with learning delays, mostly caused by lack of access to ongoing educational opportunities. Migrant culture is poorly understood by teachers and staff because of its complexities. There is no doubt that children feel the repercussions of negative cultural stereotypes and as a result become disenfranchised and absent learners. Due to the many adversities they confront, these children quickly become mistrustful of people outside their culture. It is not surprising, then, that rural migrant youth are among "the most disadvantaged students in America" (Romanowski, 2003, p. 27).

So who's responsible for assuring the rights and protection of migrant workers and their families? Government and voluntary agencies provide an array of services for migrant and seasonal laborers; however, this population has needs far exceeding the resources available to help them (Romanowski, 2003; Waldman et al., 2010). Health and safety regulations are established but are rarely enforced. Mistrust and fear prevent migrant workers from asking for help even when in dire need.

Schools are natural environments to reach children of migrant workers. Yet powerful attitudinal and curricular barriers prevent schools from successfully reaching them, and also inhibit children and families from accepting outreach. To counteract barriers, Romanowski (2003) suggests that teachers express a desire to learn about migrant culture directly from students. Storytelling is one way to learn about the lives these children lead. A flexible curriculum should begin where children are, rather than fit them into preordained grades and coursework. Bilingual and culturally relevant curriculum is also likely to engage children in their learning and advance their education.

Coming back to the question of who's responsible for assuring the rights and protection of migrant workers' children: We all are. But first we must raise their visibility as human beings who deserve not to be forgotten.

THE CULTURES WITHIN

Thus far this chapter has focused on newcomers—immigrant and refugee children, parents, and families who are relocating to American cities, towns, and rural communities. Multiculturalism, however, equally applies to populations who have been US and Canadian citizens for generations and, in the case of First Nations people, those who resided in America well before Europeans settled here.

In America, the vast majority of professional social workers (89 percent) and other mental health practitioners are white, Anglophone, middle-class, and American (Congress, 2001). Most of the knowledge taught in professional schools that informs child-centered practice and normative development theory is based on research conducted with white, middle-class families of European ancestry. Moreover, television, the Internet, and popular magazines are rife with *advice du jour* about how to raise healthy children. Most of these popular models are based on approaches relevant to white, middle-class, heterosexual, traditionally married or traditionally divorced family structures.

White American families are as unique as any other cultural group, and like other populations they have distinctive cultural beliefs and practices. For example, child-rearing goals are embedded in concepts of self-sufficiency, individualism, and independence (Hess & Hess, 2001). Healthy children in this culture are therefore guided to develop self-reliance and healthy differentiation from their families of origin. Those who do not want to leave their home community may be viewed as having "separation difficulties" or considered immature. This perception of normative development contrasts with collectivistic cultures, where the choice by young adults to stay close to their families is interpreted as maintaining appropriately close relational ties. Moreover, children from white, Western cultures are considered successful if they achieve material success and job status. Conversely, nonwhite, non-Western cultures may view community service and responsibility to family as more important than material gain.

Twenty-first-century trends in white American child rearing are child-focused, and many parents afford youngsters a significant say in decision making. For example, four-year-olds may be asked what they want for dinner or be given two or more choices in what they wish to wear. This is done to encourage independence and to avoid power struggles. In other cultures children are expected to defer to adults without question. Chinese and Chinese American cultures, for instance, promote obligation to family over individual desire. Respect for elders is central to family functioning. Children who defy these traditional values may be shamed or chastised for not being appropriately deferential to adults and ancestors.

Family decision making is also informed by culture and custom. While white Anglo-American families presume that biological, foster, and adoptive parents undertake primary child-raising responsibilities, African Americans and other racial or ethnic groups may rely equally on grandparents or other kin to rear their children. Boyd-Franklin (2006) argues that integrating extended family members and other caring adults into the raising of children should be seen as a strength in African American families as well as in other cultural groups who function from collectivist perspectives.

This was the situation in Alicia Fallon's home. Alicia, a thirteen-year-old African American eighth grader, asked to be referred for counseling. "It's my grandmother," she told the young white social worker. "She insists that I stay home on Friday nights. I want to be with my friends, but Grand doesn't let me and my mother does nothing about it."

The social worker empathized with Alicia's situation. "You need to let Grand and your mother know how you feel," she confidently suggested. They agreed to invite Alicia's mother to their next meeting to address this perceived injustice. The social worker was prepared to advocate for her client's autonomy and educate the mother about the importance of adolescent differentiation. She planned to tell her how healthy it was for Alicia to strive for independence.

The meeting turned out to be quite different than the social worker expected. Instead of championing Alicia's cause, she was caught off guard by the mother's quiet yet firm clarity. "We are a deeply connected family," Alicia's mother explained. "My daughter knows to respect and obey her grand. My mother has as much right to guide Alicia's actions as I do. She's taken care of Alicia and her brother since they were babies. I insist they respect her wishes, and I ask you to do the same."

Responsive practice for working with First Nations parents and families begins with respect for their indigenous knowledge, spiritual practices, and tribal differences, and recognition of their political struggles. Traditional tribal values commonly embrace "being versus doing" and living in harmony with nature (Anderson, Putnam, Sinclair-Daisy, & Squetimkin-Anquoe, 1999; Dixon & Portman, 2010). Raising children is a community responsibility; thus many people outside of the biological family are considered aunties, uncles, cousins, and so forth. The natural environment is also connected to family. Mother nature is intricately connected to the livelihoods, spirituality, social lives, and belief systems of tribal cultures.

Important as well to understanding First Nations people is appreciation for their history of oppression and exploitation by white explorers and powerful constituencies who sought to destroy American Indian and Aboriginal cultures through dislocation and disconnection from their families and their land. Substance abuse, chronic health conditions, and economic disparities are some of the tragic fallout of historical and continuing injustices perpetrated on Native American families and communities. It is thus understandable that First Nation and Aboriginal parents may distrust outside helpers. Developing trust in these relationships requires humility, patience, consistency, and genuine respect for tribal beliefs and practices.

There is nothing inherently improper about the norms constructed for twenty-first-century white American family cultures. What is problematic, however, is when these norms supersede cultural responsiveness and unwittingly influence our work with families and parents from other cultures and racial groups. Differences between us are neither good nor bad: they simply are, and to deny them is not helpful to the clients or communities that we serve. Indeed, recognizing and naming our differences is often a powerful step in developing trusting and effective multicultural alliances.

PRACTICE CONSIDERATIONS

Cultural knowledge and understanding continue to transform as the world and its people become increasingly interconnected. As mentioned earlier, cultural competence has come under scrutiny as a useful concept. Indeed, there is increasing consensus across mental health, education, and social service disciplines that the notion of "competence" contradicts principles that prioritize people's self-determination, antidiscrimination, and "beginning where the client is" (Johnson & Munch, 2009). Thus the culturally responsive practitioner seeks to balance informed not-knowing with respectful inquiry, while conveying that he or she has important knowledge and skills to share.

Examination of one's biases and presumptions is equally essential to the development of cultural humility. Active reflection explores cultural beliefs and values, the sources that influence them, and the ways that they are applied in practice situations. When done successfully, critical examination deepens personal responsibility for learning from, with, and about our clients (Sisneros, Stakeman, Joyner, & Schmitz, 2008). The result is that workers are accountable for prejudices and stereotypes that might impede their service to clients from unfamiliar and diverse cultures.

Practicing from a standpoint of cultural humility prepares workers for vexing ethical dilemmas. Value dilemmas and ethical issues are ever present in the work we do, especially with families whose child-rearing practices and health perspectives do not conform to dominant social norms and institutional policies. It is readily apparent that when cultural values collide, ethical dilemmas ensue. Ethical decision making includes self-awareness of how our values shape the decision-making process. Another consideration is how values, and whose values, are translated into action (Strom-Gottfried, 2008).

On a recent trip to Ghana, I asked a group of students about the treatment that mentally ill children receive in their country. A young physician in training replied that for the most part Ghanaians do not speak of mental health problems because they are so stigmatized. Institutions exist for children and adults with developmental disabilities and other serious functional impediments. However, concerns over psychological and emotional problems more often than not remain unspoken.

Let's take a moment to reflect upon what it would be like to work with a Ghanaian child referred for emotional or behavioral difficulties. Or perhaps let's consider what could be done if you thought a child needed mental health services, and his or her parents or family elders refused. Would it be wise to insist on mental health diagnosis and treatment, knowing that this child might be stigmatized within his or her family or cultural community? Would it suffice to support the family's views and find other more culturally attuned methods to address his or her needs?

These questions are difficult to answer, and such cultural dilemmas arise fairly often when an alternative view of health seems to interfere with a child's welfare. This happened with Mrs. Ly, a young Hmong mother, and her three-year-old son, Liko. Mrs. Ly was called in to speak with a mental health counselor at Head Start. The teachers were concerned about Liko's bouts of inconsolability, dreaminess, and withdrawal. They agreed among themselves that he needed medical and psychiatric assessments for conditions such as autism, a seizure disorder, and cognitive delays.

Although Mrs. Ly appreciated and respected the teachers' concerns, she had already consulted her shaman, who associated Liko's symptoms with ancestral failings. He suggested that the family seek support from community elders to retrieve Liko's soul. The family was also prescribed medicinal teas and tinctures to give to their son. Mrs. Ly had naturally consulted with her mother and grandmother, who insisted she engage in spiritual rituals before taking Liko to see Western healers. In other words, she had diligently sought help for her son.

The Head Start counselor wondered whether she should report Mrs. Ly to CPS for medical negligence. Instead she consulted with the local hospital's multicultural health clinic, where she learned that Mrs. Ly was following traditional customs of care. Working with Mrs. Ly and learning from her about her views eventually led to a compromise, and Liko was seen by a Hmong psychologist who helped with evaluation and service planning.

This case illustrates the value of addressing the health perceptions and practices of child clients and their families without judgment or reactivity. Stepping back with curiosity and concern allows workers to refrain from injuriously imposing their own beliefs. Culturally informed consultation aids in avoiding common assessment errors, for example, stereotyping cultural practices. Armed with understanding, workers can work with clients and their support systems to promote optimal mental health care.

At the same time, however, practitioners must consider the potentially harmful impact of doing nothing when faced with children's troubling behaviors. Along these lines, Walker (2005, p. 50) cautions that practitioners "employing anti-discriminatory principles may simplistically try to reinforce apparent cultural norms that are not applicable, or explain disturbed behaviour in terms of cultural features that are irrelevant." Thus workers must weigh and balance how treatment suggestions are made and to whom, and to what extent they will advocate treatment protocols that defy a family's beliefs and customs.

Expressive modalities seem to work well with children across cultures (see chapter 7). As St. Thomas and Johnson (2007, p. 12) have observed, "play is the best opportunity that humanity has to offer our children." Play and peer-centered group work helps youth navigate troubled waters while supporting each other. This is especially advantageous for children who have been torn from their families or silenced by the devastation of war, community violence, and other human atrocities. Skillful play sessions allow children to enact their struggles and find new strategies to overcome them.

Storytelling also affords children opportunities to imaginatively and constructively work through their feelings and experiences. Through storytelling, children can organize painful and complex experiences, which helps them attain regulation, master difficult emotions and memories, and in some cases move toward post-traumatic growth. Storytelling has been found particularly effective for work with immigrants and refugees because it incorporates their traditions, myths, and history and validates their cultural identity (St. Thomas & Johnson, 2007).

Multicultural peer-support groups provide opportunities for children to share their stories within a safe and structured environment. Group settings permit children to experience a sense of belonging that cannot take place in a one-to-one relationship. Hearing their own voices and receiving support-ive feedback from other youth helps them become aware of their resilience. In the case of refugees, immigrants, asylum seekers, or children of migrant workers, group recollection allows children to recall trauma, share their sor-rows, and name the injustices that they have experienced.

St. Thomas and Johnson (2007) recount a group experience where boys from the Sudan and Somalia were able to transform feelings of anger and distrust into a game of hide-and-seek that fostered feelings of connection to their homelands and to each other. "Within the group the game created an atmosphere of fun and trust building. There was lots of laughter and there were no incidents of aggressive behavior. At one point block printing was introduced and the oldest Somalian boy who had not shared much about himself eagerly engaged in the process. With great effort he took a T-shirt and hand printed Somalia on one side and his home village of Buuhoodle on the opposite side. Unprecedented as an event, this was the first time that this boy had either stopped running or focused his attention on something positive and relaxing" (p. 91). The power of the group was transformative for this youngster. It allowed him as well as the other children to recognize strengths in their survival and hope for their future.

One last thought before ending this chapter. People from diverse back-grounds and cultures living in the United States and Canada become social workers and mental health practitioners. Very little research has looked at the bidirectional effect on the therapeutic alliance of being a practitioner of color, ethnic minority, or non-Western nationality. Are practice outcomes improved when clients and workers share cultural background or race? Should agencies attempt to provide ethnic matching? Do particular strains or strengths arise when diversity interacts with therapeutic connection?

These questions have yet to be sufficiently addressed. It seems that a worker's cultural identity and background can be influential, but it may not be—like all therapeutic alliances, much of what works is particular to an individual, family, or group. In Mrs. Ly's case, having a Hmong psychologist made the difference between Liko's receiving or not receiving help. For other clients, cross-cultural alliances may present too many relational barri-ers to be successful.

On the other hand, the therapeutic alliance can provide incredible opportunities for people from culturally different backgrounds to authenti-cally connect. It offers a forum to debunk racial, ethnic, sexual-orientation, and religious stereotypes. Indeed, such relationships could provide connec-tions that are foundational to ameliorating discriminatory attitudes and build-ing bridges between parents, their children, and their families.

SUMMARY

Many of the children now seen in therapeutic practices across the United States and Canada are from diverse backgrounds. Applying cultural knowl-edge, humility, and responsivity to real-world situations with culturally diverse children and families is highly complicated. The best of intentions may fall short. Cultural respectfulness can result in a child's not receiving the care he or she needs. Cultural ignorance can do the same.

Willingness to travel into the worlds of diverse children and families and to look through their eyes is the first step in building cross-cultural alliances. Awareness of one's cultural biases and assumptions is the second, and third is knowing when and how to transcend cultural boundaries when a child is at risk. When these factors align, productive human interaction is possible, and the seeds of peace are sown.

Notes

1. On June 15, 2012, the Obama administration announced that the United States would halt deportation of young undocumented immigrants who would qualify for the Development, Relief and Education for Alien Minors Act. The DREAM Act proposes federal legislation that allows children of undocumented immigrants who graduate from high school to earn conditional permanent residency if they complete two years in the military or at college.

2. People who immigrate to Canada can become permanent residents but would not be considered Canadian citizens. A permanent resident has rights and privileges but retains citizenship in their home nation. To obtain citizenship, a person must be eighteen or over and have lived in Canada for three consecutive years. Children become citizens if one parent, including an adoptive parent, is a Canadian citizen.

3. Locating appropriate translation services for mental health counseling is challenging for newcomer populations. Family members should not serve as translators because of conflicts of interest and client confidentiality.

References

Adichie, C. (2009, October). *The danger of a single story speech* [Video]. TED: Ideas Worth Spreading. Retrieved from http://tinyurl.com/yf8w2tp

Airhihenbuwa, C. O. (2007). *Healing our differences: The crisis of global health and the politics of identity.* Lanham, MD: Rowman and Littlefield.

Anderson, L., Putnam, J., Sinclair-Daisy, F., & Squetimkin-Anquoe, A. (1999). American-Indian and Alaskan-Native single parents. In C. L. Schmitz & S. Steiger Tebb (Eds.), *Diversity in single-parent families: Working from strength* (pp. 35–68). Milwaukee, WI: Families International.

Boyd-Franklin, N. (2006). *Black families in therapy: Understanding the African American experience* (2nd ed.). New York: Guilford Press.

Bronstein, I., & Montgomery, P. (2011). Psychological distress in refugee children: A systemic review. *Clinical Child and Family Psychology Review, 14,* 44–56.

Congress, E. P. (2001). Ethical issues in working with culturally diverse children. In N. B. Webb (Ed.), *Culturally diverse parent-child and family relationships: A guide for social workers and other practitioners* (pp. 29–54). New York: Columbia University Press.

Dean, R. G. (2001). The myth of cross-cultural competence. *Families in Society, 82*(6), 623–630.

Dixon, A. L., & Portman, T. A. A. (2010). The beauty of being Native: Native American and Alaska Native identity development. In J. G. Ponterotto, J. M. Casas, L. A. Suzuki, & C. M. Alexander (Eds.), *Handbook of multicultural counseling* (3rd ed., pp. 215–226). San Francisco: Sage.

Dogra, N., Karim, K., & Ronzoni, P. (2011). Migration and its effects on child mental health. In D. Bhugra & S. Gupta (Eds.), *Migration and mental health* (pp. 196–208). Cambridge: Cambridge University Press.

Edwards, B. (2002, September 26). Profile: Deaths of 14 migrant workers in Maine lead to questions about status of non-agricultural workers [Radio broadcast]. In *Morning Edition*: 1. Washington, DC: National Public Radio.

Goldenberg, I., & Goldenberg, H. (2004). *Family therapy: An overview* (6th ed.). Pacific Grove, CA: Brooks/Cole.

Goodman, J. H. (2004). Coping with trauma and hardship among unaccompanied refugee youths from Sudan. *Qualitative Health Research, 14*(9), 1177–1196.

Hess, P. M., & Hess, H. J. (2001). Parenting in European white families. In N. B. Webb (Ed.), *Culturally diverse parent-child and family relationships: A guide for social workers and other practitioners* (pp. 307–336). New York: Columbia University Press.

Huemer, J., & Vostanis, P. (2010). Child refugees and families. In D. Bhugra, T. Craig, & K. Bhui (Eds.), *Mental health of refugees and asylum-seekers* (pp. 225–242). New York: Oxford University Press.

Johnson, Y. M., & Munch, S. (2009). Fundamental contradictions in cultural competence. *Social Work, 54*(3), 220–231.

Laird, J. (1998). Theorizing culture: Narrative ideas and practice principles. In M. McGoldrick (Ed.), *Revisioning family therapy: Race, culture and gender in clinical practice* (pp. 93–110). New York: Guilford Press.

Luster, T., Qin, D., Bates, L., Johnson, D., & Rana, M. (2009). The lost boys of Sudan: Coping with ambiguous loss and separation from parents. *American Journal of Orthopsychiatry, 79*(2), 203–211.

Luster, T., Qin, D., Bates, L., Rana, M., & Lee, J. A. (2010). Successful adaptation among Sudanese unaccompanied minors: Perspectives of youth and foster parents. *Childhood, 17*(2), 197–211.

McIntosh, P. (1989, July/August). White privilege: Unpacking the invisible knapsack. *Peace and Freedom*, 73–75, 80

Miville, M. L. (2010). Latina/o identity development: Updates on theory, measurement, and counseling implications. In J. G. Ponterotto, J. M. Casas, L. A. Suzuki, & C. M. Alexander (Eds.), *Handbook of multicultural counseling* (3rd ed., pp. 241–252). Thousand Oaks, CA: Sage.

National Association of Social Workers. (2001). *NASW standards for cultural competence in social work practice*. Washington, DC: NASW Press.

Perreira, K. M., Chapman, M. V., & Stein, G. L. (2006). Becoming an American parent: Overcoming challenges and finding strength in a new immigrant Latino community. *Journal of Family Issues, 27*(10), 1383–1414.

Piedra, L. M., & Engstrom, D. W. (2009). Segmented assimilation theory and the life model: An integrated approach to understanding immigrants and their families. *Social Work, 54*(3), 270–277.

Romanowski, M. H. (2003). Meeting the unique needs of the children of migrant farm workers. *Clearing House, 77*(1), 27–33.

St. Thomas, B., & Johnson, P. E. (2001). Migration and health: Child as healer. *Migration and World Magazine, 89*(5), 33–39.

St. Thomas, B., & Johnson, P. E. (2007). *Empowering children through art and expression: Culturally sensitive ways of healing trauma and grief.* London: Jessica Kingsley.

Sisneros, J., Stakeman, C., Joyner, M. C., & Schmitz, C. L. (2008). *Critical multicultural social work.* Chicago: Lyceum Books.

Statistics Canada. (2012). *Ethnic diversity and immigration.* Retrieved from http://www.statcan.gc.ca

Strom-Gottfried, K. (2008). *The ethics of practice with minors.* Chicago: Lyceum Books.

Suárez-Orozco, M. M., Suárez-Orozco, C., & Sattin-Bajaj, C. (2010). Making migration work. *Peabody Journal of Education, 85*, 535–551.

Trask, B. S., Thompson, L., Qiu, W., & Radnai-Griffin, D. (2009). Understanding the immigration experience through a lifecourse lens: Four personal stories. In R. Dalla (Ed.), *Strengths and challenges of new immigrant families* (pp. 53–69). Lanham, MD: Lexington Books.

UN General Assembly. (1989, November 20). *Convention on the Rights of the Child* (United Nations, Treaty Series, 1577:3). Retrieved from http://www.unhcr.org/refworld/docid/3ae6b38f0.html

US Census. (2010). *Census of population and housing, 2010: Summary population and housing characteristics: Maine.* US Census Bureau, Washington, DC. Retrieved from http://www.census.gov/prod/cen2010/doc/nsfrd.pdf

Vasquez, M. J. T. (2010). Ethics in multicultural counseling practice. In J. G. Ponterotto, J. M. Casas, L. A. Suzuki, & C. M. Alexander (Eds.), *Handbook of multicultural counseling* (3rd ed., pp. 127–145). Thousand Oaks, CA: Sage.

Waldman, H. B., Cannella, D., & Perlman, S. P. (2010). Migrant farm workers and their children. *Developmental Medicine and Dentistry Reviews and Reports.* EP Magazine. Retrieved from http://www.eparent.com

Walker, S. (2005). Towards culturally competent practice in child and adolescent mental health. *International Social Work, 48*(1), 49–62.

Webb, N. B. (2001). Working with culturally diverse children. In N. B. Webb (Ed.), *Culturally diverse parent-child and family relationships: A guide for social workers and other practitioners* (pp. 3–28). New York: Columbia University Press.

Yohani, S. C., & Larsen, D. J. (2009). Hope lives in the heart: Refugee and immigrant children's perceptions of hope and hope-engendering sources during early years of adjustment. *Canadian Journal of Counselling, 43*(4), 246–264.

Epilogue

A voice has to be listened to.

Carol Gilligan, interview with Christina Robb,
This Changes Everything

RELATIONSHIP, REFLECTION, AND EMPATHY

Reflexive (or self-reflective) practice is described as the capacity to observe and evaluate oneself in the process of working with another. Reflexivity is considered essential when working with any client, but especially when working with people who are from cultures different from our own. Empathy is a critical aspect of relational reflexivity. Irene Stiver describes empathy in this way: "In empathy you're saying, 'I'm going to be with you in your experience so you don't have to be alone in that experience.' And if somebody's with you, all things can evolve" (quoted in Robb, 2006, p. 173). Like relationship and research, commitment to reflexive practice contributes to effective and ethically sound practice behaviors.

Reflexivity in action was brought home to me by a friend who served on my doctoral committee. During a relatively stressful exchange with committee members, he slipped a tiny piece of paper to me under the table. On it was a quote by Zuang Zi, a Chinese philosopher, written in almost illegible script. It said, "Don't listen with your ears, listen with your mind. No, don't listen with your mind, listen with your spirit. Listening stops with the ears, the mind stops with recognition, the spirit is open and receptive and waits on all things."

Afterward I asked him about the quotation. He said that people are too busy talking and not listening. And even when they listen, they are preoccupied with telling others what they know rather than being open to receiving unexpected knowledge from unexpected sources. "Listening" he said, "involves so many dimensions of ourselves." I've kept that little piece of paper in my desk drawer ever since.

As my friend predicted, I have learned so much from so many unexpected sources. This knowledge would have been unavailable to me had I not been willing to embrace reflexive practice. Much of this found knowledge is illustrated in the case stories distributed throughout this book. Without disciplined reflection, for example, I don't think I could have worked effectively with youngsters like Sarina or with families like the Barrons. More importantly, I wouldn't have gained the critical knowledge they, and Sarah, whose letter begins this text, had to share.

Carol Gilligan doesn't use the term *reflexivity* but nonetheless describes the process well. She sees it as the capacity to remain open to many sides of a story and to hold these different perspectives all at the same time. The ability to juggle different perspectives and tolerate uncertainty, she believes, creates opportunities for unanticipated insight. Gilligan suggests that "instead of trying to sort through and come to a conclusion, you open your mind and wait to think, feel, and listen your way to finding out more" (cited in Robb, 2006, p. 222).

This is how I think about working with children, their parents, and families. Conversations with children permit me to learn firsthand about the complexities of their lives. Children, parents, and families share wondrous and sometimes tragic stories, often told from an unfamiliar vantage point. Colleagues add to these, and in the end we pull together often conflicting and sometimes confounding information—to tidy it up and make sense of it. Sense making is often extremely challenging and never quite provides a full portrait of the people whose lives we're asked as professionals to positively change or redirect.

Learning with, from, and about children takes place in a myriad of ways. We enter their worlds through play, improvisation, imagination, and invention. Going back to Gilligan's description of an open mind, workers must be capable of playfulness, which involves the ability to authentically think, feel, and listen to children on our way to finding out more. At the same time, we must maintain adult eyes and ears as we watch, listen, and reflect upon what children tell us. Similarly, when parents and caregivers open their doors to us and their worlds, we should enter respectfully, have faith in their wisdom, and stay with them so they know they're not alone.

NEXT STEPS

Given the depth and scope of research available to inform practice, it's disappointing that health institutions, rather than embracing relational models, are moving away from them. It's my hope that the combined scientific evidence, social science research, and practice wisdom offered in this text will provide readers with both knowledge and inspiration for critical changes in the way we think about and offer services to children and their families. Becoming agents of change on their behalf is especially important, given the increasing number of children in the United States and Canada identified with mental health problems, many of which arise because life is simply too hard or unfair. It's our responsibility to work with and for these youngsters because they have no visibility in local, state, province, or federal program and policy development.

Responsibility for advocacy and change occurs on all practice levels: through direct practice with child clients and families to combat disconnection and discrimination; through organizations to enact changes in unresponsive health, education, mental health, and social service systems; and through political and social action for broader societal changes that support and protect the needs and rights of children, families, groups, and populations. Equally important is to work collaboratively with parents and caregivers. Families especially in need of early-intervention services are rarely asked what they want. As the stories in this book reflect, these children and families often come from the least understood and most marginalized populations. Most struggle with the interplay of social disadvantages as well as traumatic hardships such as domestic violence, mental illness, and addictions, all of which set the stage for relational disconnectedness. Furthermore, children and families disenfranchised by extraordinary life circumstances (e.g., migrant laborers, addicted mothers) experience what the relational-cultural theorists call chronic disconnection—a state of overpowering sociocultural discrimination and disrespect.

When I was in Ghana, I met an extraordinary teacher who said to me: "It's not just the medicine you give, it's the hands that give the medicine." *What* we do is important. *How* we do it is equally and at times more important. Another phrase that resonates with me as I end this book comes from my mother. She said it so often that I grew up thinking she had made it up herself. My mother was the neighbor lady who made sure that when cupboards were empty, food would find its way there; when babies were born, they always had hand-knit sweaters to wear. And when people were sad, she was there to listen. "Shelley," she'd say, "one hand washes the other."

We're in this together. Relationships matter.

Reference

Robb, C. (2006). *This changes everything: The relational revolution in psychology*. New York: Farrar, Strauss and Giroux.

Index